THE POLITICS OF PLURALISM

THE POLITICS

A Comparative Study

DAVID R. SMOCK

OF PLURALISM

of Lebanon and Ghana

AUDREY C. SMOCK

ELSEVIER

New York / Oxford / Amsterdam

ELSEVIER SCIENTIFIC PUBLISHING COMPANY, INC.
52 Vanderbilt Avenue, New York, N.Y. 10017

ELSEVIER SCIENTIFIC PUBLISHING COMPANY
335 Jan Van Galenstraat, P.O. Box 211
Amsterdam, The Netherlands

Library of Congress Cataloging in Publication Data

Smock, David R
    The politics of pluralism.

    Bibliography: p.
    Includes index.
    1. Lebanon—Politics and government. 2. Gha-
na—Politics and government—1957- 3. Pluralism (Social sciences) I. Smock, Audrey C., joint
author. II. Title.
JQ1825.L4S57   320.3   75-8278
ISBN 0-444-99008-9

Manufactured in the United States of America

To our daughters, Erica and Kristina

Contents

Preface

The genesis of our interest in the politics in the new states lies in our earlier research in Nigeria, where the problem of ethnic conflict and the civil war to which it gave rise constituted subjects of particular concern to us. To gain additional perspective and insight into this complex subject of communal conflict in pluralistic states, we thought it useful to look at fragmented states other than Nigeria. Ghana's experience with ethnicity in some respects resembles that of Nigeria, but ethnic conflict in Ghana has proved somewhat more manageable. The choice of Lebanon for comparative purposes provided a religiously plural, as opposed to an ethnically plural state. Moreover, Lebanon is also a state which has opted to grapple with its communal problems in dramatically different style than Ghana and most other plural states. Being an Arab and Middle Eastern country, Lebanon also provides striking cultural contrast to Ghana.

Thus this book analyzes the dynamics of political and social life in two pluralistic societies, one of which is fragmented along religious lines and the other along ethnic lines. We have accorded particular attention to the strikingly different approaches these two states have adopted in seeking to manage communal tension and to create stable polities. Ghana under Nkrumah attempted to eliminate ethnic distinctions and thereby forge a unified society. While the leaders of Ghana's subsequent regimes have not adopted the same approach, they have tended to share Nkrumah's conviction that ethnic identities are minor impediments to nation-building and will disappear as modernization progresses. Lebanon's leaders, on the other hand, have explicitly recognized the strength of primordial attachments and have devised a socio-political system built on communal blocks which promotes intergroup equilibrium rather than assimilation. It is our conviction that the Lebanese approach, while not totally adequate and not exportable in toto, has much to offer other states confronting serious problems of religious, ethnic, and racial conflict.

Although we first visited Ghana in 1962, the bulk of our data on Ghana was gathered during two and a half years of residence there from 1969 to 1972. Visits to Lebanon in 1968 and 1971 helped prepare the ground for a 15 month period of concentrated research in Lebanon during 1972–73. Research material has been gathered by a variety of methods, including survey research and elite interviewing in both countries. In the collection and analysis of data we were very ably and faithfully assisted by Dr. Marius Deeb and Mary-Jane Deeb in Lebanon and by Albert Fiadzigbey in Ghana, as well as by university students who assisted with the administration of questionnaires. We both had formal affiliations with the American University of Beirut and one of us had a faculty appointment at the University of Ghana during our periods of residence in each country, and university officials, faculty members, and students at both those institutions gave us invaluable support.

We are particularly indebted to Courtney Nelson, the Ford Foundation Representative in Beirut, who first suggested studying Lebanon as a comparative case and then helped arrange Ford Foundation support for the project. While we gratefully acknowledge this financial support by the Foundation, we hasten to add that neither the Foundation as a corporate body nor Courtney Nelson individually tried to influence our interpretations and thus they share no responsibility for the viewpoints expressed.

Many friends and academic colleagues have generously given of their time to read and comment on portions of the manuscript, and we hope they will consider the final product commensurate with the efforts they expended. Among those who have been particularly helpful in this regard are Malcolm Kerr, Michael Hudson, William Zartman, Aristide Zolberg, Nathan Glazer, Milton Esman, Kwamina Bentsi-Enchill, Kofi Ankomah, Victor LeVine, Adu Boahen, Gilbert Ansre, Iliya Harik, Kamal Salibi, Cecil Hourani, Elie Salem, Nafhat Nasr, Yusuf Ibish, Fuad Khouri, and Jeswald Salacuse. Various staff members of the Ford Foundation in Beirut, Samir Khalaf of American University of Beirut and Salem Zablith of Lebanese University all gave helpful advice about conducting research in Lebanon. Mrs. Mona Na'man and Mrs. Asha Mathur both competently and good naturedly handled all the secretarial responsibilities.

New York
November, 1974

Introduction

POLITICIZATION OF PLURALISM

The 1960s which, at their inception, were heralded as the development decade, might more aptly be described from a world perspective as the period of the politicization of pluralism. Country after country, both industrialized and developing, some before and many after 1960, have experienced strains wrought by the competing demands of communal groups within their borders. Attachments to parochial communities within the state reflecting religious, ethnic, linguistic, regional, and racial differences have become more salient reference points in the political process. As Nathan Glazer and Daniel Moynihan have written, "ethnic identity *has* become more salient, ethnic self-assertion stronger, ethnic conflict more marked everywhere in the last seventy years."[1] States widely considered to have passed the threshold of national integration, like Britain, France, Belgium, and Canada, suddenly again confront basic issues relating to the fundamental nature of the union of their constituent components. In some other states, like the Soviet Union, evidence suggests that the process of integration has been reversed, although without giving rise to open conflict.[2] Newspaper headlines have attested to the fragility of African states in the face of ethnic or tribal struggles. The human toll of the two and a-half year war in Nigeria and the intermittent slaughter of Hutus in Burundi provide just two examples of the human tragedy resulting from the insufficiency of a wider loyalty to a national community above and beyond the parochial communal group. Nor has Asia been free of the ravages of politicized pluralism. In a few cases, notably Lebanon and India, these communal forces have been harnessed within the context of a competitive political system, but in others, like Pakistan and Ceylon, they have split asunder a country and disrupted the functioning of the political process. No continent and virtually no nation is now immune to the impact of claims for special status and privileges made on behalf of communal groups. Concomitantly, few states can assume that allegiance to the national community in a time of crisis will supersede more particularistic sources of commitment. For a world in which, according to one survey, only 9 percent of all states can be considered essentially homogeneous from an ethnic point of view and as many as 40 percent are divided into at least five major ethnic components,[3] the politicization of communal subgroups obviously has widespread repercussions. Hence, the states of the world have entered a critical period in which the search for accommodation and cohesion of their constituent elements must claim high priority.

Lebanon and Ghana, the two states on which this study focuses, have both experienced the consequences of politicized pluralism. Religious groups in Lebanon and ethnic groups in Ghana constitute the major political forces infusing the dynamics of the political system. With a population approximately half Christian and half Muslim and with Christians and Muslims further subdivided into several sectarian groups in an area of the world in which religion has been a historical obsession, Lebanon has had to cope with the management of communal competition during its entire existence. Twice in a century (1860 and 1958), civil war has erupted, and in 1969 and 1973 fighting between Palestinian commandos and the Lebanese army had communal overtones as well. Lebanon's political institutions give more explicit recognition to the primacy of parochial loyalties than perhaps any other system. Ghana's borders encompass thirty four different language groups and more than two-hundred traditional states. Although communal tensions in Ghana have not been as acute as in Lebanon, Ghana has suffered from even greater political instability, much of which has had its roots in ethnic confrontation. According to one analysis, Ghana ranks eleventh of thirty two sub-Saharan African states on a scale of communal instability as measured by civil wars, rebellions, irredentism, and ethnic violence.[4] The severity of its communal problems are thus not atypical of many other African states.

The politicization of plural subgroups and the significance of its political implications have caught many social scientists unprepared. Their analytical models and their optimism that development was an ongoing, forward-moving process predisposed them to assume that communal loyalty was only a transitional phenomenon, a kind of temporary nuisance that would inexorably disappear as tradition gave way to modernity. Thus, an analysis of most of the literature on nation-building published during the 1960s reveals that scholars either ignored the issue of communalism or assumed that it constituted a minor impediment to effective integration.[5] According to one anthropologist, the reason that communalism and ethnicity have not received sufficient attention by social scientists is that "many sociologists and social anthropologists are still influenced by the evolutionary formulations of the great sociologists of the turn of this century who have seen all social change leading in one direction: from status to contract (Maine), from community to association (MacIver), from *gemeinshaft* to *gesellshaft* (Tonnies), from mechanical solidarity to organic solidarity (Durkheim)."[6] The preoccupation of political scientists with social classes as the "real" structure of society and ideological formulations as the only legitimate form of modern politics has also caused them to underrate or ignore religion, ethnic group, race, language, and region as enduring bases of division.[7] Because some scholars interested in national integration have posited a model of successive stages, each of them more depluralized than the preceding, they have tacitly assumed that new states would gradually move from one level to another and that the older nations would not regress.[8]

Events of the last decade attest to the fact that communal attachments do not quietly wither away with exposure to modernizing influences. Quite the contrary, modernization often creates the very conditions necessary for the incubation of strong communal identities and sets the stage for communal competition.[9] Milton Esman among others has concurred that contrary to expectations that modernization brings in its wake universal perspectives and values that facilitate integration, "among the many benefits that modernization brings, communal harmony cannot be included."[10] In traditional societies groups live side-by-side in considerable isolation, each relatively sufficient unto itself. The purveyors of modernization—the roads, schools, mass media, market economy, and participant politics—pierce the shell of communal autonomy and erode the inward orientation that accompanies it. As the psychological universe of individuals and groups expand, they experience the contacts with outsiders from which communal distinctions become more clearly defined. Without this interaction communal identities remain implicit rather than explicit. The emergence of a sense of distinctiveness and the recognition of boundaries between one's group and outsiders depend on exposure to a social universe beyond the confines of isolated traditional units. Hence, the intensity of communalism may reflect the pace of modernization and not the absence of change; the more people are brought into a wider network of interaction with other groups the more they may become aware of the differences that divide them.

Modernization also sets the stage for communal competition by endowing societies with new opportunities and resources. The economy of scarcity, which exists in most new states, tends to generate intense conflict among groups who, for the most part, correctly perceive that they are engaging in a zero sum game. In the absence of strong class consciousness or of political parties with a class or ideological base, communal groups naturally become the organizing structure of competition for political office and amenities. A history of unequal access and differences in the cultural receptivity to modernization have created disparities in the level of development of groups in all societies. These inequalities among communal groups reinforce distinctions and engender conflict.[11] Even in the more economically advanced states, which do not suffer from extreme economic deprivation, economic growth rarely satisfies expectations or results in a totally equitable distribution of wealth.

Industrialization and economic development may give rise to nontraditional forms of social differentiation like class and occupation, but the introduction of these new social categories does not necessarily weaken communal bonds. The resilience of communal identities combined with the limited industrialization of most new states have inhibited the emergence of strong class consciousness. Moreover, communal and noncommunal identities may coexist within an individual—each activated in different contexts. For instance, an ardent trade unionist at the factory may be a confirmed communalist in political interaction. An analysis of the contemporary political situation in several industrialized countries, like Belgium, Britain, the United States, Canada, and the Soviet Union, suggests that communal distinctions have much greater tenacity than most analysts had predicted.

Recent political changes have also stimulated communalism. The transition to independence has left multiethnic, anticolonial movements bereft of their source of unity and brought with it new foci for societal divisions in the scramble for the political and economic positions formerly held by the colonial power.[12] Attempts of governments in new African and Asian states to establish effective control throughout the states' territories have further intensified communal awareness. To some extent a similar process of increasing centralization of political power in more developed systems has also fostered a communal backlash. In the former case, the visibility of the new political system helps to expand the horizons and expectations of individuals and groups as well as to encourage their sense of competition with other communal groups. In the latter, the centralization of political power has so advanced that the citizen feels almost naked before the anonymous and distant government and craves some form of identity in which to clothe himself to impart meaning to his existence. In the absence of a strong sense of class consciousness and of voluntary associations and political parties which arouse strong loyalties, the communal mode of thinking asserts itself. An infrastructure of communal blocs thus provides the most compelling form of social and political organization in many states. While transitional systems have not arrived at the point in their economic development where class can be the rallying cry, the industrially advanced societies seem to be shedding their class character. According to Daniel Bell, among others, this disintegration of the older effective social class units which once provided a source of emotional attachment in the industrialized states has turned the "quest for community"[13] in the increasingly centralized political systems toward communal entities.[14]

The period of politicized pluralism has prompted the belated recognition by some social scientists of the importance of communal attachments. A considerable and pessimistic body of literature has come forth displacing the optimism of the early 1960s. Alvin Rabushka and Kenneth Shepsle relentlessly stress the sources of division and inherent instability in communally plural societies. They doubt that it is possible to manage, let alone integrate, communally fragmented political systems and adjudge that the practice of politics along ethnic lines is incompatible with democracy. They offer one small hope—that confederation will minimize the deleterious effects of ethnic politics by relegating key issues to lower levels and thus reducing tensions.[15] Cynthia Enloe claims that the nation–state orientation of other political scientists reflects an integrative and assimilative bias. In contrast, she considers plural states to be artificial collectivities often sustained by oppression rather than by worthwhile goals of political development.[16]

Neither the early optimism nor the current pessimism seems warranted. It seems clear that communal allegiance will not be swept away in the tide of modernization. Yet the existence of communal attachments does not doom a political system to conflict and instability. Within a given political system, communalism need not necessarily be translated from a social into a political phenomenon. Even racial distinctions, the most striking basis for communal differentiation, do not always become politically salient.[17] As described above, within the last decade the political environment in many states has encouraged a recasting of the role of communal groups from the social to the political, but the emergence of political communalism still does not foreclose the possibility of national accommodation, with the Netherlands and Switzerland serving as two examples. Although group solidarities based on religious, ethnic, racial, or linguistic identities often evoke more emotional, uncompromising, and strident political behavior than associations reflecting other types of social cleavages, they can be managed. Man does not stand helpless before a leviathan of unleashed communal solidarities. The issue should be cast in the mold of how it is possible to manage pluralism or, more specifically, how it is possible to achieve communal accommodation within the framework of a plural political system. When communalism enters the political arena, a political system may contain it within a competitive framework; alternatively, the communal forces can generate destructive conflict uncontrolled by the political system which may constitute a threat to the political order.

To learn more about the manner in which pluralism affects political systems and how national accommodation can be promoted, this study focuses on a comparison of the experiences of two states, Lebanon and Ghana. We selected these two countries to compare the dynamics of religious communalism and ethnic communalism; to contrast the experiences of states, one of which explicitly recognized the communal allegiances of its citizens as basic components of the system, and the other sought to ignore or eradicate them; and to include examples from two different cultural zones. The Lebanese and the Ghanaian political systems typify alternative approaches to the problems that confront communally divided societies. Perhaps more than any other state, the constitutional order in Lebanon legitimates the communal loyalties of its members by explicitly recognizing the need to placate communal interests. A basic agreement reached between leaders of the two largest sects on the eve of independence carefully distributes all political offices to reflect the proportional composition of the religious communities in Lebanon. This national pact continues to underlay the operation of the political system. In contrast, the goal of Ghana's political leaders after independence was to create a unitary mobilizing political system in which ethnic distinctions would be eradicated in favor of a common

Ghanaian nationality and a homogeneous political culture. The two regimes that followed Kwame Nkrumah's fall from power in 1966 adopted an attitude of benign neglect vis-à-vis ethnic conflict. Another factor that sets Lebanon and Ghana apart as much as their commitment to different political orders has been their respective levels of concern. For Lebanon the problem of communal conflict and balance has verged on an obsession. For none of the Ghanaian regimes has ethnic conflict been the central focus of governmental attention. Although this reflects differences in terms of the relative seriousness of communal conflict in the two countries, it also stems from differing political philosophies and differing assessments of the character of communalism generally.

We also chose Lebanon and Ghana in order to have data on two different cultural areas, namely the Middle East and Africa, both of which have experienced problems deriving from the politicization of pluralism. The civil wars in Nigeria, the Sudan, and the Congo (now Zaire); the massacres in Burundi; the expulsion of Asians in Uganda; and racial oppression in southern Africa provide the most obvious manifestations of Africa's communal problems. The severity of Ghana's problems does not compare with those in some other parts of Africa, but they are nonetheless serious. In the judgment of one Ghanaian professor, journalist, and former cabinet member, "There can be no field of research and social investigation deserving a greater pride of place on our list of priorities than the subject of ethnic unity and disunity. The prevalence and depth of ethnic consciousness, prejudice, animosity, and discrimination are worthy and urgent areas of study for our social scientists, psychologists, statisticians, etc."[18] Although communal conflict in Lebanon may be more serious than that in most other countries of the Middle East, virtually every state of the area, including Israel, confronts some measure of friction among communal groups. Recent research contradicts the once popular notion to the contrary and points to deep divisions in several states beneath a superficial veneer of unity.[19] Iliya Harik, for example, concludes from his survey of the area that, "In the Middle East serious ethnic problems exist regardless of the strong integrative character of the Islamic religion and culture."[20]

Despite major differences, Lebanon and Ghana do share certain elements. Both are relatively small in size with respective populations of about 2,500,000 and 8,500,000. The constituent communal groups can be grouped into two categories, each of which comprises approximately half of the population—Christian and Muslim in Lebanon and Akan and non-Akan in Ghana—but frequently in both systems the various actors pursue more particularistic paths in which this basic dualism is not salient. Relative to many other states in their regions, Lebanon and Ghana achieved independence early and have had the advantage of greater affluence and a higher level of literacy and education. The two have experienced extensive internal migration of their own citizens and immigration from adjacent countries with the resulting intermixing of communal groups, particularly in urban areas, and the presence of large communities of foreign residents.

In addition to the contrasts that led us to decide on the two countries —between the salience of religion and ethnic ties, between the approaches the governments have pursued, and between the cultural zones—other elements distinguish the two systems— the character of their colonial experience, the language configuration, the level of economic and social development, and the type of communal pressures to which they have been subjected. The colonial interlude lasted longer in Ghana with a more thorough impact on the society. Within Lebanon knowledge of Arabic imparts a common cultural bond and facilitates communication throughout the country whereas Ghana still relies on English as the official language in the face of thirty-four different vernacular languages; neither English nor any Ghanaian language provides a lingua franca through which all Ghanaians can converse. Although both Lebanon and Ghana have had the advantage of greater prosperity than many of their neighbors, the absolute level of development in Lebanon surpasses that of Ghana. Consequently, we explicitly eschew any claim of strict comparability and instead hope that an examination of the two cases will help illuminate the nature of communal interaction and the advantages and disadvantages inherent in the methods the two have adopted to deal with politicized pluralism.

COMMUNALISM AND PLURAL SOCIETIES

Communalism, the overriding attachment to groups sharing inherited bonds based on religion, ethnic descent, language, race, or regional origin, rests on the foundations of man's need for identity and belonging. This so-called quest for community to confer social meaning and purpose to life seems to be rooted in human nature. In the search for social definition, ascriptive communities have some kind of inexorable drawing power. As Clifford Geertz has perceptively explained, communal ties, or as he calls them, primordial attachments, stem from the "givens of social existence. . . . These congruities of blood, speech, custom, and so on are seen to have an ineffable, and at times overpowering, coerciveness in and of themselves. One is bound to one's kinsman, one's neighbor, one's fellow believer, *ipso facto*; as the result not merely of personal affection, practical necessity, common interest, or incurred obligation, but at least in great part by virtue of some unaccountable absolute import attributed to the very tie itself."[21]

Central to the communal syndrome of identifying with a particular ascriptive group is the resulting inclination for members to consider those in the society who do not partake of the same background as outsiders. Communal sentiments depend on the subjective drawing of a boundary between the ingroup and outgroup. Objective differences between groups count much less than the manner in which these discrepancies are selectively translated into patterns that the actors regard as significant. What Frederik Barth has said about ethnic groups characterizes other types of communal interactions as well: "Some cultural features are used by the actors as signals and emblems of differences, others are ignored, and in some relationships radical differences played down and denied."[22] Thus, some rigid boundaries actually reflect minimal cultural variations while others articulate major cleavages. Communal divisions may involve an element of arbitrariness, but members tend to feel their integrity to be inviolate.

Within the context of a national political system, the existence of strong communal attachments means that the primary loyalty of citizens is likely to be to constituent subgroups, and in a conflict between the interests of particular groups and the national society, members will probably support the former. Moreover, the tendency to perceive others who do not partake of the same background as outsiders rather than as fellow citizens reduces the inclination of any community to moderate its demands, and this increases the strains on the political system. The relative lack of concern with the commitment to shared membership in the national community often weakens the ability of the government to impose a national perspective in the resolution of problems. Thus, communally fragmented or plural societies cannot easily compensate for the deep divisions through vigorous political action. Although a society beset by communal divisions differs from more integrated systems, few of the independent states currently grappling with communalism fit the most popular typologies of fragmented or plural societies in the literature, which either optimistically posit that the multiple affiliations of the members produce a democratic equilibrium, or pessimistically assume that the absence of a homogeneous culture inevitably produces conflict and domination by a minority.[23] Neither of these models adequately applies to the widespread situation in which a number of communal groups live side by side in a common political system to which none owes primary allegiance and over which no minority has imposed its political control.

The equilibrium model of pluralism derives from an idealization of the American experience in which crosscutting loyalties and multiple affiliations moderate demands and effect a form of democratic integration through the fluid interplay of political interests. However, communally divided societies rarely manifest the political consensus which underlies the equilibrium model, and the imbalance in the attachment to communal groups precludes other associations from adequately countervailing the influence of communalism. As Walker Connor has pointed out, "The depth of the cleavage represented by separate national [communal] identities is more profound than are cleavages based upon religion, social class, and the like, and may, therefore *not* be susceptible to Madisonian concepts of cross-cutting interests under the rubric of cultural pluralism."[24] One of the characteristics of new polities tends to be the relative weakness of modern associations especially when they bridge communal boundaries. Even when other types of social cleavages exist, the salience of communal identities dwarfs the role that class, occupational, and ideological associations can play. According to one thoughtful critic of the pluralist model, Eric Nordlinger, "If cross-cutting differences are to engender feelings of being cross-pressured, they must be equally salient and simultaneously experienced."[25] When communal and noncommunal commitments conflict with each other, the competition is rarely between equal forces, each of which has an equal opportunity to determine the outcome. Instead, an individual frequently compartmentalizes his class and occupational identities and allows them to influence his behavior in only a narrow sphere. Furthermore, in many communally oriented societies cleavages reinforce rather than counterbalance each other. Unequal access to the benefits of modernization and differences among groups in their receptivity to innovations has frequently created major disparities in their levels of development. In cases where a communal group is economically disadvantaged, the advancement of a particular individual may be more dependent upon group action than on individual initiative, thereby strengthening communal bonds.

In the conflict model, as propounded by M.G. Smith, cultural diversity and value variances preclude any form of cooperation or shared activities. With the total absence of common institutions, only political domination by a cultural minority can hold the society together.[26] The preconditions for

Smith's model, a rigid hierarchical ordering of groups, the lack of any crosscutting associations or interests, and a closed political system, do not inhere in most communally divided societies. Class structure virtually always intersects communal groupings, and cross-cutting associations, although weak, do exist. Very few of the contemporary plural societies have a political leadership drawn exclusively from the members of a single community. Even in the racially plural societies of the West Indies on which Smith based his theories, other researchers have pointed out that "what is ordinarily at stake in a racially divided society is not domination but the desire to promote or protect specific identifiable interests."[27] Smith's model seems more applicable to the colonial order in which an alien white minority was superimposed over the system, and, in fact, Smith did directly draw his inspiration from J.S. Furnivall's analysis of colonial policy and practice.[28]

Therefore, there is a need to revise these somewhat extreme images of the manner in which communal groups interact. To do so it seemed advantageous to study two of the most prevalent forms of communalism, sectarianism and ethnicity. By comparing and contrasting the manner in which sectarianism in Lebanon and ethnicity in Ghana affect their respective societies and penetrate the political arena, we hope to contribute to the knowledge of pluralism. In the subsequent chapters dealing with the history, social and cultural framework, political structure and processes, and governmental policies we will attempt to clarify the following issues among others:

1.   The relationship between the depth of cleavages and the types of intercommunal social relations.
2.   Whether social, spatial, and institutional separation facilitate or hinder accommodation.
3.   The circumstances under which individuals and groups alter their communal identities and the implications of these changes for the political system.
4.   The manner in which centrifugal and centripetal communal pressures differ in their effect.
5.   How the political structure, processes, and governmental policies affect the search for accommodation.

Both the equilibrium and conflict models of pluralism consider the existence of crosscutting relationships and ties a critical variable; in the equilibrium model they provide the integrative mechanism that holds the society together and in the conflict model the presumed total absence of any shared institutions dooms the society to the imposition of authoritarian controls by a minority. Arend Lijphart's research on the Netherlands has led him to question these assumptions about crosscutting loyalties. Lijphart suggests that in a society with deep, mutually reinforcing social cleavages, self-containment, and mutual isolation can be more beneficial for stability and democracy than a high incidence of overlapping affiliations. Lijphart finds considerable virtue in the same social conditions that cause other analysts to preclude the possibility of establishing a democratic system and even to foresee the potential for inherent conflict. The essential element in Lijphart's formulation is the question of elite cooperation. He writes that in a communally fragmented society, cooperation at the elite level may compensate for the weakness of countervailing loyalties in the masses.[29]

Lebanon and Ghana have different patterns of crosscutting relationships, self-containment, and mutual isolation. Lebanese have established a considerable network of modernized sectarian institutions; for the Ghanaians the primary infrastructure of ethnic separateness comes in the remnants of the traditional political systems. Although neither of the two countries is an extreme example, Ghana has greater homogeneity than Lebanon in the spatial location of groups. Professional associations, trade unions, class structure, schooling, exposure to the mass media, and, in the case of Ghana, religion intersect communal divisions in both societies with varying effectiveness. We will consider the relative impact of social forces prompting separation and those conducive to integration of communal groupings in order to assess better Lijphart's thesis that crosscutting affiliations are not a requirement for accommodation.

Contrary to the assumption that communal groupings represent fixed patterns on the social landscape, ample evidence exists that they ebb and flow in response to changing conditions and opportunities.[30] This has significant implications for the dynamics of communal interaction. As the environment in which social intercourse takes place alters, individuals and groups may modify their perceptions of themselves and of other communities. Within an expanded field of interaction, cultural differences that once loomed large between two contiguous communities may no longer be considered sufficient to establish a boundary, with the two groups then choosing to emphasize the common elements they share vis-a-vis the others within the system. This has occurred, for instance, in the assertion of a new Akan identity in Ghana fusing the once-antagonistic Fanti and Ashanti ethnic groups. Moreover, many of the most significant communal entities now vying for men's loyalties are not traditional in origin. The scale of most traditional societies and their communal components was much smaller than the states of today, and in the few far flung empires decentralization and local autonomy prevailed. In both Ghana and in Lebanon, long part of the Ottoman Empire, the traditional horizons of an individual rarely extended beyond neighboring villages with whom he had frequent contact. Within a contemporary urban center, though, and even more so in the context of the national political system, the traditional communal groups often prove to be too limited to be effective groupings for political competition. Thus, communal groups have tended to expand in scope to incorporate members of similar communities. With the decay of the feudal system in Lebanon and the fusion of the villages into the national political system, generalized bonds grew between members of the same religious sect. Similarly, inclusive ethnolinguistic blocs defined by linguistic boundaries have gradually emerged as political forces in Ghana. Thus, with the expansion in scope of communal identities, individuals and groups retain their original primary ties, but new bloc identities are superimposed over layers of more traditional orientations.

At any point in time, an individual in a plural society is potentially a member of more than one communal group since several types of ascriptive categories exist and the boundary defining a specific kind of communal entity may be drawn at varying levels of inclusiveness. With these alternative traditional and nontraditional forms of self-definition, the perimeter of the group to which an individual feels bound may change as a reflection of the field of social interaction. The particular environment, the issue involved, the size of the arena, the timing, and the nature of the antagonist all influence the communal bonds an individual or group emphasizes. Political or economic expediency may introduce an element of conscious choice among the options open.[31] The concept of situational identity refers to the phenomenon of the specific context determining the nature of identity.[32] Which form of identity at which level of inclusiveness individuals habitually find most salient for political competition obviously has important implications for the political system, and this will be another subject we consider. Whether members of Muslim or Christian sects in Lebanon perceive themselves primarily in accordance with their specific sectarian identities or more generally as Muslims or Christians vitally affects the dynamics of communal interaction. Similarly, the frequency with which the broader ethnolinguistic bloc identities supersede the more traditional frames of reference in Ghana has significant repercussions for the management of communalism in that country.

Historically, Lebanon has experienced centripetal pressures toward some form of federation with other Arab states, while in Ghana centrifugal pressures exerted by specific ethnic groups for greater autonomy and preferential treatment have been the key issue. As a consequence, foreign policy questions arouse communal cleavages in Lebanon far more than in Ghana, and the boundaries between international and domestic politics remain more fluid. The manner in which these two kinds of pressures mold societal relations and the strains they impose on the two political systems provide another of our themes.

Analysts often consider Lebanon to be a classic case of the problems wrought by politicized pluralism, but observers of Ghana have sometimes minimized the depth of ethnic cleavages there. Our assessment of these two systems takes issue with these polarized views, but historically communalism has been a greater political problem in Lebanon. Despite this, the Lebanese have developed more of a will to live together than Ghana's constituent groups, which show signs of increasing ethnocentricity and intolerance. How this has come about and its implications will be a subject to which we return at several points in this study.

NATIONAL ACCOMMODATION

The nature of the political institutions, political processes, and governmental policies to a great extent structure the kinds of social and political relationships that ensue in a communally fragmented society. In a society characterized by deep communal divisions individuals naturally prefer and promote the interests of their own group. Through the careful management of communalism, a political system can channel this group ethnocentrism into peaceful, supportive political competition. By negligence and mismanagement it can be allowed to degenerate into destabilizing conflict and violence. The mere existence of communal cleavages in no way predetermines political or social patterns. National accommodation refers to a political strategy for communally fragmented societies in which the political system accommodates the communal groups at the same time that it attempts to promote a measure of common loyalty to the national community. By incorporating communal groups into the political system and giving them a stake in its survival, it moderates conceptions of communal self-interest. National accommodation has as its goal the achievement of unity in diversity. In a political system in which communal groups have a sense of security and mutual toleration, loyalty to the national community can be entirely consistent with the maintenance of the integrity of communal entities. National citizenship and communal membership should not be considered as irreconcilable alternatives. Even in the most developed industrial society, people retain intermediate attachments mediating between the individual and the national community. Past experience, including that of Ghana, has shown that it is generally not feasible to obliterate communal ties in favor of instilling a total commitment to the nation. Nor would it be desirable to coercively unify the population, given the psychological and emotional costs this would entail. Thus, the strategy of national accommodation that we articulate and recommend recognizes that communal groups have something positive to offer in the way of making life meaningful and secure as well as providing an infrastructure for political competition based on socially relevant cleavages. We believe that by promoting national accommodation, a sense of national citizenship can be imposed over existing networks of subnational loyalties.

What we refer to as the system of national accommodation encompasses both a *means* of managing communal tensions and promoting improved intergroup relations as well as to the *character* of those improved relations. It does not describe any existing political system, and thus refers to an idealized type. Yet it does embody elements that have been productively employed by one or another fragmented political system. In articulating this idealized system, we draw heavily upon the experiences, both successful and unsuccessful, of our two cases, Ghana and Lebanon. The full character of the national accommodation system only becomes clear in subsequent chapters, but we can outline its principal components here.

Most of the existing literature does not address itself to how it is possible to attain communal accommodation within a plural political system. As mentioned earlier, some social scientists have often underestimated the tenacity of communal distinctions while others have pessimistically assumed that communal identity and national loyalty stand as opposed and irreconcilable forces. For both of these groups the depluralization of society precedes the achievement of greater unity. Studies of national integration, as for example Karl Deutsch's seminal work, usually have as their focus the amalgamation of two or more previously independent territories rather than the unification of a plural society.[33] When they do consider the subject of national unity, their models tend to be preindustrial European states, which tends to give their formulations an assimilationist bias. But examples of assimilation that occurred prior to the advent of the age of nationalism have little relevance for contemporary plural states.[34] The adoption of a unitary political system that does not make any concessions to the plural nature of the society in the hopes that it will promote cultural homogenization as it did several centuries ago in England or France, appears to be an inadequate, even a misguided, strategy in the age of politicized pluralism.

Some analysts, such as Eric Nordlinger, have argued that efforts to promote national integration are doomed to failure and are counterproductive because they often exacerbate segmental loyalties in their wake. Nordlinger proposes a new approach which he calls conflict regulation. To obviate intense or severe conflict in a plural society, Nordlinger defines six strategies available to a nonrepressive political regime: stable government coalition, the principle of proportionality, the mutual veto, purposive depoliticization, compromises on the issues that divide the conflict groups, and the granting of concessions.[35] As the first systematic work on the management of conflict in fragmented societies and as an antidote to much of the unfounded optimism in earlier social science literature, Nordlinger's study is an important contribution. However, Nordlinger's attempt to encompass in his analysis societies fragmented either by class or communal divisions, his failure to address himself specifically to communally oriented societies, and his choice of case material upon which he builds his theory limit the applicability of his conclusions.

Arend Lijphart has suggested that the management of conflict depends on structured elite predominance by leaders who accept the need for reconciliation. Lijphart's model of a consociational democracy emphasizes four characteristics of the elite as a prerequisite to the containment of communal tensions: a recognition of the dangers inherent in a fragmented political system, a commitment to maintain the system, a willingness (at least on some occasions) to transcend cleavage lines, and an ability to formulate nondivisive solutions to the demands of the constituent groups.[36]

Milton Esman attempts to extend Nordlinger's analysis to the peculiar characteristics of communally plural societies.[37] Esman identifies four classes of regime objectives: institutionalized dominance, induced assimilation, syncretic integration, and balanced pluralism. The first type, composed of those states committed to maintaining the institutionalized dominance of a particular communal group, resorts to networks of control and coercive techniques along with the institutionalization of preferential access for the elite to positions of educational, economic, and political ascendance in order to perpetuate the inferiority of the subordinate communities. In contrast, a regime bent on induced assimilation offers the carrot rather than the stick.

Through noncoercive incentives it attempts to induce those outside of the dominant community to give up their identity and adopt the language and culture of their governors. Those willing and able to acculturate then become absorbed on a nondiscriminatory basis. Through a policy of syncretic integration the elites of the third kind of regime aspire to replace communal loyalties with a transcendent new national identity and in the process, create the foundations for a genuinely integrated nation-state. For the exponents of this strategy, expressions of communal solidarity need to give way to loyalty to the state. Again, in a kind of dialectical movement the fourth approach, balanced pluralism, accords legitimacy to parochial solidarities within the society by incorporating them into the political system. This group-oriented system attempts to manage stresses and conflict through structured bargaining and the proportional allocation of resources and opportunities among the communal entities. Esman's interpretation of the principle of proportionality incorporates five of Nordlinger's six processes of conflict regulation: stable conditions, proportionality, compromises, mutual veto, and depoliticization. Esman's favored type of system, balanced pluralism, creates the conditions for open competition and for the management of conflict, but he does not foresee, at least in this article, that something more will evolve out of these arrangements. Esman implies that the dynamics of interaction in communally divided societies will remain almost indefinitely informed by communal interests alone.

Esman goes beyond his formulation of balanced pluralism in his study of administration in Malaysia.[38] Here he acknowledges that the adoption of a political system akin to his model of balanced pluralism did not solve Malaysia's problems, at least partially because the government responded to communal conflict rather than anticipating it. He proposes a guidance model of conflict management in which the government (1) goes beyond merely reacting to communal crises to forestalling it, and (2) stimulates and structures intergroup communication to promote accommodative habits of thinking, decisions, and behavior in the population. In its basic thrust Esman's guidance model bears resemblance to our system of national accommodation: we concur in the need to institutionalize procedures in the political system, enabling participation by the basic communal groups in the society, and simultaneously to pursue policy initiatives that strengthen the will to live together as members of a common political system.

The achievement of national accommodation depends on the nature of the political structure, political processes, and governmental policies. The appropriate political structure for a communal society can reduce the propensity for communal conflict and transform it into system supportive communal competition by incorporating communal groups in the society in a meaningful manner. The achievement of a sense of security is a subjective matter; psychological and emotional interpretations of political events are often more important than the facts of a situation in determining reactions. For this reason, adoption of a formula for sharing political power has many advantages over leaving the composition of the government to the vicissitudes of political dynamics.

Participation can help to impart a stake in the success of the system and can confer a sense of security deriving from the awareness that interests are protected. The institutionalization of the following mechanisms, possibly by explicitly writing the provisions into the constitution, would facilitate the direct incorporation of the communal groups into the political system: (1) the distribution of political offices and administrative positions to the major communal groups approximately proportional to the percentage of the population they constitute, (2) the allocation of amenities and economic resources in an equitable manner so that each group or region gets its fair share, (3) the establishment of channels of communication with groups in order to allow them to articulate their demands, (4) the maintenance of institutional forums in which representatives of various groups meet for discussion and bargaining, and (5) the adoption of an electoral system that reduces incentives for communal appeals and increases pressures for cooperation.

Political processes would facilitate national accommodation in a communally fragmented society to the extent that they (1) provided for communal coalitions and (2) linked the masses with political leaders. The political dynamics of a system of national accommodation bring together members of the major communal groups in some kind of alliance either through common institutions, like political parties, or through permanent elite coalitions. In some communally oriented political systems political parties have managed to establish a base transcending a single communal entity, but in many other states conditions are not conducive to the institutionalization of any effective political parties, let alone those that can incorporate members of diverse communal blocs. In the absence of effective mass parties with multicommunal support, the best alternative seems to be the institutionalization of a network of patron–client relationships at various levels of the political system which link together leaders of the several communities. Although Lijphart's model of consociational democracy also emphasizes elite cohesion, our system of national accommodation reflects the belief that the viability and harmonious operation of most fragmented political systems require more than a desire on the part of the elite that the system functions well. Mechanisms for distributing political power equitably must be institutionalized and means must be sought for promoting not merely elite cohesion, but improved intergroup relations and greater national cohesion at the mass level as well.

National accommodation depends on skilled political governance and self-consciousness. Governmental policy can facilitate national accommodation when political leaders act with an awareness of the implications of their decisions for communal relations and with the intention of promoting intergroup reconciliation. Well-intentioned political leaders sometimes wreak havoc rather than promote development precisely because they lack the foresight to consider how their policies will be received. At another level, to foster national accommodation decision-makers must be able to anticipate communal issues in order to study the problems and try to resolve them in advance.[39] Politicians and administrators must go beyond being managers of the present to be more imaginative molders of the future. A competitive political system is more likely to bring forth such consummate political managers than a more authoritarian regime, and civilian politicians generally have greater political skills than their military counterparts.

A system that effectively promotes national accommodation will also openly pursue measures to instill greater national unity. Often, however, the characteristic mode of action with regard to national unity is to do little and then suddenly undertake too much too abruptly.[40] Three policy areas stand out as deserving special attention: economic, educational, and language. Economic policy has particular sensitivity because communal tensions often reflect cumulative disparities in economic development.[41] Furthermore, an unstructured scramble for amenities and development projects frequently exacerbates proclivities toward communal conflict.

The government in a system successfully promoting national accommodation assumes an active role as an agent of national political socialization. Political socialization refers to the process through which people acquire their political values, orientations, and habits. In a pluralistic society in which people have no long history of living together as members of a common system, the political outlooks of the various communal groups tend to be quite different. For this reason the literature emphasizes two forms of discontinuities in these states. First, parents prepare their children for participation in the traditional local patterns rather than in the national political system, with the result that children do not learn the appropriate norms and skills required of citizens of a modern state.[42] Second, the political culture of these systems is fragmented because it reflects the distinct orientations of the constituent groups, and this lack of consensus leads to difficulties in the functioning of the political system.[43] Such a situation implies that a critical vacuum exists with regard to the interests of the national community as distinct from the parochial constituent groups. But it is possible to balance socialization into the subcultures by exposing members of the society to learning experiences that impart a more national perspective. A national system of education provides the most feasible means of instilling this social learning. To use the educational system in such a way requires effective national control over the curriculum and in most countries a substantial reform of the content of social studies in order to effectively inculcate national awareness and pride, tolerance toward other groups, and appropriate political values. The educational systems in the United States, the Soviet Union, and to some extent, the Philippines have been consciously and successfully employed in this manner.[44]

Language policy constitutes another critical sphere—pluralistic societies like Ghana cope with a mélange of languages as well as different cultures. Without the government promoting a lingua franca, citizens may lack a means of communication with each other, something which obviously inhibits that growth of contacts, understanding, common experience, and cooperation so vital to the evolution of national accommodation.

The achievement of national accommodation is a gradual process in which communal relations move along a continuum from continuous conflict to more frequent cooperation. National accommodation cannot be attained once and for all; it requires constant dedication and watchfulness. There is no threshold or take-off point beyond which the possibility of reversion to intense conflict does not exist. Moreover, progress toward national accommodation does not bring in its wake the resolution of all major political issues. Nevertheless, a significant measure of accommodation is genuinely worth striving for, as an end in itself and to provide a context within which the state can come to terms with its other major political problems.

There are no precise ways of measuring the pace at which national accommodation is advancing, and progress in all spheres cannot occur simultaneously. As a political system moves toward accommodation, it will be characterized by decreasing strife and instability arising from communal confrontation, increasing attachment to the political system, more accommodative behavior on a personal level, greater acceptance of a national frame of reference, and convergence in basic political values pertaining to the major goals of the national system. Through this process citizens will retain their attachment to communal groups, but the repercussions of these communal divisions for the national political system will be quite different from what they are in most contemporary fragmented societies. Communal interests will express themselves through peaceful political competition, which implies an acceptance of the legitimacy of the political system and its rules. Citizens will be imbued with a will to live together, which will moderate their demands and orientations, and they will have a sense of belonging to a common national community.

NOTES

1. Nathan Glazer and Daniel P. Moynihan, "Why Ethnicity?" *Commentary* 58 (October 1974), p. 39. For a similar statement see also Samuel P. Huntington, "Foreword," in Eric A. Nordlinger, *Conflict Resolution in Divided Societies* (Cambridge, Mass.: Harvard University, Center for International Affairs), Occasional Papers in International Affairs, No. 29, January 1972.
2. Richard Pipes, "Reflections on the Ethnic Problems in the Soviet Union," unpublished paper presented at the Conference on Ethnic Problems, American Academy of Arts and Sciences, Boston, 1972.
3. Walker Connor, "Nation-Building or Nation-Destroying," *World Politics*, XXIV (April 1972), p. 320.
4. Donald G. Morrison, Robert C. Mitchell, John H. Paden, and Hugh M. Stevenson, *Black Africa: A Comparative Handbook* (New York: Free Press, 1972), p. 126.
5. Walker Connor's article is a devastating criticism of this false optimism. See pp. 319–355.
6. Abner Cohen, *Custom and Politics in Urban Africa: A Study of the Hausa Migrants in Yoruba Towns* (Berkeley and Los Angeles: University of California Press, 1969), p. 197.
7. On the former, see Robert A. Dahl, *Polyarchy: Participation and Opposition* (New Haven; Yale University Press, 1971), pp. 106–107.
8. See, for example, Ali A. Mazrui, "Pluralism and National Integration," in Leo Kuper and M. G. Smith, eds., *Pluralism in Africa* (Berkeley and Los Angeles: University of California Press, 1969), pp. 333–349 and Ali A. Mazrui, *Cultural Engineering and Nation-Building in East Africa* (Evanston, Ill.: Northwestern University Press, 1972).
9. On this point, see Clifford Geertz, "The Integrative Revolution: Primordial Sentiments and Civil Politics in the New States," in Clifford Geertz, ed., *Old Societies and New States* (New York: The Free Press of Glencoe, 1963), pp. 105–153; Robert Melson and Howard Wolpe, "Modernization and the Politics of Communalism: A Theoretical Perspective," in Melson and Wolpe, eds., *Nigeria: Modernization and the Politics of Communalism* (East Lansing: Michigan State University Press, 1971), pp. 1–42; Milton Esman, *Administration and Development in Malaysia: Institution Building and Reform in a Plural Society* (Ithaca: Cornell University Press, 1972); Rajni Kothari, *Politics in India* (Boston: Little, Brown

and Co., 1970), pp. 224–245, 250–257; Iliya F. Harik, "The Ethnic Revolution and Political Integration in the Middle East," *International Journal of Middle Eastern Studies*, 3 (July 1972), pp. 303–323; John N. Paden, "Urban Pluralism, Integration, and Adaptation of Communal Identity in Kano, Nigeria," in Ronald Cohen and John Middleton, eds., *From Tribe to Nation in Africa: Studies in Incorporation Processes* (Scranton, Pa.: Chandler Publishing Co., 1970), pp. 242–270.

10. Milton Esman, "The Management of Communal Conflict," *Public Policy*, 21 (Winter 1973), p. 69.

11. On this point, see Aristide R. Zolberg, "Tribalism through Corrective Lenses," *Foreign Affairs*, 51 (July 1973), p. 733.

12. See Rupert Emerson, *From Empire to Nation* (Cambridge, Mass.: Harvard University Press, 1960).

13. William Peterson uses this term in his "Ethnic Structures in Western Europe," unpublished paper presented at the Conference on Ethnic Problems, Boston, 1972.

14. Daniel Bell, "Ethnicity and Social Change," unpublished paper presented at the Conference on Ethnic Problems; Daniel Bell, *The End of Ideology: On the Exhaustion of Political Ideas in the Fifties* (Glencoe, Ill.: Free Press, 1960).

15. Alvin Rabushka and Kenneth A. Shepsle, *Politics in Plural Societies: A Theory of Democratic Instability* (Columbus, Ohio: Charles E. Merrill, 1972).

16. Cynthia H. Enloe, *Ethnic Conflict and Political Development* (Boston: Little, Brown and Co., 1973).

17. For a discussion of this point, see Victor C. Ferkiss and Barbara Ferkiss, "Race and Politics in Trinidad and Guyana," unpublished paper, n.d.

18. G. Adali-Morty, "Facing the Music of Tribalism," *Daily Graphic*, March 25, 1972, p. 9.

19. Philip C. Salzman, "National Integration of the Tribes in Iran," *Middle East Journal*, 25 (Summer 1971), pp. 325–336; Frank R. Golins, "Patterns of Libyan National Integration," *Middle East Journal*, 24 (Summer 1970), pp. 338–352; Michael H. Van Dusen, "Political Integration and Regionalism in Syria," *Middle East Journal*, 26 (Spring 1972), pp. 123–136; Aryeh Rubinstein, "Israel's Integration Problem," in Benjamin Rivlin and Joseph S. Szyliowicz, *The Contemporary Middle East: Tradition and Innovation* (New York: Random House, 1965), pp. 388–396; Albert Hourani, A *Vision of History: Near Eastern and Other Essays* (Beirut: Khayats, 1961), pp. 71–105.

20. Harik, op cit., p. 303.

21. Geertz, op.cit., p. 104.

22. Frederik Barth, "Introduction," in Frederik Barth, ed., *Ethnic Groups and Boundaries: The Social Organization of Cultural Differences* (Boston: Little, Brown and Co., 1969), p. 14.

23. Leo Kuper, "Plural Societies: Perspectives and Problems," in Kuper and Smith, eds., op.cit., pp. 10–16.

24. Walker Connor, "The Politics of Ethnonationalism," *Journal of International Affairs*, 27, 1 (1973), p. 20. Emphasis is in the original.

25. Nordlinger, op. cit., p. 26.

26. M. G. Smith, *The Plural Society in the British West Indies* (Berkeley and Los Angeles: University of California Press, 1965); M. G. Smith, "Institutional and Political Conditions of Pluralism," in Kuper, op. cit., pp. 27–65.

27. Ferkiss and Ferkiss, op. cit.

28. J. S. Furnivall, *Colonial Policy and Practice* (London: Cambridge University Press, 1948).

29. Arend Lijphart, *The Politics of Accommodation: Pluralism and Democracy in the Netherlands* (Berkeley: University of California Press, 1968), pp. 199–211.

30. On this point, see Aristide R. Zolberg, "Patterns of National Integration," *Journal of*

Modern African Studies, V (December 1967), pp. 449–468; Paul Mercier, "On the Meaning of Tribalism in Black Africa," in Pierre L. van den Berghe, ed., *Africa: Social Problems of Change and Conflict* (San Francisco: Chandler Publishing Company, 1965), pp. 483–501; various essays in Barth.

31. See, for example, Audrey C. Smock, *Ibo Politics: The Role of Ethnic Unions in Eastern Nigeria* (Cambridge, Mass.: Harvard University Press, 1971), pp. 203–207; Melson and Wolpe, op. cit., pp. 5–6; Cohen, op. cit., pp. 186–190, 198–200.

32. John N. Paden, "Situational Ethnicity in Urban Africa with Special Reference to the Hausa," unpublished paper presented at the African Studies Association meeting, New York, 1967.

33. Karl W. Deutsch, et. al, *Political Community in the North Atlantic Area: International Organization in the Light of Recent Experience* (Princeton: Princeton University Press, 1957).

34. Connor, "The Politics of Ethnonationalism," op. cit., p. 20.

35. Nordlinger, op. cit., pp. 1–37.

36. Arend Lijphart; "Typologies of Democratic Systems," *Comparative Political Studies*, I (April 1968), pp. 22–23; Lijphart, "Consociational Democracy." *World Politics*, 21 (January 1967), p. 221.

37. Esman, "The Management of Ethnic Conflict," op. cit.

38. Esman, *Administration and Development in Malaysia*, op. cit., pp. 246–283.

39. Ibid., p. 266.

40. Critics of efforts to achieve greater national unity can point to cases where an attempt to foster national unity was counterproductive, but what they fail to realize is that the problem usually derives from the manner in which the political system handled the subject rather than the aim in itself.

41. On this point, see Zolberg, "Tribalism through Corrective Lenses" op. cit.; Robert H. Bates; "Ethnicity and Modernization in Contemporary Africa," Social Science Workshop Paper, No. 16 (Pasadena: California Institute of Technology, 1972).

42. Robert LeVine, "Political Socialization and Cultural Change," in Geertz, ed., op. cit., pp. 282–285.

43. Gabriel A. Almond and G. Bingham Powell, Jr., *Comparative Politics: A Development Approach* (Boston: Little, Brown and Co., 1966), pp. 63–72.

44. Jeremy R. Azrael, "Patterns of Polity Directed Educational Development: The Soviet Case," in James S. Coleman, ed., *Education and Political Development* (Princeton: Princeton University Press, 1965), pp. 233–271; George L. F. Beresday and Bonnie B. Stretch, "Political Education in the U.S.A. and U.S.S.R.," *Comparative Education Review*, 7 (June 1963), pp. 9–16; Robert D. Hess and Judith Torney, *The Development of Political Attitudes in Children* (Garden City, N. Y.: Doubleday and Company, 1968); Carl H. Lande, "Patterns of Polity Directed Educational Development: The Philippines," in James S. Coleman, ed., pp. 313–349.

 *2*

The Creation and Viability
of the Two States:
A Historical Perspective

LEBANON

In August 1920, four months after the Allied Supreme Council granted France mandatory authority over Lebanon and Syria, France announced the creation of the new State of Greater Lebanon. The boundaries of this new state, which coincide with those of contemporary Lebanon, diverged considerably from the portion of the Ottoman Empire that had constituted the area previously referred to as Lebanon. France's decision in 1920 doubled Lebanon's land area and increased its population by half, from 400,000 to 600,000. More critical still, the residents of the annexed areas differed significantly, particularly in terms of religion, from those of the core area. The former state, consisting principally of the area of Mount Lebanon, was composed primarily of Maronite and Greek Orthodox Christians and Druze, while most of the residents of the annexed areas were Shiite and Sunni Muslims. Given the social, economic, and political significance of religious identity in the area, this new configuration had enormous import for the viability of the enlarged state. In attempting to assess the problems of national integration faced by the new state, it is essential to look backward in time and to analyze the relationships that existed between the constituent religious or confessional communities prior to 1920.

24

Territorial Extent

At first glance it appears that the new State of Greater Lebanon was an artificial creation of the French with few historical foundations, differing both territorially and demographically from the Lebanon that was incorporated into the Ottoman Empire from 1518 to 1918. The division of the area of Greater Lebanon during most of the four centuries under Ottoman hegemony into three separate Ottoman provinces, each of which included other territories as well, seems to lend further support for this interpretation. Deeper historical analysis reveals, however, that the new State of Greater Lebanon was considerably less fragile and artificial than these facts suggest, both because during various periods of its history Lebanon enjoyed autonomous or semiautonomous status with Ottoman administrative control kept to a minimum, and because at various times in the past all of the area of Greater Lebanon had been under some form of Lebanese control.

It is difficult to be precise about the geographical extent of Lebanon prior to 1920 for several reasons. First, during the eighteenth and nineteenth centuries the boundaries shifted, alternately expanding and contracting. Second, what may have been officially recognized by the Ottoman Sultan as constituting Lebanon did not necessarily coincide with the expanse of territory under either the influence or control of the Lebanese emirs. Third, the Ottoman rulers were often not exact in defining Lebanon's geographical boundaries.

For the full period of its existence from 1516 to 1697, the Ma'n dynasty controlled the Chouf area of Mount Lebanon. But during the early part of the seventeenth century, the Ma'n emir Fakhr al-Din II extended Ma'n domination over an expanse of territory extending somewhat beyond current Lebanese borders on the north, east, and south. Despite the rather tenuous and short-lived nature of this hegemony, this period can be considered the beginnings of rudimentary political integration of the area now constituting Lebanon. Ma'n rule had a sustained, albeit weak, integrative impact on the central mountainous core of Mount Lebanon. From the Ottoman's perspective, the Lebanese emirate of the Ma'n dynasty and the Chehab dynasty, which succeeded the Ma'n in 1697, roughly corresponded with the southern two-thirds of Mount Lebanon. However, the coastal cities of Beirut, Sidon, and Tripoli all came under Ma'n sway for varying lengths of time, and Beirut was in the Chehab sphere during a portion of the eighteenth century. The

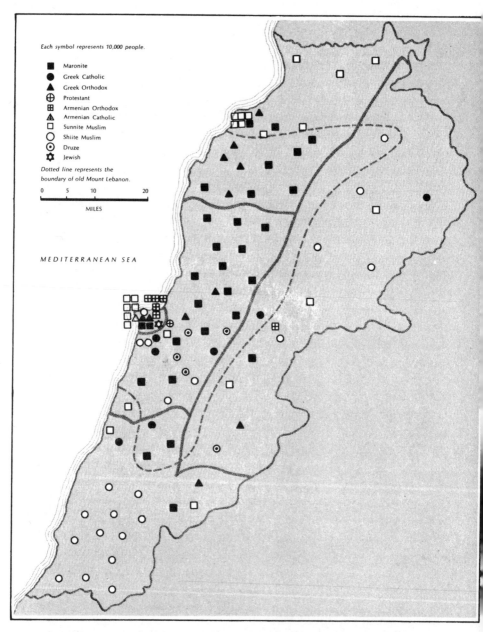

FIGURE 2-1 *Ottoman Mount Lebanon and Recent Distribution of Major Lebanese Sects*

After Pierre Rondot, *Les Institutions Politiques du Liban* (Paris: Imprimerie Nationale, 1947), p. 32.

SOURCE: Michael C. Hudson, *The Precarious Republic: Modernization in Lebanon* (New York: Random House, 1968), p. 26. Reprinted by permission of Random House and Pierre Rondot.

central and southern portions of the Bekaa valley were almost continually dominated by the Ma'n and Chehab emirs, although they officially constituted part of Damascus. Even the northern Bekaa, which was never in the orbit of the rulers of Mount Lebanon to the extent that the rest of the Bekaa was, felt the impress of Ma'n and Chehabi influence. Thus, those portions of Greater Lebanon annexed to Lebanon by the French in 1920 had important historical ties to Mount Lebanon.

Despite the truth of this assertion, it is erroneous to suggest, as some historians have, that present-day Lebanon constitutes a single national unit which has enjoyed historical continuity for the past three hundred years. Although areas like Beirut and Tripoli at one time or another did come within the orbit of the Mount Lebanon emirs, their control remained intermittent. Moreover, following the fall of the Chehab dynasty in 1842, the territorial expanse of Mount Lebanon was much more carefully defined and circumscribed, and this situation persisted from 1842 to 1918. Thus, the annexed areas of northern and southern Lebanon and the Bekaa had substantially fallen outside the sphere of influence of Mount Lebanon for nearly eighty years prior to their annexation in 1920. Finally, the territorial dominion of the Ma'n and Chehab emirs, when it did extend beyond Mount Lebanon, did not cover an area necessarily coterminus with Greater Lebanon. During some periods it fell significantly short of those boundaries, while at others it exceeded those borders, with, for example, Bashir I (1697–1707) holding sway over Galilee and Bashir II (1788–1840) controlling large portions of present-day Syria. So while the historical analyst needs to avoid thinking of Greater Lebanon in 1920 as being merely an artificial creation of the French, the other fallacy of complete historical continuity must also be eschewed.

Despite the fact that historical Lebanon, that is, Mount Lebanon, was part of the Ottoman Empire, it enjoyed a unique degree of autonomy. This resulted from the popular support the residents of the area gave to their emirs and from the military prowess of the mountain-dwelling peasants. During the rule of Bashir II, the population of Mount Lebanon barely conceded that they did not constitute an independent state. However, the form, strength, and degree of autonomy of the government of Lebanon during the Ottoman period changed frequently.

Until about 1840 a feudal system prevailed with the emir superimposed on a hierarchy of politico-economic classes. The emir's government performed a limited role during the Ma'n dynasty. As in other feudal systems, the emir did not have direct contact with the citizenry, but worked through his vassals. However, under the Chehabs, and particularly under Bashir II, the emir exercised considerable control throughout his domain.

Steady growth in governmental centralization, legitimacy and autonomy did not characterize the history of Mount Lebanon from 1516 to 1920. Even though Fakhr al-Din II had been the single ruler for the whole of his expanded emirate, when the Chehab dynasty gained control, they initially bifurcated Mount Lebanon into autonomous northern and southern emirates, ruled by two separate emirs. In 1770 Emir Yusuf became emir of a united Mount Lebanon, but it later was divided into two parts again, until it was reunited by Bashir II in 1807. Although Bashir II proved to be an independent and effective nation-builder, following the Egyptian invasion in 1832 the invaders effectively manipulated him to serve Egyptian ends. Bashir III, who succeeded as emir in 1840, was so weak and ineffective that the Chehab dynasty fell and the Ottomans attempted to impose direct Ottoman control over Mount Lebanon during the period of 1842 to 1860. Although the Lebanese notables had previously selected their own emir, the new governor in 1842 was a foreigner, a Croat, who was appointed directly by the Ottoman Sultan. During this period the Ottomans redivided the country again into two provinces, the northern portion headed by a Lebanese Maronite and the southern province by a Lebanese Druze, each reporting to the governor. Thus, during the period of the so-called Double Kaymakamate, Lebanon was forced to submit to both internal division and foreign control. Following the Christian–Druze massacres of 1860, the French, Russians, British, and Austrians forced the Turks to establish a more effective form of government, which resulted in the Règlement Organique adopted in 1861 and subsequently revised in 1864. Under the Règlement Organique Lebanon enjoyed a greater autonomy with its own army, police, and courts, and a centralized government replaced the two federated provinces. However, the governor was non-Lebanese and was directly responsible to Istanbul, and this seriously compromised the autonomy. This arrangement persisted until 1920, when Greater Lebanon was created under French mandatory control.

The Confessional Communities, 1697 to 1920

The dichotomy between urban dweller and desert nomad, a recurrent theme in the Middle East, to some degree characterized Lebanon as well, since Lebanon in the eighteenth and nineteenth centuries had cities along the coast as well as bedouin nomads in the interior. But the range of mountains running the length of the country imposed important distinctive qualities on Lebanon's social and economic structure. The mountain dwellers, who constituted the majority of the country's inhabitants, tended to reside in largely self-sufficient, nucleated agricultural villages, with the mountain peaks and valleys inhibiting trade or easy social intercourse among villages. During most of this period these mountainous agricultural areas were organized along feudal lines, with a village usually being composed of a dominant aristocratic family and that family's tenant farmers. The residents of particular villages tended to be predominantly of a single religious group, but nearby villages often represented divergent faiths.

From a historical perspective, to assess the potential viability of the newly created State of Greater Lebanon in 1920, one must focus upon the relations between the religious, that is, the confessional communities. In speaking of these confessional groupings in 1947, Pierre Rondot stated that: "Le problème des institutions politiques libanaises semble donc résider, essentiellement, dans le difficle passage des communautés traditionelles`a l'etat moderne, ou plus exactement dans le laborieux ajustement de ces entités apparement mal conciliables."[1] What was true in 1947 was even more the case in 1920. The significance of confessional identification was by no means unique to Lebanon, but characterized nearly the whole of the Near East. For most of its duration the Ottoman Empire considered itself a religious state, with the predominant element naturally being Sunni Muslim. Non-Muslim minorities, although not granted full equality, were recognized and organized as separate communities or "millets," and were accorded considerable autonomy in handling their own civic and religious affairs. In the early years of the Empire these minorities were regarded primarily as religious communities, but as Albert Hourani has described the situation: "As time went on . . . the barriers between the different communities grew higher and harder to cross, and what had been religious tended to become national groups. Their basis became not so much religious belief as the fact that one's ancestors had held that belief; ties of filial piety, intermarriage, and loyalty grew stronger; for a man to leave his community was looked upon as an act of treason."[2] The sense of separateness and of suspicion vis-a-vis other confessional communities was not simply a matter of Muslim versus Christian. Differentiation within the Christian community, primarily between Greek Orthodox, Maronite, Greek Catholic, and Roman Catholic; and within the Muslim community, primarily between Sunnis, Shiites, and Druze, became almost as great as that between the larger Christian–Muslim groupings.

During the three hundred years preceding 1920, social and economic differentiations played important roles in Lebanese history, but it was confessional identification that was the most clearly, most consistently, and most self-consciously defined. The most serious confessional conflict in Lebanon took place from 1840–1860, culminating in the Druze–Christian civil war of 1860. Even in periods of less overt conflict, confessional identity usually constituted the principal axis of collective activity, and this was especially the case from about 1800 onwards.

Even the more limited area of Mount Lebanon had a fairly complex confessional configuration for although the Maronite Christians and the Druze constituted the two principal confessional groups, Greek Catholic and Greek Orthodox communities were also of significant size. Prior to the seventeenth century the Maronites were concentrated in northern Mount Lebanon and the Druze in the south, while Shiites controlled large areas of land in central Mount Lebanon. During the seventeenth and eighteenth centuries large numbers of Maronites migrated to the south and southern Mount Lebanon became confessionally mixed, while the Shiites lost most of their land to the aggressive Maronites and Druze. Greek Catholics and Greek Orthodox, along with small Sunni pockets, were also scattered in various parts of Mount Lebanon. The Double Kaymakamate, established in 1842, attempted to divide Mount Lebanon into two confessionally homogeneous provinces, but the actual composition of the two provinces reveals the extent of the geographical mixing of confessional groups. Within the Maronite Kaymakamate 56 percent of the people were Maronite, 8 percent Druze, 19 percent Greek Catholic, and 17 percent Greek Orthodox. The Druze Kaymakamate contained 47 percent Maronites, 18 percent Druze, 21 percent Greek Catholic, and 14 percent Greek Orthodox.[3]

When we consider the areas outside of Mount Lebanon, the confessional configuration becomes even more complex. In the eighteenth and nineteenth centuries the Bekaa area contained Shiite, Maronite, Sunni, Druze, and Greek Orthodox settlements, as well as confessionally mixed towns. The coastal cities of Sidon, Beirut, and Tripoli contained large numbers of Sunnis, as did the rural areas north of Tripoli, while the areas south of Sidon and the Bekaa tended to be predominantly Shiite in composition with various Christian sects also represented in small numbers.

Given the fundamental importance of the relations among Lebanon's various confessional communities in determining the viability and in shaping the destiny of the new state of Lebanon, it is instructive to look at the character of these relations prior to 1920. Our principal focus outlines the nature of these relationships during the nineteenth century, but some illustrative material is also drawn from the eighteenth century, using as a somewhat arbitrary starting point the commencement of the Chehab dynasty in 1697. We attempt to make only a rather rudimentary classification of relationships and to assess the factors principally determining the character of these relationships. The first to be covered are examples of intergroup conflict.

Intergroup Hostility and Conflict

During the Chehab dynasty suspicion or conviction on the part of the Druze that one or another of the Chehab emirs favored the Maronites to the detriment of the Druze frequently provoked intergroup hostility and conflict. To the Druze this provided clear evidence of confessional favoritism and could be explained by the fact that the later Chehab emirs were themselves Maronites. One of the most clear-cut examples of Druze hostility aroused by suspicion of anti-Druze discrimination came in 1824 when Bashir II destroyed the property of the principal Druze leader, Bashir Junbalat, and later had him killed. The emir was motivated by a desire to eliminate his principal rival, and similar action could have as easily been taken against a Maronite opponent. The Druze, however, interpreted his actions as being anti-Druze, and as is so often the case in matters of this kind, the perceived intention was of greater historical significance than the actual motive.

A closely related but logically distinct source of intergroup hostility and conflict in Lebanon had its origins in the suspicion by a particular confessional community that a foreign ruling power discriminated against them to the advantage of other communities. For example, Maronite-Druze conflict during the later years of Bashir II's reign resulted in large measure from the policies imposed upon the emir by Ibrahim Pasha, the Egyptian overlord who controlled Lebanon and Syria from 1831 to 1840. For political reasons Egyptian policy clearly favored the Maronite community, to the detriment of the Druze. The Maronites consequently prospered during the Egyptian period, while the Druze were forcibly disarmed and conscripted in large numbers into the Egyptian army. Druze opposition to Egyptian policy led to an insurrection of both Syrians and Lebanese Druze in 1838, following which many Druze leaders were forced into exile. Further ill will was created when a Maronite army organized by Bashir II assisted the Egyptians in putting down the Druze rebellion.

A third and closely related cause of intergroup hostility and conflict came in the interventions on behalf of a particular confessional community by one of the numerous European powers who maintained a close interest in the affairs of Lebanon. Such intervention was almost invariably motivated by the political interests of the European power. For instance, in 1835–1836 a British diplomatic agent in Lebanon attempted to encourage Druze antagonism against the Maronites. In cooperation with the Turks the British supplied weapons to the Druze in 1841 and promised protection of Druze interests in any Druze–Maronite conflict. The British acted with the intention of weaning the Druze community away from their friendly relationship with the French.

We must now consider those factors contributing to intergroup hostility which had their origins within the groups themselves. In a variety of ways economic forces and economic interests affected the character of intergroup relations, and in some cases contributed to conflict. To an important degree the Druze–Christian civil war of 1860–1861 had its origins in economic conflict between peasants and landlords. Although the peasant revolt in the Kisruwan area pitted Maronite peasants against Maronite landlords, when this peasant restiveness spread to southern Lebanon it aroused Maronite peasants against Druze landlords, since most of the landlords in the area were Druze. The Druze landlords interpreted the conflict in confessional rather than economic terms and rallied the Druze peasants of the area to support them against the anticipated Maronite rebellion. Also contributing to the confessional character of the 1860 conflict was the deterioration (starting early in the century) of feudal economic and political relationships, which up to that point had laid the basis for considerable interconfessional cooperation.[4] With feudal ties weakened, confessional loyalties tended to replace fealty as the basis for corporate political action.

Another source of confessional conflict derived from the energetic efforts of Maronite clergymen to strengthen confessional ties within the Maronite community during the latter part of the eighteenth century and the first part of the nineteenth century. The clergymen's activities were largely motivated by their desire to enhance their own power and to improve the status of the Church. The clergy, particularly the Maronite Patriarch, wanted Lebanon to be a Christian state with a Christian emir, and as part of this effort the Patriarch brought Maronite leaders together in 1841 and had them pledge their support for the political struggle in which the Church felt itself engaged. Communal passions among the Maronites were aroused against the Druze community to such a pitch that when Maronites burned fourteen Druze villages in 1845, the Patriarch proclaimed the attacks to be part of a holy war against the Druze, and Maronite bishops even assisted in mapping battle plans.[5]

Closely related to the arousal of communal loyalties by the clergy in the early nineteenth century and the clerical efforts to increase their status and influence, was the urge, in this case on the part of the Maronites but in other cases on the part of other confessional communities, to attain increments in their political power. Most of the Maronites who migrated to southern Lebanon went there as impoverished peasants subject to Druze landlords. However, as they attained greater wealth they sought a sociopolitical status commensurate with their improved economic situation. This new status naturally had to be won at the expense of the Druze community, which had to that point dominated local politics in southern Lebanon. As bonds of communal loyalty became stronger in the nineteenth century, instances of political competition often became occasions for competition between confessional groups, which in turn gave rise to intergroup friction and conflict.

Intergroup Peace and Cooperation

The volume of scholarly material covering the turbulent period 1840–1861 might create the incorrect impression that the history of Lebanon was dominated by intergroup conflict, particularly between Maronites and Druze. But the eighteenth century and the latter part of the nineteenth century are notable for their lack of communal conflict. The intergroup friction that did arise was usually effectively contained. As background to an understanding of intergroup relations after 1920, it is enlightening to assess those factors that contributed to periods of relative tranquility.

During most of these periods the political system maintained a substantial degree of political control, first through feudal ties and then through greater centralization of power. During the eighteenth century an effective feudal system still prevailed, based upon strong vertical linkages. Political allegiance passed from peasant to feudal lord and from feudal lord to the emir, regardless of the confessional affiliation of the actors.[6] A Maronite peasant in southern Lebanon was thus generally partisan to the political position assumed by his feudal lord, whether that lord was Druze, as he generally was, or Maronite.[7] By the middle of the nineteenth century when the principal axis of political action shifted from feudal to confessional ties, the maintenance of interconfessional peace came to depend upon centralized political control. The fact

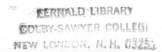

that Bashir III proved incapable of asserting this kind of control during 1840–1842 and the fact that the Ottoman authorities were unwilling to impose such control during 1860 explain in part why intergroup conflict during these periods developed to the disastrous levels that it did. In contrast, during the period 1861–1900, the European powers pressured the Ottoman authorities to assure that the governor of Lebanon had both sufficient means and the authority to maintain confessional peace.[8]

The equitable distribution of political power among the confessional communities provided another basis for peaceful coexistence during certain periods. The first systematic effort to incorporate balanced representation came in 1841 when Bashir III, with Ottoman encouragement, organized an advisory council for himself composed of ten representatives from Lebanon's various confessional communities. In order for the division of the ten council seats to roughly approximate the confessional composition of the population, three went to Maronites, three to Druze, and one each to the Greek Orthodox, Greek Catholic, Shiites, and Sunnis.[9] After the division of Lebanon into two Kaymakamates in 1842, the governor of each of the two Kaymakamates named an advisory council consisting of representatives of the various confessional communities.

Under the Règlement Organique introduced in 1861 the principle of confessional representation became more firmly and successfully established. Not only did the Representative Council, which contained two representatives from each major confessional community, permit each confessional community to have its voice heard, but the Council itself developed into an effective and cohesive political unit which often presented united interconfessional opposition to the non-Lebanese governors who ruled during this period.[10] The head of each of the six provinces also had an advisory council composed of two representatives from each major confessional group. The revised government structure initiated in 1864 abolished the provincial councils and reapportioned the seats in the central Representative Council. Under the revised formula the Maronites had four seats, the Druze three, the Greek Orthodox two, while the Greek Catholics, the Sunnis, and the Shiites each had one.[11] Not only did this form of government persist with few revisions from 1864 to 1918, but many of these concepts came to be embodied in the constitution of 1926, as we shall see when we reach that point in our discussion.

At certain points in Lebanon's history, shared politico-economic interests among members of different confessional communities also encouraged interconfessional cooperation. For instance, in 1841 Druze and Maronite nobles organized a common front to oppose Bashir III because they believed that he consistently opposed their interests, favoring the clergy and the commoners at their expense. In doing so the nobles defended primarily their political and social status interests, but their common economic interests came into play as well. Economic class interests were also important factors in the Maronite peasants' subsequent agitation against their Druze feudal lords in the south. Since the Maronite peasants were unable to convince their Druze counterparts that their real motivation for rebellion was the economic exploitation that they jointly suffered rather than confessional animosity, Druze peasants remained loyal to their Druze feudal lords. A sense of geographical or regional solidarity which cuts across confessional divisions provided another basis for interconfessional cooperation from time to time.[12]

Mention was made in an earlier portion of this chapter of the extent to which different emirs, various foreign rulers, and the European powers contributed to intergroup conflict within Lebanon, sometimes intentionally and sometimes not. But there have also been periods in which the opposition of the populace as a whole to a ruler was so intense that the various confessional groups cooperated to achieve the common end of ousting him from power. For instance, during the period of Egyptian control from 1832 to 1840, the repressive policies of Ibrahim Pasha and Bashir II relating to their extraction of taxes, their organization of forced labor, and their conscription of young men into the Egyptian army aroused the enmity of both Maronites and Druze, as well as of the minority groups. In 1840 a revolt broke out and although the Maronites were in the forefront, it was truly an interconfessional effort of national magnitude through which the populace succeeded in bringing down Bashir and his Egyptian masters.

Of considerably greater significance was the common opposition to Ottoman rule which developed in the late nineteenth century and continued to build until the Allies ended Turkish control of Lebanon in 1918.[13] Following the Christian–Druze civil war in 1860, a group of Christian intellectuals in Beirut began to agitate for Lebanese or Syrian–Lebanese independence from the Ottoman Empire on the basis of a secular Arab nationalism. They felt the need both for relief from the oppressive Islamic Ottoman state and for a secular approach to statehood which would avoid the kinds of sectarian conflicts which had been plaguing Lebanon. Some of these Christian Arab nationalists desired the establishment of an independent Christian Mount Lebanon, while others wanted a united Syria and Lebanon.

Another nationalist movement developed later in the nineteenth century under Muslim leadership with a somewhat different program. This movement sought a greater recognition of the Arab people within the Ottoman empire, more political autonomy for the Arab portions of the empire, and increased use of the Arabic language. In their emphasis upon the Arabic language and culture and in their dissatisfaction with the way the Turks were governing the Empire, the Christian and the Muslim nationalists spoke from a common platform and their efforts reinforced one another. Unlike the Christian nationalists, however, the Muslim nationalists of the late nineteenth century did not endorse the dismemberment of the Ottoman Empire or independence for Lebanon and Syria. For an orthodox Muslim the Ottoman empire fulfilled the Muslim dream of an Islamic state. To suggest complete independence for Lebanon and Syria would risk European intervention and it would also constitute a repudiation of the sacred office of the Caliph. Moreover, Arab nationalism among Muslims was not totally secular, and thus in certain fundamental respects was at odds with the nationalism of the Christians. Both Christians and Muslims faced a dilemma over whether Arabism and Islam were separable, either logically or emotionally. If they were not, then Arab nationalism excluded non-Muslims. If they were separable, then it still was not clear that Arab nationalism would have a broad appeal.

The Turkification policy instituted by the Young Turks in 1909 brought the two movements closer together. Turkish efforts to concentrate power in Istanbul and to vigorously promote the Turkish language and culture at the expense of the Arabic language and culture led the Arab Muslim elite to reconsider their attitude toward the Empire. The Young Turks showed themselves to be more Turkish than Muslim, and consequently after 1909 strong support for political independence developed among the Muslims of Lebanon and Syria. The Christians and Muslims still differed over the character and territorial extent of the desired independent state or states, with the Christians envisaging an independent Lebanon or a Lebanese–Syrian state and most of the Muslim nationalists thinking in terms of a pan-Arab empire based both on ethnic and religious loyalties. Nevertheless, the fact that the Christian and Muslim nationalists agreed on a radical political restructuring gave them a basis for cooperation. In 1915 the Turkish administration executed twelve nationalists, both Christians and Muslims, for supposed seditious activities, and in 1916 twenty-two more members of various confessional communities suffered a similar fate. These political executions outraged the whole of the Lebanese and Syrian populations, and the nationalists rededicated themselves to their joint cause.

Other Aspects of Community Interaction

Although some observers have cited opposition between Christians and Muslims as the principal source of intergroup conflict, denominational differentiation within these two larger communities often prompted more serious antagonisms than differences between Christians and Muslims as a whole. For example, their common identity as Christians did not necessarily induce the Greek Orthodox to champion a Maronite cause, which they refused to do during the Maronite–Druze conflict in 1841. Yet the Maronite community enjoyed considerable Shiite support against the Druze in 1860, despite the fact that the Druze and the Shiites both have their roots in Islam. Shiites frequently considered themselves unjustly treated by Sunni authorities of the Ottoman Empire, and in turn were frequently resentful of Sunni domination. Many of Lebanon's Greek Catholics fled to Lebanon from Syria in the eighteenth century because of discrimination there at the hands of Greek Orthodox. The Druze exhibited considerable ambivalence regarding whether or not they were Muslims, and they never felt particularly close to either Sunnis or Shiites. The fact that the Sunnis and Greek Orthodox tended to be city dwellers, while the Maronites, Druze, and Shiites were most often farmers further contributed to the differentiation within the Christian and Muslim groups. In terms of religious dogma, some of the minor points distinguishing Christian sects loomed very large in Christian minds, and the same held for differences between Sunni and Shiite dogma as well.

The possibility of conversion, or change of religious faith, theoretically can blur social differentiation among confessional communities. In a comparative analysis of confessionalism and ethnicity the possibility of changing one's religious identity comprises perhaps the most significant distinguishing element between ethnicity and confessionalism. Throughout Lebanese history cases of conversion provided an important aspect of relations among Lebanon's confessional communities. During the Mamluk (pre-Ottoman) period' for example, persecution of non-Sunnis led many Christians, Druze, and Shiites to convert to the Sunni faith. Later, a tendency could be observed for conversions to Christianity, away from Islam. For instance, in the Chehab family Emir Mulhim's sons converted from being Sunnis to being Maronites in 1756, and by the end of the eighteenth century most members of the ruling branch of the Chehab family had converted. The situation of the Chehab family was complicated by the fact that for a long period they did not reveal their conversion from Islam to Christianity, and for many years they presented themselves as being Druze to assure support from the Druze population. Following the Maronite migration from northern to southern Lebanon in the seventeenth and eighteenth centuries, some Druze, particularly members of the Druze aristocracy, converted to the Maronite faith. In many of these instances as with the Abillama' family, the leading Druze family of Matn, this conversion process affected a whole clan. Although it is difficult to accurately assess the motivations for these conversions, it seems clear that the change in religious identity was as often related to politics and status considerations as to changes of theological conviction. We can once again see the extent to which religious affiliation was socially and politically significant, and we can conclude that confessional identity entailed much more than simply personal religious faith.[14]

Mention has already been made of the fact that although the confessional groups tended to be concentrated geographically, they were by no means geographically segregated or out of contact with one another. Many parts of the country contained confessionally mixed populations and even when a particular group dominated an area, representatives of other sects were usually in evidence as well. Population movements also occurred with considerable frequency, which added to interconfessional contact and intermingling. Historically, the migration of Maronites into southern Lebanon during the seventeenth and eighteenth centuries probably had the broadest ramifications. The Maronite migrants were usually successfully integrated into the existing Druze villages, becoming either farm laborers or clerks for the Druze aristocracy. Maronites also emigrated into the predominantly Greek Orthodox areas near Tripoli, and some Maronites relocated in Tripoli itself, joining the Sunnis and Greek Orthodox already there. Maronites also appeared in Beirut, Sidon, and Tyre, as well as among the Shiites of Baalbeck and among the Sunnis of Akkar and the northern Bekaa. Often when Maronite settlements developed, Greek Orthodox settlers came soon thereafter and in some cases Greek Catholics followed as well.

Another aspect of the Lebanese situation that provided common bonds internally and which differentiated Lebanon from neighboring territories was that the vast majority of Lebanon's population had at one time been a persecuted minority group which found refuge in Lebanon. In many cases groups of people emigrated from other territories in search of the religious freedom for which Lebanon was noted. For instance, sizable numbers of Greek Catholics left Aleppo and other parts of Syria for Lebanon in the eighteenth century to escape persecution, principally at the hands of Greek Orthodox. Persecution of other Christian groups by the Ottoman authorities in Syria early in the nineteenth century provoked additional migration. Bashir II encouraged this influx, and was equally hospitable to a large group of Druze who sought refuge in Lebanon after being persecuted in Syria. In the eighteenth century a small group of Armenian Catholics from Syria resettled in Lebanon with assistance from the Maronites, and in the early part of this century waves of Armenian refugees fled persecution in Turkey and resettled in Lebanon. Of all of Lebanon's confessional communities only the Sunnis had not been a persecuted minority group at one time or another, although with the creation of the State of Greater Lebanon the Sunnis of the area became a minority group within Lebanon.

Ties to Foreign Powers

The significant role the European powers played in Lebanese history, seeking their own political ends by intervening frequently in the political life of the country, affected the relationships among the sects. We have already discussed instances in which these powers contributed to intergroup conflict within Lebanon. Another and probably equally important consequence of European interest in Lebanon has been the differing perspectives and orientations among the confessional communities which have arisen as a result of European influence. The most striking example of this comes in the French influence on the Maronite community. From the sixteenth century France considered herself to be the protector of the Maronite community in Lebanon, primarily because the Maronites were uniate Catholics, and France was the leading Catholic power. This protective relationship also extended to the Greek Catholic community, but the bonds were not as strong. By the eighteenth century the Franciscans, Jesuits, Lazarists, and Carmelites all had active missions in Lebanon which promoted the interests of the Maronite Church and community within Lebanon, and encouraged the assimilation of French culture within the Maronite community. As a consequence of the French missionary control over educational institutions in Maronite areas, knowledge of the French language and appreciation for French culture were widespread among Maronites well before the time of the French Mandate, and tended to create a significant degree of cultural differentiation between the Maronites and the other confessional communities. Maronite–French friendship also led the Maronite community to sympathize with Napoleon Bonaparte's abortive attempt to gain control of Lebanon and Syria in 1799. As we shall see in our later discussion of the Mandate period, the Maronites were also much more favorably disposed toward the French Mandate than were the non-Catholic communities.

The Russians, competing with the French for influence in Lebanon, established protective ties with the Greek Orthodox community. Although the cultural impact of these ties was not nearly as noticeable as French influence on the Maronites, the Russians did assist Greek Orthodox schools, and a generally favorable attitude toward the Russians developed among the Greek Orthodox of Lebanon.[15] In an attempt to counterbalance French influence over the Maronites, the British assiduously cultivated the Druze community during the nineteenth century. The depth of the Druze–British friendship never equalled that of the Maronite–French friendship, but the relationship did have some cultural byproducts. For instance, the British at an early date offered scholarships to children of leading Druze families to study in Britain. Moreover, the Druze generally welcomed British and American Protestant missions into their midst, after these same missions had been found unacceptable by the Maronites. The resultant tendency for schools in Druze areas to be American or British and Protestant and for schools in the Maronite areas to be French and Catholic led to quite different educational experiences for Druze and Maronite school children.

The Sunnis tended to enjoy their status as adherents to the state religion of the Ottoman empire and neither sought nor welcomed ties with powers outside of the Empire. The bonds of religion that existed between Lebanese Sunnis and the Ottoman authorities underlay their reluctance to join the push for political independence in the late nineteenth century, until the Young Turks came to power and convinced the Lebanese Sunnis that religious bonds were of considerably less importance to the Turkish rulers than were national or ethnic identity.

Historical Trends in Intergroup Relations

During the major part of the eighteenth century intergroup relations were stable. Despite evidence of sectarian self-consciousness, overt conflict rarely erupted. Relatively successful political management by the Chehab emirs as well as the strength of the feudal sociopolitical structure reinforced vertical loyalties, from commoner to feudal lord to emir, and kept interconfessional conflict to a minimum. In the first part of the nineteenth century, however, the feudal system started to crumble and the Maronite clergy began to assert itself as a political force and aroused a sense of intense communal loyalty on the part of the Maronite community. Until the Egyptian intervention in 1832, Bashir II managed to maintain the state on an even keel, but the ineptness of Egyptian rule between 1832 and 1840, combined with the growing sense of communal loyalty and the crumbling of the integrative feudal ties led to intergroup conflict, particularly between Maronites and Druze. The intensity of anti-Egyptian sentiment provided a basis for an interconfessional national revolt in 1840, but this cooperation was short-lived and interconfessional conflict led to serious clashes in 1841. The ineffectiveness of the Double Kaymakamate, the meddling of European powers in Lebanon's affairs, the weakness of Ottoman control, and the interclass conflict between peasants and feudal lords all contributed to increased tension and the eventual Christian–Druze civil war of 1860, which left nearly 15,000 dead.

Increased governmental effectiveness under the Règlement Organique, inaugurated in 1861, including an effort to distribute political power equitably among the confessional communities, as well as growing economic prosperity, brought stability once again to intergroup relations. When Turkish rule became more repressive toward the end of the century, various Arab nationalist movements developed. Anti-Turkish sentiments provided some ground for cooperation among the political elites of the Muslim and Christian communities, but the programs of the Christian nationalists (particularly Maronite) and Muslim nationalists (particularly Sunni) diverged significantly. It was only after the Young Turks came to power in 1908 and attempted to Turkify the Arab portions of the Empire that the Christian and Muslim nationalists came to agree on the need for political independence. Important differences remained, however, in their views regarding the character and scope of the independent state. Yearnings for political independence were frustrated for twenty three additional years beyond the end of Turkish rule by the French Mandate which was imposed on Lebanon and Syria in 1920. The next portion of our discussion focuses on the impact of these twenty three years.

The Period of the Mandate, 1920—1943

We have mentioned that the State of Greater Lebanon, created by the French soon after they assumed mandatory control in 1920, was considerably

larger in both territorial expanse and population than the Mutesarrifate of
Mount Lebanon as it existed from 1861 to 1918. Greater Lebanon did have
the virtue of relatively well-defined geographical boundaries, with the river
Nahr al-Kabir constituting the northern border between Syria and Lebanon,
the crest of the Anti-Lebanon Mountains forming the division between Syria
and Lebanon on the long eastern border, and the Mediterranean Sea providing the western boundary. Natural geographical boundaries do not, however,
contribute very much to the viability of a state. Although the relations
between the Maronites and Druze of Mount Lebanon had been relatively
quiescent from the time of the civil war in 1860 to the beginning of the
Mandate, the new Lebanon contained a completely new combination of
peoples. Several portions of the annexed territory had had historical ties with
the core area of Mount Lebanon, but these ties had been tenuous and
intermittent. Little sense of Lebanese nationality existed to draw the diverse
social groupings, particularly the divergent confessional communities, together into a cohesive national unit. No accurate population figures exist for
the year 1920, but according to the 1932 census 50 percent of Lebanon's
population was Christian and 49 percent Muslim, with the Christians subdivided into six major denominations and the Muslims composed of Sunnis,
Shiites, and Druze.

In large measure the French created Greater Lebanon in order to
strengthen the position of Lebanon's Maronite community as well as to
reward the Maronites for their faithful allegiance to France. By separating
Mount Lebanon from Syria the French assured that the Maronites would not
be engulfed by Syria's predominantly Sunni population. By annexing additional territories to Mount Lebanon to create Greater Lebanon, the French
saw themselves securing the economic viability of the new state.

For the most part the Maronites enthusiastically welcomed both the creation of Greater Lebanon and the granting of the Mandate to France. In fact,
various Maronite delegations travelled to Paris and Versailles during 1919 and
1920, the most important one being led by the Maronite Patriarch, to plead
for the creation of a French-controlled Greater Lebanon. When the Maronites foresaw the collapse of the Ottoman Empire, they feared that in the
political restructuring that would follow, they would be swallowed up by a
pan-Arab Islamic state in which they would have less autonomy and fewer
rights than they had under the Ottomans. These fears increased when they
witnessed the encouragement the British gave Sharif Hussayn in his plans for
a pan-Arab kingdom. The Maronites saw the French as the only power that
could or might rescue them from this fate, and the French did. Disagreement

did arise among the Maronites over the wisdom of creating Greater Lebanon as opposed to granting autonomy to Mount Lebanon. Within the Lebanese Mutesarrifate of 1861 to 1918 the Maronites had constituted approximately 59 percent of the total population, while within Greater Lebanon they were only 29 percent of the population. Despite their loss of majority status in Greater Lebanon, most Maronites favored its creation and felt assured of their continued ascendance because they expected support from the French and because they still constituted the largest single confessional community in the new state.

Most of the Sunni elite favored a united and independent Lebanon–Syria, that might be joined to the rest of the Arab world in a pan-Arab Islamic state. They consequently deeply resented the creation of a separate Greater Lebanon under French Mandate, fearing that this would permanently cut them off from other parts of the Arab–Muslim world. Moreover, since the Maronites constituted the largest confessional community in Greater Lebanon and since the French were partial to the Maronites, the Sunnis feared that they would be perpetually dominated by the French, the Maronites, or both. Sunni distrust of the French was long-standing, and derived both from the French partisanship to the Maronites and from fears regarding France's long-term interests in the area. Despite basic Sunni consensus on these points, some of the more conservative Sunni elements regretted the dismantling of the Ottoman empire and the loss of ties to the non-Arabic Islamic world which this entailed. Even among those who championed independence, disagreements arose over how extensive the new state should be, who should lead it, and the role that Islam should play in its organization and operations.

As for Lebanon's other confessional communities, the Greek Catholics concurred with the Maronites and consequently were pro-French and favored the creation of Greater Lebanon. In contrast, the Greek Orthodox held diverse views and were less sure of their stand. Compared to the other Christian communities, the Greek Orthodox were more pan-Arab in orientation and many of them supported the Sunni position. The generally anti-French and anti-Maronite sentiments of most Greek Orthodox reinforced this predilection. Yet, many Greek Orthodox were not anxious to be swallowed up in an overwhelmingly Sunni state. The Druze tended to share the ambivalence of the Greek Orthodox although, like the Greek Orthodox, they inclined toward the Sunni view. Likewise, the Shittes tended to be pro-Syrian, anti-Greater Lebanon, and anti-French, but not so uniformly or emotionally as the Sunnis.

The two largest confessional communities, namely the Maronites and the

Sunnis, were obsessed by a fear of being subordinated to the other and suffering under their oppressive control. This apprehension led the Maronites to advocate a Lebanon separate from Syria, and similarly brought the Sunnis to the opposite position, namely the merging of Lebanon with Syria. For the other confessional communities of Lebanon the issue was not so clear-cut, since they would hold minority status in whatever configuration of territories and states emerged.

From the beginning, the French accorded Lebanon's diverse confessional communities explicit recognition. For instance, in 1920 the Governor appointed an advisory council composed of seventeen members who were selected to represent their respective confessional communities. In 1922 the advisory council was replaced by an elected representative council whose seats were distributed along confessional lines. Of its thirty members, ten were Maronites, two Greek Catholic, four Greek Orthodox, six Sunni, five Shiite and two Druze, with one for the remaining minorities.

On May 24, 1926 a new constitution was promulgated which established the Lebanese Republic. It provided for a Chamber of Deputies and a Senate, and the confessional communities were proportionally represented in both. The later practice of allocating the presidency to a Maronite and other key posts to members of other confessional groups was not immediately adopted. The first President, Charles Dabbas, was a Greek Orthodox who remained in office from 1926 to 1933. His candidature was proposed by the French because they thought he would be more acceptable to the Muslims than a Maronite. However, the French refused to allow the Chamber to select a Muslim, Sheikh Muhammad al-Jisr, as President of Lebanon in 1932. A Maronite, Habib Pasha al-Sa'ad, was elected in 1933, and except for one brief period lasting six months, all subsequent presidents have been Maronites. The first Sunni premier was selected in 1937, and he has been followed by an uninterrupted succession of Sunnis. The first Shiite president of the Chamber of Deputies was chosen in 1943, and since that time the post has been reserved for Shiites.

At the time that self-government was achieved in 1943, the new Maronite President, Bishara al-Khuri, formulated an accord with the Sunni Premier, Riyad al-Sulh, the provisions of which constituted the so-called National Pact. Since the pact was a verbal and hence unwritten agreement between the two men, its details were never fully elucidated. But the main elements of the National Pact have provided the basis for political cooperation among Lebanon's confessional communities from 1943 to the present. As the principal representatives of the Christian and Muslim portions of Lebanon's population, these two men agreed that henceforth the Christians of Lebanon would recognize Lebanon as being an Arab country and would seek cooperative relations between Lebanon and her Arab neighbors. Moreover, the Christians would not seek European protection, and in turn they would not advocate political or military pacts with Western powers. For their part, the Muslims would accept Lebanon's existing geographical boundaries and would relinquish their advocacy of a union of Lebanon with Syria or any other Arab state. Moreover, the friendly relations that would be sought with Syria and other Arab states would not entail undue influence by these states on Lebanon's internal political life. Finally, they stipulated that future Lebanese presidents would be Maronites and future premiers would be Sunnis. While they found sectarianism to be distasteful, they recognized the need to maintain an equilibrium by means of this pact at least as a transitional arrangement. [16]

Following the attainment of self-rule in 1943, Lebanon gained full independence by steady increments between 1943 and 1946. On August 1, 1945 the *troupes spéciales* were turned over to Lebanese control, and by the end of 1946 all the French troops had left the country.

In many respects during the period of the Mandate the French were the key to the character of the relations among Lebanon's confessional communities. As French policy changed and as French relations with particular communities changed, so the relationships among the communities changed. In the early years of the Mandate the warm relations between the French and the Maronite community and French favoritism toward the Maronites aroused intense hostility on the part of the Muslims, particularly the Sunnis. By 1927 growing disenchantment among the Christians of Lebanon regarding French rule brought the communities somewhat closer together. Christians shared Muslim disappointment in 1926, for instance, that the constitution did not bring Lebanon closer to self-rule and independence. Further common opposition to French rule surged in 1932 and then again in 1939 when the Governor abrogated the constitution and dismissed the cabinet.

Probably the high point of intergroup harmony, either before or after independence, came in November 1943 when the French disbanded the Chamber of Deputies and arrested the president and members of the cabinet in retaliation for their amending the constituion in an attempt to terminate French control. This repressive action by the French aroused the whole Lebanese nation. Political organizations of whatever shade of political opinion or of whatever confessional affiliation cooperated in organizing a national strike, which convinced the French of the depth of the opposition. On November 22 the president and the members of the cabinet were released from prison and reinstated in office and the French authorities agreed to the constitutional amendments.

Despite these periods of national unity arising out of hostility toward the French, intergroup relations under the Mandate were frequently discordant. Christian–Muslim disagreement over the character of a French–Lebanese treaty in 1936 led to riots in Beirut in which four were killed and many more persons injured. When elections to the Chamber of Deputies were being organized early in 1943, President Thabit tried to enfranchise Lebanese emigrants living abroad, most of whom were Christians. Since this plan was clearly intended to increase the strength of the Christian electorate to the detriment of the Muslims, it provoked violent Muslim protests, which in turn forced the removal of Thabit from office and the abandonment of his plan. Maronite and Sunni manoeuvres to achieve their conflicting political ends continued throughout most of the Mandate.

Although some of the basic disagreements between the confessional groups regarding the Mandate and the future character of the Lebanese state remained unaltered, some important changes also occurred during the Mandate period. In the early years of the Mandate Sunni hostility to the creation of Greater Lebanon continued unabated. As an expression of their opposition, most of Lebanon's Sunnis boycotted the Representative Council elections in 1922. The formulation of the 1926 constitution involved the acceptance of Lebanon's boundaries, and consequently the Muslim leaders from Beirut and Tripoli refused to serve in the Constituent Assembly. The only aspect of the constitution that Muslims found palatable was the provision it made for the distribution of parliamentary seats on a confessional basis, although the precise formula for this distribution aroused considerable controversy.

The Muslims were not, however, totally united. For instance, some Sunnis focused their attention on the unification of the annexed areas with Syria, while others dreamed of a pan-Arab state. Additional differentiation came in the viewpoints of the various Muslim subcommunities. Although at the beginning of the Mandate period the Shiites were generally supportive of the Sunni demands for the dismantling of Greater Lebanon, their enthusiasm for this position waned as time passed. They were not anxious to submit themselves to a state dominated by Sunnis, remembering some of their disquieting experience under Ottoman control. Shiite attachment to Greater Lebanon was enhanced in 1926 when the community was granted the right to have its own personal status courts, separate from those of the Sunnis.

By the time of self-rule in 1943 the Sunni position had evolved considerably from what it was at the beginning of the Mandate. The idea ᵓf unity with Syria still aroused considerable emotional fervor among the Sunnis, but their position was tempered by several factors. They became increasingly aware of the unlikelihood that the territorial boundaries of Lebanon would be changed. They also had difficulty recommending a viable institutional formula for strengthening Lebanon's ties with Syria. Moreover, the election of Bishara al-Khuri as the President instead of the Francophile Emile Edde gave the Sunnis grounds for believing that they could cooperate with the Christian leadership. Evidence of this came in agreement on the National Pact, and the Pact further allayed Sunni fears, since it accepted the principle that Lebanon was an Arab state and would have friendly and cooperative relations with other Arab states, particularly with Syria. Nevertheless, the Sunni community approached the idea of an independent Lebanon at best with ambivalence, and many Sunnis remained hostile to the idea.

The Druze and the Greek Orthodox continued to be somewhat ambivalent, but their doubts concerning Greater Lebanon slowly subsided. By 1943 few members of either community openly espoused the breakup of Greater Lebanon. An important motivating factor for each was their small size. They realized that as a minority they were better situated in a country composed of minorities than being part of an overwhelmingly Sunni Syria.

Most Maronites remained firm supporters of Greater Lebanon and unalterably opposed to union with Syria. Their greatest apprehensions about the viability of Greater Lebanon arose from doubts regarding the possibility of sustained Muslim–Christian cooperation and uncertainty over Sunni loyalty to an independent Lebanon. Some Maronite extremists still favored separation of a predominantly Maronite Mount Lebanon from the rest of Greater Lebanon and Syria. Emile Edde's Constitutional Bloc proposed close ties with France as a guarantee against Lebanon's being pushed or drawn into a pan-Arab empire, but the major part of the Maronite community was satisfied with Greater Lebanon as it was constituted and their increasing estrangement from France led them to become anxious to end all formal links with France. They realized at the same time that Lebanon's future was not likely to be tranquil.

GHANA

The creation of Ghana, or the Gold Coast,[17] as a British colony involved the contrived imposition of collectivity upon a group of traditional states which, prior to that time, had not considered themselves to constitute a unique political entity. The geographical area designated as constituting Ghana contained disparate ethnic groups speaking thirty four distinct and mutually unintelligible languages,[18] and the peoples of this area were divided into more than two hundred traditional states.[19] In many places the European boundary-makers were more concerned with geometric symmetry than with ethnic homogeneity, with the consequence that the boundaries separating Ghana from the French and German colonies surrounding it bisected many ethnic communities. David Kimble, the author of a highly regarded work on Ghana's history, described the peoples of Ghana in the nineteenth century in this way: "They lived in a large number of isolated, self-contained societies, isolated by difficulties of transport, by fear of warfare and slave-raiding, by a relatively self-sufficient economy, and by a tightly knit sense of community and kinship."[20]

From this description of precolonial Ghana it would appear that Ghana confronted a task of nation-building of truly overwhelming proportions. The focus of this section is an assessment of Ghana's potential for nationhood at the commencement of colonial rule and later at independence. In the process we shall draw some conclusions regarding whether the barriers to national accommodation were as overwhelming as one might surmise from Kimball's statement and others like it. Our treatment of Ghana differs in important respects from the discussion of Lebanon. In considering the historical factors affecting the potential for national accommodation in both Lebanon and Ghana, we are concerned with the character of intergroup relations and the potential viability of the state at the time of independence, but the situations in the two countries were not the same. During the precolonial period the territory and social groups of the state of Lebanon had been part of the Ottoman empire, often a semiautonomous enclave, since the fifteenth century. Moreover, although Lebanon's different confessional communities were concentrated in particular portions of its territory, considerable inter-mixture also occurred. Therefore Lebanon's principal problem of national integration consisted of reconciling and drawing together the various confessional communities that had coexisted over an extended period, sometimes within a common political framework, often living side by side in the same towns and villages. In the case of Ghana the state had to forge bonds of cohesion and identity among geographically divided ethnic groups which, during the precolonial period, had comprised a multitude of independent traditional states. At times one or another of these states had gained ascendance over several others, but at no time prior to the imposition of British colonial rule had all the ethnic groups which today make up Ghana shared a common political structure. For the most part their relations resembled those among foreign powers.

As can be deduced from the map, Ghana's ethnolinguistic geography is complex. Three principal groups inhabit what is now the southern portion of Ghana: the Gas and Adangbes, the Ewes, and the Akans. The Gas and Adangbes are distributed in communities along the coast in the vicinity of Accra. Although they do not constitute a large group, their domination of the capital area has heightened their importance. East of the Volta River and extending over into Togo come the Ewe settlements. Some Ewe communities also reside on the western side of the Volta, but the major portion of the Ewes are located east of the Volta and in areas that had constituted part of the German colony of Togoland before World War I. After World War I the League of Nations divided this German-controlled area into British- and French-mandated areas, with the British area eventually being absorbed as part of Ghana.

The majority of people in southern Ghana belong to one or another Akan subgroup. All of these groups speak a dialect of Akan and many have had a sense of cultural and linguistic affinity. Nevertheless, the individual Akan subgroups have been important political actors in Ghana's history, and in turn these subunits have provided significant sources of ethnic identification. Of these Akan subgroups, Fanti communities lie along the central coast of Ghana, the Akwapim people and the Akim people live north of Accra, while the Ashanti dominate the center of Ghana surrounding Kumasi. Other Akan-speaking peoples are found across the western border of Ghana in Ivory Coast. Some Akan-speaking groups, such as the Akwamu and the Denkyira which are mentioned in this chapter as being important forces at various points in Ghana's history, do not appear on the ethnolinguistic map because they are no longer sufficiently self-conscious or clearly enough differentiated from their neighbors to warrant separate identification.

The largest and most elaborately structured ethnic groups in the north are

FIGURE 2-2 *Ghana's Ethnolinguistic Groups*

SOURCE: Kwamina B. Dickson, A *Historical Geography of Ghana* (Cambridge: Cambridge University Press, 1969), p. 16. Reprinted by permission of Cambridge University Press.

the Dagomba, the Gonja, and Mamprusi. Considerable linguistic fragmentation in other portions of the north makes the ethnic demarcation very complex, and it is often difficult to draw a line to divide one group from another. The north, along with the linguistically fragmented area north of Ewe territory, particularly complicates Ghana's ethnolinguistic geography.

The first part of our discussion of Ghana's potential for nationhood covers the period up to 1900, essentially the precolonial era. The selection of this date is admittedly somewhat arbitrary since portions of Ghana came under British control earlier, but at the turn of the century most of what constitutes present-day Ghana (excluding British Togoland, which was administered as part of Ghana only after 1922) became a British colony[21] composed of approximately 1,700,000 persons.[22] In this discussion of Ghana's potential for nationhood in 1900 we concern ourselves particularly with the character of the relationships among Ghana's constituent traditional states. Moreover, we analyze certain critical aspects of these interactions which we posit were among the important indices of how much difficulty Ghana would face in becoming a viable state with a lively sense of nationhood. The factors analyzed are: (1) degree of interregional trade and economic interdependence; (2) degree of peaceful contact, communication, and interchange; (3) cultural similarity; (4) linguistic homogeneity; (5) migratory movements leading to ethnic accommodation; and (6) intermarriage between distant groups and other structural linkages.

Precolonial Ghana: Trade and Economic Interdependence

For the most part, as asserted in the quotation from Kimble above, the villages of Ghana during the precolonial era enjoyed economic self-sufficiency, since most of Ghana's present-day interregional trade developed later. But this is not the complete picture: the extent of trade prior to 1900 should not be underestimated. It created important economic links between various parts of Ghana, as well as with areas beyond Ghana's borders. For the four-century period from 1400 to 1800 the town of Begho in what is now the Brong-Ahafo Region served as a pivotal trade center, where gold, kola nuts, and slaves from the south were traded for such products as cloth and brass from the north.[23] Trade routes linked Begho to Elmina, Cape Coast, and Accra on the coast. The desire of the Sudanic states and of Hausaland in Nigeria for gold and forest products from the Akan areas of Ghana brought these peoples into commercial, cultural, and political contact as well. A thriving trade in coastal salt also developed in the southern, forested portions of Ghana.[24]

During the seventeenth century a radical transformation took place in both the geography and content of Ghana's commercial activity. Despite the continuing importance of trade with the northern Sudanic states and with Hausaland, a substantial trade in gold and slaves developed with European traders on the coast. With the elimination of the international slave trade during the nineteenth century and the exhaustion of most of the gold mines, a significant drop occurred in the volume of the trade with European merchants on the coast. However, as warfare subsided late in the nineteenth century and as Ashanti control over trade routes relaxed, new internal trading opportunities developed.[25] By the end of the nineteenth century production of cocoa had commenced, which eventually revolutionized Ghana's economy and trade patterns.

Despite the basic economic self-sufficiency of the traditional states, a vigorous interstate trade thrived from at least the fifteenth century. Trade flourished more during some periods than others, but commercial activity and economic interdependence became widespread phenomena in Ghana long before the imposition of colonial rule. Before drawing the conclusion, however, that this economic activity provided the basis for later development of a strong national economy and a sense of national cohesion, some less advantageous dimensions of this commercial activity should also be noted. For instance, the development of trade led to empire building by such groups as the Ashanti, Akwamu, and Denkyira, which implied an increased level of interstate warfare. Thus, the attractiveness of the new trade increased inter-state conflict. Moreover, one of the most valued trade items were slaves, with Ghana contributing about 10,000 slaves a year to the international slave market during the height of slave trading.[26] This capturing and trading of human beings, and the raiding and interstate warfare that it entailed, hardly fostered healthy and harmonious relationships.

The trade of precolonial Ghana created economic interdependence not only among the traditional states within Ghana, but also between these states and those of the Western Sudan and northern Nigeria. Although the "internal" trade was more significant than the "external" trade, one must still recognize that Ghana's eventual boundaries did not represent the limits of precolonial trade. Granting these various qualifications, one can still reasonably assert that trading activities in precolonial Ghana provided the rudiments of economic interchange and interdependence which developed further after 1900.

Warfare and Conquest

According to some accounts of Ghanaian history, the peoples of precolonial Ghana spent most of their lives in armed combat with each other. This depiction represents a gross exaggeration which disregards long periods of peace, but one must also concede that warfare and conquest, often very divisive forces, constitute important themes in Ghana's past. Although the great states of Denkyira, Akwamu, and Ashanti achieved some of their size by creating alliances with neighboring states, most of their expansion resulted from conquest. At its height early in the eighteenth century Akwamu controlled Ga, Adangbe, Akim Abuakwa, and Akwapim. By 1800 the Ashanti empire included all the areas north of Fanti and west of Akim plus Gonja and Dagomba to the north. Ashanti threatened the coastal areas of Ghana almost continually during the period 1800–1826, including attacks on Akim, Akwapim, and Fanti areas in 1806, 1811, and 1814; and in 1863 Ashanti tried to push south through Denkyira, Wassaw, and Akim to Cape Coast. At the height of its power Ashanti dominated most of Ghana and a small portion of the Ivory Coast. During both eighteenth and nineteenth centuries frequent wars also occurred in the north, like the ones Gonja conducted against the Mamprusi, Dagomba, and Nanumba to extend its borders.

Insofar as this warfare and military conquest enflamed interethnic or interstate hostility, they were negative factors in the later development of Ghana as a nation. Evidence that the hostility engendered by military conflict and conquest persisted in many cases long beyond the end of the fighting can be seen in the frequency with which many of Ashanti's tributary states, including Akim, Akwapim, and Wassaw, attempted to attain their independence through rebellion against Ashanti rule. Moreover, since the capture of slaves became an important byproduct of many of these wars, military conflict led to long-term personal hardship and to sustained interstate hostility.

But the long-term consequences of military conquest did not all fall on the negative side. For instance, through the creation of large states by military conquest, a single political structure encompassed disparate ethnic and linguistic groups. Despite the decentralized structure of the Akwamu and Ashanti empires, the existence of a far-flung political and military framework for the empire increased interethnic interaction, communication, and cultural transfer. An instructive example of interethnic cooperation resulting from military conquest is the case of Akwapim. Following the collapse of the Akwamu empire in 1730, the Guan, Akwamu, and Akim communities, which had been forced by conquest into contact with one another, decided to join together in a new voluntary political association, which constituted the origins of the Akwapim state.[27] In the face of aggressive military action by Ashanti and other imperial states of precolonial Ghana, their opponents often forged broadly based military alliances. Many of these defensive coalitions brought together ethnic groups that otherwise would not have had much contact; and in some cases these defense alliances provided the basis for voluntary state formation, the creation of the Fanti Confederacy in the 1860s being one example.[28]

Military conquest resulted in two types of population movements. On numerous occasions a group about to be defeated in battle fled to a distant area to avoid capture, and settled there among the people indigenous to the region. The conquering power, particularly in the case of the Ashanti, also sometimes forcibly transplanted defeated peoples to distant parts of their empire to thwart rebellious movements and to achieve the kind of ethnic amalgamation conducive to the development of a unified state.[29] The creation of large states through military action also had important consequences for trade, communication and transportation. Trade within the expanded empire generally surpassed that in the tributary states prior to their incorporation into the empire, and the same held for transportation and communication. However, the aggressive military activities of an empire frequently disrupted interstate trade and communication in areas beyond its borders.

Ethnic Intermingling and Assimilation

The suggestion of Kimble and others that Ghana's traditional states remained largely in isolation from one another is cast into doubt by another important feature of social life in the precolonial period. Even disregarding various exotic theories regarding migration,[30] it is clear that population movements occurred frequently, and this resulted in some acculturation and cultural levelling as well as interstate communication.

Jack Goody's description of the composition of the Gonja area illustrates the complexity of some of these movements and of the resulting cultural intermingling:

> The present ruling class of Gonja were Mande-speaking invaders who adopted the language of the Guan-speaking indigenes. Of the Gur-speaking groups who are also subject to Gonja rule, the Grusi speakers migrated from the Sisala area sometime before this invasion. . . . At present a further migration of Mossi speakers from the

Ivory Coast is taking place. Senufo-speaking peoples form a minor element in the extreme southwest; they probably arrived from the Banda area before the Gonja rulers, as did the Mande-speaking Ligbi.[31]

The long-term accommodation between migrants and host varied from instance to instance. Mande-speaking intruders who assisted with the establishment of the Dagomba and Mamprusi states became fully absorbed into the indigenous societies. They adopted most of the customs and the language of those among whom they settled, while passing on their concepts of statecraft.[32] More recently other population intermixtures in northern Ghana have resulted in considerable cultural intermingling, for instance, between the LoDagaba and the Sisala. In most of these cases effective amalgamation appears to have eventuated, although in some instances the migrant group constituted an overwhelming cultural presence and absorbed the group indigenous to the area. In southern Ghana the common system of clanship found among all Akan-speaking states served as a convenient mechanism for the absorption of migrant Akans.[33]

However, many stranger groups remained unassimilated for long periods of time. Meyer Fortes, in analyzing this phenomenon among the Muslim residents of Kumasi in the early years of the nineteenth century, asserts that they did not desire Ashanti citizenship since this would have necessitated severing their ties with their societies of origin. Moreover, he maintains that it would have been difficult, if not impossible, to absorb these strangers into the Ashanti clan structure.[34]

Although the rate and completeness of absorbing strangers varied from place to place, virtually all of Ghana's traditional states had established mechanisms for assimilating outsiders.[35] If a stranger was prepared to consider his place of resettlement as his permanent home (which the early Muslim settlers in Kumasi apparently were not) the settler or his descendents could usually be incorporated over a period of time. To provide the legal rationale for assimilation into the clan structure, fictitious kinship ties were frequently proffered and accepted.

Language

In contrast to Lebanon where Arabic is almost universally spoken, precolonial Ghana included thirty four different language communities, and thus suffered considerable linguistic fragmentation. Yet, 40 percent of the popula-

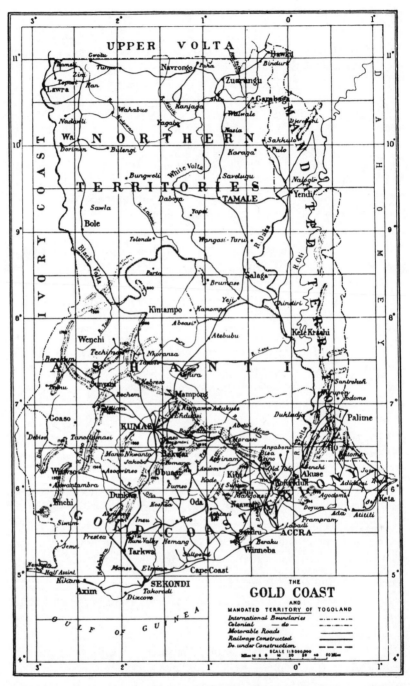

FIGURE 2-3 *The Gold Coast, 1927–published by the Survey Department, Accra*

SOURCE: David Kimble, *A Political History of Ghana* (Oxford: Clarendon Press, 1963), p. 555.

tion spoke one or another dialect of Akan as a mother tongue, which meant that a sizeable part of Ghana's southern population belonged to a single language community. Despite the fact that the northern portion of the country had serious linguistic fragmentation, many of the northern languages were closely related. The sharpest linguistic division came between north and south; most of the southern languages belonged to the Kwa subfamily of the Niger–Congo language group and most of the northern languages belonged to the Gur subfamily.

In attempting to assess the frequency of interstate communication in precolonial Ghana, the use of lingua francas and the extent of multilingualism must be considered before it is possible to determine the degree to which linguistic fragmentation inhibited interregional communication. Unfortunately, information on these subjects remains very sketchy. Cardinall claims that he discovered Moshi to be a lingua franca in the north soon after 1900,[36] but this is difficult to substantiate. From the present-day linguistic situation in parts of Akwapim, we can infer that in precolonial times persons of the Guan-speaking communities were already bilingual in Akan. In what is now Volta Region, Ewe served as a lingua franca in the south among non-Ewe-speaking communities and Akan as a lingua franca among the northern communities of that region.[37] Although Akan was widely spoken in Ghana well before the rise of the Akwamu and Ashanti empires, the incorporation of non-Akan states within these two empires promoted the broader usage of Akan both as a lingua franca and as a first language. Nevertheless, linguistic fragmentation remained a serious barrier to effective communication among many of the states.

Cultural Continuities and Discontinuities

The degree of differentiation among the cultures of Ghana's ethnic groups has served as one determinant of the character of their interaction. The central role of kinship in Ghanaian traditional societies has given rise to the often cited distinctions between ethnic groups on the basis of patterns of descent. Most of the northern societies plus the Ga and the Ewe are generally thought to trace descent along patrilineal lines; the Akans, matrilineally. These differences in patterns of descent have implications for lineage and clan structure, succession to office, inheritance, and patterns of marriage and residence.

But this generalization misrepresents the actual situation, because the social systems prevailing in the precolonial societies of Ghana were not rigid. Although the pace of adaptation and restructuring has increased during the present century, structural change occurred during the precolonial era as well. In the north some societies were in the process of moving from a system based on patrilineal descent to a system based on matrilineal descent, while other societies in the north that had been matrilineal were shifting toward a system of double descent or toward the recognition of some components of each system.[38] Furthermore, to describe these societies simply as matrilineal or patrilineal suggests too sharp a distinction, since these systems frequently share common features. Many of Ghana's basically patrilineal societies do accord matrilineal descent a role in the system and reciprocally matrilineal societies generally do not exclude completely patrilineal inheritance.[39]

In countries such as India, village exogamy, or the convention that individuals should find marriage partners from outside of their own localities, creates social linkages between different regions of the country and the nation's social fabric is thereby strengthened. In precolonial Ghana, however, one was generally expected to locate a marriage partner within one's own village or very close to it, and this expectation minimized the interethnic and interlocational linkages which marriages might otherwise have generated. Two studies have revealed interesting recent statistics regarding such marriage patterns. In 1962 in the Ewe villages of Woe and Akakple 94 percent of the marriages joined local people and 63 percent of all marriages linked people from the same section of the village.[40] In the 1960s in the Guan village of Larteh 88 percent of all marriages were between Larteh residents.[41] The likelihood is that in the precolonial period these percentages were even higher. An important exception to this pattern came in portions of the north where some ethnic groups practiced village exogamy, and as a consequence, a high proportion of their marriages incorporated persons from relatively distant places.[42]

Although certain structural variations resulted from the differing kinship and marriage systems, on the whole, the social structures of the societies of precolonial Ghana bore marked resemblence to each other, with lineage and clan units generally serving as the basic building blocks. Of equal importance for nation-building was the virtual absence of sharp socioeconomic stratification. Both sharp stratification and divergent bases of stratification among different groups might have obstructed the creation of a cohesive national society. Although slave families did generally constitute a lowly stratum, slaves were never completely ostracized, and by the beginning of the colonial era domestic slavery persisted on only a limited scale. Differences in wealth existed, but no rigid system of economic classes had evolved. Even royal lineages enjoyed only slightly greater status than commoner lineages. The vast majority of people were independent peasant farmers. Hence, the major structural problem that faced the new nation in 1900 in its effort to achieve viability and integration resulted from horizontal differentiation, or the multitude of distinct ethnolinguistic and political units, rather than from hierarchical differentiation.

From what has already been said it is clear that considerable fragmentation characterized the political organization of precolonial Ghana. The division of a population of less than two million persons into two hundred states meant that most, although not all, of the political units were necessarily small. When the Ashanti empire reached its peak in the 1820s, however, a majority of persons resident in the territory now constituting Ghana lived in states that were either part of the Ashanti empire or under strong Ashanti influence. If the European powers had not frustrated their intention, it is possible that by 1900 Ashanti would have achieved control over the whole of Ghana. In addition to Ashanti, such states as Gonja, Dagomba, Mamprusi, and the short-lived Fanti confederacy represented relatively large-scale political systems as well.

Virtually all of Ghana's traditional states fell into one of four basic organizational molds, namely, the Akan, the Ga, the Ewe, and the northern systems. Thus there was considerably more homogeneity of type than the large number of states might suggest.[43] Of these the Akan predominated and characterized not only the Akan-speaking states but, in slightly modified form, the three large northern states of Gonja, Dagomba, and Mamprusi as well. The Akan model also influenced the Ewe systems significantly and the Ga city-states to a lesser degree. Moreover, certain basic themes ran through all four types of traditional Ghanaian states, providing some cultural continuity in Ghana and beyond its borders throughout much of West Africa. First, kinship units rather than territorial boundaries constituted the basic delineation of membership in the state. For someone to become a member of another state, the society had to create the legal fiction of his membership in one of the state's component kinship units. The second common element was decentralization of power and the importance of broad consultation in decision-making, even for the paramount chief. Third, a close relationship inhered between the religious and the political systems, with the chief in many cases serving as priest as well, and in some instances being considered semidivine. Consequently, the types of sanctions at the disposal of the state were often ritualistic and supernatural, although secular and physical sanctions were also utilized. A final common element stemmed from the overriding importance accorded conciliation in judicial proceedings. In disputes between individuals and groups, even when crimes had been committed, the central theme was that of achieving reconciliation through arbitration, rather than imposing retribution through punishment.

Although the details of religious belief and practice varied from locality to locality, the traditional religious systems can be divided into the same four principal types—northern, Akan, Ga, and Ewe. Behind these generic types lay principles common to most of the religious systems not only of Ghana but the whole of West Africa. Each community acknowledged a multitude of deities, usually represented by shrines, who had to be coaxed, cajoled, and placated through sacrifices. A belief permeated these religious systems that the ancestral spirits, who played an active role in all aspects of the community's life, were among the most important supernatural beings. A final common element was the close interconnection between religious activities and political and judicial life; religion was not a remote category of experience.

Local variations on these common themes persisted largely because traditional religious practice in Ghana did not entail proselytizing. Certain elements of one system might be adopted by adherents to another system, but usually not because one community succeeded in promoting the broader adoption of its beliefs and practices. Widespread religious tolerance prevailed, with people generally accepting the relativity of religious beliefs and conceding that however different a neighboring system might be, it was probably as adequate in meeting the needs of its followers as was their system in meeting their needs. Moreover, given the fact that the ancestors were deified and played a prominent role in each system, groups with different ancestors necessarily could not worship common deities. So despite the variations in religious practice, traditional religious systems did not create serious obstacles to interethnic understanding and cohesion in the new nation of Ghana.

The spread of Christianity and Islam gave further indication of religious openness, but the introduction of these two world faiths did add new elements to the situation. Their adoption imparted common belief systems to large areas of the country and thereby provided both ritualistic and institutional linkages across ethnic lines. Moreover, as world religions, they uprooted religious belief from particular localities and individual social systems and propounded a faith open and applicable to all. However, insofar as Christianity spread primarily in the south and Islam primarily in the north, these new religions contributed an additional dimension to the cultural divergence between north and south. As aggressive and proselytizing faiths, they introduced the possibility of religious conflict in a place where religion had not previously constituted a source of intergroup dissension.

Cultural Contrasts between Ghana and Neighboring Territories

Just as cultural and linguistic homogeneity enhances the development of national cohesion, so cultural and linguistic contrast between the peoples within the nation and those living adjacent to it also contributes to national identity and national cohesion. We have pointed out that some of the traits common to the political or religious systems of Ghana's traditional states were indigenous to other parts of West Africa as well. The political borders drawn for Ghana in 1900 certainly did not coincide with sharply drawn cultural boundaries. Furthermore, the national boundaries drawn for Ghana bisected some ethnolinguistic groups, with the result that some people having the same culture and language lived both in Ghana and in the adjoining territories. For example, the Nzimas have members living on both sides of the Ghana–Ivory Coast border, and the Baule–Anyi people in Ivory Coast are Akan-speaking and are similar in culture to the Akans in Ghana. The border between Ghana and Togo divides the Ewe into two different national groups, and Ghana's borders with the Ivory Coast, Upper Volta, and Togo partition the following ethnic groups found in northern Ghana: the Garensi, the Dagari, the Birifor, the Isala, the Kasena, the Aculo, the Degha, the Konkomba, the B'moba, the Bedjebib, the Tchakosi, the Nafana, and the Busanga.

West Africa is characterized by cultural bands running in an east–west direction paralleling the Ghanaian coast, with the principal differentiation occurring between the peoples living in the southern forest zone and those living in the northern savannah. Since Ghana is shaped in rectangular form with the longer side of the rectangle running perpendicular to the coast, these cultural bands run across the country. If Ghana's shape had been such that its width were greater than its height so that it followed the borders of the cultural bands, it would have been characterized by greater cultural homogeneity and by more striking cultural differentiation from neighboring countries.

Most of Ghana's major traditional empires, such as Ashanti, Akwamu,

Denkyira, Dagomba, Gonja, and Mamprusi, lay almost completely within
the territory that later came to constitute Ghana. Thus, considerable traditional political differentiation existed between Ghana and her neighbors.
Moreover, since most interstate trade, transport, and communication occurred in the north–south direction utilizing the southern coastal ports,
Ghana achieved greater cohesion and intercultural contact from these
sources by running north and south than it would have if it had stretched
primarily in an east–west direction. These factors of political organization,
trade, transport, and communication, which contributed to migrations and
cultural diffusion, therefore went some distance toward giving a natural
definition to Ghana's national borders and compensating for the relative
absence of cultural contrast between Ghana and neighboring territories.

Ethnic Awareness

In precolonial times, a sense of loyalty and allegiance rarely extended
beyond the political unit of which the person was a part. The ethnic awareness
and conflict that have developed in the twentieth century certainly had roots
in the precolonial period. But prior to the twentieth century intergroup
relations primarily involved politically defined relations among a multitude of
states.[44] Among the segmentary societies in the north primary loyalty went to
one's locality; beyond that unit any sense of belonging gradually diminished
as the distance increased. Even though today we refer to the Tallensi or the
Lowili as identifiable and self-conscious ethnic groups, they had no consciousness of themselves as distinct ethnic or linguistic groups during the
precolonial period, and this was true of most of their neighbors as well.[45] The
development of a Pan-Ewe awareness or identity postdated 1900 as well.[46]
Only with the development of urban centers where Ewes came into contact
with diverse ethnolinguistic groups and with other Ewes did they develop a
sense of their uniqueness as Ewes. For the most part traditional group
identification among Akan-speaking peoples coincided with the composition
of state units, and thus there was little Pan-Akan consciousness. In some cases
ethnic awareness extending beyond individual political units did develop, as it
did among the Fanti. This Fanti identity derived primarily from a myth of
common origin, a distinctive dialect, and a shared religious cult,[47] which was
heightened in the nineteenth century by the military threat from the Ashanti
to the north.

It should be evident from the material presented here that some of the popular notions regarding precolonial Ghana need revision. There was unquestionably considerable artificiality in the creation of Ghana by Britain in 1900. Yet Ghana's nationhood had some cultural and historical foundations. Although there is some validity in the statement of David Kimble quoted at the beginning of the chapter regarding the isolation, self-sufficiency, fear of outsiders, and tightly knit character of the two hundred states that constituted precolonial Ghana, to emphasize these aspects alone is to give a seriously distorted picture. Slave raiding and interstate warfare did occur and they did have an impact on interstate and interethnic relations. But one can also cite innumerable examples of peaceful coexistence, mixing and contact, interstate trade, migration, acculturation, and assimilation. A map of precolonial Ghana, which has clearly delineated boundaries drawn around each of Ghana's thirty four ethnolinguistic groups, or "tribes," does not do justice to the realities of the situation either. Such a map implies that each of these ethnic groups comprised a closed and internally cohesive social system, but, in fact, considerable interaction and interchange occurred among them. Furthermore, many of them had little internal cohesion or sense of identity. Thus, such a map exaggerates both the degree of internal cohesion and underrates the frequency of interaction across linguistic lines.

Period of Colonial Rule

Although the details of the early assertion of British colonial authority are not relevant to this discussion, three aspects of this movement do have a bearing on the legacy of the colonial period.[48] First, explicit British colonization of Ghana came in stages. Colonial ascendance over the south (the Colony) was gradually extended after 1874; colonial subjugation of Ashanti dated from 1901; control over the Northern Territories was claimed in 1901 but was not completely effected until 1911; and hegemony over the Togoland area came only in 1922 when the League of Nations granted it to Britain as a mandated territory. It will become apparent later in this discussion that the gradual extension of British colonial control and then the lack of effective administrative integration of these four regions until the 1950s created serious difficulties for Ghana's subsequent attempts to achieve national integration.

A second factor of importance was the differing reactions of the four parts of Ghana to the prospect of colonial rule. Colonial control over the south (Colony) involved a rather slow assertion of authority and proceeded with relative amicability. The coastal peoples enjoyed their trading relations with the British and appreciated the role British authorities sometimes played in settling local disputes. More importantly, following the Ashanti attack on the Fantis in 1807, the Fantis and other coastal peoples sought and received British protection against the continuing threat of Ashanti aggression.

Because of the turbulent history of British–Ashanti relations, the Ashanti had no desire to be subjugated to British rule. The decisive and final military encounter between the British and the Ashanti came in 1896 and resulted in the British capturing and forcing into exile the Ashanti head of state, the Asantehene. Then in 1901 the British annexed Ashanti as a separate unit of the Gold Coast.

Colonial control over the Northern Territories resulted from agreements reached between British authorities and local leaders, as well as from an accord in 1898 among the British, the French, and the Germans, all of whom had sought control over portions of the area. In 1901 the British officially declared the Northern Territories to be part of the colony of the Gold Coast, but it took the better part of a decade for the area to be brought under complete military control because of conflicts among the region's various traditional political units and because of the plunderous activities of alien slave traders. Even then British hegemony made little noticeable impact on the everyday lives of most of the area's residents.

From 1886 to 1914 the Togoland region was a part of the German colony of Togoland. During World War I the British attacked the German forces in Togoland from the west in concert with a French invasion from the east, and Togoland quickly came under British and French control. The Paris Peace Conference divided Togoland into British and French mandated areas. This redistribution of territory reunited under British rule some ethnic groups in the north that had previously been divided between the Gold Coast and Togoland. However, the Ewes in the south, who had also been divided between the Gold Coast and Togoland, were now subjected to a further partition, with some in the Colony of the Gold Coast, others in the British mandate, and others in the French mandate. The impact of this three-way division was mitigated to some extent in 1923 when the British decided to administer British Togoland as an integral part of the Gold Coast, but Ewe displeasure over the division persisted for many more years.

Decentralization constituted the dominant theme of the administrative and legislative structure the British adopted for the Gold Coast. Although the governor of the Gold Coast retained ultimate authority over the four regions, the administrative structures and procedures for the four regions varied considerably. These ranged from an essentially military approach adopted in the early years in the Northern Territories to quasi-representative government in the Colony. The Legislative Council that flourished in the Colony was extended to cover Ashanti and the Northern Territories in 1946, and only in 1954, three years before independence, did the Northern Territories send elected representatives to replace those previously appointed by the British.

Beyond decentralization to the regional level the British colonial administration also delegated considerable authority to the many traditional states within each region. This system of indirect rule recognized the traditional authority of the chiefs in each of these states.[49] In addition to utilizing existing traditional political units and authorities, in a few areas, particularly in Togoland, colonial officials tried to encourage small traditional units to federate into larger units. In the 1920s the colonial authorities also organized provincial councils for the chiefs from the various traditional states of the Colony. Despite these limited efforts to expand traditional political horizons, the British generally emphasized the stabilization of traditional political units under the control of traditional authorities. The role of the Legislative Council, the most broadly encompassing representative institution, was limited by the fact that prior to 1946 its geographic coverage was confined to the Colony.

This decentralized system had two principal consequences for intergroup relations and national accommodation. First, by building upon the traditional units and by reinforcing authority at the local level, interethnic and interregional political competition at the center remained minimal until about 1945. With relatively little interethnic political interaction at the national level, Ghana suffered from little ethnic conflict between 1900 and 1945. But because decentralization precluded extensive interethnic contact and political interaction, little progress toward national integration was evident by 1945. The governmental structure adopted by the British in the Gold Coast minimized conflict without promoting harmony, which meant that benefits were limited and short-term in promoting national accommodation.

Nevertheless, the colonial era witnessed many new forms of interethnic contact and the forging of many horizontal linkages. Among those who developed a new sense of shared interests bridging traditional boundaries were the educated elite, although before 1940 this development was largely confined to the Colony. Two important organizations brought together members of the educated elite; namely, the Aborigines' Rights Protection Society (organized in 1897 and active until the early 1920s), and the National

Congress of British West Africa (from 1920 to 1930). Although it was strongest in the Gold Coast, the Congress also included members from Nigeria, Sierra Leone, and the Gambia, the other British colonies in West Africa. An important source of common identity and interethnic association among some members of the educated elite came from the government bureaucracy, once Africans started to be recruited for senior posts. In 1938 only 41 Africans held senior civil service posts, but this number increased to 171 in 1949, to 916 in 1954, and over 3000 at the time of independence in 1957.[50]

Although colonial relations in West Africa were never characterized by the intensity of racial hostility that prevailed in east, central, and southern Africa, the racial element still comprised an important boundary in setting the governed off from the governors and in creating some bonds of common identification among Ghanaians and among British West Africans generally. More important than the racial differences between the British and those they were governing was the simple fact of alien control. The chiefs and the educated elite prior to World War II did not aggressively push for complete self-rule, but they did consistently plead for a greater role in managing their own affairs.

After World War II, the independence movement mushroomed and the bonds forged across ethnic lines by common opposition to British rule constituted a powerful integrative force, although it once again affected the Colony more deeply than the rest of the country. The United Gold Coast Convention, Ghana's first political party, was an elitist party that was not deeply rooted. In contrast, the Convention People's Party, which Kwame Nkrumah organized in 1949, soon became broadly based and did provide important horizontal ties. Its early popularity became evident in the 1951 elections when the CPP won thirty four of the thirty eight seats being contested. As Dennis Austin asserts, by the time of independence in 1957 the CPP "could justly claim to have aroused and extended a sense of nationality which in 1946 was still inchoate."[51] As in Lebanon and many other territories under colonial control, one of the high points of national cohesion during the struggle for independence came when nationalist leaders were imprisoned. In Ghana this happened in January and February of 1948, when riots against high prices and against colonial rule resulted in the imprisonment of Kwame Nkrumah and five other leaders of the independence movement.

Fifty years of British colonial rule did implant a noticeable measure of common identity among many Ghanaians. Exposure to the English language and to British institutions, the development of crosscutting linkages, involvement in some shared national institutions, and an eventual widely shared opposition to colonial rule made Ghana a more self-conscious and potentially viable state than it had been in 1900. As K.A. Busia has written of the colonial period, "A vastly greater number of people have been brought into effective social relations."[52] The fact that all the surrounding territories were under French administration also contributed to this incipient awareness of Ghanaian national identity.

Despite the strength of horizontal ties forged for limited or sustained periods among such groups as chiefs, the educated elite, political party supporters, ex-servicemen, and cocoa farmers, Ghana still faced formidable obstacles to national accommodation. The depth of ethnic and regional attachments became particularly clear in the years just prior to independence. Once independence was assured, the veneer of national unity that had been created during the nationalist struggle was seriously disturbed by debates on the relationships that would inhere among the country's various ethnic groups in the independent state. Moreover, the regional and ethnic coexistence that had prevailed during a period of limited popular participation, decentralization, and indirect rule disappeared when the country's various regional and ethnic groups started competing for power and the allocation of resources at the center.

Underlying these disturbed relations was the residue of fear of the Ashanti on the part of those in the Colony. This fear carried over from the nineteenth century when the Ashanti posed an almost continual military threat to the south. Although little overt conflict occurred, doubts remained regarding Ashanti intentions once the British left. These fears of the Ashanti persisted in part because the system of colonial government adopted by the British entailed separate administration of the Colony, Ashanti, the Northern Territories, and Togoland. Moreover, many of the voluntary associations and horizontal linkages that developed during the colonial era were concentrated in the Colony, and consequently did little to tie the Colony to Ashanti or the other portions of the country. For their part, the Ashanti did not forget their history either. In 1953 the Ashanti members of the National Assembly pressed for representation in the Assembly well in excess of the numbers to which Ashanti's population size entitled them. In the debate over this issue Ashanti representatives argued that Ashanti deserved larger than normal representation because Ashanti constituted a nation in itself with a glorious history.[53]

The Prelude and Aftermath of Independence

As the prospect of independence loomed on the horizon, sharp conflict developed along ethnic lines, with ethnic-based political movements developing among the Ashanti, the northerners, and the Ewe. The unifying issue of independence had largely passed, and now the divisive question of the constitutional character of the new state had to be confronted. The strongest threat to the push by the governing Convention People's Party (CPP) for rapid independence and a unitary state came from Ashanti in the form of the National Liberation Movement, organized shortly after the 1954 elections. The National Liberation Movement (NLM) gained its initial strength from cocoa farmers displeased with the government's policies regarding cocoa pricing, and the NLM later absorbed protest groups from other parts of Ghana as well. But the central core of the NLM consisted of Ashanti loyalists whose concerns were less economic than ethnic. The NLM demanded that the date for independence be postponed and that Ghana adopt a federal constitution with each region managing most of its own affairs. A federal arrangement would have permitted the Ashantis to use their region's wealth to benefit themselves rather than to subsidize development in less affluent parts of the country and it would have facilitated the preservation of Ashanti institutions and a sense of Ashanti identity. K.A. Busia, a NLM leader and later Prime Minister, declared that "any constitution which fails to recognize the identity of the Ashanti nation will arouse violent feelings against it. The demand for a federal union arises from this consideration."[55]

Dissension between the NLM and the CPP resulting from their differing political ideologies led to a series of violent clashes in and around Kumasi, some of which involved political bombings and even assassinations. The strong opposition of Nkrumah and his CPP to the NLM arose in part because the NLM represented a threat to CPP control, but more fundamentally they feared that a federal system would foster subnational political socialization and encourage ethnic and regional conflict.[56] The CPP hoped to promote vigorously national consciousness and, insofar as possible, to eliminate ethnic identities.

The NLM's agitation prompted the British to insist on national elections in 1956 to determine popular wishes regarding the date of independence and the character of the independence constitution. The CPP managed an overall victory in this election, but not in Ashanti where the NLM won twelve seats against the CPP's eight.[57] Following their electoral defeat, the NLM joined the Northern People's Party in threatening the secession of Ashanti and the Northern Territories unless their demands for a federal constitution were met. To avoid this frightening prospect, Nkrumah agreed to a constitution with a provision for regional assemblies. This compromise permitted a temporary resolution of the impasse and provided a basis for the granting of independence in 1957. However, soon after independence Nkrumah pushed through a constitutional amendment abolishing the regional assemblies, thereby creating the unitary and centralized state he desired.

While the NLM called for the postponement of independence as part of its strategy for promoting the concept of a federal constitution, the Northern People's Party (NPP) appeared to prefer indefinite continuation of the status of northerners as "protected persons" under British control.[58] The prospect of the north being controlled by a sophisticated southern elite terrified many northern leaders. They feared that the southern-dominated CPP would make them "servants" in their own territory. Furthermore, unlike the Ashanti who wanted the allocation of government resources to be commensurate with revenues collected in the region, the NPP wanted special status for the north as a basis for receiving additional government subventions. They believed that the depressed state of the north warranted that it be assigned a disproportionate share of government revenues. The popularity among northerners of the NPP position became clear when it won twelve of seventeen seats in the 1954 election and then again when it captured fifteen of twenty nine seats in the 1956 election.

Nkrumah's response to the NPP's 1954 electoral success presaged his later reaction to ethnically and regionally based politics. Although the NPP constituted the largest opposition block in the National Assembly in 1954, Nkrumah strenuously objected to the NPP being recognized as the official opposition because it represented an ethnic-regional movement rather than a national political party. Thus, its very existence was inconsistent with the national perspective which to him provided the only acceptable basis for a viable modern state.[59]

An ethnic–separatist movement of a different variety developed in Togoland. As we have noted, the Ewe people were divided between the Gold Coast proper, the British mandated portion of Togoland, and the French mandated portion of Togoland. In the mid-1940s an All-Ewe Conference advocated the unification of Eweland as an independent territory. Subsequently, other organizations appeared with the same basic motive, the most important of which was the Togoland Congress.[60] In pursuit of its objectives the Togoland Congress entered Gold Coast politics in the 1950s and won three seats in the 1954 election and two seats in the 1956 election. The legal resolution of the issue came in May 1956 when the United Nations organized a plebiscite to determine the wishes of those living in British Togoland. A majority of those voting favored full amalgamation of British Togoland with the Gold Coast, and this is what happened. However, in the Ewe portions of British Togoland 58 percent of those voting preferred separation from the Gold Coast and reunification of the two Togolands as an Ewe homeland. As a consequence of this vote, doubts on the part of other Ghanaians regarding the loyalty of Ewes to Ghana lingered for several years.

It is obvious that although the CPP won the 1956 elections handily, parties based primarily on ethnic-regional appeals demonstrated their popularity and strength in particular portions of the country. In the immediate aftermath of independence in 1957, Ghana faced even more energetic challenges from communally based movements. The most serious threat arose in the former British Togoland, presently the Volta Region. An unwillingness on the part of the leaders of the Togoland Congress to accept the results of the 1956 United Nations plebiscite led them to organize military training and to plot attacks on government offices. By military action and public disturbances they apparently hoped to attract the United Nations' attention and have the question of Togoland reunification reconsidered.[61] The government responded by sending three regiments of troops to the area and placing some localities under martial law. This was probably an exaggerated response to the actual threat but it indicates the seriousness with which the government reacted to the possibility of Ewe secession. Although the preindependence threats of secession by Ashanti leaders soon disappeared, antigovernment sentiment among the Ashanti still festered. Ashanti hostility toward the CPP was of such magnitude that some observers feared that a civil war might even erupt there.[62] For as long as a year after independence, most CPP leaders considered a visit to Ashanti to be too dangerous to undertake. In Accra a new ethnically based movement developed among the Gas, who predominate there. The Ga Adangbe Shifimo Kpee had as its objective the protection of the interests of the Ga people, since the members did not believe that the CPP government showed sufficient interest in their welfare. A strike by Ga taxi and lorry drivers and violent demonstrations organized by the new movement caused the government to declare a state of emergency in Accra in August 1957, only a few months after independence.

NOTES

Notes on sources on Lebanese history: Footnotes have been used to indicate a particular debt to an individual author. In terms of general background on this subject, we have benefited particularly from the following sources: K.S. Salibi, *The Modern History of Lebanon* (London: Weidenfeld and Nicolson, 1965); Iliya F. Harik, *Politics and Change in a Traditional Society* (Princeton, N. J.: Princeton University Press, 1968); William R. Polk, *The Opening of South Lebanon, 1788–1840* (Cambridge, Mass: Harvard University Press, 1963); and Stephen Hemsley Longrigg, *Syria and Lebanon Under French Mandate* (Beirut: Librairie du Liban, 1958).

In addition to these sources and to the ones cited in footnotes, we have also found the following to be useful: M. Jouplain, *La Question du Liban* (Paris: Arthur Rousseau, 1908); Jacques Nantet, *Histoire du Liban* (Paris: Les Éditions de Minuit, 1963); Charles Churchill, *The Druzes and the Maronites Under Turkish Rule from 1840 to 1860* (London: Bernard Quarith, 1862); P.K. Hitti, *Lebanon in History* (New York: St. Martin's Press, 1967); Panos S. Jeranian, "Catholic Armenia and Maronite Religions in Mount Lebanon 1720–1840," unpublished M.A. Thesis, American University of Beirut, 1971; Mounir R. Sa'adah, "The Fifth Lebanese Legislative Assembly, 1943–44," unpublished M.A. Thesis, American University of Beirut, 1945; Mary-Jane Anhoury Deeb, "The Khazin Family: A Case Study of the Effect of Social Change on Traditional Roles," unpublished M.A. Thesis, American University of Cairo, 1972; Albert Hourani, *Syria and Lebanon* (London: Oxford University Press, 1946); Michel Chiha, *Politique Intéreiure* (Beirut: Trident, 1964; George Haddad, *Fifty Years of Modern Syria and Lebanon* (Beirut: Dar al-Hayat, 1950); T.E. Holland, *The European Concert in the Eastern Question* (London: Oxford University Press, 1885); Dominique Chevallier, *La Société du Mont Liban à l'Epoque de la Révolution Industrielle en Europe* (Paris: Librairie Orientaliste P. Geuther, 1971); Leila M.T. Meo, *Lebanon: Improbable Nation* (Bloomington, Indiana: University of Indiana Press, 1965); Lahad Khātir, *Ahd al-Mutaṣarrifīn fī Lubnān 1861–1918* (Beirut: Al-Jāmi'at al-Lubnāniyyah, Qism al-Dirāsāt al-Tarīkhiyyan, 1967); Ismā'īl Haqqī, *Lubnān Mabāhith 'Ilmiyyah wa-'Ijtimā'iyyah.* (Beirut: Al-Matba'at al-'Arabiyyah, 1969); Ahmad Muṣṭafā Ḥaydar, *Al-Dawlat al-Lubnāniyyah 1920–1953* (Beirut: Al-Najma Press, 1954); Kamal Salibi, "The Lebanese Identity," *Journal of Contemporary History*, 6 (No. 1, 1971), 76–84; and Robert M. Haddad, *Syrian Christians in Muslim Society* (Princeton: Princeton University Press, 1970).

1. "The problem of Lebanon's political institutions seems to reside essentially in the difficult transition of the traditional communities into a modern form, or more precisely in the laborious adjustment of these apparently incompatible entities." Pierre Rondot, *Les Institutions Politiques du Liban* (Paris: Institut d'Etudes d'Orient Contemporain, 1947), p. 21.
2. A.H. Hourani, "Race, Religion and the Nation-State in the Near East," in Abdulla M. Lutfiyya and Charles Churchill, eds., *Readings in Arab Middle Eastern Societies and Cultures* (The Hague: Mouton, 1970). p. 4.
3. Hitti, op. cit., p. 435.
4. Malcolm Kerr, *Lebanon in the Last Years of Feudalism, 1840–1868: A Contemporary Account by Antūn Ḍāhir Al-Aqīqī* (Beirut: American University of Beirut, 1959), p. x.
5. Noel Spencer, "The Role of the Maronite Patriarchate in Lebanese Politics from 1840 to the Present," unpublished M.A. Thesis, American University of Beirut, 1963.
6. Harik, op. cit., p. 74.
7. Polk, op. cit.

8. For a description of the governor's military and police power, see Gabriel Charmes, *Voyage en Syrie: Impressions et Souvenirs* (Paris: Levy, 1891), pp. 256–257.
9. In asserting that the council had ten members, Harik (p. 251) has revised earlier assertions that the council had twelve members.
10. Albert H. Hourani, "Lebanon from Feudalism to Modern State," *Middle Eastern Studies*, 2 (April 1966), p. 259.
11. J.P. Spagnolo, "Constitutional Change in Mount Lebanon, 1861-1864," *Middle Eastern Studies*, 7 (January 1971), p. 43.
12. See, for instance, Polk, op. cit., pp. 60–69.
13. For a fuller discussion of the Arab nationalist movement of this period, see Albert Hourani, *Arabic Thought in the Liberal Age, 1798–1939* (London: Oxford University Press, 1962); Zeine N. Zeine, *Arab-Turkish Relations and the Emergence of Arab Nationalism* (Beirut: Khayat's, 1958); and George Antonius, *The Arab Awakening* (London: Hamish Hamilton, 1938).
14. See for instance the discussion of the Chehab conversions in K.S. Salibi, "The Lebanese Emirate," *Al-Abhāth*, 20 (Sept. 1967), pp. 14–15; and Salibi, *The Modern History of Lebanon*, op. cit., pp. 11–12.
15. These friendly relations persisted to a considerable degree even after the 1917 Revolution in Russia, and Russian sympathies among Greek Orthodox Lebanese probably explain in part the left-wing political orientation of many Greek Orthodox today.
16. For translation of the principal statement Riyadh al-Sulh made regarding the National Pact, see George Dib, "Selections from Riad Solh's Speech in the Lebanese Assembly, October 1943," *Middle East Forum*, 34 (January 1959), p. 6.
17. For the sake of consistency and simplicity "Ghana" is used in the first part of this chapter to refer to the country during both colonial and independence periods, rather than using "Gold Coast" to refer to the country during the colonial period and "Ghana" to refer to the independent country.
18. B. Gil, A. F. Aryee, and D. K. Ghansah, *Special Report 'E': Tribes in Ghana, 1960, Population Census of Ghana* (Accra: Census Office, 1964).
19. The term "state" is used to refer to traditional political units which existed during the pre-colonial period. The terms "nation" and "country" are reserved for use in reference to the Ghana of 1900 and after, which drew together the traditional states under a single administration.
20. David Kimble, *A Political History of Ghana* (Oxford: Clarendon Press, 1963), p. 125.
21. In 1896 Ashanti was forced to submit to British protection; in 1899 agreement was reached on a Gold Coast–Togoland border; and in 1902 both Ashanti and the Northern Territories were officially joined to the coastal Colony, which had come under British control in 1874.
22. Robert Szereszewski, *Structural Changes in the Economy of Ghana, 1891–1911* (London: Weidenfeld and Nicholson, 1965), p. 125.
23. Ivor Wilks, "A Medieval Trade-Route from the Niger to the Gulf of Guinea," *Journal of African History*, III, 2 (1962), p. 338.
24. Kwame Yeboa Daaku, *Trade and Politics on the Gold Coast, 1600–1720* (London: Oxford University Press, 1970), pp. 5–6.
25. Jack Goody, "Introduction" to J.A. Braimah, *The Two Isanwurfus* (London: Longmans, 1967), p. vii.
26. J.D. Fage, *Ghana: A Historical Interpretation* (Madison: University of Wisconsin Press, 1959), p. 48.
27. Ivor Wilks, "The Growth of the Akwapim State," in Jan Vansina, R. Mauny, and L.V. Thomas, eds., *The Historian in Tropical Africa* (London: Oxford University Press, 1964), p. 403.

28. Francis Agbodeka, "The Fanti Confederacy, 1965–69," *Transactions of the Historical Society of Ghana*, VII (1964), pp. 82–123.

29. Ivor Wilks, *The Northern Factor in Ashanti History* (Legon: Institute of African Studies, University College of Ghana, 1961), p. 20.

30. See, for instance, Eva L.R. Meyerowitz, *The Akan of Ghana* (London: Faber and Faber, 1958), pp. 15–18.

31. Jack Goody, "The Ethnography of the Northern Territories of the Gold Coast, West of the White Volta," (Cambridge, 1952, mimeographed), p. 13. See also M.J. Field, *Religion and Medicine of the Ga People* (London: Oxford University Press, 1961), p. 40, for a discussion of the ethnic mixture in the town of Labadi.

32. R.S. Rattray, *The Tribes of the Ashanti Hinterland* (Oxford: The Clarendon Press, 1932), p. 549.

33. A. Adu Boahen, "Asante and Fante A.D. 1000–1800," in Ade Ajayi and Ian Espie, eds., *A Thousand Years of West African History* (Ibadan: Ibadan University Press, 1965), pp. 160–161; M.J. Field, *Akim-Kotoku: An Omar of the Gold Coast* (London: The Crown Agents for the Colonies, 1948), p. 36.

34. Meyer Fortes, "Some Aspects of Migration and Mobility in Ghana," *Journal of Asian and African Studies*, VI (January 1971), pp. 5–6.

35. See, for instance, Madeline Manoukian, *Tribes of the Northern Territories of the Gold Coast* (London: International African Institute, 1951), p. 49.

36. A.W. Cardinall, *The Natives of the Northern Territories of the Gold Coast* (London: George Routledge and Sons, 1920), p. ix.

37. Madeline Manoukian, *The Ewe-Speaking People of Togoland and the Gold Coast* (London: International African Institute, 1952), p. 9.

38. J.R. Goody, *The Social Organization of the LoWili* (London: HMSO, 1956, Colonial Research Studies No. 19), pp. iv. and 52.

39. For a discussion of northern ethnic groups in this regard, see Madeline Manoukian, *Tribes of the Northern Territories of the Gold Coast*, op. cit., p. 25; about the Ewe, see G.K. Nukunya, *Kinship and Marriage Among the Anlo Ewe* (London: The Athlone Press, 1969), pp. 46–48; and regarding the Fanti, see James B. Christensen, *Double-Descent Among the Fanti* (New Haven, Conn.: Human Relations Area Files, 1954), p. 4.

40. Nukunya, op. cit., pp. 72–74.

41. David Brokensha, *Social Change at Larteh, Ghana* (Oxford: The Clarendon Press, 1966), p. 219.

42. Polly Hill, *The Occupations of Migrants in Ghana* (Ann Arbor: University of Michigan, Museum of Anthropology, Anthropological Papers, 1970), pp. 61–62; and Christine Oppong, "Local Migrations in Northern Ghana," *Ghana Journal of Sociology*, 3 (February 1967), pp. 12–13.

43. See B.D.G. Folson, "The Traditional Political System," n.d., mimeographed, 9 pp.

44. See William Tordoff, *Ashanti Under the Prempehs, 1888–1935* (London: Oxford University Press, 1965), p. 15, for a discussion of how the Ashanti leadership attempted to arouse a sense of Ashanti identity among newly conquered populations.

45. See Meyer Fortes, *The Web of Kinship Among the Tallensi* (London: Oxford University Press, 1949), p. 1.

46. Manoukian, *The Ewe-Speaking People of Togoland and the Gold Coast*, op. cit., p. 30.

47. Kwame Arhin, "Diffuse Authority Among the Coastal Fanti," *Ghana Notes and Queries*, 9 (November 1966), p. 70.

48. It is difficult to set a date for the commencement of British colonial rule in Ghana. British traders built forts along the Ghana coast as early as the mid-seventeenth century, but only between 1821 to 1828 and then again after 1843 did the British crown assume responsibility

for these trading settlements. Then in 1844 the first of a series of treaties was signed between British authorities and cheifs among the coastal peoples. The first explicit British recognition of colonial control came in 1874, but even then British intentions and plans were not clear. (For an account of this period, see Fage, op. cit., pp. 64–65 and pp. 76–77.)

49. For a full account of indirect rule, see David E. Apter, *Ghana in Transition* (New York: Atheneum, 1963), pp. 131–158; and Amon Nikoi, "Indirect Rule and Government in the Gold Coast Colony 1844–1954," unpublished Ph.D. Diss., Harvard University, 1956.

50. F.M. Bourret, *Ghana: The Road to Independence, 1919–1957* (London: Oxford University Press, 1960), pp. 68 and 178.

51. Dennis Austin, *Politics in Ghana, 1946–1960* (London: Oxford University Press, 1964), p. 43.

52. See K.A. Busia, *The Position of the Chief in the Modern Political System of Ashanti* (London: Oxford University Press, 1951), p. 138.

53. Quoted in Austin, op. cit., pp. 178–179.

54. Kimble, op. cit., p. 554.

55. Quoted in Victor Effah-Apenteng, "Gold Coast Politics: The Federalist Agitation, 1954–57," unpublished M.A. Thesis, Institute of African Studies, University of Ghana, 1970, p. 63.

56. For a discussion of the opposing arguments on the federal question, see "Report from the Select Committee on Federal System of Government and Second Chamber for the Gold Coast" (Accra: The Government Printer, 1955).

57. Much of the support for the CPP in Ashanti Region came in the Brong area where the CPP supported the people's wish for a separate region.

58. See, for instance, J.A. Braimah, *The Two Isanwurfos* (London: Longmans, 1967), pp. 97–98.

59. For a partial explanation of his position, see Kwame Nkrumah, *Ghana: The Autobiography of Kwame Nkrumah* (Edinburgh: Thomas Nelson and Sons, 1959), pp. 176–177.

60. For a full discussion of these events and their significance, see Claude E. Welch, Jr., *Dream of Unity* (Ithaca, N.Y.: Cornell University Press, 1966), pp. 134–136.

61. See Austin, op. cit., p. 181; and "Statement by the Government on the Report of the Commission Appointed to Enquire into the Matters Disclosed at the Trial of Captain Benjamin Awhaitey before a Court Martial, and the Surrounding Circumstances," Government White Paper No. 10 of 1959 (Accra: Government Printer, 1959).

62. Apter, op. cit., p. 341.

The Social, Cultural, and Religious Framework of The Lebanese State

Religious differences constitute one of the major determinants of Lebanon's social and political life. The religious affiliation of an individual Lebanese does far more than merely define his theological position or determine the ritual practices he observes, for membership in a particular religious community provides a prolegomenon to his basic life patterns and the network of his social and political relationships. An observer must guard against exaggerating the role that religion plays in Lebanon's social structure and political system, but it is nonetheless a factor of enormous significance. Given this fact, and the fact that the focus of our analysis of Lebanon is upon religious pluralism in that country, it is appropriate for our discussion of the social and cultural framework of the Lebanese state to commence with an analysis of the beliefs, social organization, and life styles of Lebanon's various religious communities or sects.

Of fundamental importance to an understanding of Lebanon's various religious communities is a recognition that there are many such groups and that no one sect constitutes more than 30 percent of the country's total population: the Lebanese Government officially recognizes seventeen different sects. Lebanon's religious sects can be thought of in terms of two broad groupings, Muslim and Christian, but the subdivisions within these group-

75

ings are several and significant. According to the 1932 census, which was Lebanon's last official census, the Maronite community constituted 29 percent of the total population, Greek Orthodox 9 percent, Greek Catholics 6 percent, Sunnis 22 percent, Shiites 20 percent, and Druze 7 percent.[1] The remaining 7 percent was primarily made up of smaller Christian denominations. In 1932 the number of Christians slightly exceeded the number of Muslims, and this is reflected in the fact that since that time parliamentary seats have been divided in a ratio of 6 : 5, with Christians being assigned six seats for every five designated for Muslims.

In the absence of any recent census no reliable figures can be offered either for Lebanon's total population or for the size of the various sects. The Ministry of Planning estimated that Lebanon's total population in 1970 was 2,126,325 of which 10 percent were foreigners.[2] This appraisal excludes more than one million emigrant Lebanese, most of whom have retained a Lebanese passport even when taking out citizenship in the country in which they have settled.[3] Whether the Lebanese residing abroad should be counted as part of the Lebanese population in the event of a new census has fueled a never-ending debate among the sects—the Christians generally in favor and the Muslims against the inclusion of the predominantly Christian emigrants. The widespread reluctance in Lebanon to organize another census reflects uncertainty regarding the precise nature of the demographic shifts among the sects since 1932.

Some sources have portrayed the Lebanese population as now being about equally divided between Christians and Muslims.[4] It is quite likely, however, that the Muslims outnumber the Christians in Lebanon, both because Christians tend to have a higher rate of permanent emigration and because they tend to have a lower birthrate. The relative strength of the individual sects has undoubtedly changed since 1932 as well. For instance, the Shiite community may now outnumber the Sunnis and possibly the Maronites as well. Results of a survey undertaken by the Family Planning Association of Lebanon on a national sample of approximately three thousand married Lebanese women confirms that Shiites have a higher fertility level and a lower proportion of contraceptive users than other sects. The average number of living children each woman reported range from 2.83 for non-Catholic Christians, 3.57 for Catholics, 3.71 for Druze, 4.38 for Sunnis, to 5.01 for Shiites. Percentages of women refusing to employ any contraceptive methods follow a similar sectarian pattern with 24 percent of the Catholics, 25 percent of the other Christians, 28 percent of the Druze, 38 percent of the Sunnis, and 54 percent of the Shiite respondents being nonusers. Shiite women also wanted to have more children than respondents from other sects with 41 percent of them indicating that their preferred family size was five or more children in contrast with 11 percent of the non-Catholic Christians, 12 percent of the Druze, 20 percent of the Catholics, and 21 percent of the Sunnis.[5] These findings have obvious and important long-term implications for the relative size of Lebanon's various communities.

Various sects have issued their own population estimates from time to time, but each has had an incentive to inflate its own size. Shiite sources place the number of members of their sect in Lebanon at 755,000,[6] which in a population of 2,126,325 would comprise 35.5 percent, or 15 percent more than in 1932. Statistics issued by the Vatican list the Catholic population of Lebanon as 32.8 percent of the total,[7] which would mean a decline of approximately 5 percent since 1932 in the combined percentage of Maronites, Greek Catholics, Armenian Catholics, and Latins (Roman Catholics). Druze claim to have increased from 7 to 8 percent of the population.[8]

ECCLESIASTICAL ORGANIZATION

Lebanon's religious communities constitute a major component of the social and political systems primarily by providing a focus for loyalty, self-definition, and social identification. Theological differences count for much less than the social labels associated with membership in a sect. In fact, most Lebanese would be hard-pressed to delineate the major dogmas distinguishing one sect from another. Thus, a decline in religiosity and an increasingly secular orientation would not necessarily decrease the role of the sects in Lebanon's social and political life.

Ecclesiastical organization of the sects has implications fo the political system primarily in three ways. The degree of centralization and the authority of the head of the sect affect the kind of political role religious leaders of that community can play. Ecclesiastical organization varies considerably in this regard, and it seems more than coincidental that the Maronite Patriarch, who presides over the most centralized church hierarchy in Lebanon, historically has also had the greatest tendency to serve as the spokesman and defender of a community. A second factor to be noted relates to the international bonds that the various Lebanese religious groups have forged. An examination of the structure of the sects also shows the interplay between the religious and political spheres in Lebanon and the difficulty of drawing a sharp dividing line between church and state.

Both the Maronites and the Greek Catholics, the two largest components of the Catholic community in Lebanon, are Uniate Churches in that they recognize the Pope and are tied to Rome but are allowed to keep their own liturgies, liturgical language, and ecclesiastical customs, especially as to the marriage of the clergy. The Maronite Church, headed by a Patriarch resident in Lebanon, traditionally has been the most hierarchically structured and centralized of all the religious communities of Lebanon.[9] Today the Maronite Church comprises ten dioceses, each headed by a bishop, and 850 parishes, most of which have a resident priest. As supreme head of the Maronite Church, subject only to the Pope, the Patriarch has full jurisdiction over all subordinate bishops and clergy. An electoral college constituted by all Maronite bishops meets nine days after the death of a Patriarch to elect his successor. In order for the successful candidate to assume his new role, he must also receive a papal pallium and confirmation of his election.

The Greek Catholic Church is also headed by a Patriarch, but his headquarters is in Damascus, not Lebanon, and his jurisdiction extends throughout what formerly constituted the Arab portions of the Ottoman Empire. The Greek Catholic Church is divided into thirteen dioceses, of which six are located in Lebanon. Within the Greek Catholic Church a bishop enjoys greater administrative and financial independence in his diocese than his Maronite counterparts, with the result that the sect is less centralized than the Maronites. As in the Maronite Church, after the death of an incumbent, an electoral college of bishops selects a new Patriarch.[10]

The Greek Orthodox Church is not a uniquely Lebanese institution either. Both the Greek Catholic and the Greek Orthodox Churches have their headquarters in Syria, and their structure as a transnational institution limits the ability of the church to act as a spokesman for the community in Lebanon in social and political matters. The Greek Orthodox of Lebanon belong to the Church of Antioch. For a long time the hierarchy of the Church of Antioch remained Greek, but the last two patriarchs have been Arabs. The Church of Antioch is divided into fourteen sees governed by metropolitans. Within the Greek Orthodox Church the Patriarch has no executive power over the bishops in the diocese; he is merely considered the first among equals. For this reason, the Greek Orthodox Church is the least centralized among the major Christian sects.[11] During the twentieth century the Church of Antioch has suffered from several scandals relating to poor church management, which also had the effect of weakening ecclesiastic influence and prestige among many Lebanese Greek Orthodox.[12]

Islam has never had an ecclesiastical hierarchy comparable to Christian churches because Islam is an organic religion which, as Donald Smith has pointed out, tends to equate itself with the structure of the entire society. In contrast to Christianity, for which a church structure with a separate identity is essential, ecclesiastical organization in Islam is secondary to the embodiment of sacral law in the society.[13] Islam professes to erect no clerical barriers between man and God. The need to interpret the law has given rise to a clerical class of *ulema*, or learned teachers, who derive their authority from their education in one of the centers of Muslim law, but they do not assume the role of parish clergymen. To the extent that a distinction now exists between clergyman and layman among Muslims in Lebanon, it has, according to the Sunni Grand Mufti, in large part been forced on Muslims by the necessity of having leaders to serve as defenders of the group in a political system in which Christian clergymen fulfill this function.[14] Historically Islam has made no distinction between religion and state and under the Ottoman Empire the Sunni Muslims, as the majority community, came directly under both the political and religious jurisdiction of the caliphate; Sunni Muslims in Lebanon did not have any separate territorial organization. During the initial period of the French Mandate, the Sunnis considered themselves at a disadvantage vis-à-vis the Maronite community, whose Patriarch could unite and represent his sect. The French encouraged the establishment of a centralized administration by creating the Supreme Islamic Council and the office of the Grand Mufti. In 1936 the Muslim community invested the Mufti of the Republic of Lebanon with the spiritual and temporal powers necessary to enable him to compete on more equal terms with the leaders of the Christian communities in the defense of Muslim rights.

A Lebanese law passed in 1955 created a more centralized Sunni hierarchy than traditionally existed.[15] By legislative decree the Mufti is the leader of all Sunnis in Lebanon and the representative of the community vis-à-vis the Lebanese authorities as well as head of all *ulema* and *waqf* (religious endowments) with the power to appoint, promote, and dismiss all officials of Sunni religious institutions. The same law defines membership in the Higher Islamic Sharia Council and it functions. Lebanese law also establishes the procedure for the election of the Mufti by an Islamic Electoral Assembly. Interestingly, many who hold political office are designated by the law as being members of the Islamic Electoral Assembly. For example, the law prescribes that membership include the incumbent Premier, all former Premiers who were Sunnis (thus all of them), all incumbent Sunni deputies, all Sunni ministers, and Sunni presidents and members of municipal councils in Beirut and the capitals of the provinces. Along with the Sunni muftis, Sunni Sharia judges, members of the Sharia Court, and members of the Higher Islamic Sharia Council, the law stipulates that representatives of professional and business organizations also be included as members. The same law established the conditions for the election of the local muftis for the provinces and districts, who look after the religious *waqf* and social affairs of their designated areas.

The Shiite community traditionally lacked any kind of centralized organization. Under the Ottomans the Shiites did not have the status of a separate millet, or community, entitled to regulate its own affairs because of the orthodox attempt to bring the Shiites back into the Sunni fold. The Shiites first received the privilege to organize their own judicial system during the early years of the Christian-oriented French Mandate. Until 1969, with the establishment of the Higher Shiite Islamic Council, there was no Shiite organizational unity. Then the impetus derived from the perception of political and social needs rather than from religious considerations. [16] Despite the creation of the Shiite Islamic Council, the community still lacks much internal cohesion.

As in the case of the Sunni organization, Lebanese law regulates the membership and functions of the Higher Shiite Islamic Council. [17] According to the law, the central purpose of the Higher Shiite Islamic Council is to take charge of the affairs of the Shiite community and to safeguard its interests. This function is vested primarily in the President of the Council in consultation with the Sharia and executive boards. The President also represents the Higher Council and the Shiite sect in its relationships with the Lebanese government. Under the 1969 law, the Sharia and executive boards elect the President for a renewable term of six years. The executive board of the Council consists of all of the Shiite deputies as *ex-officio* members and twelve men elected by the general assembly by secret ballot. In turn the law specifies that the general assembly, along with muftis, *ulema*, and sharia judges, include present and former Shiite cabinet members; present and former Shiite deputies; Shiite civil court judges; Shiite university professors; Shiite civil servants from the upper two grades; Shiite members of municipal councils; professionals; representatives from social, cultural, and welfare institutions; presidents and members of councils of commercial, agricultural, and industrial chambers; presidents and board members of public institutions; and presidents of labor unions. Twelve *ulema* elected by the other Shiite Lebanese *ulema* constitute the Sharia board.

Similarly, a Lebanese law promulgated in July 1962 defines the leading Druze religious bodies.[18] According to the law, the Druze shall have two Shaykh Aql as the spiritual leaders of the sect, to take into account the bifurcation of the Druze into two clans. However, the Druze now have settled on a single Shaykh Aql. All Lebanese Druze males eligible to vote in parliamentary elections participate in the selection of the Shaykh Aql through a secret ballot. A Madhabi Council legally exists as the representative of the sect in its mundane and financial affairs. The council consists of two types of permanent members: the Council of Mashiyikhat al-Aql and all present and former Druze cabinet members and deputies. It also has several categories of elected members, including representatives of professional associations.

In terms of our interest in the interrelationships between Lebanon's religious communities and Lebanon's political system, three principal points emerge from the above discussion of the organization of the religious communities. First, in terms of structural variation among the religious bodies, it is difficult to measure centralization precisely; but impressionistically, the degree of centralization (leaving aside the Druze about whom little is known) in descending order appears to be: Maronite, Greek Catholic, Sunni, Greek Orthodox, Shiite. Second, all of Lebanon's sects have international links of some kind. The Maronites and Greek Catholics recognize the Pope in Rome as having ultimate authority over their Patriarchs and churches. The Greek Catholic ecclesiastical organization covers territory beyond Lebanon, and the Greek Catholic Patriarch sits in Damascus. Similarly, the Greek Orthodox of Lebanon are part of the Church of Antioch, and their Patriarch also resides in Damascus. The Lebanese Sunni community constitutes a structurally independent entity, but its members retain strong emotional ties with Sunnis in other countries. The same is true of Lebanon's Shiite community; Lebanon's Shiites have a sense of commonality with Shiites elsewhere, particularly in Iran and Iraq where the spiritual head of the Shiites, the Al-Maria, resides, but there is no international Shiite hierarchy formalizing these relations.[19] In a country whose national political and social life is so frequently influenced by events and persons outside of Lebanon, the international character of Lebanon's religious bodies is obviously an important factor. Third, in addition to the influence of sectarian groups on political representation and authority, the state regulates the organization of three of Lebanon's major religious communities, namely, the Druze, the Sunnis, and the Shiites. Thus, politics is not only deeply influenced by religion, but to some extent the state has politicized religious administration.

DIFFERING LIFE STYLES AND PATTERNS OF SOCIALIZATION

The majority of Lebanese seem to spend much of their lives in a social milieu in which they are surrounded predominantly by other members of their own religious group. No precise figures are available, but it seems that although many villages have some sectarian mixture, most villages are preponderantly composed of persons from a single sect. In urban areas some segregation in residential patterns also occurs since people often prefer to live near coreligionists. Everywhere in Lebanon the evolution of extensive networks of sectarian institutions enables Lebanese to interact within organizations whose members come from similar religious backgrounds. Thus, many agencies of socialization, which in other societies have a national perspective (for example, schools and youth associations), reenforce a particularistic orientation in Lebanon. Furthermore, within Lebanon the overwhelming role of the family tends to diminish the impact of other agents of socialization which might foster more broadly shared values and experiences. The existence of separate and government-endorsed personal status codes for each sect has also helped to preserve some cultural differences, particularly with regard to the role of women.

Nevertheless, in discussing life styles and patterns of socialization it is important to note that all Lebanese, irrespective of sectarian affiliation, partake of certain fundamental features of Arab culture, a culture that owes much to Islam but which is not exclusively Muslim. Moreover, with the exception of the Armenians, virtually all Lebanese speak Arabic as their mother language, and most Armenians now know Arabic as a second language. According to one scholar, "the culture of the Christian villagers is very close in tone and color to that of the Muslim villagers in spite of the religious cleavage between them."[20] Christian Lebanese may more frequently look to the West for models or may profess their Phoenician backgrounds or their Greco-Roman heritage, but they still speak Arabic and share many of the essential elements of Arab culture with their Muslim countrymen. Some Christians, particularly the Greek Orthodox, openly identify with their

Arabic roots while others, particularly the Maronites, sometimes try to minimize them. Inversely, the Muslims in Lebanon exhibit certain cultural elements that distinguish them from their coreligionists in other parts of the Middle East deriving from the European and Christian contributions to the shared Lebanese culture. Especially when a comparison is made with other plural societies, among them Ghana, the shared heritage of Lebanon's sects stands out against the traditional linguistic and cultural fragmentation with which many pluralistic countries must cope while attempting to achieve national accommodation.

To comprehend the role of sect in influencing life styles and patterns of socialization, the fact that Lebanese believe that religious background counts for a great deal must be considered. Subjective perceptions often influence people more than objective differences. Most Lebanese adhere to a view of their own society as one in which sectarian membership determines to a significant extent an individual's character and preferences, and they also believe that the orientations of members of other religious communities diverge from their own. As evidence of this, 61 percent of the respondents we interviewed in a carefully stratified national sample of one thousand Lebanese adults (the administration of which is discussed in detail in the Appendix on Survey Methodology) indicated that the attitudes and values the respondents were teaching their children differed from those taught by persons in other confessional groups. Although some real subcultural distinctions related to sect do exist, many Lebanese exaggerate the depth of the chasm setting apart one group from another and, as elsewhere, the stereotyped images some Lebanese hold of members of other sects emphasize distinctive characteristics at the expense of shared elements.

Religious ritual and custom provide one of the most visible reminders of sectarian differences. The call from mosques to prayer five times each day and the loud pealing of the church bells on Sundays constitute only part of an environment shaped by the observance of religious obligation. Each of the sects has its own religious calendar, and members publicly celebrate the major holidays as a badge of social identity. Thus, the date on which a family marks Christmas indicates whether they are Catholic or Orthodox. Similarly, whether or not someone solemnizes Ashura, the commemoration of the death of Hussein at the Battle of Karbala, reveals if he is a Shiite. At the present time all major religious festivals have become public holidays as well. This policy has probably enhanced toleration and mutual respect, but it has also heightened awareness of sectarian distinctions. Lebanese may exaggerate sectarian variations in their images of other groups because they are based on such considerations as the holidays they keep and the institutions to which they belong.

On such sensitive topics as marriage, separation, divorce, custody of children, and inheritance no civil law exists in Lebanon and sectarian laws governing these subjects diverge considerably from sect to sect, particularly with regard to the rights of women.[21] Each person registers with the government as a member of a particular sect and is then subject exclusively to the statutes and courts of that community on issues of personal status. Sects vary in their attitude toward marriage and in their prescriptions regarding who may be elected as a suitable marriage partner. Christians consider marriage a sacrament and celebrate the ritual publicly, whereas Muslims generally confine the marriage ceremony merely to the signing of a contract between two families. Another major division between Christians and Sunnis and Shiites with regard to marriage practices relates to the permission for up to four wives that the Sharia gives. However, polygamy now is very much the exception.[22] Muslim divorce and inheritance laws also differ significantly from Christian practices, particularly with reference to the rights of women. The simple contractual nature of marriage enables Muslim husbands to easily divorce their wives, whereas Sunni and Shiite women can ask for a divorce only if this right was explicitly written into their marriage contract. In contrast, Maronites and Greek Catholics completely forbid divorce and other Christian denominations impede divorce by setting more stringent conditions. Muslim rules of inheritance limit the share of the estate that can go to the wife or daughter of the deceased whereas Christian patterns of inheritance do not discriminate between the sexes.[23]

Lebanon's religious pluralism finds social expression in the panoply of institutions related to specific sects. Many of the organizations that are secular and governmental in most other countries, like schools, hospitals, dispensaries, and presses, have a religious base in Lebanon. This burgeoning of sectarian institutional life enables an individual, if he wishes, to pass his entire life in schools, youth organizations, and voluntary associations with only members of his own faith. Organizations like the boy scouts, which usually have a secular orientation elsewhere, in Lebanon become explicitly affiliated with sects, so that now there are as many different types of scouts in Lebanon as there are religious sects.

To describe something as sectarian in character does not imply that its goals are explicitly religious. It may not even explicitly adopt as its purpose the furtherance of the interests of the members of that sect. Here the label sectarian refers to the fact that members of the organization are recruited from one religious community. Some of these sectarian organizations seek to unite members of the faith throughout Lebanon in some common cause, but many of them are confined to persons from a specific locality. Many of the organizations combine an ascriptive membership base with modern organization and goals. For example, the Islamic Makassed Society, which has focused on uplifting and advancing the Muslim community through the provision of education, has played a major role in the emergence of a modern, upwardly mobile Sunni middle class,[24] and the Amiliyah Islamic Benevolent Society aspires to similarly mobilize Shiites to self-improvement.[25] The achievement of many of the goals of these organizations depends primarily on mobilizing internal resources and does not necessarily come at the expense of other groups.

To make the discussion about the role of sectarian institutions concrete, it will be useful to cite some statistics. The development of education in Lebanon until well after independence came almost entirely through the aegis of private schools, most of which had a religious affiliation. Today, a majority of students, some 60 percent, still attend private schools.[26] Catholic schools alone enroll a total of 162,256 students, comprising approximately 14 percent of the student population in primary, complementary, and secondary schools in Lebanon.[27] Since private schools generally, and Catholic schools in particular, have a reputation for maintaining higher educational standards, their importance exceeds their student enrollment. Catholic religious orders serve as the proprietors of thirteen hospitals, twenty three orphanages, twenty five dispensaries, three old-age homes, and assist at many other hospitals, dispensaries, and orphanages.[28] In Tripoli the property of the Sunni community includes a hospital, a secondary school for boys and another for girls, five Muslim cemeteries, stores, orchards, a village and its lands, a large office building and private apartments, as well as twenty five mosques.[29] The predominantly Sunni Makassed Benevolence Society operates thirteen elementary and six secondary schools in Beirut, eighty five schools in rural districts, a commercial training center, a press, a teacher training institute, a nursing school, and one of the largest hospitals in Beirut.[30] The Shiite organization, the Amiliyah Islamic Benevolent Society, has seven schools, two of which are secondary schools.[31] The Maronite Mar Mansur maintains thirty four schools.

It seems likely that a majority of all types of voluntary associations have a sectarian base. Moreover, those with a sectarian character usually have greater endurance. It is difficult to precisely ascertain the proportion of voluntary associations that have a religious affiliation, especially since many organizations whose members belong to a single sect do not adopt an overtly religious title. Nevertheless, an analysis of the titles of the registered social welfare organizations in 1965 and the names of their officers reveals that out of a total of 405 at least 182 have an explicitly sectarian or ethnic character.[32]

It is useful to reiterate that socially and politically relevant differences between sectarian groups rarely derive from their theological beliefs. In fact, most Lebanese seem incognizant of the doctrinal disagreements that theoretically provide the basis of religious division within the country. Our survey results and other studies also indicate that the Lebanese are less religious than might be assumed for a country in which so much seems to revolve around sect.[33] However, the significance of sect as a badge of social identity and as an infrastructure for political action makes it unlikely that a decline in religiosity or that increasing cultural homogenization will weaken sectarian distinctions.

Answers of our respondents in both the adult and the student surveys we undertook in Lebanon (see the Appendix on Survey Methodology) to questions concerning their religiosity reveal that the winds of secularization are beginning to blow through Lebanon as elsewhere in the world. Only 32 percent of the adult respondents considered themselves to be devoutly religious; an equal number characterized themselves as being little or not at all concerned with religion. Similarly, 28 percent of the students described themselves as being religious, 49 percent as moderately religious, and 21 percent as uninterested in religion. Traditionally, Islam has provided more than a religious creed to its adherents; through the Sharia it prescribed a life style as well. According to the representations of the adult respondents, though, Christians in general and Maronites in particular retain a religious orientation to a much greater extent than Muslims. Maronites, more than other groups, moreover, ranked their sect as of importance to them and as providing a source of pride. One can only speculate on factors affecting religiosity and pride in sect, but it should be remembered that for Christian Lebanese, particularly Maronites, religion has constituted the primary rationale for the independence of Lebanon within the Arab world, as a haven for minorities and for their political position within Lebanon. Christianity's greater separation of the sacred from the secular also obviates for them many of the difficulties devout Muslims face in reconciling prescriptions of the Sharia with the demands of life in a period of rapid social change.

One of the central elements of Lebanese culture shared by all groups, but which at the same time divides Lebanese from each other, relates to the significance of the family and kinship organization. According to Samir Khalaf, "If there ever has been a culture with an exclusive kinship orientation, Lebanon comes close to being such. Kinship has been and is likely to remain, Lebanon's most solid and enduring tie. . . . Lebanese society is predominantly a kinship culture. Society starts with the family and is fashioned after it."[34] The pervasiveness of family loyalty comprises one of the most frequent themes in the social science literature on Lebanon. Groups may differ on the degree to which this basic cohesion and solidarity extend to distant relatives, but not on the salience of the family in the web of obligation. Moreover, social change has not yet undermined the sovereignty of the family. Despite the rate of urbanization and economic development the family still reigns as the major component and security device in the society. Through all upheavals, the family serves "as a tranquilizer pill, a confessional stand, a safety valve, and a 'security blanket' all put together."[35] Irrespective of sectarian differences, for all communities, loyalty to one's kin constitutes virtually a sacred value.

Our survey results confirm the influence of the extended family. Students uniformly rated the family as their primary loyalty and source of identity. When asked to rank in terms of their importance to them the place they came from, their sect, Lebanon, the Arab nation, and their extended family, adult respondents considered the family second only to their country. More than half of those interviewed, 54 percent, placed the family as either first or second on the scale. Among the sects the Shiites adjudged the family to be of greater significance to them than their country.

The family has not been bypassed by social and economic change because it has adapted to new opportunities and needs. Family associations, probably the most common type of organized group or association in Lebanon, have clothed the extended family in the structural garb of the modern voluntary organization, utilizing a written constitution, a formal commitment of membership, payment of dues, and election of officers. These associations, which seek to unite within a single voluntary organization members of the same extended family living in different parts of the country, have appeared throughout Lebanon. Beginning in the nineteenth century, family associations have worked to raise the educational and cultural standards of the family so that members could better compete in the modern sector. Once they have achieved their initial aims they have tended to disband or become inactive. Most of those now operating are probably Shiite, the most economically and educationally deprived group.[36] In some cases the extended family, which was often a traditional economic production unit in the countryside, has now also taken on the formal dressing of the modern corporation. A majority of Lebanese corporations give legal expression to business concerns owned and operated by members of an extended family. Moreover, some of the largest firms in size and capital invested representing the most important industries in Lebanon are family firms.[37]

In all societies the family serves a critical role as the formative agent in early childhood socialization. Then as the child grows older other agencies, among them schools, peer groups, and mass media, eventually supplant the family as inculcators of norms, values, and orientations. In communally fragmented societies in which there is likely to be a discrepancy between the particularistic orientations of constituent groups and a national frame of reference, family and friends generally articulate the parochial outlook.[38] A national system of public education often provides the most effective media for plural systems to counterbalance the influence of the constituent subgroups through a process of social learning that emphasizes the legitimacy of national concerns. Our survey results suggest that in Lebanon the family tends to maintain its paramountcy throughout. In contrast with many other countries, including some as diverse as the United States and Soviet Union, in which schools comprise the most important agency for political socialization,[39] our student and adult respondents considered the effect of their formal education to be limited relative to other sources of information about the political system and relative to other molders of values and orientations. Family, books and newspapers read out of school, and personal observation outranked schooling as molders of political values and views for the students. Similarly, the adult respondents cited family, friends, books, and newspapers more frequently than their schooling. In response to a question concerning what helped the students to understand and interpret current events, they placed family, television, friends, and radio ahead of school: the adults cited newspapers, members of the family, books, and the radio in that order as the sources of their knowledge about the political system, with schooling far down on the list.

The inability of schools in Lebanon to serve as more effective vehicles of national political socialization results from elements of Lebanese culture and from the nature of the educational system. As will be discussed in Chapter 5, the Lebanese government has never attempted to employ the educational system as an instrument of national accommodation and many aspects of the educational system, particularly its extreme decentralization, make the schools manifestly unsuited for fulfilling this role. Most children attend schools in which the student body is relatively homogeneous in terms of sect and in which textbooks interpret Lebanese history through a sectarian perspective. To the extent that schooling contributes to the process of political socialization, therefore, it often reinforces the particularistic perspective of family and friends.

INTERGROUP RELATIONS

The Middle East has traditionally, and particularly during the Ottoman period, accommodated sect differences through compartmentalizing each one into its own sphere. The Ottoman millet system ceded to each religious community the right to administer itself. Aspects of the contemporary Lebanese political system follow the Ottoman pattern, as for example, legal autonomy of the sects with regard to personal status laws. People still associate mostly with members of their own or related sects, and interactions between adherents of different religious groups, particularly between Christians and Muslims, remain superficially cordial in a more-or-less stylized manner. Intersectarian relations occur primarily for economic reasons or on formal social occasions like weddings, funerals, and festivals. One indication of the importance of religious affiliation to intergroup relations is the fact that when a Lebanese meets someone for the first time he usually makes a special effort to determine his sectarian affiliation, which he can usually do on the basis of his name.[40] To feel socially at ease and to eschew uncertainty, people pursue a policy that one Lebanese social scientist has described as "mutual avoidance."[41] Yet when intersectarian social exchanges do take place, they tend to be correct and formally cordial.

Contemporary patterns of social relations result from a complex interplay of historical, cultural, institutional, and economic factors. Many of the subjects already discussed in this chapter clearly affect intergroup relations, among them the networks of sectarian institutions and associations, the subjective and objective cultural differences, and the role of the family. We will now take up three more topics bearing on the relationship among the sects: tolerance, intermarriage, and urbanization.

Historically, Lebanon opened its gates as a sanctuary of religious freedom for many persecuted minorities. The existence of seventeen officially recognized sects attests to the diversity of groups that took advantage of the opportunity offered to them to practice their faith in relative peace with other communities. Today Lebanon still evinces exceptional tolerance. Professor Charles Malik, former Foreign Minister and once President of the General Assembly of the United Nations, expressed with pride the uniqueness of his country when he asserted, "Here and only here can a Christian feel as free as in Bonn and Boston and a Muslim as absolutely free as in Karachi and Mecca."[42] For many Lebanese this tolerance constitutes an integral element in the Lebanese system and represents its greatest accomplishment and contribution to the world.

Official tolerance of theological and religious diversity finds expression in individual behavior as well. According to Fuad Khuri, "However critical of their own beliefs, the Lebanese villagers never speak openly against the beliefs of others, nor discourse with them over religious topics; rather, the Lebanese mildly and privately observe, sometimes suppressing altogether, these peculiar rites and prejudices, the exposure of which may challenge the beliefs and religious dogmas of others."[43] This formal pattern of civility reflects widespread agreement that Lebanon is a multiconfessional society in which each community must respect the religious integrity of all other communities.

When conflict does occur between confessional communities, religious intolerance conceived in a doctrinal sense is usually not a major factor.[44] In those cases where tension has arisen between the communities over religious issues, it has usually erupted between one Christian sect and another or between the two Muslim sects. For instance, most efforts by foreign Christian missionaries in the nineteenth century to convert individuals to one denomination or another were directed at other Christians, rather than at Muslims or Druze. Similarly, the Sunnis under the Ottoman Empire tended to regard the Shiite community as deviants who should be pushed to return to Sunni orthodoxy. The Shiites were first granted the legal and institutional autonomy enjoyed by other communities during the Mandate period.

As one expression of religious tolerance in Lebanon, only certain small Protestant groups still actively proselytize. Most conversions today result from intermarriage, with the wife adopting the husband's faith. The major Protestant denominations and Greek Catholic Churches have both ceased their previously active proselytization activities among the Greek Orthodox. Since the 1930s the Catholic Churches have agreed to prohibit conversion of persons from one Catholic sect to another. As an expression of their fraternal links resulting from a common origin, the Greek Catholics have also stopped attempting to make inroads into the Greek Orthodox community.

Widespread tolerance and acceptance of a diversity of religious creeds does not mean that most Lebanese accept all religions as being of equal worth. As with people elsewhere, Lebanese tend to assume the superiority of their own approach to the sacred. Among certain Christians the preference for their own sect accompanies a denigration of things Muslim. A few of our interviews revealed that hidden behind the veil of a public profession of tolerance and the mask of an urbane manner, a few Christian leaders harbored an intense disdain for Islam as a religion and as a civilization. Despite their cordial relations with Christian colleagues, some Muslims voiced a bitterness against Christianity for its role in the imperialist expansion of the West and for its tendency to cast certain aspects of Islam in Lebanon in its own image, such as the introduction of an ecclesiastical hierarchy. Ghassan Tueni, the editor of *al Nahar*, Lebanon's most prominent newspaper, has pointed out that, "Christians say two things and Muslims say two things: What they say to themselves and what they say to others."[45]

Anthropological studies show that endogamy has been the accepted practice of all of Lebanon's confessional communities. Traditionally, marriage partners were selected within the ancestral village, often from members of the same lineage or clan, and Muslims preferred patrilineal first cousin marriages whenever feasible. Frequently parents of the prospective mates made the selection. Many factors militated in favor of endogamy. In a plural society like Lebanon, endogamy within the sect bound the progeny of succeeding generations to the religious and cultural heritage of the community. The practice of local endogamy reflected the relative isolation of the village with the concommitant uncertainty inherent in going beyond the known circle of social relations. Since marriage in Lebanon traditionally has united two families as well as two members of those families, parents were understandably reluctant to countenance a union with a relative stranger. Similarly, the pressure to marry a relative resulted from the quest for ensuring a successful affiliation of families. Another factor was the desire to prevent the dispersion of property outside the extended family; for purposes of inheritance, cross-cousin alliances retained family property within the family. With the erosion of village autonomy, local endogamy seems to be weakening,[46] and the role of the family in selecting partners seems to be declining.[47]

Legal barriers have generally inhibited members of two different faiths from marrying unless one of them has converted. As Victor Ayoub indicates, religious endogamy "is not maintained because it is explicitly prescribed that a person must marry within the religious community, but because there is no other simple recourse."[48] Analysts commonly assert that virtually no intersectarian marriage takes place. "Impossible in the villages because of social and communal pressure, Christian–Muslim marriage is still a rare phenomenon in the cities like Beirut, Tripoli, and Saida."[49] "Perhaps the most emphatic identification with the religious group is expressed in the marriage situation. Here the boundary lines are clear, the barriers thick, and no crossing is permitted."[50] Yet, despite the legal difficulties and the traditional prohibitions, inter-sect marriages do occur. Intermarriage generally involves conversion of one partner, usually the wife, and, with the change of religious affiliation, assimilation to different religiocultural practices. Sects have been more permissive when a man from within their community proposed taking a wife from another group because they assumed that the wife would convert and the children be raised in accordance with the faith of the husband. Muslim law, for example, clearly distinguishes between two types of inter-marriage. It tolerates matrimony between a Muslim man and a Christian woman and even allows the woman to retain her religion if she agrees to bring up the children as Muslims. In contrast, Muslim law does not recognize the marriage of a Muslim woman to a Christian man; if a woman enters into such an alliance in effect she ceases to be Muslim. Christian groups, while acceding to Christian interdenominational unions, enjoin wedlock between Christians and Muslims.

Virtually all village studies, except for the single one on the Druze, cite cases of such mixed marriages.[51] However, the more radical the departure of the union from accepted practice, the less willing the villagers have been to discuss it, which partially accounts for an underrated percentage of intermarriage. Another reason for underestimation was that women did not have to register or indicate their religion until after independence in 1943. And since most women eventually converted to their husband's faith, the end result masked the different origins of the partners. The highest number of intersectarian marriages is between members of two Christian denominations. In 1970, of the 4472 marriages performed by all Catholic churches in Lebanon, 431, or 9.7 percent, united two people of different sectarian backgrounds.[52] Since Catholics are often more hesitant than other Christian denominations to marry outside their group, it is quite possible that their figures for 1970 reflect current trends in Lebanon. Intermarriage will certainly remain the exception rather than the rule for the foreseeable future. Only 18 percent of the respondents in our student survey, for instance, indicated a willingness to marry someone from another religious group.

Urbanization with its movement of people from a traditional to a more modern milieu carries the promise of social change. Some social scientists have assumed that urbanization and its concommitant transition to new patterns of life would inaugurate widespread social mobilization leading to the erosion of former clusters of loyalty.[53] Lebanon has experienced rapid urbanization in the post-World War II period. At the present time 58 percent of the Lebanese population live in places that can be considered urban with a population of more than 10,000 persons, and 45 percent of all Lebanese citizens reside in Beirut and its suburbs.[54] Furthermore, 52 percent of the population have migrated at least once during their lifetimes, two-thirds of whom moved to Beirut or its suburbs.[55]

Urbanization, however, does not generally level sectarian differences and may accentuate rather than reduce sectarian identity. Some evidence suggests that when villagers emigrate to Beirut or Tripoli, the sect assumes many of the social functions that village ties formerly fulfilled for them in the rural areas; by determining residential patterns, by providing a network for mutual assistance and aid, by helping to find jobs, and by structuring political participation. Samir Khalaf and Per Kongstad conclude in their study of Hamra, the central district in Beirut, that "Urbanization in Beirut thus far has not been associated with a large measure of decline of kinship or weakening of traditional ties and communal attachments. . . . One may perhaps infer that the intensity and increasing scale of urbanization has not been accompanied by a proportional degree of urbanism as a way of life."[56] Khalaf and Kongstad attribute the salience of traditional ties and communal attachments to the relative recentness of the large-scale urbanization in Beirut and to the maintenance of a nostalgic commitment to rural values in general and the home village in particular.[57] The urban resident typically considers himself a transient who will eventually return to live in his home village. This assumption draws the urban resident back to his village for festivals, for rites of passage, and for vacationing.

Most districts in Lebanon's two major cities, Beirut and Tripoli, are identified as being predominantly for members of a particular sect or more generally for Christians or Muslims. Thus, an urban migrant tends to be drawn to a part of the city inhabited by his coreligionists. A study of low-income families in Beirut showed that 68.7 percent of the Armenians lived in one Armenian section, 74.2 percent of the Maronite respondents resided in one largely Christian district, and 79 percent of the Sunnis were in a single quarter.[58] One of the two adjacent suburbs of Beirut that Fuad Khuri researched was primarily Shiite and the other predominantly Christian.

According to Khuri, by living among his coreligionists, a rural migrant "feels at home" and reduces to a minimum the kinds of adjustments he has to make to the patterns of suburban life.[59]

Although urban residence increases the salience of sectarian identity, this does not imply an increase in intersectarian conflict or tension. The patterns of urban sectarian segregation seem to be part of the general practice of mutual avoidance or limited contact to reduce possible sources of friction. Faud Khuri suggests that the greater role of the sect in an urban setting represents an intermediary stage between family and national identity and, as such, reflects the weakening of family attachments rather than the reduction of national loyalty.[60]

Lebanon represents an extreme case of the universal tendency for people to gravitate toward the known and avoid the unknown, which in this social system, means that people generally socialize, reside, join organizations, attend schools, and marry within a relatively narrow sphere usually defined by sectarian boundaries. Since distinctions between groups result from subjective perceptions based on social rather than religious factors, the decline in religiosity and increasing urbanization will not, by themselves, alter present patterns. On the whole, although they occur, intermarriage and religious conversion cannot be considered significant factors mitigating against sectarian exclusiveness. If Lebanon were to pass a law enabling prospective mates to opt for civil marriage, the incidence of intersectarian unions might significantly increase. For just this very reason, however, the leaders of all religious communities strenuously oppose the introduction of such a reform.

SECT AND SOCIOECONOMIC DEVELOPMENT

It is clear from the discussion thus far that religious differences in Lebanon involve more than merely variations in dogma; the communities tend to have separate institutions and some distinctiveness of life style. This section will explore the extent to which social and economic variables reenforce sectarian boundaries. For purposes of this analysis, it will be helpful to describe the contemporary geographic distribution of sect members in Lebanon. Table 3-1 shows the regional composition based on 1956 population estimates prepared by Al-Nahar.

Despite this geographical mixing of sects, the geographical distribution is by no means even. In Beirut proper the Sunnis constitute the largest single

TABLE 3-1 *Lebanese Population by Sects and Province (1956)*

SECTS	BEIRUT	MOUNT LEBANON	NORTH LEBANON	SOUTH LEBANON	BEKAA	TOTAL
Sunnis	76,116	24,423	118,203	29,889	37,067	285,698
Shiites	17,062	22,716	1,337	148,446	61,044	250,605
Druze	2,457	71,569	19	6,893	7,193	88,131
Maronites	18,101	224,921	111,917	39,509	29,260	423,708
Greek Catholics	3,617	21,520	3,864	23,147	35,630	87,778
Greek Orthodox	25,276	32,239	62,767	10,784	17,861	148,927
Protestants	5,482	3,945	1,357	2,493	1,088	14,365
Latin	2,771	963	330	265	117	4,446
Armenian Catholics	8,809	3,722	345	298	1,448	14,622
Armenian Orthodox	42,762	15,600	1,579	1,833	1,905	63,679
Chaldeans	1,178	62	29	8	189	1,466
Syrian Catholics	4,757	40	194	3	705	5,699
Syrian Orthodox	2,745	257	150	5	1,641	4,798
Jews	5,382	95	40	1,108	67	6,692
Others	215	447	6,064	206	261	7,193
TOTAL	216,730	422,519	308,195	264,887	195,476	1,407,807

SOURCE: Reprinted from Michael W. Suleiman: *Political Parties in Lebanon.*
Copyright c 1965, 1967 by Michael W. Suleiman. Used by permission of Cornell University Press.

TABLE 3-2   Predominant Community by Province

Beirut	56% Christian
Mount Lebanon	78% Christian
North Lebanon	60% Christian
Bekaa	52% Muslim
South Lebanon	67% Muslim

SOURCE: Percentage computed from the figures in *al-Nahar*,
April 26, 1956, p. 1.

sect with the Armenian Orthodox and the Greek Orthodox respectively the
second and third in size. However, the Christians have a slight overall
majority in the province of Beirut. Mount Lebanon has a majority of Maronites, some 53 percent. Maronites also form the most numerous sect in North
Lebanon, 36 percent of the population of the province. In the Bekaa and
South Lebanon the Shiites predominate, the respective figures being 30 and
56 percent. By district *(qada)*, employing the 1932 census results which are
the last available breakdown: Maronites are in the majority in two districts in
Mount Lebanon, Kisrwan and Metn; two districts in North Lebanon,
Zagharta and Batroun; and one in South Lebanon, Jezzine. Greek Orthodox
are in the majority in the Koura district of North Lebanon. Districts with a
majority of Shiites include two in South Lebanon, Sidon and Tyre; and two in
the Bekaa, Baalbeck and Hermel. Sunnis have a majority only in two districts,
Tripoli and Akkar, both in North Lebanon, because Beirut, where many
Sunnis reside, is not divided into districts. Druze do not have a majority of 'he
population in any district, but they have a proportion of 30 percent or more in
Chouf and Aley in Mount Lebanon and in Rachaya in the Bekaa.

It is difficult to document precisely the differences in economic status and
in educational achievement among the different sects. It is clear that considerable variations of economic status and educational achievement exist
within each individual religious community. Thus, one hesitates to make
broad generalizations about the groups as a whole. From our survey data it
would seem that the Christians as a whole fare better economically and
educationally than do the Muslims, largely because of the depressed condi-
tion of the Shiites. Sunnis compare favorably with several Christian denominations.

A comparison of geographic regions provides one rough index of sectarian
differences, since regions tend to have a majority of one religious group or

another. One of several problems with this kind of analysis is that the predominance of Christians or Muslims in a particular province is not generally sufficient to enable the analyst to draw definitive conclusions about the religious communities from regional data. The IRFED Mission report describes in some detail Lebanon's unbalanced regional development. They classify 70 percent of the localities in the central zone, which corresponds to predominantly Christian Beirut and Mount Lebanon, as being in the developed category and only 5 percent as underdeveloped. In contrast, 46 percent of the localities in the North are considered nondeveloped or underdeveloped. The same report considers 35 percent of the localities in Bekaa as nondeveloped or underdeveloped and 30 percent in the South. All the districts in Lebanon that IRFED considers nondeveloped are located in the North and the Bekaa. The largest number of districts classified as underdeveloped districts are in the North. All of the districts in South Lebanon are described either as underdeveloped or partially developed.[61]

Education constitutes one of the most critical variables in determining the level of development of a geographic area or a sect. An analysis of the educational statistics for Lebanon indicates that predominantly Christian Mount Lebanon and Beirut form an oasis of educational advancement. In regard to the number of students attending both public and private schools, Mount Lebanon stands out as the province with the greatest commitment to education. Beirut boasts the highest proportion of students in public and private educational institutions in relation to its total population. North Lebanon, the Bekaa, and South Lebanon all have proportionally fewer students, particularly in private schools and they rank in that order. For private education the relative position of the Bekaa is third after Beirut and Mount Lebanon, with North Lebanon fourth and South Lebanon fifth. An analysis of the geographic distribution of secondary schools, a crucial element in the development of the elite, shows Beirut the largest center, with Mount Lebanon also having a significant number, but with North Lebanon, South Lebanon, and the Bekaa being less favored.[62] According to our adult survey data, Christians were far more likely than Muslims to attend private schools generally and private religious institutions particularly. More than 60 percent of all Greek Catholics and Maronites, for example, described themselves as graduates of private religious school, whereas only 29 percent of Sunnis and 24 percent of Shiites and Druze similarly listed their educational backgrounds. These differing percentages reflect both the unequal distribution of private educational facilities and the preponderantly Christian nature of the private schools in Lebanon.

In any country the ability to speak foreign languages opens a window on the world. For the Lebanese, knowledge of French has traditionally constituted the link with western culture. Because the Lebanese have frequently considered knowledge of foreign languages as a sign of good education, educational curricula emphasize languages, and rates of bilingualism and trilingualism in Lebanon are exceptional. According to statistics issued by the Ministry of Planning, 40 percent of the Lebanese population, particularly those resident in Beirut and other urban centers, know French, and 14 percent English.[63] Among our adult respondents, Shiites, Sunnis, and Druze (in that order) were more likely to be limited to Arabic. Maronites had the greatest tendency to know French, Sunnis and Greek Orthodox to speak English, and Greek Catholics to be trilingual.

Along with the regional educational and economic discrepancies mentioned above, other evidence reconfirms that, in general, Christians have a better economic status. In 1968 67 percent of the national income came from commerce and services, 22 percent from industry and construction, and only 11 percent from agriculture. At the same time almost half of the Lebanese population derived their income from agriculture.[64] It would seem warranted to assume that the two least urbanized provinces, South Lebanon and the Bekaa, have the highest proportion of people depending on agriculture as their source of income, and therefore the lowest income. According to the IRFED study, agricultural workers earn only about one-third of the average national income whereas laborers in the industrial and transport sectors receive close to the average. In contrast, business, commerce, and services constituted the most prosperous sector of the economy. The income of businessmen ranges well above the Lebanese average.[65] This boom sector has traditionally been Christian-dominated. Yusif Sayigh's study of the entrepreneurs of Lebanon reflects this sectarian imbalance. In his representative sample of entrepreneurs, four-fifths were Christian and only one-sixth Muslim. Muslims had a larger share of the agricultural sector and held a slightly better position in industry than they did in finance and services. Christians in Lebanon have historically dominated in the spheres of finance, trade, and services, and they have established the requisite networks of business contacts and entrepreneurial traditions. There are indications that Muslim business leaders now have, by industrial enterprise, an outlet for their frustrations at finding much of the opportunity in foreign trade, finance, and services seized by their Christian counterparts. But Christians, according to Sayigh's sample, nevertheless dominate by a factor of five to one in industry as well.[66]

CROSSCUTTING TIES AND ASSOCIATIONS

Lebanese who are divided on the basis of sect share many cultural, occupational, and professional links. Class structure also cuts across sectarian affiliation. Moreover, Lebanon is a small country tied together by a relatively good road system: few villages are more than a two-hour drive from the capital. The central influence of Beirut radiates throughout the country, giving Lebanon something of the atmosphere of a city-state. The small size of the country, the close relationship parliamentarians maintain with their constituents, and a high exposure to mass media combine to make politics a broadly shared national pastime. According to our adult survey results, a common sense of national citizenship also unites many Lebanese. Of our respondents, 67 percent attributed greater significance to pride in their citizenship than to pride in their residence, sect, or Arab identity, and 51 percent ranked Lebanon as more important to them than their locality, sect, extended family, or the Arab nation.

A high rate of exposure to mass media emanating from Beirut provides another element of continuity. Our adult survey results indicate that 89 percent of our respondents listened to news broadcasts on the radio (as many as 65 percent daily), 78 percent watched television, and 80 percent read newspapers (61 percent daily). Most of those interviewed, 82 percent, received their news from Radio Lebanon. Furthermore, in a country that may have the largest number of newspapers per capita in the world, one daily has managed to capture a large share of the reading public. More than half of our respondents, 55 percent, read *al-Nahar* (another 21 percent are not regular readers of any newspaper), and the preference for *al-Nahar* grew with greater education. The role of *al-Nahar* looms large in Lebanon because so many people rely on newspapers to learn about the political system; more of our respondents turned to newspapers for their information on the Lebanese political system than to any other source. Respondents who read newspapers frequently tended to be more politically oriented, less sectarian, less likely to vote as did the rest of their family, more likely to say that their political attitudes had changed in the last ten years, more likely to have different attitudes and values than their parents, and more likely to believe that their own views deviated from those of other members of their group.

Despite the relative ineffectiveness of schools as agents of political socialization compared with the role of education elsewhere, the educational system does make some contribution to instilling a national orientation. According to our survey results, the influence of the family declined in relationship to the amount of education an individual had. Although even a university education did not displace the paramountcy of the family, it opened respondents to other agents. With greater education the receptiveness to schooling and to books as molders of views increased somewhat. When analyzing the sample as a whole, the level of education rarely correlated with the beliefs and attitudes of respondents, but when the sample was divided into Christians and Muslims on a few key questions, as will be discussed in Chapter 5, the more the education, the greater was the tendency for the responses in the two groups to converge. In light of the pronounced tendency of the curricula to avoid sensitive issues and to abjure inculcating a shared orientation to national citizenship, the convergence may result from the indirect effect of further education widening horizons, fostering exposure to common influences, and increasing intersect contact.

Despite the disparities among confessional communities in economic well-being, class structure nevertheless bisects sectarian affiliation. Village studies commonly describe differences in status and economic position among members of the community. IRFED's analysis classified 4 percent of Lebanon's population as rich, 14 percent as well-to-do, 30 percent as average, 40 percent as poor, and 9 percent as destitute.[67] Statistics on educational differentiation within the labor force provide another indication of the pyramidal nature of the class structure in Lebanon. A survey of the Lebanese labor force was undertaken by the Ministry of Planning in 1971. This survey estimates the size of the labor force in Lebanon as 27 percent of the total population. Of these 572,000 workers, the vast majority of whom were men, 29.4 percent were illiterate; 50.5 percent had an elementary education; only 15.8 had a high school education, and the university graduates comprised not more than 4.3 percent. Most of the university graduates filled high status and income positions in technical and liberal professions, such as engineering, medicine, and law. Among the country's peasant farmers, 93.3 percent were either illiterate or only had the equivalent of a primary school education.[68]

To objectively recognize the existence of class differences and to subjectively utilize them as the basis of social action are not the same. Despite the obvious gradations in income and status among the classes, class consciousness in Lebanon is relatively low, and the inclination to translate this consciousness into viable political and social movements is even lower. In an article on the class structure in Lebanon, Fuad Khuri cautions that, "It is still inappropriate to use the concept of class to study social structure in Lebanon, the more so if this study involves power structures."[69] Samir Khalaf concludes in both his research on the middle class residing in the Hamra section of Beirut and his study of the labor movement that there is little class consciousness and solidarity. According to Khalaf, the survival of traditional kinship attachments has prevented the Lebanese middle class from developing the cohesion and self-consciousness that characterized the growth of the middle class in other societies. Similarly, continuing loyalty to the family, sect, and ethnic group has militated against the emergence of class consciousness and weakened the commitment of workers to labor unions.[70] Thus, the salience of vertical kinship and religious ties has so far blocked the construction of networks of social loyalty on a nonascriptive horizontal grid.

Nevertheless, many nonascriptive organizations do exist, the two most important kinds being the labor unions and the professional associations, both of which play significant roles as spokesmen for the interests of their members. Since its inception at the beginning of the twentieth century, the Lebanese labor movement has focused on the improvement of working conditions within the existing economic and social system. Unlike the labor organizations in other transitional societies, the trade unions in Lebanon have rarely become involved in wider political issues. At the present time only 15 percent of the potential nonagricultural labor force, some 57,000 persons, are members of one of the 169 licensed unions. Many of these 169 licensed unions are affiliated to one or another of the nine labor federations now existing in Lebanon.[71]

The Lebanese labor movement still remains a relatively weak vehicle of change within the Lebanese politico-economic system. Unions suffer from the low class consciousness and solidarity as well as from their own organizational deficiencies. The fact that many companies are family firms with a disposition to hire workers from the same sect or locality reinforces kinship and confessional ties at the expense of class militancy. Moreover, employers' paternalistic attitudes and the general lack of sympathy of the government toward strikes does not provide a favorable climate for industrial action.[72]

The organizational deficiencies of the labor union movement are myriad. To begin with, only a small proportion of the labor force has been unionized. Because unions generally fail to apply consistent criteria for membership, many unions join together white-collar clerks and manual members at the expense of harmony and effectiveness. Neither the internal structure of the local unions nor that of the federations follow exclusively craft or industrial lines. The labor movement also remains divided by regional differences and by personal rivalries of union leaders. Each of the nine labor federations has a regional base: one in the North, one in the South, and seven in Beirut. The high frequency of unsuccessful strikes manifests the general weakness of the union movement.[73]

Although professional associations represent a far smaller proportion of the labor force than trade unions, their elite membership and greater cohesiveness accords them a more significant role. There is no comprehensive list of professional associations available, but it seems that many, if not most, professional, technical, and commercial groups have formed syndicates. Some of the most important of these professional associations are the Beirut and Tripoli Bar Associations with 1800 members,[74] the Lebanese Association of Architects and Engineers with 3500 members, and the Lebanese Medical Association with approximately 1400 members.[75] There are also the Pharmacists Syndicate, the Syndicate of Dentists, the Lebanese Association of University Professors, the Lebanese Chamber of Commerce, the Lebanese Manufacturers' Association, and the Lebanese Management Association. As well as representing the interests of their members vis-a-vis employers and the government, many of these professional associations have been granted statutory self-regulatory powers.

In interviews, members of the professional associations denied that sectarian considerations entered into the operations of their organizations or the selection of officers. Instead they stressed the overriding focus on professionalism. Nevertheless, an analysis of the lists of incumbent and past officers of various associations reflects the preponderance of important posts that Christians have held within the professions, particularly in law and in medicine. It would seem that little effort has usually been made, particularly on the part of the Beirut-based associations, to achieve sectarian balance in official positions. Since their inception, for example, the Beirut Order of Advocates has never had a Muslim president and the Medical Association has had only one.[76] The Order of Engineers and Architects has a better record of electing Muslim officers, perhaps due to their greater representation in the profession.[77] Some labor groups, however, try to choose officers in a manner that will reflect the sectarian composition of the total membership. For example, in the 1972 election of officers for the Syndicate of Bank Employees, each of the two opposing lists had a careful distribution among the religious communities. The successful list included eight Christians, four Muslims, and one Shiite; the other had seven Christians and five Muslims.[78] For specific figures on the religious identity of officers of key professional associations, see Table 3-3.

TABLE 3-3   *Incumbent Officers of Professional Associations in 1972, by Sect*

	NUMBER OF CHRISTIANS	NUMBER OF MUSLIMS
Beirut Medical Association[1]	10	2
Beirut Order of Advocates[1]	20	—
Tripoli Order of Advocates	2	3
Beirut Order of Engineers & Architects[1]	6	2
Tripoli Order of Engineers & Architects	1	8
Pharmacists Syndicate	7	2
Beirut Order of Dentists	4	—
Tripoli Order of Dentists	2	2
TOTAL	52	19

[1]The jurisdiction of the Beirut order extends to all parts of Lebanon except the province of North Lebanon.

SOURCE: Interviews; articles on the lawyers association in *Travaux et Jours*, 42 (Janvier-Mars 1972); articles on the architects and engineers association in *Ttravaux et Jours*, 43 (Avril-Juin 1972) and on the dentists' syndicate, *L'Orient-Le Jour*, Novembre 20, 1972, p. 2.

Thus, trade unions and professional associations constitute relatively weak vehicles for fostering ties across sectarian boundaries. The strength of sect and family has blocked the emergence of the class consciousness that underlies successful labor movements. A greater sense of occupational unity in the professional associations has not made them into effective pressure groups. A tendency for Christians to predominate in the leadership of many of the professional associations also reduces their potential for intersectarian linkages.

A survey of the social, cultural, and religious framework of the Lebanese political system provides convincing evidence that sectarian considerations pervade life in the country. Membership in a sect brings with it certain distinctive elements of life style, participation in a network of institutions and associations, and sometimes a particular perspective and syndrome of attitudes. Sectarianism maintains its hold on the Lebanese people as an arbiter of social and political interactions despite signs of a decrease in religiosity. Thus, increasing secularization or greater cultural homogenization will probably not dethrone religious identity from its paramount role. The complex interplay between the sects and the state enables the government to legally regulate the composition and election of the leadership of several of the sects and yet to abdicate to the sects responsibility for the legislation and enforcement of laws relating to personal status.

Despite all of the sectarian differences in socioeconomic status and cultural patterns, Lebanon's religious communities have accommodated in many important respects to the needs of a plural society. Lebanese who are divided by sectarian identity still have much uniting them. Significantly, Lebanese exhibit a will to live together and to make their multisectarian experiment a success. The extreme outward show of politeness to members of other religious groups constitutes one element in this determined effort to avoid tension. As countless Lebanese are themselves aware and as many have related in interviews, this commitment to good relations comprises one of the most significant factors in the Lebanese experience and is also the element least exportable to other fragmented societies.

NOTES

1. Official census for 1932, cited in A. H. Hourani, *Syria and Lebanon* (London: Oxford University Press, 1946), p. 121.
2. *L'Enquête par Sondage sur la Population Active au Liban, Novembre 1970* (Beirut: Ministère du Plan, 1972), pp. 60, 69. The estimate of the United Nations for the same year was 2,614,000. See *Population Bulletin of the United Nations Economic and Social Office in Beirut*, No. 3 (July 1972), pp. 39–40.
3. In 1961 the Mission IRFED gave a figure of 1,089,041 emigrés. For statistics on emigration see Mission IRFED (Institut International de Recherche et de Formation en vue du Développement intégral et harmonisé), *Besoin et Possibilites de Développement*, Tome I (Beyrouth: Ministère du Plan, 1961), pp. 49–51. The IRFED report was officially commissioned and therefore its findings have semiofficial status. A more recent estimate of 1,575,000 emigrés appears in Jean Bas, "L'Emigration Libanaise et la Double Nationalité," *L'Orient-Le Jour, Vie Moderne, Culture, Jeunes*, No. 97, du 14 au 20 Avril 1963, p. 111.
4. See, for example, Norman Horner, "A Statistical Survey of Christian Communities," Beirut, 1972, mimeographed, p. 21. The above source is sympathetic to the Christian viewpoint and had access to records of the Catholic Church.
5. The Family Planning Association of Lebanon gave permission to the authors to use the data it collected in its 1972 survey. The Family Planning Association based its sample on a scientifically drawn subsample of a household survey of the Ministry of Social Welfare. The Family Planning Association plans to publish the findings in a report written by Miss Wadad Abi-Nader. For an earlier study of demographic trends also showing higher birthrates for Muslims, see David Yaukey, *Fertility Differences in a Modernizing Country* (Princeton, N. J.: Princeton University Press, 1971), pp. 29, 43, 79, 81.

6. 'Alī Ḥasan al-Amīn, "Al-Shī 'a fī Lubnān" (**"The Shiites in Lebanon"**), 1972, (mimeo).

7. "Les Prêtres Catholiques les plus fidéles à leur sacerdoce sont les Libanais," *L'Orient-Le Jour*, February 21, 1973, p. 2.

8. Interview with Shaikh Muhammad Abu Shaqra, Sheikh 'Aql of the Druze community on January 30, 1973.

9. On the Maronites, see Pierre Dib, *History of the Maronite Church*, trans. by Seely Begianni (Beirut: Imp. Catholique, 1971); Pierre Rondot, *Les Chrétiens d'Orient* (Paris: J. Peyronnet and Cie, n.d.); Joseph Dibs, *Perpétuelle Orthodoxie des Maronites*, trans. by Vazuex (Beirut: Imp. Moderne D'Arras, 1896); Adrian Fortescue, *The Uniate Eastern Churches*, 2nd ed. (New York: Ungar, 1957).

10. Interviews with Greek Catholic Bishop Grégoire Haddad, January 5 and 11, 1973; Donald Attwater, *The Christian Churches of the East*, Vol. I, *Churches in Communion with Rome* (London: G. Chapman, 1961), pp. 58–59.

11. Interview with Greek Orthodox Bishop George Khodr, January 4, 1973; "Greek Orthodox Church," *Encyclopedia of religion and Ethics*, Vol. VI (New York: Charles Scribners, 1955), pp. 425–431.

12. Mary A. Kilbourne, "The Greek Orthodox Community of Syria and Lebanon in the Twentieth Century," unpublished M.A. Thesis, American University of Beirut, 1952, pp. 113–114.

13. Donald E. Smith, *Religion and Political Development* (Boston: Little, Brown and Co., 1970).

14. Interview with Shaikh Hasan Khalid, the Sunni Mufti, February 12, 1973.

15. "Marsūm Ishtirā 'ī Raqam 18 Ṣādir bi-tārīkh 13 Kānūn al-thānī Sanat 1955 ma 'a al-ta 'dīlāt al-Muqarrara 'alā ba 'ḍ mawāḍiḥ min qabl al-Majlis al-Shar 'ī al-a'lā bi mawjib al-qarār raqm/5/ tarīkh 21 dhī al-qa 'da 1386 H. al-Muwāfiq 2 ādhār 1967 a.d." (The Legislative Decree No. 18 of 13th of January 1955 with the Amendments of 2nd of March 1967) mimeographed in *Dār al-Fatwā* provided by the Higher Islamic Sharia Council from *Al-Jarīda al-Rasmiyyah (Official Gazette)*; No. 22, 16th of March 1967 (Beirut: Government of Lebanon).

16 Interview with Imam Moussa Sadre, President of the Higher Shiite Islamic Council, January 8, 1973.

17. Al-Majlis al-Islāmī al-Shī 'ī al-A 'lā (The Higher Shiite Islamic Council). "Qānūn Inshā' al-Majlis al-Islāmī al-Shī'ī al-A 'lā" (Law on the Establishment of the Higher Shiite Islamic Council), (Beirut: Sadir Press, 1969).

18. "Qānūn Ṣādir bi-Tārīkh 13 Tammūz Sanat 1962 bi-Intikhāb Shaykh 'Aql al-Tā' ifa al-Durziyyah." "Qānūn Ṣādir bi-Tārīkh 13 Tammūz Sanat 1962 bi-Inshā' al-Majlis al-Madhhabī lil-Tā' ifa al-Durziyyah." (Law promulgated on the 13th of July 1962 concerning the election of Shaykh Aql of the Druze Sect; Law promulgated on the 13th of July 1962 on the establishment of a Madhhabi Council for the Druze sect.) *Al-Jarīda al-Rasmiyyah (Official Gazette)*, Vol. 101, Part II, No. 29, 18th of July (Beirut: Government of Lebanon), pp. 1088–1097.

19. "Al-Majlis al-Islāmī al-Shī'ī al-A'lā fī Lubnān," (The Higher Islamic Shiite Council of Lebanon) untitled, undated pamphlet.

20. Raphael Patai, *The Republic of Lebanon* (New Haven, Conn.: Human Relations Area Files, 1956), p. 18.

21. Maher Mahmassani and Ibtissam Messara, eds. and trans., *Statut Personnel Textes en Vigueur au Liban* (Beirut: Faculte de Droit et de Sciences Economiques, 1970).

22. Fuad Khuri, "Two Suburbs of Beirut," unpublished manuscript, 1972, p. 140; Jamal K. Harfouche, *Social Structure of Low-Income Families in Beirut* (Beirut: Khayats, 1965), p. 80.

23. For Christian laws of inheritance see "Qānūn Sādir bi Tārīkh 23 Hazīrān Sanat 1959, Qānūn al-Irth li-Ghayr al-Muhammadīn" (Law issued on the 23 June 1959, Law of Inheritance for the Non-Muslims), Al-Jarīda Al-Rasmiyyah (The Official Gazette), No. 31, 24th of June 1959, pp. 730–749.

24. Linda Schatkowski, "The Islamic Maqased of Beirut: A Case Study of Modernization in Lebanon," unpublished M.A. Thesis, American University of Beirut, 1969; Samir Khalaf and Linda Schatkowski, "The Convergence of Tradition and Modernity: The Case of the Islamic Maqased of Beirut," unpublished paper, 1969.

25 Evelyn A. Early, "The Amiliyah Society of Beirut: A Case Study of an Emerging Urban Za'im," unpublished M.A. Thesis, American University of Beirut, 1971.

26. Statistiques Scolaires Annees 1969–1970, 1970–1971 (Beyrouth: Le Bureau de la Statistique, 1972), pp. 28, 142.

27. Interview with Msg. Ignace Maroun, head of Catholic Schools in Lebanon, June 19, 1972.

28. Horner, op. cit., p. 22.

29. John Gulick, Tripoli, A Modern Arab City (Cambridge, Mass.: Harvard University Press, 1967), p. 47.

30. Schatkowski, op. cit., pp. 120, 137.

31. Early, op. cit., p. 53.

32. Jam'īyāt al-Khidmat al-Ijtimā'iyya fī-Lubnān (Social Welfare Oranizations in Lebanon) (Beirut: Ministry of Planning, 1965).

33. See, for example, Kilbourne on the Greek Orthodox; Toufic Touma, Un Village de Montagne au Liban (Paris: Mouton and Co., 1958), p. 139 on a Maronite community; and Judith R. Williams, The Youth of Haouch el Harim: A Lebanese Village (Cambridge, Mass.: Harvard University Press, 1968), p. 14 on a Sunni village.

34. Samir Khalaf, "Family Associations in Lebanon," Journal of Comparative Family Studies, II (Autumn 1971), p. 236.

35. Ibid., p. 237.

36. Ibid., pp. 236–250; Fuad I. Khuri, "A Profile of Family Associations in Two Suburbs," unpublished paper presented to Middle East Social Anthropology and Sociology Conference, Nicosia, 1970.

37. Sameh K. Farsoun, "Family Structure and Society in Modern Lebanon," in Louise Sweet, ed., Peoples and Cultures of the Middle East, Vol. I (Garden City, New York: The Natural History Press, 1970), pp. 267–272.

38. On discontinuities in the socialization process in fragmented societies, see Robert LeVine, "Political Socialization and Cultural Change," in Clifford Geertz, ed., Old Societies and New States: The Quest for Modernity in Asia and Africa (New York: The Free Press of Glencoe, 1963), pp. 280–304.

39. See, for example, Robert D. Hess and Judith V. Torney, The Development of Political Attitudes in Children (Garden City, N.Y.: Doubleday and Co., Inc., 1968).

40. Levon Melikian, "By Their Names," Middle East Forum, XXXIX (April 1963), pp. 34–39.

41. This is a term Fuad Khuri employs in "Two Suburbs of Beirut."

42. Interview with Professor Charles Malik, December 1972.

43. Khuri, "Sectarian Loyalty in Two Suburbs," op. cit., p. 6.

44. Jawad Boulos, "L'Influence des données géographiques et historiques sur la personalité du Liban," Action Proche-Orient, XXI (Juin 1963), p. 23.

45. Translated from al-Nahar, November 30, 1969, p. 10.

46. See, for example, John Gulick, "Conservatism and Change in a Lebanese Village," in Abdulla M. Lutfiyya and Charles W. Churchill, eds., Readings in Arab Middle Eastern Societies and Cultures (The Hague: Mouton and Co., 1970), pp. 317, 326.

47. Levon H. Melikian, "The Family in Lebanon," in *Cultural Resources of Lebanon* (Beirut: Librairie du Liban, 1969), pp. 162, 164.

48. Victor Ayoub, "Resolution of Conflict in a Lebanese Village," in Leonard Binder, ed., *Politics in Lebanon*, (New York: John Wiley & Sons, Inc. 1966), p. 121.

49. Mounir Chamoun, "*La Famille au Liban*," *Travaux et Jour*, 25 (Octobre–Decembre 1967), p. 31, our translation.

50. A. I. Tannous, "Group Behavior in the Village Community of Lebanon," in Lutfiyya and Churchill, eds., op. cit., p. 106.

51. See, for example, Anne H. Fuller, *Buarij: Portrait of a Lebanese Muslim Village* (Cambridge, Mass.: Harvard University Press, 1961), p. 66; John Gulick, *Social Structure and Cultural Change in a Lebanese Village*, op. cit., p. 131; Tannous, op. cit., p. 106; Emrys L. Peters, "Aspects of Rank and Status among Muslims in a Lebanese Village," in Sweet, ed., op. cit., p. 96; Teny Anoushavian Simonian, "Assimilation Patterns of Rural and Urban Armenian Communities in Lebanon," unpublished M.A. Thesis, American University of Beirut, 1971, p. 143. Fuller's study is of Sunnis, Gulick's of Greek Orthodox, Tannous's of Greek Orthodox and Maronites, Peters' of Shiites, and Simonian's of Armenians.

52. "Les Prêtres catholiques les plus fidèles."

53. Karl W. Deutsch, "Social Mobilization and Political Development," *American Political Science Review*, **IV (September 1961)**, 493–514.

54. *L'Enquête par Sondage sur la Population Active au Liban*, op. cit., p. 59.

55. *L'Enquête par Sondage*, op. cit., pp. 69, 73.

56. Samir Khalaf and Per Kongstad, *Hamra of Beirut: A Case of Rapid Urbanization* (Leiden: E. J. Brill, 1973), p. 170.

57. Khalaf and Kongstad, op. cit., p. 170.

58. Harfouche, op. cit., p. 79.

59. Khuri, "Two Suburbs," op. cit., pp. 30–37.

60. Fuad Khuri, "Sectarian Loyalty in Two Suburbs: A Stage Between Family and National Allegiance," unpublished paper, n.d.; p. 1.

61. IRFED, Tome II, op. cit., pp. 76–77.

62. *Statistiques Scolaires* (Beyrouth: Ministère de l'Education 1972), pp. 28–33, 142–148.

63. *L'Enquête par Sondage sur la Population Active au Liban*, p. 106.

64. Samir Khalaf, "Lebanon," draft version of article prepared for *Encyclopedia Britannica*, 1971, p. 1.

65. IRFED, Tome I, op. cit., pp. 81–95.

66. Yusif A. Sayigh, *Entrepreneurs of Lebanon* (Cambridge, Mass.: Harvard University Press, 1967), pp. 69–80. Sayigh's sample of 207 businessmen was carefully chosen in order to be representative of the business community as a whole.

67 IRFED, Tome I, op. cit., p. 43.

68. "Survey on Lebanese Labor Force Revealed," *The Arab World Weekly*, April 22, 1972, 13–15.

69. Fuad Khuri, "The Changing Class Structure in Lebanon," *Middle East Journal*, 23 (Winter 1969), 29–44.

70. Samir Khalaf, "Lebanese Labor Unions: Some Comparative Structural Features," *Middle East Economic Papers* (Beirut: American University of Beirut, 1968), 111–138; Samir Khalaf, "Industrial Conflict in Lebanon," *Human Organization*, 24 (Spring 1965), 25–33; Khalaf and Kongstad, op. cit., p. 96.

71. Khalaf, "Lebanon," op. cit., p. 15.

72. On government policy, see Tawfiq Bawarshi, "The Lebanese Labour Scene," *Middle East*

Forum, XXXIX (June 1963), 21–24.

73. Khalaf, "Lebanese Labour Unions," op. cit., pp. 120, 121, 126.

74. Naoum Farah, "Le Barreau en Crise," *L'Orient-Le Jour: Vie Moderne, Culture, Jeunes*, Supplément, 15–21 Avril 1972, II–V.

75. Interview with Mr. Ibrahim Trak.

76. We analyzed the sects of the presidents from lists appearing for the lawyers in the Farah article and articles in *Travaux et Jours*, 42 (Janvier-Mars 1972) and for the doctors from interviews.

77. René Chamusay, "Les ingénieurs Libanais à la recherche de leur profession," *L'Orient-Le Jour: Vie Moderne, Culture, Jeunes*, Supplément, 24–30 Juin 1972, II–V.

78. "Deux listes aux élections du syndicat des employés de banque," *L'Orient-Le Jour*, May 18, 1972, p. 2.

4

Sectarianism and the Lebanese Political System

In a political system whose most fundamental guiding principle is that of maintaining an equilibrium among the country's various confessional groups, checks and balances are all-pervasive.[1] Yet, it is essential that one political officeholder be the final arbiter for certain key issues so that equilibrium does not become synonymous with inactivity. In the Lebanese system the president assumes this position. To be a successful arbiter, however, he must work closely with the two other key officeholders, the premier and the speaker of the parliament, the first of whom is a Sunni and the second a Shiite. But he must also collaborate with the cabinet, parliament, and various nongovernmental interest groups and individual actors. One of the lessons painfully learned from the 1958 civil war was the necessity that the president share power with the premier, particularly when the political interests of the principal confessional groups are at variance. To a certain extent, the president benefits from being a member of the country's most prominent confessional group, but he is also constrained by the fact that the other religious groups continually suspect that his action may be motivated by a desire to favor the Maronites at the expense of the other communities. Therefore, the president holds frequent and broad consultation to ensure that his policies will have interconfessional backing.

Second in importance and closely related to the imperative of continual consultation, is that the president symbolizes and promotes national unity. Because the president is always from the same confessional group, this task becomes more difficult and more important. Although he represents the Maronite community, he is supposed to stand above all confessional, as well as other controversies, and to promote reconciliation and peaceful intergroup relations. As one author has described it, the president "is expected to speak of 'Arabism' to broaden the political outlook of the Christians and of 'Lebanism' to strengthen the concept of sovereign state among the Muslims."[2] Although he does not always succeed at this task, the Lebanese population expects that these considerations will significantly influence his behavior. The president's behavior constitutes the key to the maintenance of the equilibrium upon which the whole system is based.

In playing his role the president tries to give the impression of being above controversy and partisan politics. Generally, presidents have only issued occasional statements to the press or official pronouncements on controversial issues, although the incumbent, President Suleiman Franjieh, has inaugurated a monthly press conference.[3] Instead, the president acts in public like a ceremonial head of state, endeavoring not to project or reveal the authority he actually holds and exercises. The manner in which he conducts himself promotes the myth that day-to-day political and policy issues rest in the hands of the premier and members of his cabinet, rather than with the president in consultation with his cabinet. By this means the president can symbolize unity and reconciliation and remain, at least in the public's mind, above the cut and thrust of politics. If some governmental policy becomes too controversial or objectionable, the president can merely ask his cabinet to resign, letting the ministers assume responsibility, while maintaining his own image of impartiality and noninvolvement.

The fact that the National Pact allocates the presidency to the Maronites has several important implications for intersect relations. Probably the most consequential is that competition for the post becomes primarily intraconfessional rather than interconfessional. When parliament elects a new president every six years, a Sunni does not challenge a Maronite for the post, and in turn the Sunnis and the Maronites do not line up behind their respective candidates and compete for the office along sectarian lines. Instead, competition for this office takes place within the Maronite community, with various Maronites contesting against each other. The legitimacy of a candidate and his success in a presidential election usually depends upon having the backing of a strong interconfessional coalition. The first announcement of support for General Fuad Chehab as a candidate in 1970 came from a group of five composed of a Sunni, two Shiites, a Maronite, and a Greek Orthodox. The nucleus of the Center Bloc that was working to promote Frangieh's candidacy included a Sunni, a Shiite, and a Greek Catholic. In many such alliances the Sunni member has his eye on becoming premier if his candidate for president is successful, and the Shiite member has designs on the speakership. The National Pact, along with Lebanon's electoral laws, thus turns what would potentially be divisive interconfessional electoral competition into interconfessional cooperation and intraconfessional competition. Encouragement of intraconfessional competition is not necessarily healthy in itself, but this type of competition is much more easily contained and presents much less of a threat to the viability of the Lebanese state than interconfessional competition.

Writers and orators frequently call for the abolition or amendment of the National Pact, particularly its reservation of the three top political posts for particular sects. Nevertheless, when consideration of various candidates for the presidency is underway, rarely is a non-Maronite candidate proposed. During the 1958 civil war rumors circulated that the insurgents wanted Kamal Jumblatt, a Druze, for the presidency once President Camille Chamoun stepped down. But Jumblatt adamantly denied this.[4] In 1964 rumors surfaced again of Jumblatt as a possible candidate, but the presumed source of this threat to the Pact, Sunni Premier Rachid Karami, disclaimed any interest in deviating from the Pact.[5] Again in the 1970 election a few people mentioned non-Maronite candidates and Rachid Karami has suggested he might be a candidate in 1976, but to a remarkable extent the reservation of the presidency to the Maronites has gone unchallenged, at least by those in a position to change the system. As a result, all five presidents who have held office since independence have been Maronites.

In keeping with one of the major themes of Lebanese political life, members of parliament generally hope that they can elect the president on the basis of a consensus or even by unanimous vote to minimize the disruptive impact of the election within this religiously divided society. In 1964 President Charles Helou was elected by a vote of ninety two out of ninety nine votes, and the three preceding presidents were also elected by overwhelming majorities. Occasionally, however, no consensus develops and these instances are instructive in terms of revealing the basis upon which electoral contests are fought. Particularly interesting was the election of President Frangieh in

1970, when he defeated his chief rival, Elias Sarkis, by a vote of fifty to forty nine. In large part, this election involved competition between two coalitions of political leaders, whose members were struggling to gain cabinet posts and the kind of political patronage that sustains their political power, but competing political philosophies were at stake as well. As already indicated, these two coalitions were interconfessional in membership, and yet a careful analysis reveals that Frangieh obtained a majority of the Christian votes (thirty four out of fifty four Christian parliamentarians), while Sarkis was backed by a majority of the Muslim parliamentarians (twenty nine out of forty five).[6] The divergence was particularly striking between Maronite and Sunni voters. Since both Sarkis and Frangieh are Maronites, the preference of Maronite deputies for Frangieh and the Sunni and Shiite support for Sarkis did not reflect confessional prejudice. What was important were the presumed and stated differences in policy positions of the two candidates, and the extent to which these orientations coincided or diverged from those favored by the various confessional communities. Frangieh was generally thought to be more likely to restrict activities of the Palestinian commandos on Lebanese soil and on the whole not to be as sympathetic to Arab nationalism as Sarkis. Attitudes on the commando issue constituted the most timely and pertinent reflection of long-standing Maronite–Sunni differences over Lebanon's role in the Arab world.

Mention has already been made of the close relationship between president and premier, and the extent to which, especially since 1958, these two office-holders have shared responsibility for most major government decisions. Their relationship symbolizes and gives substance to the Christian–Muslim partnership and particularly the Maronite–Sunni pact upon which the Lebanese sociopolitical order is built. The position of the premier in this relationship is weakened, however, by the fact that he serves at the pleasure of the president, and does not enjoy a fixed term of office as does the president.[7]

The dual expectation of the premier that he serve as a national leader sharing national responsibilities with the president while also representing the Sunni community in the highest councils of government often creates serious role conflicts. Particularly in times of interconfessional tension, a Sunni premier who appears to remain loyal to the Maronite president who appointed him to his post tends to be perceived by segments of the Sunni community as being disloyal to community interests, or at least not sufficiently assertive of the community's point of view. In 1958 Sami al-Solh, who remained at the side of President Chamoun during the civil war, was virtually declared an outcast by his coreligionists; in 1969 Rachid Karami felt compelled to resign as premier when he could not reconcile his two roles. Another special burden placed on the premier results from his position as nominal head of the government. Although the president may be the author of a particular policy, the public and the parliament usually hold the premier responsible. The premier's responsibilities frequently surpass his power, while the president is not always held publicly accountable for all of his authorized activities.

The president in consultation with the premier-designate appoints the cabinet, although the actual selection process usually involves extensive soundings of opinion among political groupings and political notables, and in some cases among religious, business, and other interest group leaders as well. The prevailing tendency is for the cabinet to be composed of as broad a cross-section of parliament as possible, taking into account confessional identity, regional representation, political bloc or party membership, and ideological persuasion. Cabinet members need not share all or even many of the president's or the premier's political viewpoints, thus making the cabinet an unwieldy body for executive action. Yet it constitutes a relatively effective body of opinion for consultation by the president and the premier. Given its size (nearly one out of every six members of parliament was a member of the 1972 cabinet) and its broadly representative character, the cabinet serves as a kind of mini-parliament and thereby assumes some of the tasks that parliament would perform if it were a stronger organ. One of the major advantages the cabinet has over parliament in handling important issues derives from the secrecy of its proceedings. Hence, sensitive issues, particularly in terms of their impact on interconfessional relations that have been carefully side-stepped by parliament, can be considered by the cabinet. By attempting to give representation within the cabinet to each of the major political and confessional groupings, most members of parliament are assured that their interests and those of their constituents will be represented there. In turn, most cabinets receive overwhelming support in their initial vote of confidence.

By bringing together within the cabinet persons with diverse political followings and often holding divergent points of view, the president usually hopes that accommodation and reconciliation will be achieved, even if decisive policy formulation cannot be. Probably the most extreme example of this approach came in President Chehab's first cabinet following the 1958 civil war, to which he named two Maronites, one of whom was a leader of the

Christian-dominated counterinsurrectionist forces, and two Sunnis, one of whom was a leader of the Muslim-dominated insurrectionists. In addition to permitting each point of view to be heard in the central government councils, this approach also gives all major political factions a stake in the system, in terms both of feeling a part of the core of the system and also in having patronage at their disposal to enhance their political futures. Moreover, political notables or blocs that do not have a member in a particular cabinet know that their chances are good of attaining such representation in forthcoming cabinet reshuffles.

One of the most important aspects of cabinet formation concerns the effort to achieve proportional representation of the confessional communities. Article 95 of the constitution requires that the country's various confessional communities be equitably represented, but does not specify a formula for proportional representation. Through tradition and precedent, however, a pattern has evolved that is almost invariably followed. Once it has been decided how many members the cabinet will have, reference is made to precedent to determine how these posts should be distributed among the communities. For instance, all those cabinets since 1943 with six members (1943, 1944, 1945, and 1956) have been composed of the following: one Maronite, one Sunni, one Shiite, one Greek Orthodox, one Druze, and one Greek Catholic. All but one of the cabinets with ten members (1951, 1952, 1954, 1955, 1956, 1964, 1966, 1968) have had three Maronites, three Sunnis, one Shiite, one Greek Orthodox, one Druze, and one Greek Catholic. All the cabinets of 14 members (1958, 1961, 1964) have included the following: three Maronites, three Sunnis, two Shiites, two Greek Orthodox, two Druze, and two Greek Catholics, except that in 1958 instead of two Greek Catholics there was one Greek Catholic and one Armenian Catholic. Similar precedents have been established for all the other cabinet sizes, namely, cabinets with three, four, eight, and eighteen members, the latter being the predominant number since 1972. Except for three cabinets composed of three persons and one cabinet composed of nine, all the other cabinets since 1943 have had an even number. This has permitted the other aspect of the formula to work, namely, that half the members of the cabinet are invariably Christians and half are Muslim. Thus, not only is there a carefully proportioned distribution among the various sects, but an absolute balance is maintained between the two more all-encompassing confessional divisions, Christian and Muslim. Finally, in virtually all cabinets an equal number of posts are given to members of the major Christian sect and the major Muslim sect, that is, the Maronites and the Sunnis. To a certain extent, although not with absolute rigidity, certain portfolios are reserved for particular sects. For instance, the minister of the interior is usually a Sunni and the minister of defense a Druze, while the deputy premier is almost invariably a Greek Orthodox.

In appointing their cabinet following the 1972 parliamentary elections, President Frangieh and Premier Saeb Salam strictly adhered to the traditional formula for confessional representation: four Sunnis, four Maronites, three Shiites, two Greek Orthodox, two Druze, two Greek Catholics, and one Armenian Orthodox in the cabinet of eighteen. Frangieh and Salam also attempted to include as many parties and parliamentary blocs as possible so that a total of eleven of the fourteen parliamentary blocs had at least one member named to the cabinet.[8] Clearly, the guiding principle was to organize a broad coalition that would reflect the diversity of parliament rather than to choose a cabinet that could agree on a bold government program. In constituting the cabinet, Frangieh and Salam also sought balanced regional representation, but this took lowest priority. While at least two members of the cabinet came from each of Lebanon's five provinces, the precise number chosen from each province did not necessarily reflect the relative size of that province's population. For instance, despite the fact that twenty out of the ninety nine members of parliament represent constituencies in North Lebanon, only two parliamentarians from the north were named to the eighteen-member cabinet.

Proportional confessional representation is more than the mere application of numerical formulae. The cabinet of Premier Amin Hafez appointed in 1973 by President Frangieh was forced to resign by Muslim parliamentarians and supporting Muslim organizations, who complained that the Muslims named to the cabinet were not sufficiently prominent and the portfolios they held were not of comparable importance to those held by Christians.

Although this effort to maintain an equilibrium and confessional balance within the cabinet has its obvious advantages for a pluralistic society, such a system naturally extracts its costs as well. In distributing posts in a manner to satisfy the various confessional, regional, and political interests, it is difficult to additionally expect technical competence, particularly when selection is confined to the ninety nine members of parliament. One poignant example came in 1955 when a Maronite engineer was named minister of foreign affairs in accordance with the tradition that this post is reserved for a Christian, while a Sunni ex-diplomat was named minister of public works.[9] An added difficulty arises from the fact that cabinet members tend to see themselves not only as national officeholders, but also as representatives of their respective confessional, regional, and political constituents. Although he has perhaps made the point too strongly, Malcolm Kerr focused on this weakness of the system when he wrote:

> Here the fundamental tension of the entire system of Lebanese cabinet making arises again: men of sharp partisan views are brought into the cabinet in order to leash them with responsibility, but as they cannot afford to pay the full political price that responsibility entails, they strike a compromise by becoming in effect only half ministers . . . and lending to the cabinet only half the cohesion demanded of it by the formal constitutional system. [10]

One might infer from the Lebanese constitution that parliament (Chamber of Deputies) is the core of the political system. In some respects it is, but not in terms of shaping and promoting a legislative program. Several analysts have pointed out that the Lebanese parliament, not unlike parliaments in many other democracies, is not a very robust institution. One analyst has discovered that during four sample years between 1950 and 1966, not a single one of the 384 bills considered by parliament was rejected. [11] The tendency has been for the president and premier with the assistance of the cabinet to prepare the legislative program and for parliament to enact their proposals with relatively little reflection or debate.

Of fundamental importance in assessing the role of parliament, however, is the mere fact of its existence, particularly since its membership is distributed among the country's confessional and geographical subdivisions roughly in proportion to their size. Charles Rizk indicates the significance of this when he writes, "Douze communautés religieuses différentes, musulmanes et chrétiennes, y cohabitent, en vertu d'un contrat social dont le parlementarisme est l'expression politique." [12] One of the chief architects of Lebanon's constitution, Michel Chiha, stressed repeatedly in his writings the significance of parliament as a vehicle for dialogue between representatives of the country's various confessional communities. [13] This is not to contend that a completely powerless and ineffective parliament could exert a positive impact on Lebanon's political and social life, but it does suggest that additional factors should be assessed in judging its importance and its effectiveness.

The role expectations of members of parliament are not limited to lawmaking and the conduct of interconfessional dialogue. Constituents generally consider the parliamentarian's most important task to be that of performing personal services for those who elected him and whom he represents. This is part of the personal element that is so fundamental to the Lebanese political system, and which arises in part from the country's small size both in territory and population; on the average, a member of parliament represents only 24,000 people. Constituents seek out their representative to loan or give them money; to intervene for them with the bureaucracy in obtaining redress of grievances, jobs, promotions, licenses; to intervene with the police and judges in court cases; and to provide a variety of other kinds of assistance. Although this is certainly not unique to Lebanon, this form of representation is accorded particular importance in Lebanon. A survey of civil servants conducted by Marun Kisirwani revealed that sixty percent of the civil servants questioned recommended that anyone seeking to transact official government business should seek assistance from influential mediators. A counterpart survey he conducted of Lebanese citizens indicated that 65 percent of his respondents seek assistance from such influential mediators as parliamentarians whenever they have business to transact with the bureaucracy.[14] A poll of seventy seven parliamentarians conducted in 1971 indicated that most of them believed these personal services to be the most important contributing factors to their election or reelection.[15] In 1972 such key parliamentarians as Raymond Edde and Sabri Hamadé testified that their support of the government was explicitly dependent upon the services and development projects they could obtain on behalf of their constituents from the government.[16] In the majority of cases, this intervention by a member of parliament enables the ordinary citizen to solicit the hearing and services to which he is theoretically entitled, but which are normally beyond his reach, since the bureaucracy is remote and government procedures are often beyond the citizen's understanding. There are instances in which undue and illegal influence is exerted, but these are in the minority. Although in many respects this may comprise an expensive, ineffective, and sometimes unjust means of conducting government business, it has the virtue of giving virtually every Lebanese citizen the sense that he has a highly placed person, usually a member of his same confessional community, who can represent his personal interests and intervene on his behalf when he needs to encounter the remote and fearful machinery of government. This provides a different kind of representation than was envisaged in the constitution, but it is probably more meaningful to the ordinary Lebanese citizen and constitutes a critical source of governmental penetration and national cohesion.

Both the size of parliament and the number of constituencies have changed frequently since independence. What has remained constant, however, is the proportional confessional representation, based on the relative sizes of the confessional communities at the time when the last census was conducted in 1932. The most basic guiding element in the allocation of parliamentary seats is that five seats will go to Muslims for every six seats that go to Christians, a formula that has its origins in the slight numerical predominance of Christians over Muslims in the 1932 census. Following from this principle, the total size of parliament must be divisible by eleven; thus, parliament has at various times been composed of forty four, fifty five, sixty six, seventy seven, and ninety nine members. The parliament elected in 1972 has ninety nine deputies chosen from twenty six constituencies, all but one of which are multimember constituencies. The distribution of these seats among the various confessional communities is indicated in Table 4-1.

The reservation of each parliamentary seat for a member of a particular confessional group has many of the same implications as the reservation of the presidency for the Maronites. Electoral competition takes place between competing candidates of the same sect and in turn is intraconfessional. In multiconfessional constituencies interconfessional alliances are usually formed to wage electoral battle. Since all the residents of a constituency vote for each of the seats, the Sunnis of the Chouf, for example, vote not merely for candidates for the two Sunni seats, but they also have the right to choose among the candidates for the three Maronite seats, the one Greek Catholic seat, and the two Druze seats as well. In the case of the Chouf, more non-Maronite voters will be electing the Maronite representatives than will Maronite voters.

This electoral system sometimes causes voter dissatisfaction. In the 1972 parliamentary elections a young Arab nationalist, who is a member of the Nasserite Organization, was elected to fill the Greek Orthodox seat in a Beirut constituency. He won the election primarily through the backing of the Sunni voters in the district who tend to be more sympathetic than Christian voters to an Arab nationalist political position. Since most of the Greek Orthodox voters saw his political philosophy as alien to their own, both lay and clerical leaders of the Greek Orthodox community, including the Metropolitan, organized protest marches and called for amendment of the electoral law to permit only members of a candidate's confessional community to vote for him.[17]

The electoral alliances worked out in individual constituencies are called

TABLE 4-1 Confessional Composition of 1972 Parliament by Constituency

NAME OF CONSTITUENCY	MARONITES	SUNNIS	SHIITES	GREEK ORTH.	GREEK CATH.	DRUZE	ARM. ORTH.	ARM. CATH.	PRO-TEST.	MINO-RITIES	TOTAL
1. Beirut No. 1	1			1	1		3	1	1		8
2. Beirut No. 2		1	1							1	3
3. Beirut No. 3		4		1							5
4. Baabda	3		1			1					5
5. Metn	3			1			1				5
6. Chouf	3	2			1	2					8
7. Aley	2			1		2					5
8. Kesrouan	4										4
9. Jbeil	2		1								3
10. Zahle	1	1	1	1	1						5
11. Rashaya		1		1		1					3
12. Baalbeck-Hermel	1	1	4		1						7
13. Sidon		1									1
14. Jezzine-Maghdoucheh	2				1						3
15. Zahrani			1		1						2
16. Bint-Jbeil			2								2
17. Tyre			3								3
18. Marjayoun-Hasbaya		1	2	1							4
19. Nabatieh			3								3
20. Tripoli		4		1							5
21. Dunieh		2									2
22. Akkar	1	2		1							4
23. Zghorta	3										3
24. Koura				2							2
25. Bsharri	2										2
26. Batroun	2										2
TOTAL	30	20	19	11	6	6	4	1	1	1	99

"lists," which are composed of candidates for each of the seats being contested in the constituency. For example, in Tripoli, which is allocated four Sunni seats and one Greek Orthodox seat, each competing list contains four Sunni candidates and a Greek Orthodox candidate. A particularly prominent politician usually heads each list and other candidates are enticed to join his list with the prospect that their association with him will gain them votes from among his supporters. In like fashion, the list leader hopes to win votes from the supporters of those he invites to join his list. Each voter in Tripoli, for instance, can vote for four Sunni candidates and one Greek Orthodox candidate, and he is encouraged by his patron candidate to vote for the other candidates on his list. Underlying the list system, participants assume that each candidate has a group of supporters coming principally from his own confessional community who will vote for him, and that these clients will also cast their ballots for the other candidates whom he designates as being the ones with whom he has formed an electoral alliance.

This system has the advantage of minimizing interconfessional electoral competition and conflict, as well as enhancing the electoral chances of moderate candidates and working to the disadvantage of confessional chauvinists. Its disadvantages include the fact that persons who do not belong to the principal confessional groups of a particular constituency cannot stand for election. For instance, Bsharri, Batroun, and Zghorta are single sect constituencies with the seats allocated in each case to Maronites. Non-Maronites resident in those constituencies can vote, but they cannot stand for election. In multimember constituencies it is possible for a candidate from one confession to receive more votes than a candidate for another confessional seat and yet still not be elected. For example, in the 1968 parliamentary elections, in the third constituency of Beirut a Greek Orthodox candidate received 10,244 votes and was elected to the Greek Orthodox seat, while a Sunni candidate received 11,795 votes and was not elected since he was competing only with other Sunni candidates and not with the Greek Orthodox candidate.[18]

As already indicated, the formula for the distribution of seats among the confessional communities has its historical justification in the 1932 census results. Most Lebanese concede privately that the demographic situation has not remained static since then. To some the demographic change is irrelevant to parliamentary representation; the current system has proved itself workable and thus should be maintained. For others, the current distribution of seats is unjust so long as it does not take into account shifts in the relative size of the various communities.

The majority of those elected to parliament are not members of a political party and are not backed by any particular political party. For instance, in 1972, 39 percent of the members of parliament were party members. The same holds for the electorate: In our survey of one thousand Lebanese adults, 11 percent indicated that they were members of political parties and 32 percent said that they supported a political party, while the remaining 55 percent were neither members nor supporters. Candidates for parliament generally seek votes on the basis of both the political philosophy they hold and on the basis of the personal services they can provide their clients. Their ability to provide patronage to their constituents largely depends upon the kind of parliamentary coalition they organize or join and the number of coalition partners they can manage to have named to the cabinet. Blocs are generally organized by a particularly prominent parliamentarian, and the bloc usually is referred to by the name of its leader. These parliamentary coalitions or blocs tend to be informal groupings with frequently shifting memberships, but they constitute important structural units of the Lebanese political system.

While political parties do not dominate the electoral scene to the extent that they do in most other democratic systems, a steadily growing number of members of parliament over the past twenty years have been party members.[19] Moreover, in extraparliamentary political life political parties play a significant role in articulating political protest.[20] This is particularly true of the left-wing and Arab nationalist parties. Of particular interest to the analysis here is the extent to which political parties are confessionally differentiated, as well as the relationship between party ideology and the confessional composition of the party. Some exceptions can be cited, but in general Lebanon's political parties tend to be differentiated, as are so many other Lebanese associations, in terms of the confessional identities of their members. This is not to say that all Maronites belong to a single political party, the Sunnis to another, and the Greek Catholics to a third, since there are many parties and the range of choice is broad. Christians from one socioeconomic stratum tend to be attracted to one predominantly Christian party and Christians from other strata tend to be drawn to other parties.[21] Except for those few parties whose membership is religiously defined, like the Association of Moslem Brethren, virtually all parties have members from more than a single confessional group. In most parties, however, a single confessional group predominates.

The Kataeb (Phalangists) is Lebanon's largest political party and probably the best organized. Pierre Gemayel founded the party in 1936 and remains its leader. Its ideology has traditionally emphasized "Lebanism" as opposed to Arab nationalism, and usually espouses the uniqueness of multiconfessional Lebanon within the predominantly Muslim Arab world.[22] When the party believes that those of its persuasion, most of whom are Christians, are threatened or that a conflicting ideology is likely to predominate in Lebanon, it has been prepared to call out its well-trained militia to defend its point of view by force.[23] In this respect the Kataeb resembles many other political parties in Lebanon who also have paramilitary wings. Like most other parties whose membership derives primarily from a single or from closely related confessional communities, the Kataeb leadership denies that it is a Maronite or a Christian organization and contends that its membership is relatively broadly based. But careful assessment of its membership in 1969 indicated that 80 percent were Maronites, 10 percent came from other Christian communities, and 10 percent were non-Christians.[24] Sixteen of the twenty one members of the party's central bureau in 1970 were Maronites, and all five of the remaining members came from other Christian communities.[25] In 1971 the first non-Christian, a Druze, was added to the central bureau.[26]

The Kataeb leadership repeatedly emphasizes that its differences with certain other political parties, and particularly with the Arab nationalist parties, arise from ideology, not from Christian antagonism toward Muslims. It attempts to portray the division of political opinion and political groupings in Lebanon as being between radical and conservative, between the right and left, rather than between Christian and Muslim. Moreover, it claims that the confessional imbalance in its membership is because members of certain confessional groups tend to be more favorably disposed towards its ideology than others, not because its Christian leaders prefer having Christian members. It can be argued that these assertions provide mere rationalization for what is to a considerable extent a confessionally based political party. On the other hand, it is fundamental to an understanding of the relationship between politics and religion in Lebanon to realize that members of Lebanon's various confessional communities do tend to have varying political perspectives, particularly regarding Lebanon's position in the Arab world. As a result, political groupings tend to a considerable degree to be confessionally differentiated as a direct consequence of their differing outlooks.

Two other predominantly (but not exclusively) Christian political parties are the Liberal National Party, led by former President Camille Chamoun, and the National Bloc of Raymond Edde. On the Muslim side al-Najjadah began as a Muslim response to the Christian-dominated Kataeb. Behind its leader Adnan Hakim, its 10,000–15,000 members work for the defense of Muslim rights in Lebanon and for the fruition of Arab-Islamic culture. [27] The Progressive Socialist Party (PSP) of Kamal Jumblatt draws a large portion of its membership from Druze tied to the Jumblatt family through traditional bonds of allegiance, but it also derives a substantial share of its support from other confessional groups, both Christian and Muslim. Unfortunately, accurate figures regarding the confessional identities of the members of these parties are not available.

Analysis of the confessional composition of parliamentary blocs and of party blocs within parliament is another means of determining the extent to which Lebanese parties and other political organizations are broadly or narrowly representative in confessional terms. Despite the importance of confessional factors in political activity in Lebanon, in May 1972 none of the five parties represented in parliament with more than a single member, and not one of the seven parliamentary blocs was confined to representatives from a single confessional community. Only two of these twelve blocs and parties in parliament were represented solely by Christians and only one of the twelve was exclusively represented by Muslims. Table 4-2 indicates the extent of confessional coalescence in the parliamentary setting, and evidence presented in the next chapter demonstrates that the period 1960 to 1972 witnessed a clear historical trend toward greater inter-confessional parliamentary cooperation of this nature. Thus, while confessional factors influence parliamentary activity, cooperative action among parliamentarians frequently occurs across confessional boundaries. Nor does a single confessional group monopolize leadership positions of parliamentary blocs and of party blocs in parliament. These leadership posts were distributed as following in May 1972: four Maronites, two Sunnis, two Shiites, two Druze, one Greek Catholic, and one Armenian.

Another important characteristic of some Lebanese political parties is their transnational character. These international linkages are of three different types, but in each case they represent an interest on the part of a segment of the Lebanese population to merge Lebanon or one part of it with another state. None of these parties is sufficiently active, successful, or aggressive to constitute much of a current threat to Lebanon's national identity, but their existence and their party programs are worth noting, particularly in a discussion of religious and ethnic factors in politics. The Syrian Social Nationalist Party (known as PPS) provides one such example; it contends that Lebanon is merely an artificial subdivision of the Syrian nation, which in addition to

TABLE 4-2 *Confessional Composition of Parliamentary Blocs and Party Blocs in Parliament, May 1972*

PARTY OR BLOC	SUNNI	SHIITE	DRUZE	MARO-NITE	GREEK ORTH.	GREEK CATH.	ARM. ORTH.	ARM. CATH.	PRO-TEST.	ROMAN CATH.
Kataeb (party)				5		2		1		
National Bloc (party)	1	1		3						
Liberal National Party	1	2		5	1	1				
P.S.P. and F.L.N. (party)	2	1	3	2		1				1
Tashnaq (party)							4		1	
Iraqi Baath (party)	1									
Nasserite Movement (party)					1					
Karami Bloc	3				1					
Assaad Bloc	1	7			1					
Salem Bloc	4	1								
Skaff Bloc	2	1	1	1		1				
T. Frangieh Bloc		1		4	2					
Arslan Bloc			1	2	1					
Hamadé Bloc	1	3		1		1				
Unaffiliated	4	2	1	7	2	1				

SOURCE: *L'Orient-Le Jour*, April 14, 1972; April 18, 1972; April 22, 1972; April 25, 1972; and April 28, 1972.

Lebanon, is thought to include the peoples of Jordan, Syria, Iraq, Cyprus, Kuwait, and Palestine. Significantly, the major portion of the PPS membership in Lebanon comes from the Greek Orthodox, Druze, and Shiite communities, all of which sometimes feel their interests to be slighted by the two dominant communities—the Maronites and the Sunnis.[28] Several largely Muslim parties advocate the union or federation of Lebanon with other Arab states. This category includes the Syrian-oriented Baathists, the Iraqi-oriented Baathists, and the Nasserite Movement. Examples of quite a different kind are the two Armenian parties, Tashnaq and Hunchak. Their principal ideological concerns relate to the eventual reunification of the Armenian peoples in an Armenian homeland. Although these parties present candidates for election to the Lebanese parliament, their political programs focus on transnational concerns peculiar to Lebanon's largely unassimilated Armenian ethnic minority. These Armenian parties have branches in virtually all parts of the world where Armenians have settled, and consequently their leadership is international.[29]

In a nation rent by deep pluralistic divisions, a strong government bureaucracy ideally can play at least two critical roles in contributing to national cohesion and the viability of the state. First, through sheer effectiveness, a government apparatus of competent officials operating on the basis of the disinterested principles of bureaucracy can conduct government business in a manner that cushions communal conflict among politicians. Second, a large central bureaucracy composed of a broad cross-section of the nation's population can bring representatives of the nation's component groups into intimate and continuous contact. In working together for a common purpose they can create among themselves bonds of trust and mutuality, and thereby constitute a core of citizens at the center with a national orientation.

Unfortunately, the Lebanese bureaucracy, at least until recently, has achieved these results only in limited measure. One reason is that prior to the Chehab regime (1958–1964) government operations were narrow in scope; consequently, the civil service establishment was small. Moreover, political intervention in the bureaucratic process inhibited the development of a disinterested professional ethic. Poor quality of personnel undermined both effectiveness and the development of the appropriate attitudes. Finally, selection of personnel on the basis of confessional quotas tended to reinforce confessional identities rather than promote a national perspective.[30]

Dating back to the periods of the Règlement Organique and the French Mandate, Lebanese governments have made some effort to attain confessional balance among those employed by the government. Since 1926 the constitution has contained a provision calling for the proportional distribution of government employment among the confessional communities, and this provision is presently embodied as Article 95. Despite this constitutional requirement, prior to 1958 the proportional distribution of posts was imperfectly realized. For instance, although the Maronites constituted only about 29 percent of the population in 1958, they held approximately 50 percent of government posts.[31] As a means of rectifying these imbalances, President Chehab first devised and then insisted upon the strict application of a new confessional formula in the recruitment and promotion of civil servants. Prior to 1958 the standard procedure, not always applied, was to employ five Muslims for every six Christians, but under President Chehab's reforms one Muslim had to be hired for every Christian. Although the Chehab regime devised no strict formula for allocating these positions among the various Christian and Muslim subgroups, greater effort was exerted after 1958 to see that some of the internal inequities were rectified. For instance, since 1958 Shiites have obtained a greater portion of the Muslim job quota than they did prior to that date.

The rationale for adopting confessional identity as a criterion for recruitment to government posts is multidimensional. First, such jobs constitute an important economic benefit which all the constituent groups wish to enjoy in equal or proportionate measure, since all communities are contributing taxes to pay the wages of government workers. Second, the imposition of strict quotas inhibits persons responsible for recruitment from favoring members of their own or allied communities and discriminating against members of other communities. Third, the achievement of balanced confessional representation at the higher levels of the civil service, that is, at those levels responsible for policy formulation, helps guard against the neglect of the interests of particular communities when government programs and policies are formulated.

Figures indicating the confessional composition of the civil service as a whole, which in 1969 totalled 24,230 persons, are not available. Various sources concur though that of the government work force recruited since 1959, 50 percent have been Muslim and 50 percent Christian, while some imbalances may exist among those employed earlier. We have been able to obtain precise information regarding the distribution of the highest level posts, namely those holding the rank of director general and ambassador. Table 4-3 presents this division.

TABLE 4-3   *Distribution of Class 1 Civil Service Posts (Ambassadors and Director Generals) Among the Confessional Communities*

	1946	1962	1972	1974
Maronite	12	18	28	39
Greek Orthodox	6	11	10	14
Greek Catholic	1	7	9	8
Christian Minorities	0	2	2	9
(Christian subtotal)	(19)	(38)	(49)	(70)
(Percentage Christian)	(61%)	(54%)	(52%)	(50%)
Sunni	9	24	23	31
Shiite	1	2	15	29
Druze	2	6	7	10
(Muslim subtotal)	(12)	(32)	(45)	(70)
(Percentage Muslim)	(39%)	(46%)	(48%)	(50%)
TOTAL	31	70	94	140

SOURCES: 1946 figures from Pierre Rondot, *Les Institution Politiques du Liban* (Paris: Imprimerie Nationale, 1947), p. 89.
1962 figures from Michael Hudson, *The Precarious Republic* (New York: Random House, 1968), p. 320.
1972 figures from official sources within the Lebanese government.
1974 figures from *L'Orient-Le Jour*, February 19, 1974, p. 12.

As revealed in Table 4-3, the period between 1946 and 1974 witnessed steady progress toward Christian–Muslim parity within the top echelon of the civil service. The change that took place in 1974 not only involved the establishment of the principle that Christians and Muslims should be equally represented at the top of the civil service ladder, but also that some of the key posts traditionally reserved for Christians, such as the director general of the Ministry of Education and the president of the Civil Service Board, should no longer be strictly Christian preserves. This change resulted from Muslim agitation and complaints that parity of numbers needed to be accompanied by equality of power. In tracing the development from 1946 to 1974 the most striking change has been in representation of Shiites. In 1946 Shiites held only one of the thirty one posts, while in 1974 the Shiite community was allocated 21 percent of the class-1 posts.[32] This proportion approximates the magnitude of Shiite representation in parliament. The proportion of other confessional groups holding class-1 positions in 1974 similarly reflects their parliamentary representation, and in turn the relative size of the various communities in the 1932 census count.

The utilization of confessional identity as one criterion for recruitment and promotion has had widespread repercussions. Although the Civil Service Board appoints no one who does not meet certain minimum standards, merit is not the only factor influencing who is chosen from among those eligible. If four positions of a certain type are vacant, two must be filled by Christians and two by Muslims. If the four most capable persons are Muslims, only two of them may be chosen along with two less qualified Christians. If four Muslims qualify but no Christians meet the minimum qualifications, no appointment can be made because no Christians can be appointed. The posts thus remain vacant until more candidates apply and qualify. The same holds for promotions: a Christian ready for a promotion cannot be promoted unless there is a Muslim who can be promoted simultaneously to the same grade. At the level of director general each post is generally reserved for a member of a particular sect. For instance, the director general of the Ministry of Finance is a Greek Orthodox and if he retires or is transferred, he will be replaced by a Greek Orthodox, and the same holds for the Sunni who heads the Tax Bureau. If a qualified person from that sect is not available for appointment, then the post remains vacant until a suitable person can be named.

The value of distributing civil service posts on a proportional basis among the communities is apparent, and the practice has unquestionably contributed to intercommunity accommodation. Yet the system clearly extracts its costs. The Civil Service Board, which is responsible for government recruitment and for assuring that Article 95 of the constitution is implemented, has complained about the rigid manner in which it is expected to assure proportionality. Because of confessional constraints, the Board experiences difficulty in appointing those it considers to be the most highly qualified candidates as well as in keeping posts filled.[33] As Ralph Crow has pointed out, if every sect had a surplus of well-qualified candidates for each type of civil service post, there would be no necessary contradiction between merit and sectarian recruitment, but since this is not the case confessional considerations frequently require sacrifices in quality.[34]

Government departments and ministries have also complained about the rigidity of the system. In November 1972 officials of the Ministry of Agriculture objected strenuously when they were not permitted to appoint the best qualified persons to research positions at the Center of Agricultural Research because a disproportionate number of the selected candidates were Muslims.[35] During the same month officials of the Ministry of Foreign Affairs protested that they had to leave key diplomatic posts vacant in Paris and Moscow because an insufficient number of qualified Muslims had applied, and the Civil Service Board would not permit the Ministry to appoint their Christian candidates.[36]

Considerable official attention has recently been devoted to how Lebanon can preserve the basic principle of proportional distribution while modifying its application, so that some of the shortcomings of the current system can be overcome. In 1972 the Civil Service Board recommended revisions to the cabinet that would permit the attainment of confessional balance within government employment as a whole but not require that confessional balance be maintained in each job.[37] This would permit considerably more flexibility. Although this proposal was not adopted, the cabinet did agree that top posts should not be strictly reserved for members of particular sects and that in certain technical fields confessional balance could be disregarded to assure high quality appointments.[38] Whether these decisions will be implemented is still unclear. Some adjustments seem necessary so that the principle of confessional balance can be preserved without sacrificing too much in terms of administrative quality and effectiveness.

In late 1972 religious leaders representing all three Muslim sects started demanding that another aspect of civil service personnel policy be modified to permit the full recognition of religious equality. They asserted that Friday should be a free day for all civil servants in recognition of its being the Muslim Sabbath. Since Sunday, due to its sacred character to Christians, is a nation-wide holiday for members of all faiths, they contended that by the same logic Friday should be a holiday as well.[39] The release of Muslims at 11:00 A.M. to attend prayers, which was then the practice, was not thought to be sufficient. After two years of discussion and debate, a decision was reached in 1974 to close government offices at 11:00, with Friday afternoon being free for all government employees.

Although the proposal for a holiday on Friday did not gain universal support from Muslims, it faced nearly universal opposition from Christians. Some Christians retorted that even under the existing policies a Muslim civil servant worked an average of 216 fewer hours per year than a Christian civil servant because of religious holidays and released time for prayers. They asserted that if inequalities existed, the Christians were the disadvantaged ones, not the Muslims.[40] The eventual denouement represented the kind of compromise for which Lebanon is noted, but the issue itself illustrated that Lebanon's confessional system is still in evolution and new issues will undoubtedly have to be faced periodically.

Countries faced by regionally based pluralistic divisions have two divergent responses to centrifugal forces available to them. One approach, to retain as much power as possible at the center, impedes the development of regional, and potentially secessionist, power bases. The contrasting approach, to concede a degree of autonomy to regionally based ethnic or religious groups, imparts to them a belief that they control their own destinies, which thereby gives them a stake in the national system as well. Lebanon has chosen the centralized approach, and consequently most of Lebanon's government apparatus is located in Beirut.[41] Given its small geographical size and its relatively small population, a decentralized system is probably not feasible. Moreover, additional concessions to regional-confessional interests would pose serious risks to national viability.

Despite the fact that power in the Lebanese political system is centralized, the system has trace elements of decentralization and deconcentration.[42] The country is divided into the five provinces (muhafazat) of Beirut, Bekaa, Mount Lebanon, North Lebanon, and South Lebanon. Each of these has a governor (muhafiz) assigned to it as the representative of the central government. Working closely with the Minister of Interior, he oversees the implementation of government policy at the provincial level and is also responsible for the maintenance of law and order. Consistent with the major themes of Lebanese political culture, his most important function is to serve as a conciliator at the provincial level among competing individuals, clans, confessional communities, political factions, and localities. To facilitate his effectiveness as a conciliator, the governor is rarely someone who is native to that area or even someone who is a member of the predominant confessional communities of the province. For example, a Sunni would not generally be named as governor of North Lebanon and a Maronite would not be a likely candidate for Mount Lebanon.

Although the Lebanese armed forces are not very large, numbering about 15,000 men,[43] or very well equipped, they have often exerted a positive influence on interconfessional relations. Lebanese generally consider the army to be the national institution with the best record for peaceful interconfessional relations.[44] The armed forces make an effort to keep a rough balance between Christians and Muslims among rank-and-file soldiers, and top officer posts are carefully distributed among the religious groups. Moreover, the post of Commander of the Armed Forces is reserved for a Maronite, and the Minister of Defense position is generally assigned to a Druze and only rarely given to a Christian.

On several occasions the military managed to assist with the maintenance of a national equilibrium during times of crisis. In 1958 President Chamoun ordered the Commander of the Armed Forces, General Fuad Chehab, to back the government and put down the insurrection. But Chehab permitted the army to play only a carefully circumscribed role for fear that full involvement by the army might create a Muslim–Christian split within the army, and also because he believed that President Chamoun was disrupting the country's confessional equilibrium to the advantage of the Christian half of the population. If General Chehab, a Maronite, had brought the full force of the army against the predominantly Muslim insurrectionists, irreparable damage might have been done to Christian–Muslim relations. After the 1969 crisis over the Palestinian commandos had dragged on for several months, giving rise to increased tensions between Lebanon's Christians and Muslims, the army was able to work out a settlement with commando leaders. In this intervention the army again assisted with the settlement of a political crisis that had decidedly confessional overtones.

Although military leaders and the army have usually contributed to the maintenance of internal stability and balance between the confessional communities, one striking instance can be cited of what might appear to be confessionally partisan action by an army commander when General Emile Bustani refused to accept the instructions of Premier Rachid Karami in 1967 to open a front with Israel during the Six Day War.[45] A Maronite military leader thereby acted contrary to the wishes of the Sunni Premier on an issue that sharply divided Christians and Muslims in Lebanon. More recently, when extensive fighting broke out between the army and the Palestinian commandos in May 1973, some Muslim (particularly Sunni) backers of the commando movement believed that the Army was being exploited in partisan fashion by the Maronite President and the Maronite army commander to undermine the Arab struggle against Israel.

Two aspects of the Lebanese legal system have important implications for intercommunity relations and the confessional structure of the sociopolitical order. First, a legal prohibition exists against any organization or individual writing, saying, or doing anything that has the object or effect of arousing confessional conflict. Any individual declared guilty of this offense is subject to a fine, imprisonment, and loss of certain civil rights. A person found to be a member of such a prohibited organization is subject to both a fine and imprisonment.[46] We have discussed the various kinds of social and political constraints that inhibit provocative activities, and these are undoubtedly much more important means for maintaining peaceful coexistence among the communities than these provisions of the penal code. Nevertheless, these laws are invoked on occasion to control the activities of organizations and individuals who are beyond the reach of nonlegal restraints. For instance, in 1972 the public prosecutor charged four fanatical young Christians with having formed an illegal organization called the Association for the Worldwide Unification of Christianity, which incited confessional strife through its publications, and the association was subsequently forced to disband.[47]

Another aspect of the legal system, namely, the management of personal status issues, has more profound implications for sectarianism in Lebanon. As already described in Chapter 3, the autonomy of the confessional communities gains most explicit recognition in the jurisdiction they are accorded over personal status law, which covers such sensitive and far-reaching subjects as marriage, divorce, inheritance, and adoption. Each of the recognized confessional communities has the right to "legislate" personal status laws for its own members and to handle all related judicial cases, and the communities have thus become legal entities. Each Lebanese citizen is registered with the state as being a member of a particular religious community, and he is subject to the personal status laws and courts of that community. Following a marriage, personal status issues of the couple are governed by the religious body that performed the marriage. Although most communities allow for appeal of cases to higher religious authorities or to religious appeal courts, no case relating to personal status can be dealt with by a civil court, either initially or on appeal. If uncertainty arises regarding whether the issue under dispute is actually a personal status issue or if there is confusion as to which religious court has jurisdiction over a case, the *Cour de Cassation* can make the relevant determinations, but that is the extent of the role of civil courts. The personal status laws for the three Muslim communities, namely, the Sunnis, the Shiites, and the Druze, were enacted by parliament from texts of laws referred to it by the leaders of the three communities. No legislation embodies the personal status laws for the various Christian communities, but in 1951 at the request of the government each community codified its own laws.[48] Another somewhat bizarre feature of Lebanon's system for handling personal status issues is that the final determination of some cases is made by non-Lebanese residing in distant places. Although no case before one of the Muslim courts can go beyond an appeal court in Lebanon, Maronite cases can be appealed to the Vatican in Rome, and the Greek Catholic and Greek Orthodox cases can go to their respective patriarchates in Damascus.

In many other pluralistic societies, and Ghana is a suitable example, the disparate laws governing personal status issues for the society's constituent communities remain uncodified and tend to evolve over time, adjusting themselves to the changing social and economic environment of the developing state. In Lebanon, however, personal status laws have sacred overtones, and modification and evolution are hardly compatible with a belief in their divine origins. Although some evidence suggests that marginal accommodation among the different systems is occurring through the encroachment of civil on religious law,[49] change is barely perceptible. Differences, for instance, between Catholics and Muslims regarding the propriety of divorce or the differing rights and obligations of women, are likely to persist for a long time.

Other countries manage to function reasonably well despite some discrepancies among their constituent religious or ethnic groups over issues relating to personal status. In Lebanon, however, several religious communities each hold absolute jurisdiction over the personal status affairs of the members of their communities. Religious marriage and religious divorce do not merely supplement civil marriage and divorce; Lebanon has no civil marriage or divorce. This makes life difficult for atheists or others who refuse to be identified with the legally recognized confessional communities, and most significantly, the nonexistence of civil marriage inhibits interconfessional marriage. Although a Muslim man and a Christian woman can marry in a Muslim ceremony, under Muslim law a Muslim woman cannot marry a Christian man. Christian groups generally require that both man and woman be members of the same sect.

In the past the question of the breadth of jurisdiction of the religious courts has aroused considerable controversy, as it did in 1952 when the lawyers' guild went on strike to protest a planned extension of the jurisdiction of Christian courts. In recent years, however, the principle of community autonomy in handling personal status issues has not provoked much public debate, with the exception of some dissatisfaction with the exclusive control of marriage by the religious communities. Opposition to civil marriage provides ground upon which religious leaders from all faiths can unite, constituting something of an intercommunity pressure group, as they did in countering the lawyers in 1952. The interest of religious leaders in preserving their control over marriage includes their general aversion to interconfessional marriage. A few religious leaders support the introduction of civil marriage,[50] and it seems that a majority of the population favors it as well, not the abolition of religious marriage but the offering of civil marriage as an alternative for nonbelievers or for interfaith marriages. In a recent al-Nahar public opinion poll, two-thirds favored Lebanon's adoption of civil marriage.[51]

Community autonomy in legislating and adjudicating matters relating to personal status tends to strengthen confessional identities and rigidify key differences in both belief and life style among the communities. Moreover, it appears to be increasingly apparent to the Lebanese public that the introduction of civil marriage could help relieve some of the inflexibility inherent in the current system and, in turn, enhance intercommunity accommodation. Nevertheless, this is an innovation to which many of the pillars of the confessional system remain adamantly opposed. It seems unlikely that civil marriage or any other significant modification in the management of personal status issues will be adopted within the next several years.

THE DYNAMICS OF POLITICAL ACTION

Public interest in politics in Lebanon runs very high. A majority of the respondents in our survey of one thousand Lebanese, 62 percent, described themselves as moderately or very interested in politics, and 72 percent indicated that they frequently discuss politics with friends. Moreover, an astonishingly high proportion of those interviewed correctly identified various political office holders: 99 percent knew the president, 98 percent the premier, 94 percent the speaker of parliament, and 69 percent knew all the deputies representing their constituency in parliament.

To a great extent, interest in politics derives from the intensity of confessional competition in the political arena. Although it is tempting and dangerous to overemphasize the impact of confessional identity on political behavior, careful assessment of the Lebanese social and political system inevitably leads one to conclude that confessional identity is the most important single factor differentiating political attitudes and shaping political behavior. A variety of interwoven factors, some of which have no relationship to religious group membership, mold the political attitudes and behavior of particular individuals. Many Lebanese do not let their confessional identity or the interests of their confessional group influence their political behavior whatsoever. Generally, however, confessional factors loom large.

The fact that representation within parliament is distributed proportionally among confessional groups reflects the importance accorded this factor by those who shape the electoral laws. Equally significant, the Lebanese political system's confessional arithmetic divides the top three political posts (president, premier, and speaker) among the three largest confessional groups, and balances the membership of the cabinet between Muslims and Christians, as well as among the various sectarian subgroups. Although the results of our survey showed that some aspects of the confessional system in Lebanon were distasteful to the respondents, there was fairly widespread agreement that parliamentary representation should continue to be defined in confessional terms. In answer to a question regarding possible reforms to the present system, 60 percent favored retention of confessional representation and only 31 percent advocated abolition of the system. Survey results also demonstrated concurrence that competition between confessional groups is an observable phenomenon in Lebanon; eighty percent of those surveyed believed that such competition exists.

The political salience of confessional identity derives largely from the differing political values held by the various confessional communities. Before turning to specific political issues upon which confessional groups tend to disagree, it is important to consider differences in general orientation that help explain discord on particular questions. On no question in our survey did Muslim and Christian opinion divide completely, and Christians and Muslims gave similar responses to many questions. But on several questions the distribution of responses articulated by members of these two confessional blocs tended to diverge, and in each of the cases cited these variances are at least at the .01 level of significance using the Chi square test. For instance, Muslims often portray more negative attitudes toward the Lebanese state and the government. Although the 1958 civil war represented the postindependence high point of Muslim alienation and it has never reached that level since, our survey does indicate consistent contemporary Christian–Muslim disagreement in their assessment of Lebanon and its government. While two-thirds of the Christians in the sample of one thousand did not believe that the government is responding adequately to the country's needs, as many as four-fifths of the Muslims expressed the same negative evaluation. Although 51 percent of the Christians were either partially or completely positive about current government policies, only 31 percent of the Muslims agreed with them. Muslims were also less inclined to support the government when there was a conflict between their locality and the government, and they were slightly more inclined than the Christians to believe that there are occasions upon which it is justifiable to break the law, particularly when they considered a law unjust or discriminatory.

Another important and striking difference between Christians and Muslims in their general political orientations relates to attitudes vis-à-vis the Arab world.[52] Those interviewed were asked to rank the following in terms of their importance to them personally: the locality they come from, their religious sect, Lebanon, the Arab nation, and their extended family. Sixty two percent of the Christians put Lebanon first out of these five options, while only 34 percent of the Muslims placed Lebanon first; 30 percent of the Muslims ranked the Arab nation first, while only 8 percent of the Christians did so. When asked which two persons (whether living or dead) they most admire, 43 percent of the Christian respondents named a Christian Lebanese political figure, with former President Camille Chamoun being the individual most frequently cited. Only 13 percent of the Muslims chose a Christian Lebanese political leader. They tended to state a preference for Muslim leaders, with Gamal Abdul Nasser being cited by 33 percent. Only 5 percent of the Christians replied that Nasser was the man they most admired. When respondents were asked to indicate with which other country they believed Lebanon had the most in common, 40 percent of the Muslims answered Syria or another Arab state, while the Christians were more inclined to mention a European country like France or Switzerland, with only 18 percent mentioning an Arab country.

Although on the questions cited above Christian–Muslim differences are invariably greater than divergences among Christian subgroups or among Muslim subgroups, important variances between these subgroups nevertheless exist. The most striking Muslim–Christian dichotomies generally come between the Sunnis and the Maronites, the distinctions among the other confessional groups being somewhat less marked. For instance, those surveyed were asked to rank the following in terms of the extent to which they constituted a source of personal pride: residence in their locality, membership in their sect, Lebanese citizenship, and being an Arab. Forty-nine percent of the Sunnis ranked "being an Arab" first, while only 5 percent of the Maronites did so. The Shiite percentage was identical with the Sunnis,[53] but the other major groups fell in the middle with following percentages of respondents ranking "being an Arab" first: Greek Catholic, 17 percent; Greek Orthodox, 17 percent; Druze, 20 percent.

In terms of specific policy issues that divided Christians and Muslims, mention has already been made in the discussion of the 1969 crisis of Christian–Muslim differences regarding the commandos and Lebanon's stance vis-à-vis Israel. When asked what is the most important problem Lebanon faces today, most respondents, 49 percent of the total sample (52 percent of the Muslims and 46 percent of the Christians), specified Israel/Palestine. Despite this general consensus on the significance of the Israel/Palestine problem, the question of how Lebanon should respond to the problem evokes divergent responses with Muslims generally advocating a more militant pro-commando and anti-Israeli position. Consistent with this stance, Muslim political leaders usually favor strengthening the Lebanese army to improve its defensive capabilities against Israel, including the introduction of military conscription.

Muslim respondents seem to be more negatively disposed to the existing confessional formulae. Sixty five percent of the Muslims interviewed opposed the current reservation under the National Pact of the three top political posts for the three most numerous confessional communities, as compared with 44 percent of the Christians. Regarding the confessional division of parliamentary seats, Muslim opposition (45 percent) came to approximately twice that of Christian opposition (21 percent). Although a majority of Christians surveyed favored retention of the system under which civil service posts are divided proportionally among the confessional communities, a clear majority of Muslims disapproved of the system, even though its initial intention had been to increase the proportion of Muslims in the bureaucracy.

Although the government has given more attention to economic and educational disparities since 1958, the discussion in Chapter 3 showed the extent to which regional and sectarian inequalities still exist. Being the more disadvantaged group, the Muslims accord greater import to equalization. One question in the survey asked whether it is proper for the government to take tax moneys from the rich areas of Lebanon and use them for development projects in the poorer areas. Seventy nine percent of the Muslims said that this should be common practice; 63 percent of the Christians agreed with them. In response to another question, the Muslim respondents were somewhat more inclined than the Christians to see economic competition as constituting the principal cause of confessional conflict. Consistent with Muslim concern over creating greater socioeconomic equality, Muslims also have tended to be the more active supporters of government investment in the state education system.

Earlier in this chapter we looked at certain types of parliamentary activity as one index of confessional cooperation and conflict in the political arena. Ideally, a systematic analysis of parliamentary voting patterns would provide a concrete basis for determining patterns and historical trends of interconfessional political relations within parliament. Unfortunately, since most votes are unanimous or nearly unanimous because the political bargaining precedes the voting, little data of value can be gleaned from this source. Moreover, most voting takes place by secret ballot, so that it is difficult to assess voting behavior in confessional terms. We have, however, analyzed a few parliamentary ballots where a real contest occurred and where it was possible to determine the way individual parliamentarians voted. In the vote of confidence for the new cabinet installed following the 1964 parliamentary elections, thirty three out of the ninety nine deputies voted against the new cabinet. While the overall ratio of Christians to Muslims in parliament is six to five, in this vote of confidence twenty Christians voted with the opposition along with thirteen Muslims, meaning that a slightly higher proportion of Christians voted against the government than for the government, while the reverse was the case for the Muslims. More significantly, only three out of twenty Sunni members opposed the government, while fourteen out of a total of thirty Maronite members voted against the government.[54] In the vote of confidence following the 1968 parliamentary elections, the opposition consisted of twenty four Christians and only six Muslims. Seventeen out of thirty Maronite members voted against the government, but only one Sunni out of twenty did so.[55] Both of these votes reflect the fact that the Chehabist cabinets in power from 1958 to 1970 tended to have more Christian (particularly Maronite) opponents than Muslims. Nevertheless, it is clear that both the government supporters and the opposition included substantial members of both Christians and Muslims.

Previous portions of this chapter have emphasized the extent to which both political competition and divisions of political opinion are also evident within particular confessional subgroups. During the 1958 civil war, for instance, the Druze and Armenian communities were sharply divided internally between progovernment and antigovernment sides. Contests for president, premier, and speaker also present arenas for intracommunity political competition. Intracommunity political competition at the local level naturally comes most openly during parliamentary elections, since candidates from within the same confessional community contest directly against each other. An analysis of patterns of violence that occur during parliamentary elections manifests the intensity of this intracommunity competition. Our assessment of such electoral violence is based upon cases of fighting (either armed or unarmed) between individuals or between groups, as reported in *L'Orient* for the 1968 elections and in *L'Orient-Le Jour* and *The Daily Star*, Beirut daily newspapers, for the 1972 elections. In 1968 the newspapers reported fifteen cases of such violence, thirteen of which involved fighting between supporters of two candidates who were members of the same confessional community. In most instances these supporters, that is, the antagonists, came from the same confessional community as well. In the remaining two cases the fighting took place between supporters of Christian candidates coming from different sects. In no case was there violence between supporters of a Christian candidate and those of a Muslim candidate. A similar pattern occurred in 1972, although with some variation. Out of a total of twenty four instances of reported violence, eighteen involved armed or unarmed fighting between supporters of candidates from the same confessional community, and three others resulted from conflict among Muslims of different sects or among Christians of different sects; for example, between the supporters of a Greek Catholic candidate and a Maronite candidate. The remaining three took place between Muslims on one side and Christians on the other. One of these, a clash between Maronites and Druze, led to the deaths of several security officers who tried to control the fighting. There is no question that the electoral system that pits a candidate against another member of his own confessional community contributes to this pattern of intracommunity, as contrasted with intercommunity, political conflict. Nevertheless, such violence attests to the intensity of this competition, and suggests the extent to which intracommunity political contests are a very important aspect of competitive political behavior in Lebanon.

The active role in politics played by religious leaders and religious organizations reflects and reinforces the importance of sectarianism to politics in Lebanon. In some cases religious officials involve themselves in politics in the same manner and on the same basis as laymen do, like the Maronite priest who is currently a member of parliament. On certain issues religious leaders from all faiths have formed their own interest group to promote their clerical and ecclesiastical prerogatives in the face of pressures exerted by lay groups. For instance, whenever consideration is given to the introduction of civil marriage or the curtailment of the role of religious courts in handling personal status matters, religious officials of all faiths join forces, as they did in 1952, to withstand the assault on their authority. It is more common, however, for intervention by ecclesiastical authorities and religious organizations to occur when the special interests of their constituents are at stake, or when an issue arises that puts confessional groups at odds with one another, such as controversies relating to Arab nationalism. In March 1974 Imam Moussa Sadre, President of the Higher Shiite Islamic Council, organized a mass rally of 100,000 Shiites (15,000 of whom were armed with rifles) to demand more government jobs and increased government attention to the rights and welfare of Lebanon's Shiites. A Maronite bishop has recently asserted that the Maronite patriarch has as much, if not more, of an obligation to defend Lebanon as the government does, and that he is not merely a religious leader but a civil leader as well, with a responsibility to help point the state in the right direction.[56]

Activities during the 1970 presidential elections offer typical illustrations of the involvement of religious leaders and organizations in politics. During the election period, parliamentarians backing particular candidates often consulted religious leaders in an attempt to refine their strategy or broaden their support. For instance, members of the Kataeb executive bureau met with the president of the Council of the Shiite community, Imam Moussa Sadre, in their efforts to promote Pierre Gemayel's candidacy. In the middle of the election period the Sunni Grand Mufti organized a meeting of leading Sunni politicians and representatives of Sunni organizations in an apparent effort to coordinate electoral strategy. The most overt involvement came on the part of the then Maronite Patriarch, Monseigneur Butros-Bulos Meouchy, who called a meeting of heads of all the Christian communities to discuss the election. The communique released by the Patriarch after the meeting constituted a sharp attack on the candidacy of General Chehab and expressed grave concern over the position a future president might take regarding the Palestinian commandos, whose activities he saw as a threat to Lebanon's viability. Despite efforts by the Greek Catholic Patriarch to promote a reconciliation between Chehab and the Maronite Patriarch,[57] the newspaper that was considered to voice the Patriarch's views, Nida al Watan, continued its strong opposition to the Chehabist position in the election.

Although religious leaders are generally motivated by parochial considerations in their political interventions, more disinterested interventions have also occurred. In the 1958 civil war the Maronite Patriarch, Monseigneur Butros-Bulos Meouchy, was outspokenly critical of the activities and stance of

Maronite President Camille Chamoun, who was perceived by most Maronites as having staunchly defended their interests in the face of a grave threat posed by Sunni Arab nationalists. The Patriarch's intervention in that crisis was one of the boldest and most influential actions taken by any religious figure in Lebanon. In May 1970, Imam Moussa Sadre organized an extremely effective general strike in Lebanon to dramatize to the government the plight of the population of southern Lebanon vis-à-vis the Israeli military threat.[58] If the government had not responded by establishing a Council for South Lebanon and allocating L.L. 30 million for special projects in the south, Imam Sadre had planned to have his followers occupy the presidential palace. Although Imam Sadre was promoting the interests of the Shiites, who constitute a majority of the southern population, in that particular instance the residents of the south, regardless of their religious identification, recognized him as their spokesman. He served the broader role of regional leader rather than merely that of a sectarian spokesman. During the army–commando crisis of 1973 religious leaders as a group acted as a restraining and conciliating force.

Family and clan loyalties also play an important role in Lebanese politics. Clan-based politics does not imply political competition that disregards confessional boundaries, since members of a particular extended family or clan are almost invariably members of the same confessional community. When competition occurs within a single confessional community, as it tends to during parliamentary elections, family units generally constitute the most important groups competing with one another. Particularly at the local level and in the rural areas, the family often serves as the bargaining unit in the competition for political support.[59] To seek family or clan support in the Lebanese context is not a matter of a few votes. For instance, two of the clans in Zghorta represent approximately 1500 and 1000 votes, respectively.[60] Political competition between clans both contributes to and is a function of the factionalism and feuds which are so pervasive in rural Lebanon.

Family and clan identities play an important role in parliamentary elections even in cities because urban migrants often maintain registration in their locality of origin rather than shift it to their place of urban residence, and this is often true even of second- and third-generation urban migrants. Among those questioned in our survey, one-third of those living in Beirut and Tripoli indicated that they vote in their locality of origin rather than in Beirut or Tripoli where they are resident. Most candidates in the 1972 parliamentary elections succeeded in building at least part of their electoral support along kinship lines, but in some places intrafamily factions developed as a result of the emergence of competing candidates within the same family, as was true, for instance, of the Frangieh family in Zghorta. As an indication of the intensity of some intrafamily political conflict, four of the cases of political violence during the 1972 parliamentary elections cited above and three of the cases referred to in 1968 involved intrafamily violence.

At times political competition between clans is projected to the national scene, as in the 1930s and 1940s when the Khouri and Edde clans both sought the presidency. The extent to which parliamentary seats are "inherited" along family lines provides additional manifestation of the importance of kinship ties. For instance, during some periods almost one-fourth of the members of parliament have "inherited" their parliamentary seats from older members of their families.[61]

Although it is legitimate to accord family loyalties a high position among the political values of the Lebanese citizen, one must also be wary of exaggerating the importance of family factors. In our survey 37 percent of those interviewed stated that their voting behavior consistently conforms to that of other members of their extended family. This figure was significantly lower, however, among younger voters and among urban voters, implying that family loyalties are on the decline as influencers of political behavior. Fuad Khuri's study of two suburbs of Beirut also shows that the invocation of family loyalties in political contests is sometimes only a camouflaged appeal to confessional interests.[62]

Regional loyalties are also evident as motives for political action. This has been clear in the case of the population of southern Lebanon, who feel particularly vulnerable to Israeli raids against commando concentrations in the south; and those from the south are particularly sensitive to the issue of whether the Palestinian commandos should be accorded freedom of movement. Following a clash in the south in 1969 between commando units and the Lebanese army, which was trying to curtail commando activities, Shiites, Greek Orthodox, and Druze residents of Hasbaya and Marjayoun joined in a demonstration to show their support for the Lebanese army. This was followed by an interfaith delegation of religious leaders calling on army leaders to indicate their support of the army. The period of Israeli attacks on the south in 1972 similarly brought forth expressions of interconfessional regional ties.

As an illustration of the subtle tension between regional and confessional identities, an interesting debate took place in October 1972 among Shiite parliamentarians over whether, in considering the threats facing them from the commandos and the Israelis, they should meet as Shiite deputies alone, or whether an intercommunity gathering of all parliamentarians from the south should consider the situation from a regional perspective. Some of the Shiite parliamentarians argued for a confessionally based gathering, while others contended that regional interests superseded confessional interests, at least in this instance.[63]

The existence of geographically defined parliamentary constituencies provides additional evidence of the degree to which local and regional interests are thought important. Some proponents of electoral reform have proposed a single large constituency for the whole of Lebanon, but this concept has not gained much popularity. Mention has also been made of the attempt to attain a semblance of balanced regional representation when cabinets are named. The fact that parliamentary electoral competition comes largely on an intracommunity basis helps reduce the importance of confessional conflict as a barrier to regional solidarity. For instance, in explaining the alliance he formed with a powerful Greek Catholic politician from the Bekaa, Shiite Sabri Hamade said that they shared a common interest in the welfare of the Bekaa and that, as members of different confessional communities, they were not competitors for either a parliamentary seat or for a cabinet position.[64]

A sense of common regional interest also contributes to the formation of many parliamentary blocs. Following the 1964 election five out of eleven parliamentary blocs consisted of deputies representing a single province. Following the 1968 election three of ten blocs were of this nature, and following the 1972 election six out of the twelve blocs were regionally defined. In certain cases the blocs are both regionally and confessionally homogeneous, and here regional and confessional interests are mutually supportive.

Economic status and occupational identity also play important roles as motivators of political behavior, although they do not compare in significance to confessional identity. The discussion of trade unions in Chapter 3 indicated their general weakness and the relative lack of class consciousness to sustain them. Labor federations frequently appeal to the government to check the rise in the cost of living, to improve the social security system, or to make other policy changes favorable to their members, but these requests usually have little impact. Moreover, trade unions only infrequently back particular political candidates or parties in elections, and they rarely conduct active lobbying programs or engage in strikes against the government.[65] Strikes with political implications by tobacco growers and by teachers in 1973 suggest, however, that activity by labor organizations may in time gain new importance. A recent microstudy of small businessmen's associations in Zahleh underscores this possibility of increasing political activism of an interconfessional nature by economic interest groups.[66]

Professional associations for the most part lack a political orientation, although mention can and should be made of instances of strikes organized by such associations; on one occasion by the lawyers' association and on another by a section of the engineers' association. This is not to imply that professional people are not politically active. For example, over half of the members of parliament elected in 1972 were lawyers, doctors, engineers, or members of other professions.[67] But professional people who become politically active generally do so as individuals and represent their regional, family, confessional, or ideological interests more than their professional interests. Insofar as trade union and professional associations tend to be interconfessional in membership and usually contain members from a variety of geographical locations and family origins, their limited political involvement leaves the field open to those groupings whose memberships are more heavily dependent upon primordial attachments. Nevertheless, the strength and importance of professional associations is gradually increasing and they can be expected to play a greater political role in the future.

Student organizations tend to be active and politicized, and frequent student strikes, occasionally violent, have been organized in recent years at all five Lebanese universities. The issues involved in these strikes sometimes have relevance only to the institution itself, but strikes frequently have political overtones. For instance, a strike by students at Lebanese University in 1972 that lasted several weeks focused on student demands for reformulation of government policy regarding higher education.

Class consciousness of an interconfessional nature is muted and is not a predominant factor in Lebanese politics. There is, however, one major exception to this statement, and that is among the sociopolitical elite. Although this elite is no longer confined to feudal landlords and wealthy urban businessmen, to a remarkable degree, the political elite still share comparable socioeconomic status and life styles.[68] They have many common interests and needs, despite their membership in different confessional communities. Georges Naccache, at that time editor of *L'Orient*, wrote in 1952 that Lebanon was governed by "la dictature d'un Club de Notables."[69] Some analysts have asserted that these cohesive relations and cooperation are primarily dictated by a need among elite members to exchange favors with each other in order for each to attain their individual political ends.[70] While this is undoubtedly an important factor, shared social and economic interests also lead the political elite to act cohesively to attain their common ends. Even when their political orientations and interests differ, they share a common need for the system to be preserved.

Far from engendering class conflict within Lebanese society, this cohesion among the political elite constitutes a critical factor in the maintenance of general sociopolitical stability. Each member of the political elite has a network of clients attached to him. As their patron he nurtures and sustains their allegiance through the services he provides or even through the money he gives: they in turn follow his political directives.[71] Although there may be limited horizontal cohesion within the society at large, the vertical strands of allegiances based on client-patron relations and the cohesion and accommodation that govern, on a horizontal plane, the relationships within the political elite provide a relatively stable and well-articulated framework for the Lebanese sociopolitical order.[72]

This notion can be usefully elaborated by introducing the concept of the *za'im*, the Arabic term for patron. Arnold Hottinger portrays the relationship between the *za'im* and his followers in the following fashion:

> It appears that in peacetime a *za'im* is the recognized leader of a community who has the power to speak for his clients as a group or as individuals, who is expected to take action in their and in his interest whenever necessary. In peacetime he is the man to whom an individual of a certain traditional outlook in life, will go if he has business to transact with somebody stronger than himself, and above all, with the government. The *za'im* may also have some business relationship with his clients, as landlord, as employer, or as someone who obtains employment for a client through intercession with a third party with whom the *za'im* may be involved in some way. The *za'im* will protect "his" clients and will foster his own interests at the same time as theirs.[73]

Ties of fealty, much like their feudal antecedents, cement the system of za'imship.[74]

A *za'im* can be either a rural landlord or an urban political boss.[75] A high-status *za'im* generally seeks a seat in parliament or even a cabinet post, since such positions offer special access to patronage and money for his followers. But the sociopolitical structure of patron-client relations is much more complex than merely that between parliamentarians and their supporters. A lower status *za'im* generally does not have sufficient status or support to seek a parliamentary seat, but he can bargain with higher level *za'ims*, whom he will support in an election. Considerable status and power differentiation is evident among parliamentarians as well, with parliamentarians of lesser status becoming clients of higher status parliamentarians. This finds expression in the formation of parliamentary blocs, with the bloc leader being the patron of those parliamentarians who join his bloc. Although a parliamentary seat or a cabinet post provides important underpinning to a *za'im's* status, powerful *za'ims* are able to maintain the support of their clients even if they remain outside of parliament for a few years. Powerful *za'ims* can also arrange to have their surrogates named to cabinet posts, and thereby reap patronage and financial benefits without having the responsibility of heading a government ministry.

At the grass-roots level, political patron-client relationships tend to reinforce confessional differentiation rather than forge interconfessional links. Although instances can be cited of local *za'ims* building some of their power base upon support from members of other confessional communities, most of a *za'im's* clients are generally members of his own religious group. But at a higher level of social and political interaction, political notables serve important integrative functions. Samir Khalaf refers to *za'ims* as "tension managers,"[76] who provide not only informal adjudication of conflicts among the individuals or family groups constituting their clientele, but also mediation to resolve conflicts that cross confessional boundaries. The interconfessional coalitions forged between *za'ims* for electoral or other purposes and the attachment of local *za'ims* to a higher status *za'im*, who is often from a different sect, constitute even more important interconfessional linkages. Confessionally differentiated groups of clients thereby become structurally integrated by means of their leaders at higher levels. Such forums as parliament and cabinet permit interest aggregation among the *za'ims* collected there and the clients they represent.[77] The common socioeconomic status that the *za'ims* or the political elite share, strengthen the ties which link them. Fuad Khouri sees the system of *za'imship* as an "instrument of integration, linking ordinary citizens to the national polity at large."[78]

One final factor influencing the dynamics of political activity in Lebanon needs to be mentioned, and that is the role played by foreign governments, both Arab and non-Arab. Hardly a political event occurs in Lebanon that is not influenced by foreign pressures. During the 1970 presidential election campaign, various Muslim political leaders visited Cairo and Damascus to discuss electoral strategy.[79] In the 1969 conflict with the commandos, President Nasser of Egypt mediated between the two sides, and final agreement was reached as a result of negotiations conducted in Cairo. Premier-designate

Rachid Karami even consulted with President Nasser over the composition of the cabinet he tried to form prior to the settlement. Foreign involvement is thus not always the result of foreign meddling; Lebanese political leaders frequently seek the advice and assistance of foreign statesmen in resolving domestic political issues. This foreign involvement is not unrelated to the confessional component in Lebanese politics because Western influence generally has the greatest impact on Christian leaders, while Muslim political leaders tend to be more responsive to influence exerted by other Arab states. The 1958 civil war serves as the most classic example of Western powers backing the predominantly Christian faction and various Arab states providing military and political backing to the predominantly Muslim insurgents.

We cannot posit a simple answer to the question of the basis of political behavior in Lebanon. Confessional factors inform political configurations in a variety of ways, but sectarian considerations also interplay with intercommunity political cooperation and intracommunity political competition. Moreover, interests deriving from the needs of family, region, and socioeconomic class also motivate political actors. Insofar as some sections of Lebanese society consider the welfare of the Arab world to be important, Pan-Arab interests enter into consideration as well. The relative importance accorded these various factors depends upon the issue being considered, the circumstances, and the political actors involved. Overall, however, confessional factors clearly predominate.

NOTES

1. For descriptions of the Lebanese political system, see Michael C. Hudson, *The Precarious Republic* (New York: Random House, 1968); Charles Rizk, *Le Régime Politique Libanais* (Paris: Librairie Générale de Droit et de Jurisprudence, 1966); Leonard Binder, editor, *Politics in Lebanon* (New York: Wiley, 1966); Iliya Harik, *Man Yaḥkum Lubnān (Who Rules Lebanon)*, (Beirut: al-Nahār, 1972); and Hasan al-Hasan, *al-Qānūn al-Dustūrī fī Lubnān (Constitutional Law and the Constitution in Lebanon)*, (Beirut: Dār Maktabat al-Hayāt, 1963).
2. Elie A. Salem, *Modernization Without Revolution: Lebanon's Experience* (Bloomington: Indiana University Press, 1973), pp. 58–59.
3. This seems to be one of several indications that President Frangieh is making subtle but real changes in the role and image of the presidency, moving it more toward a publicly recognized seat of power, publicly responsible for the policies the incumbent formulates.
4. Kamāl Jumblatt, *Haqīqat al-Thawrat al-Lubnāniyyah (The Truth about the Lebanese Revolution)*, (Beirut: Dār al-Nashr al-'Arabiyyah, 1959), p. 43.
5. *Al-Hahār*, June 10, 1964.

6. The voting is by secret ballot, so that there may be some slight discrepancy between these figures and actual voting patterns, but most parliamentarians indicated how they voted so that the figures are a good if not a perfect reflection of actual voting. Based on election results in *L'Orient*, August 17, 1970, p. 1; and *al-Nahār*, August 18, 1970, p. 7, and August 19, 1970, p. 2.

7. Bishara al-Khuri, the first president of independent Lebanon indicates in his memoirs that one reason he rotated the position among various families was to obtain maximum breadth of Sunni support for his government, and in turn draw as broad a cross-section of the Sunni community as possible into intimate involvement with the affairs of state. See Bishara al-Khuri, *Ḥaqā'iq Lubnāniyyah (Lebanese Truths)* Vol. 3, (Beirut: Awrāq Lubnāniyyah), p. 338.

8. *L'Orient-Le Jour*, May 24, May 25, and May 28, 1972.

9. Halim Faris Fayyad, "The Effects of Sectarianism on Lebanese Administration," American University of Beirut, unpublished M.A. Thesis, 1956, p. 80.

10. Malcolm H. Kerr, "Political Decision Making in a Confessional Democracy," in Binder, *Politics in Lebanon*, op. cit., p. 197.

11. Ralph E. Crow, "Parliament in the Lebanese Political System," in Allan Kornberg and Lloyd D. Musolf, eds., *Legislatures in Developmental Perspective* (Durham: Duke University Press, 1970), p. 294. For the meaning of urgent and double urgent legislation, see Article 58 of the Constitution, and Article 86 and 88 of the Internal Rules of the Chamber.

12. "Twelve different religious communities, Christian and Muslim, coexist (in Lebanon) by virtue of a social contract, of which their representation in parliament is the political expression." Rizk, op. cit., p. 3.

13. This point is reiterated in various portions of Michel Chiha, *Politique Intérieure* (Beirut: Trident, 1964).

14. Marun Y. Kisirwani, "Attitudes and Behavior of Lebanese Bureaucrats: A Study in Administrative Corruption," unpublished PH.D. Diss., University of Indiana, 1971, pp. 166 and 201.

15. *Al-Nahār*, July 27, 1971. See also Harik, op. cit., p. 67.

16. *Al-Anwār*, August 13, 1972, p. 3; *al-Nahār*, August 20, 1972, p. 2; and *al-Anwār*, August 27, 1972, pp. 2 and 8.

17. *L'Orient-Le Jour* and *Daily Star*, April 19, 1972.

18. *L'Orient-Le Jour*, supplement, February 12–18, 1972, p. iv.

19. Thirteen percent in 1951; 24 percent in 1953; 18 percent in 1957; 35 percent in 1960; 31 percent in 1964; 37 percent in 1968; and 39 percent in 1972. Data derived from *L'Orient-Le Jour*, April 14, 1972, April 18, 1972, April 22, 1972, April 25, 1972, and April 28, 1972; Camille Chehab; "Les Elections Legislatives de 1968," Beirut, 1968, mimeographed; Camille Chehab, "Les Elections Legislatives de 1964," Beirut, 1964, mimeographed; Abdo I. Baaklini, "Legislatures and Political Development: Lebanon 1840–1970," State University of New York at Albany, unpublished PH.D. Diss., 1972, pp. 252–253; and Michael W. Suleiman, *Political Parties in Lebanon* (Ithaca, N.Y.: Cornell University Press, 1967), p. 265. See also Jalal Zuwiyya, *The Parliamentary Election of Lebanon, 1968* (Leiden: E. J. Brill, 1972), pp. 92–94.

20. For a fuller discussion of political parties, see Suleiman, op. cit., pp. 168–202; and a series of articles that appeared in *The Arab World Weekly*, from February 1, 1969 to April 5, 1969.

21. For an interesting categorization of the predominantly Christian parties in these terms, see Karim Pakradouni, "Unité et Diversité des Partis de Droite," *Le Monde*, December 22, 1972, p. 20.

22 For statements of Kataeb ideology, see Pierre Gemayel, *Connaissance des Kataeb* (Beirut: n.p. 1948); J. P. Entelis, "The Lebanese Kataeb: Party Transformation and System

Maintenance in a Multiconfessional Society," unpublished PH.D. Diss., New York University, 1970.

23. For a statement on the party's policy regarding its militia, see Joseph Chader, "Les Kataeb au Tournant," *L'Orient-Le Jour*, supplement, Sept. 3 to 8, 1972, p. v.
24. Entelis, op. cit., p. 212.
25. Ibid., p. 230.
26. Chader, op. cit., p. 4.
27. See Suleiman, op. cit.; p. 204 and Hudson, op. cit., p. 176.
28. For an elaboration of the appeal the PPS holds for Lebanese Greek Orthodox, see Robert Haddad, *Syrian Christians in Muslim Society (Princeton, N.J.: Princeton University Press, 1970), pp.* 92–95. For a statement of PPS ideology, see Labib Zuwiyya Yamak, *The Syrian Social Nationalist Party: An Ideological Analysis* (Cambridge, Mass: Harvard Middle Eastern Monographs, No. 1 1, 1966).
29. For an account of the programs and activities of these Armenian parties, see Zaven Mequerditch Messerlian, "Armenian Representation in the Lebanese Parliament," unpublished M.A. Thesis, American University of Beirut, 1963.
30. For an analysis of bureaucratic structure, see George Grassmuck and Kamal Salibi, *Reformed Administration in Lebanon* (Beirut: American University of Beirut, 1964).
31. Kamal Salibi, "Lebanon under Fuad Chehab 1958–1964," *Middle Eastern Studies*, 2 (April 1966), p.213.
32. *L'Orient-Le Jour*, February 4, 1974 and February 9, 1974.
33. "Taqrīr Raʾīs Majlis al-Khidma al-Madaniyyah'an Aʿmāl al-Majlis Khilāl al-Sanawāt al-Thalātha 1966–1967–1968" ("Report of the Chairman of the Civil Service Board on the Activities of the Board During the Three Years 1966–1967–1968"), *Official Gazette*, Annex, No. 26, March 31, 1969, pp. 130–132.
34. Ralph E. Crow, "Religious Sectarianism in the Lebanese Political System," *Journal of Politics*, 24 (August 1963), p. 511.
35. *L'Orient-Le Jour*, November 28, 1972, p. 2.
36. *L'Orient-Le Jour*, November 2, 1972, p. 3.
37. *Al-Nahār*, July 5, 1972, p. 2. For an exposition of this general position, see Antoine Messarra, "La répartition confessionnelle permanente ou provisoire?" *Action Proche-Orient*, 23 (December 1964), pp. 35–40.
38. *L'Orient-Le Jour*, October 21, 1972, p. 1.
39. See particularly the text of the speech of Sheikh Hassan Khaled, the Sunni Grand Mufti, at the Id al-Adha feast on January 14, 1973, which appeared in *The Arab World Weekly*, January 20, 1973, pp. 18–19.
40. For the computations involved, see *L'Orient-Le Jour*, February 5, 1973, p. 3.
41. See, for instance, Pierre Delvolve, *L'Administration Libanaise* (Paris: Institut International d'Administration Publique, 1971), p. 13.
42. For general discussions of local government and field administration, see Rizk, op. cit., pp. 153–161; Adnan G. Iskandar, *Bureaucracy in Lebanon* (Beirut: American University of Beirut, 1964), pp. 57–60; and Edward Bitar, "Personnel Administration in a Developing Country: A Study of the Lebanese Bureaucracy," unpublished PH.D. Diss., Louisiana State University, 1970, pp. 123–132.
43. Riad N. El-Rayyes and Dunnia Nahas, *Politics in Uniform: A Study of the Military in the Arab World and Israel* (Beirut: al-Nahar Press Services, 1972), p. 55.
44. Rizk says, "Notre Armée est, de toutes les organisations nationales, la moins pénétrée de confessionalisme." ("Our army is, of all the national organizations, the least penetrated by confessionalism."), op. cit., p. 136.
45. See *al-Nahār*, June 8, 1967.

46. Article 317 of the Penal Code (December 1, 1954) and Article 318 (March 1, 1943).
47. L'Orient-Le Jour, December 3, 1972, p. 4.
48. The laws of the different communities are collected in Maher Mahmassani and Ibtissam Messarra, Statut Personnel: Textes en Vigeur au Liban (Beyrouth: Faculte de Droit et des Sciences Economiques, 1970).
49. Pierre Catala and Andre Gervais, eds., Le Droit Libanais (Paris: Librairie Generale de Droit et de Jurisprudence, 1963), p. 12.
50. For example, Greek Orthodox Bishop George Khodr (interview on January 4, 1973) and Greek Catholic Bishop Gregoire Haddad (interview on January 5, 1973).
51. "Al-Ṭā'ifiyyah" (Sectarianism), pp. 66–67.
52. For some additional survey data on this subject, see Baha Abu-Laban, "Social Change and Local Politics in Sidon, Lebanon," Journal of Developing Areas, 5 (October 1970), pp. 27–42.
53. It is likely that if we had been able to interview more Shiites from the south, the Arab orientation of the Shiites covered in the survey would not have been quite so great.
54. L'Orient, September 30, 1964.
55. Analysis based on roll call given in L'Orient, January 31, 1969.
56. Mgr. Khalife quoted in Robert Solé, "Liban, Bastion Chrétien," Le Monde, December 5, 1972.
57. Reported in al-Bayraq, August 10, 1970.
58. See L'Orient, May 27, 1970.
59. See, for instance, the discussion of a local election in "Tabran" in Elie Salem, "Local Elections in Lebanon: A Case Study," Midwest Journal of Political Science, IX (November 1965), pp. 376–387.
60. L'Orient-Le Jour, April 17, 1972.
61. Samir Khalaf, "Primordial Ties and Politics in Lebanon," Middle East Journal, 4 (April 1968), p. 247.
62. The family factors in politics are discussed in Fuad I. Khuri, "Two Suburbs of Beirut," unpublished ms., Beirut, 1972, Chapter 4.
63. See al-Anwār, September 28, 1972, p. 2; and L'Orient-Le Jour, October 2, 1972, p. 3.
64. Al-Anwār, August 27, 1972, pp. 2 and 8.
65. For a discussion of the political impotence of trade unions see Rizk, op. cit., pp. 49 and 67; and Antoine Messarra, "Les Legislatives," L'Orient-Le Jour, supplement, February 12–18, 1972, p. III.
66. Peter Gubser, "The Politics of Economic Interest Groups in a Lebanese Town." Washington, D.C.: mimeographed, 1972.
67. The Arab World Weekly, May 6, 1972, p. 6.
68. For evidence regarding the overlap between Lebanon's economic and political elites, see R. H. Dekmedjian, "The Entrepreneur in Lebanese Politics: A Case of Overlapping Elites," paper read at Middle East Studies Association annual meeting, Milwaukee, Wisconsin, November 9, 1973.
69. L'Orient, April 28, 1952.
70. Iliya Harik makes this assertion in "The Ethnic Revolution and Political Integration in the Middle East," International Journal of Middle East Studies, 3 (July 1972), p. 318.
71. For a detailed account of how the za'īms of Zahlah interact with their clients, see Peter Gubser, "The Zuama of Zahlah: The Current Situation in a Lebanese Town," Middle East Journal, 27 (Spring 1973), pp. 173–189.
72. Khalil Ahmad Khalil has made an interesting but not a persuasive case that the za'īm system is a form of class exploitation and submerges just below the surface intense inter-class

conflict, in "Al-Za'āmat al-Istizlamiyyah fī Lubnān" (The Leadership of Clientele in Lebanon), *Dirāsāt 'Arabiyyah*, September 1972, pp. 27–38.

73. Arnold Hottinger, "Zu'amā' and Parties in the Lebanese Crisis of 1958," *Middle East Journal*, 15 (Spring 1961), pp. 128–129.

74. Samir Khalaf, op. cit., p. 254.

75. See for instance Arnold Hottinger, "Zu'amā' in Historical Perspective," in Binder, op. cit., pp. 85–105; for an interesting account of the rise of Rashid Baydoun as an urban *za'īm* see Evelyn Aleene Early, "The 'Amiliyya Society of Beirut: A Case Study of an Emerging Urban Za'im," unpub. M.A. Thesis, American University of Beirut, 1971.

76. Samir Khalaf, op. cit., p. 259.

77. For elaboration of this concept, see Arend Lijphart, *The Politics of Accommodation: Pluralism and Democracy in the Netherlands* (Berkeley: University of California Press, 1968), p. 203.

78. Fuad I. Khuri, "Two Suburbs of Beirut," op. cit., p. 224. See also his "al-Ṭabaqāt al-Ijtimā-'iyyah fī Lubnān wa-Dawruhā al-Siyāsī" ("Social Classes in Lebanon and their Political Role"), *Revue Libanaise des Sciences Politiques*, (1970) pp. 25–32.

79. A report in *al-Hayāt* on August 10, 1970 indicated that both Hamade's trip and Jumblatt's trip were for the purpose of discussing presidential candidates with Syrian and Egyptian leaders. See also *al-Nahār* August 10 and 11, 1970.

 5

Political Change and
Reform in Lebanon

Since the creation of Greater Lebanon in 1920, the Lebanese state has
continued to face serious problems of sociopolitical fragmentation resulting
from its religious pluralism. These stresses have posed formidable challenges
to the creation of a viable state. In assessing Lebanon's potential for future
viability and the efficacy of its political system in promoting national accommodation, it is useful to consider the evidence for historical trends, particularly with regard to the following questions: What trends exist in terms of
intercommunity cooperation? Is there any evidence of a trend toward con-
vergency of political values among the communities? Is there any indication
of greater national consciousness today than in the past? What about sectarian
consciousness and commitment to the sectarian community? How about
Pan-Arab loyalties and their impact on the Lebanese state?

Various analysts have drawn their own conclusions on these issues, and
most have been pessimistic. Michael Suleiman wrote in 1967 that "the
inhabitants of what constitutes Lebanon today have rarely, if ever, had strong
feelings of loyalty to a Lebanese 'nation'."[1] Elsewhere he claims, "The state of
Lebanon and the Lebanese people as a 'nation' are purely mythological
notions to half the population at least."[2] Michael Hudson, writing in 1968, is
even more negative. Having entitled his book on Lebanon, *The Precarious*

Republic, he asserts that "as a political culture, Lebanon is a collection of traditional communities bound by the mutual understanding that other communities cannot be trusted."[3] Elsewhere he says that Lebanon enjoys only a "veneer of integration."[4] He contends that the processes of urbanization and social mobilization have tended to exacerbate intergroup conflict, rather than promote greater cooperation.[5] Edward Shils wrote in 1966 that "the Lebanese consensus is like the hedgehog; it knows only one thing, namely the National Pact, and, more particularly, the principle of proportionality and the statistical reality of the application of that principle."[6] We need to consider whether the situation is really this grim.

As the discussion in Chapter 2 indicates, during the period of the Mandate the Lebanese Republic was held together largely by the authority of the French. Most Muslims opposed the creation of Greater Lebanon, preferring that Lebanon be merged with Syria. The only basis upon which the various confessional communities were prepared to coexist, namely mutual reconciliation, received concrete expression in the National Pact. The National Pact appeared to provide an adequate interim basis for intergroup coexistence following independence, and Lebanon enjoyed relative stability during the period 1943–1958. The increasing Muslim role in the civil service, in business, and in politics gave them a steadily increasing, although still unequal, stake in the Lebanese system.

The 1958 civil war, however, represented a watershed for Lebanon.[7] To characterize this war simply as conflict between Christians and Muslims would be an oversimplification, yet the war had heavy sectarian overtones.[8] The insurgents, most of whom were Muslim. opposed the regime of President Camille Chamoun on several counts. They believed that he was attempting to impose a Maronite-controlled presidential system of government, disrupting the prevailing practice of power-sharing at the top. Moreover, they opposed President Chamoun's bringing Lebanon into a western military alliance, thereby violating the foreign policy provisions of the National Pact. The principal purpose of this westward leaning policy was Chamoun's opposition to the Pan-Arab movement being led by Nasser, and Chamoun's fear that Lebanon would be engulfed by a Sunni-dominated, Pan-Arab state. The insurgents were also reacting against economic inequities between Christians and Muslims.

Despite the immediately disruptive and divisive consequences of the war, over the long term the 1958 experience enhanced the viability of the political system. First, it exposed the fundamental fragility of the system. The veneer of national solidarity was indeed thin: in 1958 leaders were reminded that deep confessional cleavages remained, even among the educated and sophisticated strata. It became apparent that the accommodation necessary for long-term viability involved more than the kind of statistical formulae contained in the National Pact and the electoral laws. The "no victor, no vanquished" precept upon which the war itself was ended had to become a permanent feature of Lebanese political life. In 1958 Christian leaders recognized that Muslim cooperation could not be taken for granted, and that success for the Lebanese experiment depended upon a return to the kind of genuine sharing of power characteristic of the relationship between President Khouri and Prime Minister Riad Solh. Moreover, this sharing of power required that on important issues a broad interconfessional consensus be reached before action was taken. Reflecting on the 1958 conflict, Pierre Gemayel stated that "we have learned that Lebanese unity and understanding among us all is the most important thing. Also that no one group can impose its will upon the others. I repeat, we must understand each other."[9] In the field of foreign policy Christian leaders generally came to appreciate that although Lebanon should pursue an independent foreign policy, it must accept its place in the Arab world and seek cooperative relationships with other Arab states, even the more militant and radical of them. On the part of some, the new approach merely comprised an effort to achieve a more stable and equitable equilibrium. For others, there was a growing recognition of the need to move beyond accommodation and balance toward cohesion and national unity. Although his formulation sounds cynical and flippant, many agreed with the statement of Emile Bustani that "we have revolutions only about once a century (i.e., 1860 and 1958). The memory of how much they cost lasts that long."[10]

A remembrance of the costs of the 1958 conflict helped to prevent the 1969 crisis from deteriorating into civil war. However, the differing ways in which these two crises were handled reflect some of the changes in Lebanon's political culture during the intervening decade. In making such a comparison, one has to be fully cognizant of the differing sorts of crisis they were, but they were sufficiently similar in both their origins and their seriousness that such a comparison is instructive. The 1969 crisis started with riots in reaction against army moves to curb Palestinian commando activities on Lebanese soil, with most Muslims supporting freedom of movement and freedom of attack against Israel and most Christians favoring tight control of the commandos by the Lebanese army.[11] The riots led to the resignation of Premier Rachid Karami and his cabinet. A new government was finally formed seven tension-filled months later after a compromise settlement, the Cairo agreement, had been worked out. Probably the most significant difference between the crises of 1958 and 1969 was that the 1958 dispute provoked armed internal conflict, but the 1969 crisis did not. Although sporadic fighting broke out between the Lebanese Army and Palestinian commando units in 1969, and some deaths resulted from the clash between demonstrators and police at the first stage of the 1969 crisis, the country never split into two armed camps as it did in 1958. Even though the two opposing factions were more sharply differentiated confessionally in 1969 than in 1958, it proved possible to establish a dialogue across confessional boundaries and to contain the conflict. In 1969 participants evinced a widespread desire to resolve the issues on the basis of a broadly accepted compromise. Political positions were not easily cast aside, but when it became apparent that compromise was essential, partisans put the viability of Lebanon ahead of their own preferences, and over the period of the crisis common ground was reached by incremental steps.

The 1973 crisis resulting from violent confrontation between the Palestinian commandos and the Lebanese Army further substantiates the trends evident in a comparison of 1969 and 1958. Although in 1973 a difference in perspective surfaced between some Muslim and Christian leaders, the general convergence of political outlook during this crisis was noteworthy. While most leaders shared a genuine sympathy for the plight of the Palestinian refugees in Lebanon and the Palestinian cause generally, most Christians and Muslims concurred that the integrity, safety, and stability of the Lebanese state must not be sacrificed, and that a haven can be provided Palestinians in Lebanon only if it does not jeopardize the safety of Lebanese citizens and the viability of the Lebanese political system. Religious leaders played a particularly important role in working for a settlement between the army and the commandos and in assuring that the crisis did not deteriorate into the confessional confrontation characteristic of most previous Lebanese crises.

During 1974 the continuing confrontations between Lebanon and Israel and between Lebanon and the Palestinian commandos led to somewhat divergent reactions between Christians and Muslims. Muslim leaders charged that the two leading Christian political parties, the Kataeb and the Liberal National Party, were strengthening their paramilitary units in preparation for a showdown with the Palestinian commandos, and one armed skirmish did occur. Regarding Israel, many Muslim leaders wanted Lebanon to strengthen its defenses in the face of Israeli incursions and to achieve closer military coordination with other Arab states. Despite the differing perspectives between many Christians and Muslims on these issues, the external threats were seen as more threatening than the internal divisions.

Of fundamental importance to the differences between the crises of 1958 and 1969 were the changes that took place during the 1960s in Lebanon's relations with other Arab states. Lebanon enjoyed much less antagonistic relations with other Arab states in 1969 than in 1958. Although in 1969 Syria provoked some of the fighting between Palestinian commando units and the Lebanese Army, in 1958 Syria had fed large quantities of arms and ammunition to Lebanese insurrectionists. Gamal Abdul Nasser, who was seen by Christian Lebanese in 1958 as the principal antagonist, promoted reconciliation between the factions in 1969 and was instrumental in helping work out a compromise agreement. By 1969 Lebanon seemed to have much more adequately come to terms with the fact that it is an Arab state, although complete accord has not yet been reached within Lebanon regarding the kinds of relations Lebanon should establish with other Arab states.

Lebanon's changing relations with other Arab states during the 1960s resulted in large part from the shifting character of the Arab nationalist movement and its impact on the Lebanese population. First, the welding of socialism to Arab nationalism disenchanted many Lebanese Muslims, particularly the Muslim merchants and other members of the burgeoning middle class in Beirut and Tripoli, when they saw the moves in Syria starting in 1961 to socialize the economy. Despite their awareness that their economic position as a community was not equal to that of Lebanon's Christians, Lebanon's Muslims realized their advantageous economic situation compared to that of their Muslim brethren in most other Arab countries. Second, the break-up of the United Arab Republic revealed how difficult it is to achieve Arab unity. Third, the crushing and humiliating defeat of Egypt and Syria in the war with Israel in 1967 substantially undermined Egypt's aggressive leadership of the movement for Arab unity. Moreover, the focus of the Arab nationalist movement veered somewhat from the achievement of political unity to the conflict with Israel and the recapture of occupied territories. Finally, when Nasser died the movement lost the charismatic leader who had so inspired it.

Consequent to these developments, the drive for political union in the Arab world has lost much of its momentum. A realization has grown that Arab cooperation can be accomplished within the existing framework of Arab states. *Etatism* and Arab cohesion no longer appear so inconsistent, and localized nationalism has reasserted itself in Egypt and other states.[12] Many Arab nationalists in Lebanon have become increasingly reconciled to the existence and permanence of the Lebanese state, and its existence no longer poses as much of an obstacle to the achievement of their reformulated political goals.[13] As a leading Sunni scholar and civic leader told us, "The Sunni conversion to the acceptance of Lebanon is genuine." Moreover, Nasserism and Baathism have emphasized the secular nature of the Arab nationalist movement; consequently, Arabism and Islam have become more distinct.[14] Although the revolutionary leaders in Libya have tried to reassert the Islamic and unification aspects of the movement, they have not thus far succeeded in reversing the trend. In turn, Christian Lebanese feel less threatened by Arab nationalism since Arabism seems somewhat less incompatible with Lebanism.

Of enormous long-term consequence, many Lebanese have different attitudes regarding their identity as Arabs. These shifts mirror the political developments in the region mentioned above, but they surpass their significance. The trend in Lebanon is for members of all sects to perceive themselves less in the context of their family, geographical, and sect identities, and more in terms of their being Arabs. Evidence for this comes from testimony given in interviews with astute observers of the changing Lebanese scene as well as from our survey results. Because of their past reluctance to identify as Arabs, this shift particularly characterizes the Christian communities. One high-level Maronite civil servant told us that fifteen years ago he would not have admitted to being an Arab, while today he is intensely proud of this fact. Table 5-1 describes the differing attitudes on this subject shown by the responses to one of the questions in our survey. This question asked the respondents to rank the following in terms of the degree to which they provided them with a source of pride: residence in their locality, membership in their sect, Lebanese citizenship, or being an Arab. As indicated in the table, younger respondents and better educated respondents were likely to accord "being an Arab" a higher rank, suggesting that this reflects a historical trend toward a greater sense of Arab identity.

Both Muslims and Christians tended to rank "Lebanese citizenship" in the first place, according it more importance than "being an Arab." Moreover, neither age nor amount of education dramatically influenced the pride in being a Lebanese citizen. At the same time that the attachment to Lebanon was constant, the responses show a shift in the pride in being Arab, particularly among the Christian respondents. While there has been an inclination among analysts to believe that strong Arab attachment and strong Lebanese attachment are incompatible, our data lends support to a divergent interpretation. Cross-tabulations between responses given to the question in Table 5-1 with responses to a wide variety of other survey questions, show that while Arab identity is becoming stronger, attachments to family, region, and sect are in the decline. It might then be asserted that increasing Arab identity is developing at the expense of attachments to family, region, and sect. This is evident, for instance, in the tendency for those who indicate pride in their Arab identity to answer the following questions differently than those who do not demonstrate such pride: (1) Do you always vote as the rest of your extended family votes? (2) With which of the following three sorts of people do you have the most in common: someone who comes from the same part of Lebanon; someone having the same kind of employment; someone who belongs to the same confessional group irrespective of where he comes from? (3) Rank the following in terms of their importance to you: place you come from, your sect, Lebanon, Arab nation, family.

Although Lebanese Muslims are still more inclined to take pride in their Arab identity than are Christians, the growing Arab identity among both communities suggests that in the future a strong sense of common ethnic

TABLE 5-1   *Those who Ranked "Being an Arab" First or Second in Terms of Constituting a Source of Pride*

BY AGE	PERCENTAGE OF CHRISTIANS	PERCENTAGE OF MUSLIMS
20–29	46	81
30–39	47	86
40–49	37	78
50–59	31	58
60 and over	20	62
BY LEVEL OF EDUCATION		
No schooling	11	57
Completed primary school	31	74
Completed middle school	35	90
Completed secondary school	47	75
Completed university	51	89

identity may make an important contribution to the present shared pride in Lebanese nationality in providing a basis for common identity among Lebanese Christians and Muslims. In the past many Christians perceived Arab identity to be inextricably interwoven with Islam and feared that to identify with the Arab world necessitated giving up their attachment to Lebanon and to Lebanon's individuality and sovereignty. Now, however, there appears to be a growing belief that an Arab identity and a Lebanese identity are not mutually exclusive and that Lebanon can demonstrate an Arab orientation while still remaining independent and preserving a distinct national personality. Evidence of a greater Arab orientation can be seen, for instance, in the recently revised party program of the Maronite-dominated Kataeb.[15] The Kataeb has no intention or inclination of becoming Arab nationalist in orientation, but the issues dividing the Kataeb and other predominantly Christian parties from Arab nationalist parties may become less sharply drawn in the future.

Despite these shifts in Arab orientation, 60 percent of those interviewed in the survey believe that loyalty to Lebanon has increased over the past ten years. Twenty-five percent think that it has remained constant, while 14 percent estimate that it has declined. Significantly, a particularly large proportion of the Maronite respondents, 69 percent, consider loyalty to Lebanon to have increased, while 20 percent characterize the situation as unchanged, and 10 percent postulate that loyalty has decreased. The Maronite response is important because it is the Maronite community that has tended to have the greatest doubts concerning Muslim loyalty to Lebanon. If Maronite fears regarding Muslim commitment to Lebanon are being progressively allayed, then one source of interconfessional tension is being steadily eliminated.

Our survey results indicate that a sizeable number of Lebanese favor a federation of Lebanon with one or more Arab states, with Muslims more positively inclined toward such a federation than Christians. Sixty six percent of the Muslims questioned support of such a federation, while 33 percent are opposed (Sunnis were 68 percent in favor and 29 percent against). Among the Christian respondents the proportions are reversed: 24 percent favor a federation and 75 percent oppose it (among Maronites 16 percent were in favor and 83 percent against). Although the issue of a federation or amalgamation of Lebanon with other Arab states has in the past constituted the most divisive issue between Lebanese Christians and Muslims, for a variety of reasons it does not evoke quite so much contention today. First, support for a federation does not mean that the respondent thinks there is much likelihood that a federation will ever be effected. Only 19 percent of the Muslims and 14 percent of the Christians surveyed believe that a federation is likely to materialize. These figures suggest that for the vast majority of those who favor a federation, this remains a vague hope rather than an active political program. Second, while in the past and particularly during the Mandate period, a large proportion of Muslims desired amalgamation with Syria or other Arab states, the present inclination is to favor a federation in which Lebanon would retain its individual identity and many of its national institutions. Third, when we analyze responses to this question in terms of the respondent's age and level of education, it is clear that among the younger and the better educated, this issue of federation is a much less divisive issue than it is among the older and the less educated, implying that in the future it will become even less of a source of acrimonious controversy between Christians and Muslims. As shown in Table 5-2 education inclines Christians more positively toward federation and makes Muslims less favorably disposed. Hence, Christians and Muslims who have had university education differ less on this issue than do well-educated and uneducated Christians. With educational opportunities expanding steadily, greater Muslim–Christian convergence yet may be expected in the future if the current trend is sustained.

Other data from the survey indicate that a clear trend exists toward convergence of political opinion between Christians and Muslims on other issues that have separated these two groups in the past. Discrepancies still remain, but by comparing the answers of the younger respondents with those of older respondents, there is basis for concluding that within the foreseeable future many of the Christian–Muslim differences will decrease in magnitude or may even disappear. [16] In some cases of growing convergence, Muslims' views are shifting toward the Christian position while the opinions held by Christians are changing toward the Muslim outlook. This is true, for instance, of attitudes toward an Arab federation. On other issues, both Christian and Muslim opinion seems to be moving in the same direction, but greater similarity is resulting from the fact that the opinions of one group (in most cases, the Christians) are changing more dramatically than those of the other.

The perception of the Israeli/Palestine conflict as being the most important issue facing Lebanon provides another example of a growing Christian–Muslim convergence with younger Muslims being somewhat less likely than older Muslims to cite this as being Lebanon's greatest problem, while younger Christians are more likely than older Christians to describe this as the most significant political question. The same kind of trend appears in

TABLE 5-2 *Those Favoring Federation of Lebanon with One or More Other Arab States*

LEVEL OF EDUCATION	PERCENTAGE OF CHRISTIANS	PERCENTAGE OF MUSLIMS	PERCENTAGE DIFFERENCE
No schooling	15	80	65
Completed primary school	18	71	53
Completed middle school	22	61	39
Completed secondary school	28	65	37
Completed university	40	62	22

the responses manifesting attitudes toward the Palestinian commandos. Uneducated Christians more frequently cite the commandos as constituting Lebanon's greatest problem than do educated Christians. On the Muslim side there is a slightly greater inclination for educated Muslims to see the commandos as posing a threat than for uneducated Muslims, as indicated in Table 5-3.

Consistent with this Muslim–Christian convergence on issues relating to Arab nationalism, fewer educated Muslims cite Nasser as the man they most admire than do less educated Muslims, while better educated Christians are slightly more likely than less educated Christians to name Nasser in this regard. Nasser remains a more popular figure among all strata of Muslims

TABLE 5-3 *Those Who Cite Commandos as Constituting Lebanon's Most Serious Problem*

AMOUNT OF EDUCATION	PERCENTAGE OF CHRISTIANS	PERCENTAGE OF MUSLIMS	PERCENTAGE DIFFERENCE
No schooling	33	0	33
Completed primary school	18	3	15
Completed middle school	13	8	5
Completed secondary school	12	6	6
Completed university	9	5	4

than he is with Christians, but the differences are much less striking among the educated than among the uneducated. On their side, educated Christians show less inclination than less educated Christians to list a Christian Lebanese political figure as the man they most admire.

A similar pattern emerges from the analysis of attitudes toward the confessional system. Younger Muslims do not differ significantly from older Muslims in their attitudes toward the National Pact, but younger Christians are more negatively inclined toward the National Pact than are older Christians. As a result, the attitudes of younger Christians and Muslims on this issue differ less than the attitudes of older Christians and Muslims. As indicated in Table 5-4, this trend is even more dramatic when education is selected as the variable.

A similar sort of convergence appears in responses regarding the distribution of civil service posts to the various communities on a proportional basis. Better educated Christians and Muslims tend to agree more on this issue than less educated Christians and Muslims. As shown in Table 5-5, younger Christians and Muslims are also more likely to agree than are older Christians and Muslims. In fact, it is more likely that a Christian and a Muslim between the ages of twenty and thirty will concur on the advisability of eliminating this distribution of posts than it is that a Christian between twenty and thirty will answer in the same way as a Christian who is between forty and sixty years old.

It is difficult to pinpoint those dimensions of the educational system and which other aspects of Lebanese society contribute to this convergence of political values among younger and better educated Christians and Muslims.

TABLE 5-4   *Opposition to the Reservation of the Presidency for the Maronites and of the Premiership for the Sunnis*

AMOUNT OF EDUCATION	PERCENTAGE OF CHRISTIANS	PERCENTAGE OF MUSLIMS	PERCENTAGE DIFFERENCE
No schooling	21	70	49
Completed primary school	34	63	29
Completed middle school	38	72	34
Completed secondary school	42	74	32
Completed university	64	72	8

TABLE 5-5 *Opposition to the Proportional Distribution of Civil Service Posts among the Communities*

AGE	PERCENTAGE OF CHRISTIANS	PERCENTAGE OF MUSLIMS	PERCENTAGE DIFFERENCE
20–29	60	72	12
30–39	52	69	17
40–49	42	64	22
50–59	35	60	25

It is likely, however, that intercommunity contacts in school and university are important. Moreover, data from the survey indicate that better educated and younger Christians and Muslims are more likely to be exposed to the same mass media than are older and less well-educated Christians and Muslims. For instance, while university educated Christians and Muslims tend to read the same newspapers, the newspaper reading habits of more poorly educated Muslims and Christians differ significantly, with Muslims being much more likely than Christians to read newspapers with an Arab nationalist editorial bias. Younger Lebanese have also tended to have their political attitudes shaped by Lebanon's recent political history, which has been less acrimonious in terms of confessional conflict than earlier periods. Later in this chapter we assert that the educational system could profitably be reformed to enhance its ability to promote political socialization, but our survey results suggest that some aspects of the current educational system have managed to facilitate a reduction in value divergence among the confessional communities.

Two indices suggest that interconfessional cooperation is growing both in the political and nonpolitical spheres. On the political side, interconfessional political coalitions within parliament have increased in number and importance over the past decade. Looking at the composition of parliamentary blocs and party blocs in parliament just after the elections of 1960, 1964, 1968, and 1972, one finds that a growing proportion of these blocs have had a mixed confession membership in the sense that an increasingly higher percentage of them consist of at least 25 percent Christian members and at least 25 percent Muslim members. For instance, four-man blocs in 1972 were more likely than in 1964 to be composed of two Christians and two Muslims rather than of one Christian and three Muslims, one Muslim and three Christians, four

Muslims, or four Christians. Table 5-6 shows this progress for parliamentary blocs and party blocs combined: Table 5-7 shows the pattern for party blocs alone. The significance of the party bloc figures arises from the increasing number of parliamentarians who belong to party blocs. In some cases the inclusion of other sects in a bloc represents mere window-dressing, but in other instances confessionally mixed blocs are based upon strong interconfessional alliances.

On the nonpolitical side, the survey results show that the younger Lebanese are more likely to participate in interconfessional social groupings than are their elders. Of those in the twenty to forty age range who are members of social, welfare, and sports organizations, 70 percent belong to organizations with multiconfessional memberships. Of those forty years and above with

TABLE 5-6 *Parliamentary Blocs and Party Blocs Containing at least 25 Percent Christian and 25 Percent Muslim Membership (in percent)*

1960	30
1964	55
1968	58
1972	58

TABLE 5-7 *Party Blocs in Parliament Containing at least 25 Percent Christian and 25 Percent Muslim Memberships (in percent)*

1960	33
1964	33
1968	33
1972	60

SOURCES ON BLOC MEMBERSHIP: *L'Orient*, July 4, 1960, May 5, 1964, April 9, 1968, April 14, 1972, April 18, 1972, April 22, 1972, April 25, 1972, and April 28, 1972; Camille Chehab, "Les Elections Legislatives de 1960," Beirut, 1960, mimeographed; Chehab, "Les Elections Legislatives de 1964," Beirut, 1964, mimeographed; Chehab, "Les Elections de 1968," Beirut, 1968, mimeographed.

memberships in such organizations, only 52 percent have joined multiconfessional organizations. Education seems to have a direct impact on patterns of social interaction as well, with better educated members of the sample being more likely to be members of multiconfessional organizations than are the less educated.

Lebanon's confessional divisions remain deep ones, but the situation does not seem as grim as one would believe from the statements of other authors quoted at the beginning of this section. These observers have paid insufficient attention to important historical trends which suggest that intergroup cooperation both of a political and nonpolitical nature is increasing, and that there is some progress toward interconfessional convergence on political outlooks and values. The period of confessional politics has not ended, and confessional identity will be an important factor in political behavior for a long time yet. Nevertheless, if the current trends continue, we might reasonably anticipate that political crises involving sharp intercommunity conflict may occur with less frequency, and the crises that do occur may be resolved with less anguish.

THE ADEQUACY OF THE CONFESSIONAL SYSTEM

Given the depth of intercommunity suspicions at the time of independence, one of the most remarkable aspects of postindependence Lebanese history is the degree to which intercommunity conflict has been contained and communal peace maintained. Despite the numerous political issues that have divided public opinion along confessional lines, only in 1958 did open intercommunity fighting break out, and even then the conflict entailed more than communal strife. Without the explicit attempt to design a political system appropriate to a sharply fragmented society, Lebanon would have courted many more crises of the type of 1958 and might have come unstuck altogether. Although the Lebanese political system may not have aggressively promoted national integration, it has provided a context in which national consciousness has emerged, intercommunity contact and cooperation have increased, and political values have begun to converge.

The strength of the Lebanese political system derives from much more than a mere balance of power or a mathematical formula for equitably distributing political and civil service posts. Complex patterns of community interaction and accommodation are evident everywhere. The Lebanese political system calls for close consultation and cooperation between the president, the premier, and the speaker; for restraint and reconciliation in all matters that might provoke confessional conflict; for seeking intercommunity consensus in the election of the president and in dealing with other significant political issues; and for intercommunity political alliances in parliament. To be more than a sterile division of power, formulae for dealing with communal competition depend on a will that they work and a system of political values to support and articulate the formulae. The top political offices in Cyprus are divided between the Greek and Turkish communities, but the two current office-holders have rarely met with each other since taking office, thus providing an example of a formula that does not go very far toward establishing communal peace. As President Suleiman Frangieh told us, the Lebanese system for managing intercommunity relations has slowly evolved over a full century; the nature of the accommodation that has been worked out is sufficiently subtle and complex that "il faut vivre le système pour le comprendre."[17]

In addition to the political system, two other important factors have contributed to the promotion of intercommunity accommodation in Lebanon. First is the character of Lebanon's confessional pluralism. The balance in size of the two large religious groupings makes it difficult for either to impose its will on the other. More important yet, each of these major groupings is subdivided into smaller confessional communities which are clearly differentiated from each other, not only in terms of theology and religious institutions, but often in political orientation as well. Lebanon is a nation of minorities, rather than merely the combination of two monolithic blocs. As former President Charles Helou has written, "Dans un pays comme le nôtre, fait de minorités sensiblement égales et également jalouses de leurs droits, où aucun élément ne peut être prétrendre de constituer une majorité oppressive, où il ne saurait être question de régime de contrainte—la seule paix réalisable est une paix consentie, fondée sur l'entente et la collaboration, sur un état d'équilibre."[18]

In terms of economic and social development, a government that operates on the principle that near unanimity is required before action can be taken has great difficulty in performing as a vigorous mobilizing force. Malcolm Kerr points to real problems when he writes that "it is in the nature of the executive in Lebanon to avoid decisions that are political in the full sense. The government's function might be said to be judicial; it adjudicates claims and petitions in accordance with established sets of unwritten rules."[19] Economic modernization is evident, and to the extent that the political system has contributed to conflict resolution and tension reduction, it has enabled this modernization to proceed. For the most part, however, modernization has occurred in spite of the government rather than because of it.[20] The fortunate circumstance of Lebanon's having various important economic assets and a vigorous rate of economic growth means that the government's laissez-faire economic policies can much more easily be tolerated by the population there than they would be in most other developing countries.

A system oriented largely to maintaining an equilibrium among pluralistic communities is not well adapted, for instance, to the adoption of a decisive foreign policy; or to an effective policy of national defense; or to controlling and upgrading the country's schools, since such a large portion of the schools are under semiautonomous control of the religious communities. Nor can administrative reform proceed easily when it is considered necessary to maintain strict personnel quotas that reflect the confessional composition of the population, and when the control of certain government agencies is deemed the preserve of particular communities. The most striking illustration of the costs of the Lebanese system in terms of government ineffectiveness came during the 1969 crisis. Seven months elapsed with no cabinet or prime minister while a compromise solution was sought, and during this period government operations remained virtually paralyzed. On occasion, the government's search for consensus can create more problems than it resolves.

POLITICAL REFORM

Our interviews with political and religious leaders from all major communities indicated broad agreement that the emphasis upon coexistence and equilibrium embodied in Lebanon's political system has been of central importance to the relative political stability Lebanon has enjoyed. Some leaders believe, however, that the present system will not suffice for the future. Those advocating adjustments to the confessional system are not insignificant in number. And yet those calling for reform generally propose carefully phased, evolutionary change,[21] and this is true of some of the most radical reformers. This reflects a general appreciation of the success the system has had in minimizing intercommunity conflict, and a realization that a restructuring of the Lebanese political system could provoke serious societal upheavals.

Advocacy of change arises from two principal sources. First there are those, most of them Muslims, who believe that genuine community equality has not been attained. A more perfect equilibrium requires parity of political power and economic status. Many Muslims contend that they remain second-class citizens in Lebanon, even though they are at least as numerous as Christians: they call for the principles of balance and equality to be more fully realized. The reservation of the presidency, the most important political office, to a Maronite Christian provides a particularly sensitive issue. Despite the fact that a Sunni Muslim is invariably premier and a Shiite Muslim is always speaker of parliament, some critics believe that this does not constitute a just distribution of power.[22] To rectify this perceived imbalance, former Premier Saeb Salam has recommended the adoption of an interconfessional six-member presidential council as a substitute for the presidency. The chairmanship of the council would rotate among the six members, three of whom would be Christian and three Muslims.[23] Others have suggested that the presidency be open to all and that his selection be by a public election, not by parliament. Focusing his attention on what he believes to be another injustice in the allocation of political posts, a Shiite deputy has proposed that the position of premier be rotated between the Sunni and the Shiite communities.[24]

Closely related to these appeals for the redistribution of top political posts lies the question of the relative size of the different communities. Without a census since 1932, no accurate determination is possible, but many Muslims believe that they now outnumber the Christians, and among the Muslims many Shiites reckon that their sect is now more numerous than the Sunni community. Since the initial allocation of parliamentary posts and top political positions was rationalized in terms of the respective sizes of the communities in the 1932 census, a new ranking of communities in terms of size would theoretically necessitate a redistribution of political posts. Thus, the advocacy of a new census is usually synonymous with a call for a reassessment of the distribution of political power.

Although political leaders occasionally call for a new census or for a redistribution of posts, pressure in this direction is not as great as might be anticipated. In this regard, mention has already been made in the preceding chapter of how infrequently non-Maronites have been nominated for the presidency. Admittedly, some of those who disapprove of the current distribution of posts advocate the complete abolition of the confessional system, and thus the question of a new census or the reallocation of posts among the communities does not arise. Others who consider that some injustices inhere in the current allocation are prepared to forego a reconsideration of how posts are assigned, to avoid the conflict and strife which such readjustments might entail. For instance, the religious heads of both the Shiite and the Druze communities believe that a new census would reveal their communities to be larger relative to the other communities than they were in 1932, and yet they both oppose a census being held because of the delicacy of the current equilibrium. They deem it preferable to suffer some injustices in the interest of maintaining political stability.[25] Their attitude illustrates the spirit of compromise that has enabled the system to function as well as it has.

A second type of dissatisfaction with the system is expressed by those who believe that the attainment of equilibrium should be only a transitional stage in Lebanon's political development. According to them, a system built on the principle of balance has constituted a necessary interim arrangement, but the time has come to seek a more thorough-going kind of national accommodation. In pointing to what he considers serious deficiencies in the Lebanese political formula, Sheikh Michel Khouri, leader of the Destour Party, has explained, "My father (President Bishara al-Khouri, who was coauthor of the National Pact in 1943) used to assert that if we survive as a nation for twenty five years under the National Pact, then Lebanon will be safe. But that is not enough. . . . The National Pact is a negative pact. The Christians abandon the idea of protection from a foreign power, and the Muslims agree not to merge with the Arab world, but this is merely negative. . . . What we need is to create a new national consensus."[26] In agreeing with this point of view, others contend that Lebanon's sociopolitical system has had the unfortunate effect of strengthening confessional divisions,[27] and that the system requires amendment if Lebanon is to move beyond community coexistence to national cohesion. Hassan Saab, for instance, has asserted that "contractual unity is not a substitute for national identity; a traditional balance of power is not the equal of modern integration."[28] The attainment of such cohesion or accommodation might enhance political stability by reducing some systemic strain and also relieve some of the communal pressures on the political system, thereby according more opportunity to Lebanon's political institutions to grapple with other issues facing the state.

Opposing this view, many members of the Lebanese political elite believe that it is not feasible to eliminate barriers dividing the communities or to actively promote national integration. Dr. Charles Malik, former Foreign Minister and President of the United Nations General Assembly, claims that the autonomy enjoyed by each community constitutes the most precious characteristic of Lebanese sociopolitical life, and any attempt to homogenize

Lebanese society should be assiduously avoided.[29] In an interview in 1973, President Suleiman Frangieh asserted that the equilibrium system and the maintenance of community freedom will continue for the foreseeable future to characterize the essential structure of the Lebanese political system.[30]

To a certain extent, the feasibility of moving beyond a mere negative pact has become a moot issue because of the growing convergence of political values among the communities, particularly among those who are younger and better educated. This is clear, for instance, in regard to perceptions of Lebanon's place in the Arab world, which in the past has so sharply divided Christians and Muslims. The contentious character of this controversy regarding coexistence versus accommodation derives in part from the fact that most members of the elite generally remain unaware of how striking this trend toward convergence actually is.

One means recommended for promoting greater integration is to change the basis of parliamentary representation and to shift the basis of political behavior at the highest levels of government. Admittedly, members of parliament carry with them several other identities in addition to their confessional origins, for instance, their occupational and class membership, and they can be expected to represent these interests in parliament along with their confessional interests. However, proponents of this view want these varying interests to be accorded more explicit recognition and representation in order to permit a more faithful reflection of the full range of Lebanon's political interests and to augment various nonreligious identities. For instance, if trade unions or professional associations had representatives in government councils, this might help strengthen the bonds within occupational groups, bonds that usually bridge confessional divisions. Several years ago the Destour party advocated the introduction of social and economic representation to complement confessional and geographical representation. More recently the idea has gained popularity with such influential political leaders as Kamal Jumblatt, Pierre Gemayel, and Ghassan Tueni. Jumblatt proposes the creation of a Constitutional Council, which would constitute a second house. While the Chamber of Deputies would continue to have representation defined in terms of confession and geography, the Constitutional Council would be composed of representatives from major professional and occupational groups.[31] Pierre Gemayel has put the Kataeb party on record as favoring a somewhat similar social–economic council, although it would be a consultative rather than a legislative body.[32] Ghassan Tueni's views parallel those of Jumblatt in regard to a new social and economic council comprising a second house.[33] The hope implicit in this proposal is not merely that a new basis of political representation be introduced, but that a new national consensus might arise based on a perception of shared economic interests. The proposers believe that this would provide a basis for more effective governmental intervention in promoting economic development and also a means for strengthening the Lebanese social fabric.

A final group of critics contend that the political system as constituted inhibits Lebanon's political modernization. They charge that the political system props up the political position of traditional notables and blocks the recruitment of new political leadership, that it militates against the development of ideologically oriented political parties, and that it encourages corruption.[34] The confessional component of the system is usually the focus of attack for these critics, and the proposed remedies range from the abolition of the confessional system to the adoption of such electoral reforms as new forms of proportional representation, enlarged multimember constituencies, or even smaller single-member constituencies. Defenders of the present political system counter that the Lebanese political system is not feudal in character and that political recruitment is quite vigorous and open.[35] Others have argued that no fundamental alterations will be wrought in the patterns of political recruitment and influence merely by adjusting the size of constituencies, basing their conclusions in part on the marginal effect of constituency adjustments for the 1953 election.[36]

One misconception inheres in much of this criticism of the political system. The body politic in Lebanon is certainly not altogether healthy, but it is doubtful that the confessional aspect of the political system is the sole or even the major source of difficulty. To the extent that political actors are primarily motivated by a desire to promote the well-being of their own confessional communities, then sectarianism constitutes the principal motive force of political life in Lebanon. The confessional aspect of the political system has been devised as a response to sectarianism, and it is sectarianism rather than the confessional component of the political system that remains the major obstacle to some types of political reform. For instance, confessionally mixed and ideologically oriented political parties have not developed largely because of pervasive sectarian motivations and the differing political interests of the various confessional communities. Only to a marginal degree does the confessional aspect of the political system per se inhibit the evolution of more vigorous political parties. In similar fashion, the continuing political power of traditional political notables arises from other features of Lebanon's social and political structure. The confessional aspect of the political system seems to us to play only a limited role in reinforcing their political influence.

Those advocating reforms of the Lebanese political system are not confined to a radical fringe. According to the results of our survey, a significant proportion of the Lebanese population favors one kind of reform or another. In response to a question asking whether they had any suggestions for political reforms in Lebanon, 72 percent of the respondents proposed some type of reform, of which 24 percent went so far as to counsel the abolition of the confessional system. A small majority of the respondents, 52 percent, opposed retention of the current formula under which the presidency is reserved for the Maronites and the premiership for the Sunnis. However, only 31 percent favored abandonment of confessional representation in parliament.[37] On all three of these questions the Muslim respondents tended to be more negatively disposed toward the present confessional system than were the Christian respondents.

In a small-scale newspaper survey of key political figures in 1972, four of the twelve politicians who addressed the subject favored abolition of the confessional system, with two others proposing amendment but not abolition. The remaining six preferred retention of the system in its current form.[38] Significantly, all three of the responding Sunni politicians advocated abandoning the system, while major support for the system came from the Christians surveyed. In his memoirs, former President Bishara al-Khouri observes that Lebanese politicians call for the abolition of confessionalism only as long as their own confessional interests remain untouched.[39] Indecision and ambivalence vis-à-vis the confessional system are widespread. They generally do not reflect insincerity or duplicity nearly as much as an appreciation of both the strengths and weaknesses of the system; a desire for change, but also a realization of the inadequacies of all the possible alternative systems in satisfying Lebanon's needs.

EQUITABLE ECONOMIC DEVELOPMENT

Inequalities in wealth and economic opportunities among the confessional communities is clear, and has been demonstrated by data presented in Chapter 3. These disparities have serious implications for intergroup relations and for the continued viability of the political system; and they deserve as much governmental attention as reforms that are more explicitly political in character. The 1958 civil war serves as one illustration of the political implications of the economic structure of Lebanon. Among the major causes of the Muslim-dominated, insurrectionist surge was the perception of a considerable discrepancy between the socioeconomic status of the average Muslim and that of the average Christian, and the belief that the government was doing far too little to rectify these inequalities. The level of discontent among Muslims over their socioeconomic status has not in recent years reached the pitch that it did in 1958, and the gap has been somewhat narrowed since then, but the situation ought still to provide cause for governmental concern.

Probably the most effective means of promoting greater comparability of socioeconomic status among the communities would be to concentrate on equalizing educational opportunities, since education constitutes such an important vehicle for economic mobility in Lebanon. This and other aspects of educational reform are considered in a subsequent section. It will be clear in that discussion that utilization of the educational system as an instrument for enhancing community parity is severely restricted by the extent to which education is controlled privately, particularly by Christian religious bodies. Confessional communities understandably give primary attention to the needs of their own community.

Arising from his conviction that the roots of the 1958 civil war were largely socioeconomic, President Fuad Chehab focused much of his regime's attention on regional and sectarian economic inequalities. He believed that by moving away from laissez-faire economic policies to more vigorous government promotion of economic parity, the government could lay the basis for a less precarious national unity. He evidenced particular concern over the plight of Lebanon's predominantly Shiite areas. To assist his government with the assessment of the country's most pressing economic needs and opportunities, President Chehab invited Father Louis Lebret, the Director of l'Institut International de Recherches et Formation en vue du Développement Intégral et Harmonisé (IRFED) of Paris, to organize an economic survey. The survey was done in 1959–1960, and then Father Lebret was subsequently asked to undertake supplementary economic studies between 1960 and 1964 which provided the basis for the formulation of a five-year plan. The multivolume IRFED report on Lebanon's economic problems and prospects focuses primary attention on the importance of equitable economic development in promoting national cohesion. On the first page of its introduction the report asserts that in the face of strong confessional loyalties, as well as a tendency toward individualism, the birth of civic consciousness and effective national cohesion can only be realized if the diverse communities all believe that they are benefiting equitably from the national economy. [40] In pursuit of this interest the IRFED team embarked on a meticulous study of the economic needs and opportunities of each portion of the country.

Whatever inclination President Chehab had in this direction upon taking office, his predisposition was reinforced by the conclusions that the IRFED mission drew. During the Chehab regime, economic planning enjoyed heightened prestige, and consequent to the IRFED recommendations regarding the need to concentrate on regional and confessional inequalities, three different types of regional planning groups were formed. In 1963 the government decided that each of Lebanon's five regions should have a multidisciplinary planning and research team, a regional technical group, and a regional consultative planning council. [41] The proposed development expenditure for the five-year plan period 1964–1968 of L.L. 3 billion far exceeded government expenditure for any five-year period prior to that time.

The three principal programs devised during the Chehab regime to assist Lebanon's poorer regions and communities were the Litani River project, the Green Plan, and the Office of Social Development. The original plan for the Litani River project called for a dam that would provide both electric power for a large portion of the country and irrigation water for many arid and semiarid portions of the South and the Bekaa. Although the dam has been constructed and is producing electric power, a variety of political and economic obstacles have impeded implementation of the aspect of the project intended to assist poor farmers, mostly Shiites, living in the vicinity of the river and its dam. The Green Plan has met with considerable success in increasing the incomes of small, impoverished farmers. Land reclamation in mountainous areas has constituted the major thrust of the program, but the Green Plan has also assisted farmers with the construction of agricultural roads and water reservoirs, and with the improvement of orchards. At heavily subsidized rates, small farmers can contract for earthmoving equipment to clear and terrace portions of their land that they had been unable to farm productively in the past. A ceiling on each job of L.L. 10,000 assures that most of the aid goes to small farmers. Between 1965 and 1970, 12,703 farmers benefited from some aspect of the Green Plan's activities. [42] With assistance from the World Food Programme, the Green Plan is now extending its operations to cover a variety of other types of assistance to poor farmers, including assistance with construction of wells, irrigation and drainage canals, and reforestation.[43]

The Office of Social Development provides assistance to private welfare agencies as well as directly operating other welfare services for the aged, orphans, and the mentally handicapped. More important to the Chehab strategy, however, are its social development activities in rural areas. In many respects this social development program resembles conventional community development programs popular in many countries during the same period. Workers at the village level and the offer of government subsidies are expected to motivate villagers to start cottage industries, improve their agricultural practices, and build community facilities.[44] The enthusiasm of the village-level workers has often been infectious, and considerable local activity has been generated by their efforts, but their impact on the socioeconomic status of Lebanese villagers has generally been marginal.

Results from our attitude survey of one thousand Lebanese suggest public support for programs aimed at improving the economic position of depressed groups. In response to a question regarding whether it is proper for the government to take tax moneys from richer areas of Lebanon for use on development projects in the poorer areas, 70 percent of the respondents answered "often" and 19 percent said "sometimes." Only 8 percent thought that it was never proper for the government to act in this manner.

Despite post-IRFED government activity and expressions of public support, only limited progress has been made toward the noble goals of confessional and regional equality expressed in the IRFED reports. Although many poor villagers have undoubtedly benefited from the activities of the Green Plan, the Office of Social Development, and other government departments, the cumulative impact of these activities has certainly not constituted a dramatic socioeconomic restructuring of Lebanese society. Although the original concept of these programs was to concentrate on the poorest areas, politicians from each region have pressured the government to assure that rough parity is maintained in terms of government expenditure in each region.[45] Some preference appears to have been given the poor South, but the difference is not dramatic. For instance, the Office of Social Development sends six rural development units to the South and five to each of the other regions; and Green Plan expenditures have been slightly greater in the South than elsewhere. A Council for the South was created in 1969 with a sizeable budget, but this resulted primarily from Israeli attacks on the South, and its funds are used largely for reconstruction of facilities destroyed in these attacks.

Economic planning generally and regional planning particularly have never come to be firmly rooted, and since the end of the Chehab era the concept of the government playing an instrumentalist role in Lebanese economic affairs, particularly in order to promote regional and community parity, has lost much of its popularity. The most recent economic development "plan" does make mention of five major new irrigation schemes that could have an important impact on the economic level of several depressed agricultural areas in the country. On the whole, though, the plan is more a review of the general economic situation than a projection of new economic endeavors.[46] Economic planning and government intervention may not be essential in a country that enjoyed an annual growth rate of 7 percent and a per capita growth rate of 4.7 percent during the period 1964–1969, but the disparities between regions and among the confessional communities are unlikely to close dramatically without greater governmental initiative, both in terms of new tax policies and development projects.

THE EDUCATIONAL SYSTEM

Education constitutes one of the most vital policy areas for achieving national accommodation. Through no other medium does the political system have as direct a channel for influencing the values and orientations of its citizens. Research on political socialization, the process through which members of society learn politically relevant attitudes and patterns of behavior, indicates that the school system can be the most important agency to transmit fundamental orientations.[47] For example, Robert Hess and Judith Torney conclude on the basis of a study of 12,000 American school children that, "The public school appears to be the most important and effective instrument of political socialization."[48] Virtually all of the studies of political socialization also emphasize the early age at which the basic political orientations and patterns of loyalty are developed.[49] This means that even in countries in which the majority of school children receive only a primary education the school system can inculcate a sense of national citizenship and promote intergroup tolerance. Many factors influence the effectiveness of the school system as an agent of political socialization: the percentage of the population the school system reaches; the composition of the student body; the content of the social studies curriculum and the manner in which this curriculum is taught; and the amount of emphasis on social and political subjects all effect the process and the success of political socialization by schools. When cohesive cultural subsystems exist, as they do in communally divided societies, and the school system does not consciously reinforce the national frame of reference, the process of socialization tends to direct loyalty toward these more particularistic units rather than to the nation as a whole.

In Lebanon the fragmented nature of the educational system makes it difficult to employ the schools as an agent of national political socialization. For a country in which 69 percent of the population is literate and approximately 30 percent of the total population is now attending school,[50] the Lebanese Ministry of National Education plays a surprisingly limited role. Lebanese often describe their educational system as a partnership between the public and private sectors, but in that relationship the public schools and the Ministry of Education have been very much relegated to the junior position. In the thirty years since independence the Ministry of Education has failed to articulate and pursue a coherent educational policy with the following results: fewer students attend public than private schools; the Ministry has little control over private schools; it has been difficult to set curricula relevant to Lebanon's needs; and little uniformity exists in content, textbooks, and standards.

The preponderance of the sectarian-controlled private sector results from the manner in which the educational system evolved and the concern of the sects to exercise their constitutional prerogative to maintain their own schools. The tradition of private education originated during the time of the Ottoman Empire. Under the mandate the French found it convenient to leave education primarily in private hands. Article 10 of the constitution has preserved this historical freedom of education in Lebanon. According to Article 10, "Freedom of education is guaranteed, provided it does not conflict with public order and morality, or offend the dignity of any of the religions or sects. The right of the sects to operate their own schools shall not be interfered with in any way, provided they comply with the educational laws issued by the state."[51]

At a basic level, budgetary restrictions have manifested the relatively low priority accorded to public education and also limited the expansion of the public sector. Until recently the Lebanese government spent a considerably lower proportion of its budget on education than other states in the Middle East. In the mid-fifties Lebanon allocated less than 13 percent of its national budget to the educational sector, compared with the 20 to 25 percent invested by Tunisia, Iraq, Algeria, Sudan, and Morocco.[52] By 1967 the portion of the

Lebanese budget going to education rose to 15 percent, and in 1971 it took a sharp upswing to nearly 20 percent.[53] Investment in public education has come primarily at two points in the educational cycle, primary schools and a national university benefiting a much smaller group. Financial and other factors have restricted the expansion of the public sector beyond 40 percent of the total student enrollment. In fact, as shown in Table 5-8, the faster growth of private schools has actually decreased the proportion of students in the public sector during the last five years for which statistics are available.

As Table 5-9 reveals, the relatively even balance between the public and private sectors at the primary stage changes to a distinct preponderance in favor of the private schools at the higher levels. Until recently the private sector predominated to an even greater extent in higher education. At the apex of the educational system, more than two-thirds of the students attend the equivalent of foreign universities located in Lebanon: the Arab University, which is an affiliate of the University of Alexandria; the American University, which is chartered in the state of New York; and Saint Joseph University, which is partly financed by the French government.

The extent to which educational facilities are equitably distributed in a particular country has implications for the role the school system can play in promoting national accommodation. An imbalance in access to education can produce divergent attitudes among educationally advantaged and disadvantaged groups and it can also lead to economic disparities and concommitant grievances. In Lebanon residents of predominantly Christian Mount Lebanon have a distinct edge over other parts of the country due to the

TABLE 5-8   *Public and Private Schools, 1943 to 1970*

YEAR	TOTAL ENROLLMENT	PERCENTAGE IN PUBLIC SCHOOLS	PERCENTAGE IN PRIVATE SCHOOLS
1943	131,000	17.5	82.5
1959	266,900	39.7	60.3
1965	442,510	40.9	59.1
1970	732,681	38.0	62.0

SOURCE: Mission IRFED, *Besoins et Possibilités de Développement du Liban*. Tome II (Beyrouth: Ministère du Plan, 1961), pp. 61-62; *Statistiques Scolaires* (Beyrouth: Ministère de l'Education, 1972), p. 20.

historical concentration of effort by missionaries and native churches in that predominantly Christian region. With 29 percent of the total population of Lebanon, Mount Lebanon has 38 percent of all public school enrollment and 46 percent of the attendance in the private sector. Only one other region, Beirut, has a greater proportion of students attending schools than the percentage of the population it comprises. Moreover, with regard to the higher quality and more prestigious private institutions, South Lebanon, Bekaa, and North Lebanon are particularly disadvantaged. Predominantly Muslim South Lebanon, North Lebanon, and the Bekaa, constituting 55 percent of the population of Lebanon, provide only 26 percent of the total enrollment in private schools.[54] Another imbalance in educational opportunity comes in the availability of places in secondary schools. Throughout Lebanon the pyramidlike structure of the educational system restricts the number of primary and complementary school graduates who are able to continue in secondary school. A student in Mount Lebanon or Beirut, however, has a considerably better chance than his counterparts in South Lebanon and the Bekaa to gain entrance, since Beirut and Mount Lebanon, with 44 percent of the population of Lebanon, account for 69 percent of all secondary schools.[55] Moreover, the figures presented in Table 5-10 indicate that this distribution pattern is not being readjusted, but rather reinforced. The causes of these distorted distribution patterns probably include the historical advantage of

TABLE 5-9   *Public and Private School Enrollment by Type of Schools, 1970*

LEVEL OF SCHOOL ENROLLMENT	PERCENTAGE OF ENROLLMENT IN PUBLIC SCHOOLS	PERCENTAGE OF ENROLLMENT IN PRIVATE SCHOOLS
Primary	44	56
Complementary (Intermediary)[1]	51	49
Secondary	29	71
University[2]	29	71

[1]This figure is somewhat deceptive because most complementary schools are integrated with secondary schools, particularly in the private sector.
[2]An unknown proportion of those in private universities are foreigners.

SOURCE: *Plan Sexennal de Développement, 1972-1977* (Beyrouth: Ministère du Plan, 1972), p. 108.

TABLE 5-10   *Percentage of Schools in Each Region, 1966 and 1971*

REGION	PERCENTAGE OF TOTAL POPULATION[1]	PERCENTAGE OF TOTAL SCHOOLS, 1966	PERCENTAGE OF TOTAL SCHOOLS, 1971
Beirut	15	10.5	11.5
Mount Lebanon	29	36.8	38.2
North Lebanon	22	21.4	22.1
South Lebanon	19	15.3	14.8
Bekaa	14	15.9	13.4

[1]Percentages are based on figures published in *al-Nahar*, April 26, 1956.

SOURCE: *Recueil de Statistiques Libanaises*, No. 6, *Année 1970* (Beyrouth: Ministère du Plan, 1971), pp. 420-421; *Statistiques Scolaires* (Beyrouth: Ministère de l'Education, 1971), p. 25.

Mount Lebanon, the differential ability of residents of different areas to meet the costs of private education, and the regional/confessional variations in terms of responsiveness to educational oportunities.

The degree of heterogeneity in the student body and the teaching staffs of the schools may also affect the socialization process, because children who are exposed to a diversity of backgrounds may have more tolerance toward members of other groups and a greater appreciation for the cultural richness and diversity of their nation.[56] Official statistics on the confessional composition of the schools do not exist for Lebanon, but the student bodies of most private religious schools and public schools are relatively homogeneous. The tendency for a sectarian group to cluster in a particular residential area produces a situation in which most children in public primary school attend classes predominantly with members of their own sect. Since public secondary schools recruit students from a larger area, they probably achieve a wider range of sectarian backgrounds. More affluent persons everywhere attempt to send their children to private institutions, leaving the public schools to the poorer families who cannot afford private school fees.[57] Thus, differences in social background of the students in the private and public educational sectors often mirror the class structure of the community with two exceptions: many elite private schools do award a few scholarships to exceptional students from families of limited means; and a minority of private institutions, particularly some of those operated by the Catholic churches, charge only nominal fees.

Secular private institutions, which comprise only a small proportion of the schools in Lebanon, achieve the greatest diversity in their student populations. Some of the institutions operated by foreign missions also strive to recruit students from differing backgrounds in contrast with the private schools managed by Lebanese religious groups, which tend to cater primarily to members of their own sect. In our Lebanese school sample, the National Protestant College and Carmel St. Joseph, a school of the International Carmelite Order of Nuns, had a far better balance between Christians and Muslims than the other schools, particularly the Maronite and Shiite schools. On a countrywide basis, the Catholic school system with an enrollment of 162,000 children reports that 60 percent of its students are Catholic, 20 percent belong to other Christian denominations, and 20 percent are Muslim. With a few exceptions, Catholic schools do not strive for heterogeneity within particular institutions, but instead reach non-Christians by opening schools in their communities.[58] In Greek Orthodox schools in Beirut, between 50 and 80 percent of the students are Greek Orthodox, depending on the location.[59] Sunni Makassed schools have not been successful in their efforts to attract Christian students.[60] As a consequence of the fact that a preponderance of private schools are operated by Christian denominations, a large number of Muslim students seeking a higher quality private education attend Christian schools. For example, in our adult survey sample 12 percent of the Sunnis had been educated at Sunni private schools, while 18 percent were products of a Christian institution. Of the Shiite respondents, 14 percent attended a Sunni or Shiite school and 11 percent a Christian school. Twenty of the 21 percent of the Druze who went to private religious schools went to Christian schools, meaning that only 1 percent of the Druze attended private Muslim schools.

The Ministry of Education has the power by law to regulate private schools primarily through establishing the language to be employed, by setting an official curriculum, by requiring all students to sit for the same baccalaureate examinations at the end of the secondary school cycle, and by approving text books. In fact, these controls have not been utilized fully. In 1946 the Chamber of Deputies passed a series of decrees articulating the principles on which the educational system was expected to be based. These reinstated Arabic as the supreme national language to be used as the official medium of instruction in all primary schools and for the teaching of Lebanese history, geography, and civics; prescribed an official curriculum for most academic subjects; and established the examination system.[61] These laws, which basically remain unchanged, do not and were not intended to cast education in a uniform mold. Schools have the option of employing Arabic, English, or French for instruction in many subjects: that decision, to a great extent, determines the foreign educational influences to which the students will be exposed. Moreover, French medium private schools commonly ignore legislative prescriptions and teach all subjects in French. As for the official curriculum, its catalogue of topics to be covered in a particular academic year does not specify the time to be spent on each one, the developments to be emphasized, or the interpretation to be given. Nor does the official curriculum specifically exclude anything. Private schools are thus able to substantially determine what is taught.

The baccalaureate examination system offers some common framework at the secondary level, but it is not an effective unifier. In all three streams: science, literature, and classical languages, the examination concentrates heavily on the subject of specialization. According to the regulations on the Lebanese baccalaureate examinations, civics questions have constituted no more than one-fifteenth of the total and even in the literary stream, civics, history, and geography questions have comprised only two-ninths of the test.[62] Moreover, the examination questions avoid sensitive topics on which sects might disagree in their interpretation.

Laws also accord the Ministry the right to inspect and approve all textbooks adopted, but the Ministry has never enforced these provisions, even with regard to standardizing the books in the public schools. Thus, the procedure under the law for private and public schools to submit their books to the Ministry each year has resulted at most in a perfunctory investigation of particular texts against which complaints have been lodged because material in them is offensive to members of certain sects. The Ministry does not even have information as to the texts in use in each school. The result has been a lack of uniformity within even a single type of school system, and the proliferation of inadequate teaching materials. Up to eleven different history and nine civics textbooks are available for each class.[63] To indicate something about the standard of the texts, two members of a review committee for the Ministry of Education reported in 1970 that none of the existing civics texts for several school grades even followed the official program and that many of the books that did comply for other classes had serious deficiencies.[64]

Many factors combine to sustain the fragmented character of the education system.[65] Private schools zealously guard their privileges and resist any further regulation. Since virtually all members of the political elite are graduates of private institutions, the private sector is never without strong defenders. Supporters of private education stress the need for freedom and lack of controls to be able to preserve their high educational standards. Private schools undoubtedly offer higher quality education, but rather than perceiving the inadequacies of public education as the legacy of past policies, private educators often assume that public schools are inherently inferior. With a preponderance of private schools under the sponsorship of Christian denominations, Muslims often accord more importance to the public school system. The head of the Sunni Makassed schools, for example, contemplated with equanimity a future in which the public schools educated the vast majority of school children and the private schools served essentially as innovators.[66] In contrast, some Christian leaders have harbored a desire for the public sector to wither away leaving a monopoly for the private schools. In 1959 the Kataeb party actually introduced a motion into parliament calling for the establishment of a new arrangement under which every student would have the chance to attend any private school of his choice, with the Ministry of Education footing the entire bill for his school fees. The Catholic school system, which now has 60 percent as many students as the public system, would be the primary beneficiary of the dismantling of public education. Although it is less often expressed, another factor that influences private schools in their stand against further centralization is the fear that secular education might weaken the integrity of the sect.

Until the recent establishment of the Educational Center for Research and Development, the Ministry of Education did not have the collective disposition to alter the status quo. The policy of consciously employing education for promoting national accommodation and a sense of national citizenship had low priority at best, and many within the Ministry argue, as Msg. Ignace Maroun, head of the Catholic schools put it, "uniformity does not create unity."[67] One former director general of the Ministry of Education ironically ignored the French model of education, from which he otherwise very much drew his inspiration, when he asserted in an interview that the prescription of a detailed curriculum and an authorized series of textbooks was tantamount to communist-style indoctrination by the state.[68] Another factor that may contribute to the disinclination for change has been the reservation of most of the senior administrative positions within the Ministry of Education, including the central post of the director general of general education (primary and secondary schools), for Maronites, since Maronites have generally been among the communities most satisfied with the existing educational order.[69]

Moreover, the controversial nature of educational reform in Lebanon places the Minister of Education in a precarious position: few men have remained in that cabinet office long enough to formulate and implement a new policy. The three-year period after President Frangieh took office, for example, saw five different men attempting to grapple with that ministry.

The amount of time spent on social studies in the schools attests to the low priority accorded to instilling a sense of national citizenship. The number of hours allocated to civics, history, and geography ranges from three out of twenty seven at the primary level to four or five out of thirty in various years at intermediate school. In 1971 the Ministry of Education withdrew civics from the secondary school schedule due to dissatisfaction with it. Depending on the stream and the stage of secondary school, history and geography comprise two to four of the thirty one-hour program.[70] Private schools are not obliged to follow the official time schedule and some may devote even fewer hours to civics and social studies.

An analysis of the official curriculum provides further insights into the limitations of the educational system.[71] During the 1972–1973 academic year schools still substantially employed the civics, history, and geography outlines instituted in 1946. As with many other aspects of the educational system, these guidelines relied heavily on the program prevailing during the French Mandate, which was already outdated by then current French standards. According to the official curriculum, civics and morals constituted a single subject oriented toward fostering spiritual values, moral standards, and pride in the nation. But most of the time allocated to civics focused on an abstract catalogue of general moral virtues, many of which seem more appropriate for French schoolchildren of forty years ago than for contemporary Lebanese students. To give some examples, topic headings included refinement of the mind and senses, strength of will, noble character, self-control, kindness to animals, and conscience and its prerogatives. Concern with the Lebanese political system came only in one small unit comprising approximately one-eighth of the syllabus in the eighth and ninth years of education and then in the final two baccalaureate classes. In the 1960s a group of educators prepared two civic texts in conjunction with the Ministry, which were then distributed as the authorized books for these courses.[72] These books, the only texts ever designated for use by the Ministry, dealt explicitly with the Lebanese political system and attempted to instill a sense of patriotism. However, in contrast with the official point of view, both books emphasized that the sectarian nature of the political system was only a transitional stage. After a few years of use these books were withdrawn in 1971, and civics was temporarily dropped from the secondary school course pending a revision of the curriculum.

The preamble to the history curriculum recognized that "History is one of the most useful courses in consolidating national sentiments and pride,"[73] but the actual curriculum does not accomplish these aims. Lebanon occupied a central position in the history curriculum—of the nine years of formal study of history, the topics for three of them focused entirely on Lebanon and, for the remainder, half of the history unit concentrated on Lebanon. However, the one-sided, Christian-oriented presentation of contemporary Lebanon as the direct outgrowth of a Phoenician civilization that was then enriched by cultural ties primarily with the West has alienated many Muslims, and it has neglected to instill a proper appreciation in many students for the considerable contributions of the Arab world. Despite Lebanon's location in the Middle East and the integral role its relationship with its neighbors has played in its evolution, students learned little about Arab history, and the curriculum completely neglected the history of the Arab world after 1800. In contrast, for many school years, half of the course revolved around Western history. Another deficiency came through the greater emphasis on the ancient and the early modern periods at the expense of the twentieth century. By failing to update the curriculum after 1946, the Ministry denied students the opportunity to study the post-World War II years, which encompassed the critical post-independence developments. After nine years of history, Lebanese schoolchildren might understand little about why Lebanon sought its independence, the accomplishments of the state, or the problems it seeks to resolve.

Despite the dissatisfaction voiced in many quarters over a period of years with the 1946 curriculum and the establishment of several committees vested with the responsibility for reforming the history and civics courses, a new history curriculum was first introduced in the 1973–1974 academic year. The failure to reform the curriculum earlier attests to the difficulties of achieving a consensus as to how Lebanon's history and political system should be interpreted. The textbooks adopted by different schools reflect the divergence of historical and political perspective which characterizes Lebanon. It should be noted though that the differences of interpretation, as real and consistent as they are, reveal themselves through subtle nuances in the manner in which the texts deal with a particular subject. All textbooks generally follow the prescribed course outline. Moreover, the tact and politeness the Lebanese generally show to members of other groups has its counterpart in the educational system in the treatment accorded to sensitive topics in these books.

Based on our analysis of seventy two history texts used by various Lebanese schools, it is clear that the major difference in history texts is whether Lebanon's heritage is viewed as predominantly Phoenician or Arabic. Those authors, generally Christians, who advocate the Phoenician perspective devote more pages and chapters to the subject, even adding it to sections of the curriculum dealing with Arab history. They selectively emphasize the favorable aspects of the Phoenician civilization and tend to equate Lebanon's present boundaries with those of the ancient Phoenician states. Texts with a more Arab orientation, often written by Muslims, focus on the connection between Lebanon and the Arab world and subtly try to demonstrate that the ancient Phoenician city-states were not coterminous with Lebanon. Another point of disagreement comes in the discussion of the Mandate period in assessing both the motives of the French and the historical basis of Greater Lebanon. The pro-Phoenician group of texts tend to be more favorable to the French and more inclined to perceive Greater Lebanon as having deep historical roots. Although no data are available that permit a precise attribution of which texts are employed by which schools, it seems likely that Christian schools tend to adopt Phoenician-oriented texts and Muslim schools tend to use texts that are Arab-oriented.

Based on our content analysis of fifty four civics texts in use in 1972–73, it is evident that civics texts universally avoid controversy by failing to discuss the confessional nature of the political system. Descriptions of a particular political office do not mention the sect affiliation of its holder. With the exception of the two civics texts for the baccalaureate classes once issued by the Ministry of Education and later withdrawn, none of the books even hint that Lebanon has a multiconfessional plural society which has given rise to a political system of a special character. This may account in part for why respondents in our student and adult surveys, as discussed in Chapter 3, attributed so little importance to schools as agents of political socialization.

A revised history curriculum introduced in 1973–74 corrects most of the major deficiencies of the 1946 version.[74] Lebanon's Phoenician heritage occupies a less central position, and Arab history receives attention during approximately one-half of three years of history at the intermediary level and one-third of two years of secondary history. Moreover, the curriculum carries the historical strands of Lebanese, Arab, and world history through the post-World War II period. Consequently, the new history program refocuses

Lebanon into a much more balanced perspective. A new civics curriculum will be written and instituted gradually beginning with the lowest primary classes.[75] In the meantime, the Ministry of Education has suspended the teaching of civics for secondary schools, and it seems unlikely that at the projected rate of development the new curriculum will be available for that level until the 1980s.

Along with the adoption of a new history curriculum, the Ministry of Education underwent another and even more important and hopeful change with the creation of an Educational Center for Research and Development, which became operational in 1972. By creating the Educational Center for Research and Development, the government has centralized control over the following subjects in a unit that has administrative and financial autonomy: educational planning, educational research, production of textbooks and instructional materials, educational documentation, educational training of teachers, and evaluation.[76] If the new center fulfills its mandate, it could fundamentally reform the educational system of Lebanon. Its success, however, is far from assured since it faces opposition from many educators, politicians and other influential people. Moreover, private schools are not anxious to lose any of their current freedom.

In conclusion, the educational system in Lebanon does not operate as a very effective agent to socialize children to a national perspective. Instead, we would agree with Emile Valin that education in Lebanon tends to reinforce the strength of subsystems.[77] As mentioned in Chapter 3, the potential of the educational system as an agent of national political socialization is circumscribed by cultural factors, particularly the preponderant role of the family. Nevertheless, the limited influence of formal education also stems from other factors. To reiterate, in a country in which education has remained primarily in private hands, the Ministry of Education has lacked the inclination and power to impose uniform standards reflecting national needs. The sectarian affiliation of a majority of schools combined with sectarian residential patterns render most educational institutions largely homogeneous in confessional terms. Unequal distribution of educational facilities has given rise to significant regional and confessional disparities with regard to access to schools in general and the availability of quality private schools in particular. Prescription of a general curriculum for history and civics by the Ministry of Education has not prevented a particularistic interpretation of these subjects in the textbooks, reflecting the divergent views of Lebanon and its history held by the respective confessional communities. In turn, to the limited extent that schools act as agents of socialization, many of the divergent political values and orientations of the confessional communities tend to be imparted to the children. At the present time the Ministry of Education has a unique opportunity through the Educational Center for Research and Development to set a new course and to create a more national frame of reference. Even such proponents of autonomy for private schools as Professor Charles Malik concur that education should now provide a "common denominator" through greater uniformity in the history curriculum to facilitate national accommodation.[78]

In our discussion of the educational system, of civil service personnel policies, and in the discussion of political reform, we have mentioned proposed modifications of the confessional system which undoubtedly warrant consideration. By relieving some of the rigidities of the current system, carefully conceived reforms could contribute to greater governmental effectiveness. Other reforms, for instance, the proposal to give the educational system a more national perspective, could also promote the process of national accommodation. Ten to fifteen years ago experimentation would have been risky, but intercommunity coexistence has now become sufficiently stabilized so that some adjustments are possible without endangering the viability of Lebanon's sociopolitical order. Nevertheless, virtually all potential reforms raise sensitive issues: they must be conceived with care and introduced with tact. The degree of democracy and political stability that this politically fragmented state has enjoyed attest to the ingenuity of the political system and particularly the confessional component of that system. The progress Lebanon makes over the next decade in achieving greater political modernization will help test the truth of Samuel Huntington's assertion that "the non-Western countries of today can have political modernization or they can have democratic pluralism, but they cannot normally have both."[79]

NOTES

1. Michael W. Suleiman, *Political Parties in Lebanon* (Ithaca, N.Y.: Cornell University Press, 1967), p. 1.
2. Ibid., p. 34.
3. Michael C. Hudson, *The Precarious Republic* (New York: Random House, 1968), p. 34.
4. Ibid., p. 89.
5. Ibid.
6. Edward Shils, "The Prospect for Lebanese Civility," in Leonard Binder, ed., *Politics in Lebanon* (New York: Wiley, 1966), p. 5.

7. This point is emphasized by such observers as Kamal Salibi, "Lebanon Since the Crisis of 1958," *The World Today*, 17 (January 1961), pp. 32–42; and Ilya Harik, "The Ethnic Revolution and Political Integration in the Middle East," *International Journal of Middle East Studies*, 3 (July 1972), pp. 319–320.

8. The best sources on the 1958 civil war are M. S. Agwani, *The Lebanese Crisis, 1958* (London: Asia Publishing House, 1965); Fahim I. Qubain, *Crisis in Lebanon* (Washington, D.C.: Middle East Institute, 1961); Leila Meo, *Lebanon: Improbable Nation* (Bloomington, Ind.: University of Indiana Press, 1965); Robert Murphy, *Diplomat Among Warriors* (London: Collins, 1964); Desmond Stewart, *Turmoil in Beirut* (London: Allan Wingate, 1958); Camille Chamoun, *Crise au Moyen-Orient* (Paris: Gallimard, 1963); Kamal Jumblatt, *Haqīqat al-Thawrat al-Lubnāniyyah (The Truth About the Lebanese Revolution)* (Beirut: Dar al-Nashir al-'Arabiyya, 1959); Kamal Jumblatt, *Fī-Majrā al-Siyāsat al-Lubnāniyyah Awdạ̄'wa-Takhṭīṭ, (In the Course of Lebanese Politics, Situations and Plans)* (Beirut: Dar-al-Tali'a, 1960?), Ma'rūf Sa'ad and Muhammad Majdhūb, *'Indamā Qawamnā (When We Resisted)* (Beirut: Dār al-'Ilm li'l-Malāyīn, 1959); Emile Bustani, *March Arabesque* (London: Robert Hale, 1961); Malcolm H. Kerr, "Lebanese Veiws on the 1958 Crisis," *Middle East Journal*, 15 (Spring 1961), pp. 211–217; Arnold Hottinger, "Zu'amā' and Parties in the Lebanese Crisis of 1958," *Middle East Journal*, 15 (Spring, 1961), pp. 127–140; Kamal Salibi, "The Lebanese Crisis in Perspective," *The World Today*, 14 (Sept. 1958), pp. 369–380; Pierre Rondot, "Quelques Réflexions sur les Structures du Liban," *Orient*, 2 (1958), pp. 23–36; Pierre Rondot, "La Crise du Liban," *L'Afrique et L'Asie*, No. 43 (1958), pp. 45–53; Nabih A. Faris, "The Summer of 1958," *Middle East Forum*, 38 (Jan. 1961), p. 32; Francis Nour, "Particularisme Libanais et Nationalisme Arabe," *Orient*, 2 (1958) pp. 29–42; Jean-Pierre Alem, "Troubles Insurrectionnels au Liban," *Orient*, 2 (1958), pp. 37–47; Ephraim Frankel, Jr., "The Maronite Patriarchate and its Role in Lebanese Politics: A Case Study of the 1958 Lebanese Crisis,"American University of Beirut, unpublished M.A. thesis, 1971; and Na'īm al-Zayla', *Sham'ūn Yatakallam (Chamoun Speaks)* (Beirut: n.p., 1960).

9. "Forum Interviews Pierre Gemayel," *Middle East Forum*, 34 (March 1959), p. 30.

10. Emile Bustani, *March Arabesque*, op. cit., p. 86.

11. The principal sources used for background on the 1969 commando crisis include the following periodicals: *L'Orient, Al-Nahār, Al-Anwār, Al-Jarīda, Al-'Amal, Al-Muharrir,* and *The Arab World.* Also useful were Development Studies Association, *Lubnān wa'l-'Amal al-Fidā'ī al-Filasṭīnī (Lebanon and the Palestine Guerrillas)* (Beirut: Nadwat al-Dirāsā al-Inmā'iyyah, 1969); Rais A. Khan, "Lebanon at the Crossroads," *World Today*, 25 (Dec. 1969), pp. 530–536.

12. See R. H. Dekmejian, "The Arab World After Nasser," *Middle East Forum*, 47 (Autumn and Winter 1971), p. 41.

13. For an elaboration of this point see Antoine Messarra, "Notre Independance est-elle menacée?" *L'Orient-Le Jour*, supplement, November 18–24, 1972, pp. iv and v.

14. For an interesting perspective on this issue, see Edmond Rabbath, *La Formation Historique du Liban Politique et Constitutionnel* (Beyrouth: Librairie Orientale, 1973), pp. 554–563; also Albert Hourani, "Arab Nationalism," in his *Arabic Thought in a Liberal Age* (London: Oxford University Press, 1962).

15. For an assessment of the new program from an Arab nationalist perspective see "Al-Shaikh Pierre ibn Amīn al-Jumayyil Yadḥhab al-'Urūba" ("Shaikh Pierre son of Amin el Gemayel Moves Towards Arabism"), *Al-Sayyād*, 29, No. 1467, (Oct. 26—Nov. 2, 1972), pp. 28–35; see also "Al-Ṭā'ifiyyah" (Sectarianism) (Beirut: Al-Nahār, December 1972), p. 77.

16. Although it might be argued that comparing the old and young does not provide evidence of trends since as the young grow older their attitudes may become more similar to those of their elders, we feel confident about asserting the existence of a trend because similar differences appear when comparing the educated and uneducated and because recent political events provide corroborating evidence.

17. "One must 'live' the system in order to comprehend it." (Personal Interview with President Suleiman Frangieh, August 13, 1972).

18. "In a country like ours, made up of minorities which are almost equal, and equally jealous of their rights, where no community can pretend to constitute an oppressive majority, where there is no possibility of a dictatorship—the only possible peace is a consensual peace, founded on understanding and cooperation, and on an equilibrium." Le Jour, November 28, 1941.

19. Malcolm Kerr, "Political Decision Making in a Confessional Democracy," in Binder, Politics in Lebanon, op. cit., p. 190.

20. For an interesting editorial on government immobility on the economic front, see Al-Nahār, August 28, 1973.

21. In a public opinion survey conducted by al-Nahār newspaper, only 23.6 percent of those who favored the abolition of the confessional system advocated its elimination in one stroke, "Al-Ṭā'ifiyyah" ("Sectarianism") (Beirut: Al-Nahār Publishers, December 1972–January 1973), pp. 66–67. For corroborating data, see Halim Barakat, "Social and Political Integration in Lebanon: A Case of Social Mosaic," Middle East Journal, 27 (Summer 1973), p. 306.

22. See, for instance, the comments of former Premier Abdallah Yafi in "Ou s'arretent les pouvoirs du President de la Republique?" L'Orient-Le Jour, July 14, 1972, p. 4.

23. Elie Salem, "Cabinet Politics in Lebanon," The Middle East Journal, 21 (Autumn 1967), pp. 497–498.

24. Interview with Deputy 'Alī 'Abdallāh, January 22, 1973.

25. Interview with Imam Moussa Sadre, Chairman of the Higher Shiite Council on January 8, 1973 and with Shaikh Muḥammad Abū Shaqra, Sheikh 'Aql of the Druze community on January 30, 1973. The Mufti of the Sunni community, on the other hand, favors a new census being conducted. (Interview on February 12, 1973.)

26. Interview, March 24, 1973.

27. See, for instance, Joseph Mughaizil, Lubnān wa'l-Qaḍiyyat al-'Arabiyyah (Lebanon and the Arab Problem), (Beirut: Manshūrāt 'Awaydat, 1959), pp. 105–107; and Edmond Rabbath, op. cit., 554–563.

28. Hassan Saab, "The Rationalist School in Lebanese Politics," in Binder, Politics in Lebanon, op. cit., p. 279.

29. Interview, December 1, 1972.

30. Quoted in L'Orient-Le Jour, April 29, 1973, p. 1.

31. L'Orient-Le Jour, April 9, 1972, p. 3.

32. L'Orient-Le Jour, February 21, 1973, p. 3.

33. L'Orient-Le Jour, May 13–19, 1972, p. xiv.

34. See, for instance, Charles Rizk, Le Régime Politique Libanais (Paris: Librairie Generale de Droit et de Jurisprudence, 1966), pp. 106–107 and p. 168; and Michael Suleiman, "Elections in a Confessional Democracy," The Journal of Politics, 29 (February 1967), p. 109. Also interviews with Deputy Ali Khalil, January 11, 1973, and with Deputy Zaki al Mazbudi, February 2, 1973.

35. See, for instance, the data compiled by Iliya Hari, Man Yaḥkum Lubnān (Who Rules Lebanon), (Beirut: Al-Nahār, 1972), pp. 32–33.

36. See Clyde G. Hess, Jr. and Herbert L. Bodman, Jr., "Confessionalism and Feudality in Lebanese Politics," *The Middle East Journal*, 8 (Winter 1954), pp. 10–26.

37. Fourteen percent of those who favored the continuation of proportional distribution proposed an amendment to the system under which only members of the candidate's community could vote for him, meaning that the Druze in the Chouf constituency, for instance, would only vote for candidates for the Druze seats, while the election of the Maronite deputies would be determined by the Maronites.

38. *L'Orient-Le Jour*, April 9, 15, 18, 25, 28, 1972 and May 5, 6, 11, 13, and 27, 1972.

39. Bishara al-Khouri, *Haqā'iq Lubnāniyyah (Lebanese Truths)*, Vol. 3, (Harissa: Basil Brothers Press, 1961), p. 68.

40. Mission IRFED, *Besoins et Possibilités de Développement du Liban*, Tome I, *Situation Economique et Sociale* (Beyrouth: Ministere du Plan, 1961), p. 17.

41. For a description of each of these, see Georges G. Corm, *Politique Economique et Planification au Liban, 1953–1963* (Beyrouth: Imprimerie Universelle, 1964), pp. 159–169.

42. Middle East Economic Consultants, "The Green Plan: A General Evaluation of Performance" (Beirut, 1972), mimeographed, p. 18.

43. See World Food Programme, "Plan of Operations: Integrated Development of the Lebanese Mountain Areas" (Beirut, May 1971), mimeographed, p. 18.

44. For a description of their activities, see Joseph Donato, "Le Plan de Développement Social au Liban" (Beyrouth: n.p., June 1960); and Maṣlaḥat al-In'āsh al-Ijtimā'i, *al-Taqrīr al-Sanawī li'ām 1969 (Annual Report of the Department of Social Development,)* (Beirut, 1969 and 1970, mimeographed).

45. Interviews with officials of the Ministry of Planning and the Green Plan.

46. Ministère du Plan, "Plan Sexennal de Développement, 1972–1977" (Beyrouth: La Direction Centrale de la Statistique, 1972).

47. Gabriel A. Almond and Sidney Verba in *The Civic Culture: Political Attitudes and Democracy in Five Nations* (Princeton, N.J.: Princeton University Press, 1963), deal with the relationship between education and political orientations in the United States, Great Britain, Mexico, Germany, and Italy, pp. 121, 151, 152, 206, 304, 336, 352, 359, 362, 379, 380, 382. See also Richard R. Dawson and Kenneth Prewitt, *Political Socialization* (Boston: Little, Brown and Co., 1969), pp. 143–180; James S. Coleman, "Introduction: Education and Political Development," in James S. Coleman, ed., *Education and Political Development* (Princeton, N.J.: Princeton University Press, 1965) pp. 3–34; Jeremy R. Azrael, "Soviet Union," in Coleman, ed., op. cit., pp. 233–271.

48. Robert D. Hess and Judith Torney, *The Development of Political Attitudes in Children* (Garden City, N.Y.: Doubleday and Co., 1968), p. 120.

49. See Hess and Torney, op. cit., pp. 33–36; Fred I. Greenstein, *Children and Politics* (New Haven, Conn.: Yale University Press, 1965), pp. 56, 60; David Easton and Jack Dennis, *Children in the Political System: Origins of Political Legitimacy* (New York: McGraw-Hill, 1969), p. 398.

50. *Plan Sexennal de Développement, 1972–1977*, p. 107; *L'Enquête par sondage sur la population active au Liban*, Novembre 1970, Vol. 1. *Méthodes analysées et présentation des résultats* (Beyrouth: Ministère du Plan, 1972), p. 97.

51. "Al-Dustūr al-Lubnāni" ("The Lebanese Constitution") (Beirut: Bureau of Lebanese and Arab Documentation, 1969), p. 3.

52. "Statistical Data on Education and Manpower in the Arab Countries" (Paris: OECD Directorate for Scientific Affairs and Development Centre, 1966).

53. *Statistiques Scolaires* (Beyrouth: Le Bureau de la Statistique, 1972), p. 6.

54. Ibid., pp. 28, 72.
55. This analysis is based on data in *Statistiques Scolaires*, p. 25.
56. Dawson and Prewit, op. cit., pp. 168–169; Kenneth P. Langton, *Political Socialization* (New York: Oxford University Press, 1969), p. 171.
57. Private school fees range up to L.L. 2000 per year per student, which is more than Lebanon's per capita income.
58. Interview with Mgr. Ignace Maroun, head of the Catholic schools in Lebanon, June 19, 1972.
59. Interview with Archbishop Ghaphrail Salibi, February 16, 1973.
60. Interview with Hisham Nashabi, Director of the Makassed school system, June 22, 1972.
61. Decree No. 6998-Decree No. 7004, October 1, 1946.
62. Government of Lebanon Decree No. 9101, Regulations on the Lebanese Baccalaureate Exam, Beirut, 1968.
63. This information is based on a list made available by the Center for Educational Research and Development which was compiled by a staff member going to the bookshops in Beirut selling school texts.
64. Letter addressed to Head of Education Research Department, May 29, 1970.
65. The material for this and the subsequent discussion on education is based on interviews which included three former ministers of education (Professor Charles Malik, Mr. Ghassan Tueni, and Dr. Najib Abu-Haidar), two former director-generals in the Ministry of Education, the director of the Makassed schools, the head of the Catholic schools in Lebanon, former staff of the Education Research Department, and members of the new Center for Educational Research and Development.
66. Interview with Hisham Nashabi, June 22, 1972.
67. Interview with Mgr. Ignace Maroun, June 19, 1972.
68. Interview with Joseph Zarour, former Director-General for General Education (primary and secondary schools), June 23, 1972.
69. Until 1972 four of the director-generals were Maronites; a fifth for Youth and Sports was a Shiite. The new organization of the Ministry changes the sectarian balance somewhat because the new autonomous director for the Center for Educational Research and Development is a Protestant.
70. Official schedule supplied by Ministry of Education.
71. This analysis is drawn from "Manhaj al-Ta'lim" ("The Program of Instruction") (Beirut: Ministry of Education, 1946).
72. *Al-Tarbiya al-Madaniyyah (Civics)*, 2nd. ed. (Beirut: Mudīriyyat al-Ta'līm al-Mihanī, 1970); *Al-Tarbiya al-Madaniyyah*, 2nd book *(Civics)*, 2nd ed., (Beirut: Mudīriyyat al-Ta'līm, 1970).
73. Program of Instruction, 1946.
74. "Manhāj al-Ta'līm," ("Program of Instruction"), directive 2151, 1970; 14529, 1970; "Jadāwil Manhāj al-Ta'līm," ("Program of Instruction"), directive No. 13167, October 20, 1969.
75. The Lebanese Republic, Ministry of Education and Fine Arts, Legislative Decree No. 2150 specifying the curriculum for education at the primary level, Beirut, 1971.
76. Decree No. 2356, December 10, 1971.
77. Emile Jean-Pierre Valin, *Le pluralisme socio-scolaire au Liban* (Beyrouth: Imprimerie Catholique, 1969), pp. 171, 178.
78. Interview with Charles Malek.
79. Samuel Huntington, "Political Modernization: America vs. Europe," *World Politics* 18 (April 1966), p. 412.

6

The Social, Cultural, and Ethnic Framework of the Ghanaian State

The social and cultural milieu in Ghana reflects the primacy of ethnic groups as the basic ordering unit in the society. However, the nature and dimensions of ethnic groups as well as their relative importance as political actors shift from time to time like the prisms in a kaleidoscope. An ethnic community generally consists of individuals who consider themselves to share a group identity based on a common ancestry and culture. Because membership in the ethnic group is subjectively defined, the boundaries of the ethnic group are imprecise and subject to change. At any point, an individual belongs to several actual or potential ethnic groups of varying levels of inclusiveness. Which of these ethnic groups is the most salient for his self-identity and whom he perceives as sharing membership in the group depends on the situation. Within the circumscribed village environment, the less inclusive lineage or the clan may take precedence, whereas the immigrant to the city mingling with a heterogeneous population will probably identify with a larger ethnolinguistic community. With the expansion of networks of intergroup contact, cultural and linguistic differences that once loomed large may be forgotten, and common bonds may be recognized. From one perspective, ethnic group membership is more rigid than religious sect affiliation, since the possibility of

193

conversion does not arise, but from another point of view, the communal implications are made more fluid.

For the purpose of analyzing the dynamics of the national political system in Ghana and assessing the potential for national accommodation, the more inclusive ethnolinguistic communities, sometimes referred to as tribes, are the most relevant actors.[1] However, in terms of subjective perception and objective definition, the boundaries between these ethnolinguistic communities are often difficult to draw. The majority of people in southern Ghana belong to one or another Akan subgroup, but some Ghanaians embrace their common Akan heritage and others emphasize the dialectical and cultural differences among the Akan. In the Northern and Upper Regions and the northern portion of the Volta Region of Ghana, the considerable linguistic variation obfuscates linguistic and hence ethnic divisions. Overlaying this division in the Northern and Upper Regions, though, groups share many similarities in social structure and culture,[2] and a sense of common heritage and regional identity now binds together many people from this area of Ghana, particularly when they migrate to the south.

According to the 1960 census results, the various Akan groups, all of whom reside in the south, constituted 44 percent of the Ghanaian population, the Mole-Dagbani in the north 16 percent, the Ga-Adangbe around Accra 8 percent, and the Ewe in the east 13 percent.[3] At the time of this enumeration foreigners composed about 12 percent of the total Ghanaian population. Subsequent governmental efforts to discourage continued permanent residence of large foreign African communities, particularly by means of the Aliens Compliance Order of 1969, reduced the proportion of the population accounted for by persons of foreign origin to 6.6 percent.[4] Thus, the Akan now comprise close to half of the Ghanaian population. Table 6-1 presents the major groups by size of the population as reported in the 1960 census.

TRADITIONAL INSTITUTIONS

As mentioned in Chapter 2, precolonial Ghana was divided into 200 political units of varying size which were patterned into one of four basic organizational models: the Akan, the Ga, the Ewe, and the Northern. The contemporary remnants of the traditional political systems do not pose much threat to the national unity of Ghana. Despite the structural differences, these systems historically shared many common elements, and even many of the distinctive

TABLE 6-1   *Distribution of Ghanaian Population in 1960 by Major Ethnolinguistic Groups*

GROUP	PERCENTAGE	AREA OF RESIDENCE
Akan	44.1	South
Fanti	11.3	
Ashanti	13.3	
Akim	3.0	
Akwapim	2.2	
Kwahu	2.0	
Boron	4.8	
Nzima	2.6	
Other	6.9	
Mole-Dagbani	15.9	North
Dagomba	3.2	
Dagarti	3.0	
Frafra	2.1	
Other	8.6	
Ewe	13.0	East
Ga-Adangbe	8.3	South-East
Ga	4.8	
Adangbe	3.5	
Guan	3.7	Throughout country
Gurma	3.5	North
Grusi	2.2	North

SOURCE: B. Gil, A. F. Aryee, D. C. Ghansan, *1960 Population Census of Ghana, Special Report 'E', Tribes in Ghana* (Accra: Census Office, 1964), pp. xxxiii, xxxiv.

institutional features have become more similar through the influence of the Akan model and the changes wrought by colonial administrators.[5] Moreover, the preeminent position of the central political system has reduced even the once mighty Ashanti empire to a largely ceremonial and symbolic status. It would be fallacious to assume that the incumbent office-holders wield the powers once associated with their rank or that they can evoke the respect formerly accorded to their predecessors. The ceding of sovereignty to the colonial agents placed the traditional rulers in the fundamentally compromising position of being the agents of an often unpopular overlord. Both the Ghanaian politicians and military officers who succeeded them have been careful to ensure that the chiefs who were enstooled were their compliant supporters. Thus, changes in regime have been associated with destooling some chiefs and enstooling others in their place. Moreover, the imposition of another, more inclusive and powerful, political system over the traditional order has deprived the traditional office holders of much of their *raison d'etre*. The organization of many of the traditional systems, particularly the Akan, reflected the needs of one of their primary preoccupations—going to war. Peaceful coexistence has caused many traditional institutions to atrophy like a vestigial organ. Furthermore, the decisions on significant issues once made by chiefs and other traditional office-holders have been removed to other levels of the political system. Whatever significant political powers and prerogatives remained to the chiefs at the time of independence disappeared after the onslaught of the Nkrumah regime against them.

Conversion to Christianity, the development of a market economy, the introduction of modern education, and large-scale urban migration have all eroded the influence of the chief. Since the position of the chief was bolstered by religious sanctions and since many of his functions had religious import, conversion to Christianity and Islam has had political implications. In some cases early Christian converts even disassociated themselves from the remainder of the community, in an effort to lead a new life consonant with Christian teachings. In many places the royal family themselves became Christians, making it difficult for the chief to pour libations and offer sacrifices to the ancestors as his office required. The development of a market economy and the new prosperity resulting from the cocoa trade weakened the corporate unity of many communities and also frequently reversed the traditional economic hierarchy in which the chief was the wealthiest member of the community. At the same time, disputes over stool lands and poor administration often impoverished the royal lineage.[6] The opening of schools by missionaries and the establishment of a national system of education after independence have not intentionally alienated the students from the traditional political system, but they have introduced new perspectives, values, and concerns. The fact that a student spends so much time at school reduces his familiarity with the traditional political system. Also, people with modern education have generally been unwilling to remain in their rural villages. Instead, they have emigrated to urban centers in search of prestigious white-collar employment. For the integrity of the traditional political system and the concomitant status of the traditional rulers, this widespread migration has two major repercussions. Many children live away from the home community when they would otherwise be socialized into its norms and practices, and frequently, even in rural areas, a portion of the town's population are outsiders owing no allegiance to the chief.

The contemporary role of traditional political institutions was one subject explored in three surveys undertaken by the authors in Ghana and one sponsored by the Ministry of Education in association with the authors and Lynn Fischer.[7] (The Appendix on Survey Methodology discusses the surveys in some detail.) Survey results indicate that formal education does not alienate a child from his local community, but that it does make appreciation of the role of tradition more formalistic. Children and university students still respect their traditional leaders and consider them to have a place in the community, but their description of the role of the chief reflects the limited functions he now performs. Although respondents believed that traditional rulers still had some contribution to make, they did not accord high status to them. Education then does have major repercussions for traditional institutions in pushing them further from the center to the periphery of concern. Schoolchildren in Ghana, particularly at the higher levels, showed themselves to be considerably more conversant with the central political system than with the traditional political institutions, and with this change in focus, traditional institutions have been relegated to a subsidiary position.

The contemporary role of traditional office-holders varies considerably from one area to another in Ghana. The deference they can command generally depends on their traditional status and on the degree of modernization their constituency has undergone. Many answers relating to the role of traditional authorities from the surveys show the Ashanti and the northerners as currently having the most effective traditional political systems and the respondents from these areas to be more conversant with the traditional systems. Upon succession to office, the community still grants each Ashanti chief, along with his stool and ornaments of office, the mantle of respect embodying the accomplishments of the Ashanti Confederation. The vitality of the traditional political systems in the north reflects the lower level of social and economic change that has transpired in that area. In contrast, Ga neglect of traditional authorities derives from the rapid development of Accra, their home territory, and also from the decentralized nature of their traditional political system.

For purposes of our analysis, the largely symbolic existence of the panoply of traditional political systems in Ghana does not have the same significance as the institutional networks emanating from the religious sects in Lebanon, because these traditional institutions cannot provide an organizational infrastructure for as many phases of life and because they are not national in scope. Traditional leaders coexist with modern political institutions, schools, hospitals, and voluntary associations, none of which fall under their scope of authority. Aside from membership in the carefully circumscribed Houses of Chiefs, traditional leaders have not organized on a regional or national basis. The festivals and ceremonies associated with traditional institutions remain part and parcel of an individual's life, but along with this concern for things traditional, most people operate in the nontraditional institutional order as well. The horizons of most Ghanaians have expanded beyond the confines of the traditional universe.

Ethnicity remains a salient variable, and ethnic differences are still considerable, but this relates more to the process of socialization than to the strength of traditional institutions. Values and attitudes concordant with ethnic, social, and political systems have survived with greater vitality than the institutions they once served. And, as it will be shown, ethnicity in Ghana, just like sect in Lebanon, provides a ready system of social classification, a kind of shorthand method of insight into the background and mores of an individual or group.

SOCIALIZATION AND LIFE STYLES

Our research findings as well as those of other scholars lend support to the hypothesis that a Ghanaian's conception of his world strongly depends on his ethnic group membership.[8] More significant differences among respondents on our surveys resulted from ethnicity than any other variable.[9] Ethnic groups showed significant differences in all of the categories of questions on the surveys. Children apparently acquire the orientations of their ethnic group partially through the explicit teachings of their family and partially through personal observation and imitation.

However, Ghana does not conform to the models of extreme discontinuities in socialization between traditionally oriented, early childhood learning and later teaching in a more national frame of reference.[10] Such extreme discontinuities fail to occur in Ghana because the child is exposed at an early age to both parochial and national agents of socialization and because the content of political learning communicated by the family often does not conflict with a more national perspective. The child in Ghana who is born in a rural community and lives there during his formative years still has meaningful contact with the national political system and modern agents of socialization. The fairly extensive road system that connects all parts of the country together enables the child to travel to other sections of the country and brings outsiders to his own village. Moreover, the dispersal of transistor radios and the interest in newspapers leaves few communities isolated from the impact of the mass media.

In Ghana individuals comfortably retain the traditional alongside the modern, partaking of both without major social or psychological conflict. Neither individuals nor social systems exhibit the consistency of being entirely traditional or modern. As David Brokensha concludes in his study of Larteh, a Guan-Akwapim town in the Eastern Region, "Much more significant than the conflicts or 'breakdowns' is the remarkable way in which old and new forms have blended achieving accommodation in nearly all areas of social life. The outstanding feature of social change at Larteh then is not conflict but adaptation and accommodation."[11] Brokensha believes that this process of assimilation makes Larteh typical of many West African communities. Our research and other publications support the thesis that social change necessitates neither conflict nor the collapse of traditional culture. Hence, the life style of Ghanaians incorporates a subtle blend of the modern and the traditional.

Language, dress, and customs provide the most visible signs of differences in life style among ethnic groups. The language an individual speaks not only instantly types him, it also erects barriers. The various dialects of Akan, the vernacular of almost half of the Ghanaian population, are mutually intelligible but there is little linguistic meeting ground between the non-Akan languages. Although knowledge of English and Akan by the non-Akan does furnish lingua francas for interaction, it does not dissipate the emotional ties linking members of an ethnolinguistic group. Styles of traditional dress are less significant because of the extensive borrowing between groups and because of the popularity of Western clothes, especially among the men. Some southerners have even begun to wear the distinctive smock tops that once set apart men from the north. Ghanaians proudly wear "national dress" for celebrations and ceremonial occasions, and this "national dress" refers to any of the traditional patterns.

Differing customs generally do not constitute divisive barriers. As is common among traditional societies, the Ghanaian ethnic groups evolved rites and rituals to mark all the important events of life. It is now common for some of the rituals formerly performed by the family or clan, like puberty rites, to be neglected. The annual or seasonal festivals celebrated by the people of a town or ethnic group have had far more significance because they served to reinforce the solidarity of the community and to bind each generation in turn to their cultural obligations. Although missionaries initially forbade converts to participate, Christians, who presently constitute the majority in most southern communities, now frequently join with their fellow townsmen in the ceremonies. For them, the festivals seem devoid of their original religious import; instead, participation expresses pride in their heritage.[12] Unlike the celebration of religious events in Lebanon, the pageantry of these events often evokes widespread respect and interest among members of other communities.

Ghanaians, like the Lebanese, generally seek the company of members of their own group. Although in both the rural communities and the urban centers people tend to retain some social distance from members of other ethnic groups, Ghanaians do not follow a practice of "mutual avoidance" in a prejudiced manner. Unlike in Lebanon, rural communities in Ghana traditionally have been largely homogenous. The high rate of internal migration has changed this—at the time of the 1960 census in two-thirds of Ghana's local authority areas at least half of the inhabitants were not members of the indigenous community[13], but the persons living in rural villages from other groups are generally recent arrivals, whose roots remain elsewhere and who consider themselves to be transients. Typically, the urban dweller views his residence there as only temporary, as well, and assumes that he will return home at some point in the future.[14]

The social exclusiveness in urban centers often derives from insecurity. Distances measured in levels of development and historical time are far greater in Ghana than in Lebanon between the rural and urban areas. A migrant from the Northern or Upper Regions particularly traverses a psychological divide of enormous magnitude in settling in a large southern Ghanaian city. The search for the security of the known in the vast impersonal otherness of the city draws members of the same group together, despite the fact that they do not usually live in ethnically segregated neighborhoods. Among them it is possible to speak one's own dialect, practice familiar customs and patterns of living, and perhaps most importantly, receive the warmth and assistance that can make life in an alien environment tolerable.

Within the pluralistic urban society, residents generally perceive the similarities and minimize the differences that separate contiguous ethnic groups within the rural area. The inclusive ethnolinguistic communities, not their constituent subgroups, often become the relevant boundaries. Thus, in the multiethnic urban environment the boundaries of membership of the ethnic groups become extended and the migrants' in-group often is a more inclusive unit, but the tendency to favor social contacts primarily within the group does not change.

The considerable ethnic heterogeneity in residence patterns does not give rise to strong social networks that cut across ethnic divisions. Geographical intermixing generally leads only to superficial social interaction among neighbors. Even voluntary associations frequently have an ethnic base in urban areas.[15] Some interactions between persons of different ethnic groups do take place on a casual, informal basis, though, and Ghanaians generally tend to be polite and hospitable to strangers. For instance, in the study done by Margaret Peil of Ghanaian factory workers, only 5 percent of the respondents said that they never had any social relationships with workmates, and 90 percent indicated that they would invite fellow employees to a social event like a party for a new baby.[16]

It should also be kept in mind that ethnicity constitutes only one variable, albeit a significant one, influencing patterns of socialization. The results of our three surveys support the conclusions of social scientists like Robert Hess and Judith Torney, who have worked with American children, that the family need not be the most salient agent in the process of political socialization, particularly in regard to the modern system.[17] The family usually communicates the traditional orientations and outlooks of the society, which, in the case of Ghana, tend to be ethnically particularistic. Therefore, the ability of more modern agents to counter this influence in the critical early years of childhood learning imports well for national unity. Formal knowledge gained through schooling comprised the most important source of knowledge and attitudes toward the modern political system; virtually no schoolchildren or university students designated their families as the most important source of their knowledge about the modern political system. Schooling provides children from differing ethnic groups with common experiences, exposure to the same learning materials, and a joint fund of knowledge about their country. Just as modernization and intergroup contact has reduced some of the visible differences in life styles, public education has eliminated the monopoly of the family and the particularistic society over molding the child.

Although inadequacies in the present curriculum hamper the schools from playing their full role as the paramount agent of political socialization, future improvements should enable them to impart a national perspective more effectively than they are now doing.

INTERGROUP RELATIONS

Intergroup relations by definition refer to the nature of the contacts between members of different groups, but in Ghana the subject is complicated by the difficulty of designating the salient groups. To some extent, it is possible to conceptualize the situation by perceiving the individual as surrounded by a series of concentric circles of decreasing intensity of loyalty. The most compelling referent remains the extended family and then the village or town to which his family traces its roots. Beyond the village there may be a larger traditional political unit, one or more ethnolinguistic communities of varying levels of inclusiveness, for example, Fanti and Akan, and finally the nation. This model of concentric circles does not, however, accurately present the complexity of the situation; first because the salience of a particular form of identity depends to a great extent on the context in which the individual must make a decision, and second because, historically, groups have altered their self-images. Hence, ethnic identities and the social relationships flowing from them do not easily fit into a series of rigid compartments, but instead may be likened to a kaleidoscope of ever-changing hues and combinations.

There is a disagreement among scholars and among Ghanaians themselves regarding the extent to which the ethnolinguistic communities, which are often the political referents of the contemporary Ghanaian political system, have traditional roots. Certainly the territorial limits of the traditional political units did not always coincide with contemporary ethnolinguistic communities or any kind of permanent network of alliances. The Ashanti empire extended beyond the demarcation of the Ashanti. Ewes, Gas, and several northern groups lacked any traditional political unity, and some scholars claim that they did not have a sense of common identity either. Even if they did, it was certainly based only on a weak sense of cultural affinity. Only after the imposition of the colonial system increased the regularity of contacts among groups did people broaden their awareness of the linguistic and cultural similarities uniting some groups and dividing others. The emerging sense of identity based on common culture and language has not led to the creation of political monoliths. Ghana's contemporary history attests to the significance of divisions within the ethnolinguistic communities as well as between them. The cohesiveness of an ethnolinguistic community itself depends on the particular issue.

Changes in the political context of intergroup relations can themselves lead to the perception of new communities which, in turn, become political actors. The emerging sense of a Pan-Northern Regional identity provides one such example. Since independence the various northern groups have become aware of cultural similarities and of the relative neglect of their area of the country and its lower level of development. Similarly, prior to the time of the first military regime in Ghana, few people thought of themselves as Akan. Instead, the dialectal divisions within the greater Akan unit constituted the salient points of reference. The traditional hostility between the Fanti and the Ashanti seemed for a long time to be one of the givens on the Ghanaian political landscape, but by the time of the election in 1969, the Akan entity had become a political force.

One of the major factors governing the character of intergroup relations is the ability to communicate across group boundaries. The results of one of our surveys of university students indicated that people who knew another Ghanaian language were more inclined to consider members of that group as similar to themselves. Even before the political evocation of the common Akan heritage, the mutual intelligibility of all Akan dialects drew Akans together. The non-Akan communities have not established and probably cannot construct an effective counteralliance because their languages are so different from one another. The spread of English and Akan as lingua francas has made it more possible for members of ethnic groups to interact socially, but the kinds of relationships that individuals have through an alien tongue often lack closeness and emotional satisfaction. Nevertheless, the facility for learning languages in Ghana is of enormous import for intergroup relations. Unfortunately, national statistics indicating knowledge of second languages are not available. On the Ministry of Education survey, which was administered to a national sample of 1757 school children, slightly more than half of the respondents could speak English or at least one other Ghanaian language besides their own. Few students from southern ethnic groups had learned any northern languages, but 26 percent of the students from northern communities had proficiency in at least one southern language. Akans showed less inclination than other Ghanaians to acquire a second language, probably because they had less need to do so, whereas members of the small non-Ewe

ethnic communities in the Volta Region, Gas, and northerners most frequently described themselves as having the ability to speak another language.
As these respondents grow older and have more contacts with members of
other communities, an even greater proportion of them may learn other
Ghanaian languages.

The frequency of intermarriage between groups provides an index of the
nature of intergroup relations. Until relatively recently the considerable
isolation of groups from each other precluded much contact, let alone
marriage. Only with the establishment of urban centers and the increasing
rates of internal migration has intermarriage become a possibility. In Ghana,
as in Lebanon, significant social pressure still exists to marry within a narrowly defined group. Nevertheless, according to statistics based on the post-
enumeration survey of the 1960 census, interethnic marriage in Ghana at that
time occurred approximately twice as often as inter-sect marriage currently
does in Lebanon. In 1960 the vast majority of males, 82 percent, reported that
their wives came from the same tribe, with 8 percent having wives from an
entirely different group, and the remainder from related subgroups.[18] As
might be expected, more men in urban areas, almost one-fourth of the total
urban male population, chose a wife from another ethnic community.
Several Akan subgroups, particularly the Akwapim and Akim, had a
significantly above average proportion of interethnic marriages while groups
in the Volta Region (Ewe and non-Ewe) and northerners had greater than
average inclination to choose a marital partner within their own community.
Such interethnic unions may become somewhat more common in the future;
younger and better educated men more often marry a woman outside of their
own group, and Christians and Muslims, both of whom are likely to increase
their proportion in the population, are more likely than adherents of traditional religions to cross ethnic boundaries.[19] However, ethnic solidarity will
probably mitigate against any substantial increase in the numbers of interethnic marriage. Only 27 percent of the students participating in the Ministry of
Education survey indicated a willingness to marry someone without regard to
his or her ethnic background.

In an effort to ascertain more about Ghanaians' self-identity and images of
members of other groups, series of relevant questions were included on the
surveys. Some of the resulting trends in the answers have implications for
current and future ethnic relations in Ghana. Particularly, the survey results
confirm the emergence of a new sense of Akan identity. They also show a
greater level of ethnocentricity and prejudice than many Ghanaians assume

exists. Respondents consistently demonstrate stronger negative stereotypes toward Ewes and northerners than to any other Ghanaian ethnic groups. Although students cannot be considered typical of the entire population, our less systematic interviewing of adults corroborated these patterns. Moreover, as discussed in the next chapter, social and political behavior seems consistent with these results.

Only a few years ago the term Akan was more likely to be employed by scholars to refer to a linguistic grouping than by Ghanaians themselves to identify an ethnic community. Although the Akan peoples shared many cultural traits, their self-perception emphasized the historical, institutional, and cultural differences that separated the various subgroups. As the next chapter will discuss in greater detail, this sense of distinctiveness constituted one of the givens of the political landscape through the time of the Nkrumah regime, particularly the friction between the Fanti and the Ashanti. This has changed. Many of our respondents, for instance, 61 percent of the university students on one survey on open-ended questions, identified themselves or referred to another Ghanaian as an Akan rather than as being Fanti, Ashanti, or other groups. Both Joseph Kaufert and Robert Price in their recent research similarly found that the Akan cluster had real meaning within the referent sets of their Ghanaian research subjects.[20]

Contrary to the assumptions of many members of the Ghanaian elite, the results of all four surveys consistently pointed to the existence of a considerable level of ethnocentrism and probable prejudice. Increasing amounts of education, particularly when associated with moving beyond the confines of predominantly homogenous school environment into one with a more heterogeneous school population at the secondary and university levels, reduced this, but even this educated elite displayed some prejudice toward members of other groups. Moreover, in a society in which the majority is still illiterate and only 63 percent of the eligible children attend primary school,[21] the widened perspective of the educated elite probably counts for less than the attitudes of the uneducated and partially educated, especially since well-educated political leaders harboring little personal hostility to members of other ethnic communities frequently have been the ones in communally divided countries to manipulate the emotions of the masses for their own ends. When asked, for example, on the Ministry of Education survey whether it would be hard to play soccer when students from other regions were on their team,[22] only 35 percent of the primary, 49 percent of the middle, and 51 percent of the secondary students said no. With each successive grade of children at the primary school level, the percentages answering that it would be difficult actually increased. The vast majority of primary and middle school respondents preferred to attend school in their own regions, and most secondary school respondents were similarly inclined. When given a list of some of Ghana's ethnic groups, many students, particularly in primary and middle school, indicated that there were ethnic groups with whom they could not have even economic relationships: only 43 percent of the primary respondents and 52 percent of those questioned in middle school, but 73 percent in secondary school, were willing to trade with all persons irrespective of their backgrounds.

University students consistently displayed less ethnocentricity. The vast majority claimed that they were not concerned with the ethnic backgrounds of their university tutor, the prime minister of Ghana, or their future spouse. In their choice of their three closest friends, all but 13 percent of our sample went beyond the confines of their own region; 54 percent indicated that at least two of their three closest friends came from other regions. Most of these respondents had attended secondary boarding schools that had a heterogeneous student body and they met their friends there. Members of the Ghanaian elite cannot be considered ethnically blind: the university sample has the same patterns of negative stereotypes toward certain ethnic groups as the other respondents, and their ethnic identity counts for very much in explaining their conduct. However, along with this attachment to their ethnic group, many of them consider their school ties to be important. Therefore, networks of "old boys," especially from the secondary boarding schools, which link together persons from several ethnic groups, somewhat counterbalance ethnic polarization. One unfortunate effect of increasing the number of secondary schools in Ghana has been the trend toward ethnic homogeneity in many of the newer schools, which draw their student bodies only from the surrounding region.

Our survey results demonstrate the character of negative stereotypes Ghanaians hold of members of some ethnic groups, particularly of Ewes and of northern ethnic groups. Many of the respondents, with the exception of university students, considered foreigners, even the British, who of course are of another race and live on another continent, or the Hausa, who are citizens of Nigeria, as closer to them than the Ghanaian Ewe or Dagomba. Respondents on the Ministry of Education survey also cited the Ewe and the Dagomba as the two ethnic groups with which they were most reluctant to intermarry or to trade. In another study of social distance based on responses to a questionnaire given to secondary students in Ghana, Roberta Koplin's mean scores produced similar patterns, with the Ashanti along with the Fanti and other smaller Akan groups bringing the most favorable reaction and the Ewe placing last on the list. The mean distance scores that she compiled revealed that almost all of her respondents would feel more at ease socially interacting with British than they would with Nzimas, Dagombas, and Mamprusi Ghanaians.[23] Similarly, Joseph Kaufert's research on ethnic clusters based on university students' interethnic social distance scalings of 14 major ethnic groups in Ghana, showed a sharp distinction between Ewes and northerners and the remaining groups.[24]

Thus, a review of intergroup relations in Ghana does not present a simple picture. Ethnicity comprises the strongest social tie, and Ghanaians are drawn to members of their own group. The survey data revealed considerable evidence of ethnocentricity and the crystalization of negative attitudes toward Ewes and northerners. Moreover, a slight majority of university students believed that tribalism was on the ascendance in Ghana. On the other side, secondary and university students displayed more tolerance and a decreased emphasis on ethnic identity on many items, and, as will be discussed later in this chapter, students at all levels exhibited a national perspective in reference to some issues. Urbanization and increased internal migration have provided new opportunities for socializing and living with members of other ethnic communities, but their short-term effect seems to have been to foster the emergence of more inclusive ethnolinguistic blocs and to increase ethnic consciousness and distinctiveness. By bringing together persons in new economic and social relationships, urban centers have also encouraged a somewhat higher rate of ethnic intermarriage. If agents of national political socialization take a more active role, the maintenance of ethnic attachments still seems compatible with a growing commitment to the national community. However, present ethnic attitudes seem sufficiently divisive to warrant active governmental intervention. Otherwise it is possible that ethnic relations may deteriorate to a point that would make national accommodation very difficult to achieve.

ETHNIC GROUPS AND SOCIOECONOMIC DEVELOPMENT

In Ghana, as in most plural countries, there are discrepancies in the social and economic development of constituent communities. Statistics indicate the south generally, and particularly the Greater Accra, Ashanti, and Eastern

Regions, outdistance the level of development of the rest of the country with the northern areas far behind. Similarly, profiles of the ethnic groups whose traditional home is in those better developed areas, the Fantis, Ashantis, Akwapims, and Gas, attest to the advantage of earlier opportunities for education, urbanization, and cocoa production, while the groups of northern origin lag considerably behind.

Provisional returns from the 1970 census show the total population of Ghana to be 8,545,561, broken down regionally as described in Table 6-2. Statistics on the homogeneity of localities according to birthplace by regions show that the Greater Accra Region has attracted the greatest number of migrant Ghanaians. By 1970 probably less than half of the population there had originated in the region. In contrast, only 5 percent of the population in the Volta Region and 2 percent in the Northern and Upper Regions had migrated from another region in Ghana.[25] Volta and Northern and Upper Regions were the net exporters of laborers for other parts of Ghana. This population outflow also has had repercussions for the development of the three regions from which many of the migrants come, because many of their educated and skilled citizens seek employment in other parts of Ghana,

TABLE 6-2   *Regional Distribution of Ghana's Population in 1970*

REGION	1970 POPULATION	1960 POPULATION	PERCENT INCREASE (1960-1970)	AVERAGE ANNUAL GROWTH RATE PERCENT
All regions	8,559,313	6,726,815	27.04	2.4
Ashanti	1,481,698	1,109,133	33.59	2.9
Brong Ahafo	766,509	587,920	30.38	2.7
Central	890,135	751,392	18.46	1.7
Eastern	1,261,661	1,094,196	15.30	1.4
Greater Accra	851,614	491,817	73.16	5.6
Northern	727,618	531,573	36.88	3.1
Upper	862,723	757,344	13.91	1.4
Volta	947,268	777,285	21.89	2.0
Western	770,087	626,155	22.99	2.1

SOURCE: Table 3.2, *1970 Population Census of Ghana*, Vol. II, *Statistics of Localities and Enumeration Areas* (Accra: Census office, 1972), p. XXIII.

and because the economically productive sector of the population remaining there supports a larger proportion of dependents.

On the basis of eight socioeconomic indices: population density, number of cities (settlements of 5000), number of secondary schools, population per doctor in government hospital, percentage of regional population consuming electricity, gallons of water consumed per head, number of manufacturing industries, and length of standard road per 100 square miles, K. B. Dickson, a Ghanaian geographer, suggests the following regional ranking from most to least developed: Accra, Ashanti, Eastern, Central, Western, Volta, Brong Ahafo, Northern, Upper.[26] This developmental rating cannot be considered conclusive because it does not take into account agricultural productivity, per capita income, literacy, and primary and middle school attendance. Since cocoa has accounted for most of Ghana's export earnings during the twentieth century and national prosperity has often depended on the cocoa crop, the fact that in recent years more than one-third of Ghana's crop has been produced in Ashanti and none of it grown in the northern regions again points to historical economic discrepancies. In 1963–1964, the last years for which regional data on cocoa production were published, the regional breakdown was as follows: 37 percent from Ashanti, 21 percent from Brong-Ahafo, 18 percent from the Eastern Region, 13 percent from the Central Region, 6 percent from the Volta Region, and 5 percent from the Western Region.[27]

Another important index, educational enrollment, shows that with respect to primary and middle school attendance, the Eastern and Ashanti Regions have a higher percentage of school children relative to their population size and the Upper and Northern Regions a lower percentage. Accra and the Central Regions have more secondary school enrollment and the Northern and Upper Regions less than their portion of the 1970 population.[28] In 1970 the region with the highest proportion of persons in the age group six years and over who had been to school was Accra (65 percent) followed by the Eastern (54 percent), Ashanti (51 percent), Western (47.9 percent), Volta (47.4 percent), Central (43.7 percent), and Brong Ahafo (38.9 percent), with the Upper (12.1 percent) and Northern Regions (11.1 percent) recording significantly lower figures for past and present school attendance.[29]

As might be expected, standings of ethnic groups within the classification of white-collar workers reflect educational patterns. According to the 1960 census, the last one for which ethnic breakdowns were published, the ranking of ethnic groups within the classification of white-collar workers from highest to lowest was Ga-Adangbe, Akan, non-Ewe Volta, Ewe, Mole-Dagbani, and

Gurma. If only the professional and technical white-collar workers were considered, then the non-Ewe Volta groups had the highest status followed by the Akan, Ga-Adangbe, Ewe, Mole-Dagbani, and Gurma.[30]

A review of the trends of socioeconomic development in Ghana reiterates the theme, already cited in other parts of this study, of the gap between the northern and southern portions of the country. Differences in economic potential as well as historical accidents and policy decisions made in the early years of the colonial period gave rise to many of the current discrepancies in development, but what is more ominous for the future of the country is the continuation and perhaps even accentuation in some of the patterns since independence. As Ghana has become more industrialized, better educated, and more modern in other ways, the government's inclination to invest in areas with some elements of an infrastructure has frequently deepened the already existing gap. The lower level of political consciousness in the north has not as yet led to major or sustained political demands for the government to undertake a major effort to equalize development there, but it may occur. Moreover, if the south develops at a faster rate than the north and further increases the gap between them, it will become more difficult to establish a sense of common citizenship.

CROSSCUTTING TIES AND ASSOCIATIONS

In Ghana, education, religious affiliation, labor unions, farmers' associations, women's and youth groups, and class formation all provide some nexus between persons belonging to different ethnic groups. The effectiveness of these ties as integrating forces vary considerably in terms of the number of ethnic groups they embrace and in their salience. Of them, education has the most significant impact because of the common outlook and orientations that it imparts and because of the national system of social stratification that derives from it. Religion, particularly Christian denominations, divides local communities, but it also links adherents throughout Ghana. From another perspective, though, religion by reinforcing north/south differences may eventually constitute a disintegrative mechanism. Although labor unions, farmers' associations, and youth groups frequently draw their memberships from a wide base, they rarely sustain movements strong enough to challenge the primacy of ethnic bonds. Similarly, ethnic identity overshadows the class structure that bisects it, and it remains a deterrent to the development of strong class consciousness.

Education

Ghana, in contrast to Lebanon, has a national system of education cutting across ethnic boundaries. With the exception of a small number of international schools, primarily for foreign children resident in Ghana, all of the primary and middle schools form one system, including those managed by churches. As the analysis of the education system in Chapter 8 will detail, since 1958 the Ministry of Education has prescribed uniform curricula for all subjects in primary and middle schools in addition to deciding which textbooks should be used. Public primary and middle schools in Ghana—and there are very few private schools at this level—follow the same program, receive identical financing, and are staffed from a common pool of teachers. Hence, the national system of education has imparted to school attenders a shared experience and, to some extent, instilled in them common expectations and orientations.

The impact of the national education system as an agent of political socialization has been circumscribed, however, by the limited exposure of the population and inadequate curricula. Because the expansion of the educational system has been so recent, a majority of adults have not had the benefits of education, and the minority who have attended school mostly did so at a time when curricula determination was less centralized. Even today, 37 percent of the children eligible for school never enroll, and low attendance patterns coincide with other regional and ethnic disparities. In addition, the lack of concern of educationalists in Ghana with manifest political socialization to encourage a sense of national citizenship has caused the educational system to dissipate some of its potential for inculcating loyalty to and concern for the national community.

Patterns of responses to questions on the Ministry of Education survey reveal some of the strengths and weaknesses of the educational system as an agent of national political socialization.[31] National accommodation depends in part on a commitment to the national community and the evolution of a national perspective. The survey's results show that by primary class 5 or age eleven a majority of the students questioned were able to name Ghana as the nation to which they belonged. However, the vast majority of primary and middle school respondents could not respond to an inquiry as to what was their opinion of Ghanaians, possibly because they could not conceptualize a shared Ghanaian nationality beyond the distinct ethnic identities. With regard to the evolution of a national frame of reference, 43 percent of the primary students, 54 percent of the middle school students, and 59 percent of the secondary students responded that an Ewe from Ghana (the example was changed depending on the region) should feel closer to another Ghanaian from a different ethnic group than to an ethnic brethren from another African country. On the other hand, most primary and approximately half of the middle school respondents did not want to share revenues from their region with Ghanaians resident elsewhere. Primary and middle school students further exhibited insularity in admiring parochial rather than national figures. In rating whether the extended family, village, tribe, or Ghana was most important to them, respondents at the primary and middle levels preferred their families, but Ghana appeared as the second choice of even the primary students and as the primary loyalty of a slight majority of those in secondary school.

National accommodation also presumes some awareness of how the political system operates. Students in Ghana at best seem to have fragmentary knowledge. Respondents at all levels had difficulty conceptualizing the functioning of the Ghanaian political system. Most could not describe the role of such key institutions as the national assembly or respond either factually or evaluatively when asked about the role of such groups as politicians. But by the fourth primary class, the majority of students knew that the teachers' salaries were paid by the government. Respondents in middle and secondary schools consistently were able to identify Prime Minister Busia as a leader of the national government and understood that he had become prime minister by election. The timing of the administration of the survey, which occurred within two weeks after the military coup that brought Colonel I. K. Acheampong to power, provided an unusual opportunity to gauge understanding of an important political event. When asked who was the head or leader of government for all of Ghana, 11 percent of the primary, 30 percent of the middle, and 66 percent of the secondary school respondents named Colonel Acheampong or the army, indicating that they realized the implications of the coup. Slightly more than half of the primary and a third of the middle school students went without answering at all, but it is difficult to know why —whether they were confused, incognizant, or afraid—and the remainder listed Busia or another prominent person in his administration. Students generally believed that the government helped them and their families and that people could influence what the government decides to do, but there was no correlation on these questions between positive attitudes and amounts of education.

Political socialization theorists have reported that attachment to national symbols plays an important role in development and identification with one's country.[32] In a plural society in which most members have at best a dawning sense of national consciousness and partial information about the national system, such symbols could provide a particularly valuable emotional link between citizens and their nation. Survey results, however, show that Ghanaian schools fail to impart awareness of national symbols. Few respondents in the Ministry of Education survey could accurately describe from memory the Ghanaian flag: only 6 percent of primary, 25 percent of middle, and 58 percent of secondary students could do so. Even fewer were familiar with Christiansborg Castle, the seat of government and a historical landmark.

It is difficult to evaluate conclusively the impact of education in Ghana on fostering national accommodation, especially since we did not have the opportunity to test a control group of uneducated Ghanaians comparable to the educated samples. With continuously increasing amounts of education, respondents became more politically aware, nationally oriented, and somewhat more tolerant; but even secondary school students could not be described as well informed or as having national frames of reference. Primary and middle school students, who are more typical of the educational level of the adult population, were even less so. The relative ineffectiveness of schooling derives to a considerable extent from deficiencies in the curriculum, which will be assessed in greater detail in Chapter 8.

Religion

The 1960 census revealed that according to the self-identification of respondents, Christians constituted the most numerous religious group in Ghana with 43 percent of the population; believers in traditional religions were 38 percent; and Muslims were 12 percent of the adult population. Significantly, major ethnic groups in southern Ghana had a high percentage of Christian affiliation and a low percentage of Muslim affiliation, whereas the ratio of Christians to Muslims tended to be the opposite in the north.[33] Far more northerners clung to their traditional religion than did southerners. The historical diffusion of religions in Ghana accounts for this pattern. Islam entered Ghana earlier from the north through the aegis of other African groups. Christianity first came to the southern coastal areas as an adjunct of European expansion and gradually spread inland as part of the contact with other elements of Western civilization. Because colonial administrators preferred to exclude them as a potentially disruptive influence, Christian mis-

TABLE 6-3 *Religious Affiliation of Adults by Ethnic Group in 1960*

ETHNIC GROUP	CHRISTIAN	MUSLIM	TRADITIONAL
Akan	62.7	4.3	25.4
Ga-Adangbe	54.5	1.5	35.2
Ewe	48.3	0.4	45.1
Non-Ewe Volta	71.5	1.5	26.7
Mole-Dagbani	7.4	21.9	63.9
Grushi	6.1	14.2	70.8
Total	42.8	12.0	38.2

SOURCE: B. Gil, A.F. Aryee, D.K. Ghansah, *1960 Population Census of Ghana, Special Report 'E', Tribes in Ghana*, Accra: Census Office, 1964, p. LXXXV.

sionaries have established posts in most parts of the north only since independence.

Unlike many other African countries where missionaries carved out geographic or ethnic blocs in which their church proselytized without interference from other sects, denomination cuts across ethnic lines in southern Ghana. There are a few churches, like the Evangelical Presbyterian Church, which have a limited geographical base in one ethnic area, but these localized churches do not have a monopoly. Census tables show that each of the major southern ethnic groups is represented among several different Christian denominations. For example, 63 percent of Akans in 1960 described themselves as Christians. Of this group, 20 percent were Roman Catholic, 20 percent Methodist, 11 percent Presbyterian, 3 percent Anglican, 3 percent Apostolic, and 7 percent members of other Christian churches. The 55 percent of the Ga-Adangbe who similarly registered as Christians also were divided into Roman Catholics with 3 percent, Methodist with 13 percent, Presbyterian with 20 percent, Anglican with 8 percent, Apostolic with 8 percent, and other smaller church groups. Ewe Christians, who comprised 48 percent of the total ethnic group, said that they attended the Roman Catholic Church, 21 percent; the Presbyterian Church, 21 percent; and the Methodist Church, 1 percent.[34] Fragmentation among Christian sects in local communities means that in any given village or town as many as ten or more denominations may compete for adherents.[35]

The situation is different, however, with respect to the northern part of

Ghana. First, most of the population remains wedded to the traditional religion, and among those who have embraced a more universalist creed, Muslims outnumber Christians two to one. Second, one Christian sect, the Roman Catholic Church, has made much more of an effort than any other to establish a base in the north. This is shown both in the 1960 census results and by Ministry of Education data. In Ghana, as in most parts of Africa, the opening of schools usually provided missionaries with their first foothold in a community. Ministry of Education statistics on the management units for public primary and middle schools by district indicates that the major denominations have schools in virtually every district of every region, with the exception of the Northern and Upper Regions. In these two regions the Roman Catholic educational agencies manage ninety six primary schools while the Presbyterians have twelve, the Anglicans six, and the Methodists one.[36] Similarly, Roman Catholic units manage twenty two middle schools in contrast with five for all other Christian denominations.[37]

It is difficult to assess with certainty the significance of religion as an integrating or disintegrating force in Ghana. Although the churches do create a community of believers throughout Ghana and members frequently belong to active local organizations, the sects have generally not sought to create strong national lay associations or youth groups. Sectarian membership does not generally constitute a strong basis of primordial identification, and it is not uncommon for persons to change membership from one church to another for minor reasons unrelated to dogma or belief. Moreover, the fragmentation of communities in terms of general church membership does not lead to animosity. Perhaps this reflects the traditional religious tolerance noted in Chapter 2 as well as the historical development of the churches in the Gold Coast. One study observes that missionary activity in the Gold Coast was more moderate and free from the religious extremism expressed by sects elsewhere in Africa.[38] At the time when Christianity was initially introduced, converts had a sense of belonging to a separate community, but now Christians tend to exert less effort to set themselves off from the practitioners of traditional religion. In many places the children of both groups attend school together, the adults participate in the same annual rituals, which usually commemorate the unity of the town rather than ancestral spirits, and all avidly listen to transistor radios and partake of other material elements of modern life. Only the African spiritual churches tend to stimulate the close bonds and excessive self-consciousness once characteristic of all Christian communities.[39] Most Christian parents do not seem to object to their children marrying outside of the sect. On the whole, Ghanaians exhibit a great deal of religious tolerance to all other religions and sects regardless of the one to which they belong. The Christian–Muslim dichotomy could become more salient in the future, though, because it reinforces the many other distinctions between the north and south.

Labor Unions

At first glance, the trade union movement in Ghana appears to be an effective social movement cutting across ethnic lines, and to a certain extent it does serve this role. Unions exist in the major industrial enterprises, and during the last twenty years most unions in Ghana have been affiliated with one central trade union congress. In actuality, however, unions make only a marginal impact on the primacy of ethnic ties. To begin with, only a small percentage of the entire population finds employment in the industrial sector of the economy. The preponderantly agricultural economic base of the country limits the potential proportion of the overall population available to the unionists to organize to a maximum of about 12 percent of the work force. In 1960 only 330,000 persons, representing 8.8 percent of the total adult population, were employed in wage labor, which was almost the same percentage as in 1951.[40] A significant expansion of the trade unions beyond their present numbers, therefore, would be contingent upon unanticipated rapid industrial growth. Furthermore, since the early days of the independence movement, unions have suffered from political interference and governmental restrictions.

As in the case of the trade union movement in other developing countries, unions in Ghana have experienced problems with organization and leadership. In 1944 only eleven unions with a total membership of four hundred persons had been formed. By 1957, the year before the Industrial Relations Act was passed, the Trades' Union Congress claimed seventy two affiliated unions with 154,000 members. However, the TUC had little control over constituent unions, and the member unions were themselves poorly organized. The Industrial Relations Act rationalized the structure of the trade union movement by establishing one union for each industrial concern and by requiring each of the unions to join the more powerful central congress, but at the same time it sapped the vitality of the locals. Although the local branches were meant to have some autonomy, they failed to do so outside of the Accra area. Nkrumah's efforts to transform the unions from interest groups attempting to better the conditions of employment of their members into productionist-oriented units serving the general community reduced the interest of workers in trade unionism. Membership in the TUC during the Nkrumah period fell below the universality legislated for in the 1958 Industrial Relations Act. Despite compulsory dues payment, one scholar estimates on the basis of union records that only 50 percent of all workers paid their dues in 1960 with the proportion increasing to 71 percent by 1964, and many of those who joined lacked a commitment to their unions.[41] Moreover, during the Nkrumah era the TUC was considered a wing of the CPP and suffered from the same organizational deficiences as the other CPP auxiliaries —formalism, lack of adequate channels of communication, mismanagement of finances, corruption, and eventually alienation from the people.[42] In the end the CPP sacrificed genuine participation for control.

After the 1966 military coup, the Trades' Union Congress was the only wing of the party to survive the dismantling of the CPP and its auxiliaries. Under National Liberation Council, Busia, and National Redemption Council regimes, the unions still faced legal restrictions on the scope of their activities. According to figures supplied by the TUC secretariat, the total strength of the affiliated unions as of January 1, 1971 was 351,479. The largest of the seventeen constituent unions was the Industrial and Commercial Workers Union with 83,000 members.[43]

Many of the unions, even the locals, are multiethnic in composition, reflecting the employment patterns in the country. Union loyalty has not, however, fundamentally displaced ethnic allegiances. The unions cannot, at this stage of their evolution, provide the economic services and psychological assurances that ethnic ties and institutions furnish. As in the case of kinship and confessional attachments in Lebanon, primordial allegiances seriously weaken unions. A member's reflex is to look to fellow ethnics rather than occupationally defined groups as the natural unit for social and political activity. Ethnic rivalries within unions can also weaken effectiveness. In some cases employers have managed to break strikes by bringing in recruits from a group other than the one prominent in the union.[44]

Farmers' Associations

Alongside of the union movement, Ghana has experienced the somewhat unique development of national organizations of small farmers. In a predominantly agricultural country, where the preponderant proportion of the population continues to engage in small-scale farming, such an association constitutes a potentially more significant counterweight to ethnic affiliation than do trade unions servicing a small minority. As in the case of the union movement, though, the various farmers' associations have never become effective multifunctional vehicles competing for the loyalty of their members. Farmers' societies originated after World War II as cocoa marketing cooperatives to replace the European firms that had monopolized the purchase of the crop from Ghanaian growers. The colonial Department of Agriculture encouraged the formation of these cooperatives as a way of facilitating the dissemination of improved production practices. Cooperative founders contributed capital shares to establish the society, and in return they receive yearly dividends on their investment from the small deduction made for the overhead of the cooperative on each load of cocoa it sells. Cooperatives pay farmers according to the number of bags of cocoa they produce for the market, which varies from year to year.

In 1953 the CPP established the Cocoa Purchasing Company as a competing cooperative movement, but the report of the 1956 Jibowu Commission, which concluded that the Cocoa Purchasing Company was used as an instrument to force farmers to join the party, led the colonial administration to disband it. Then the CPP invested its energies in organizing the United Ghana Farmers' Council as a party auxiliary. After independence the Nkrumah regime sought to control the cooperatives just as it had the labor unions by forcing them to join a central body dominated by the party. By 1961 the United Ghana Farmers' Council achieved a monopoly in marketing the entire cocoa crop. Its membership grew from the 60,000 farmers registered with the Alliance of Ghana Cooperatives in 1960 to 300,000 because cocoa producers could find no other outlet for selling their crop.

Despite its substantial membership, the United Ghana Farmers' Council did not serve as a focus of loyalty countervailing a farmer's ethnic attachments. Joining was not actually voluntary, and the high membership rolls reflected only the marketing monopoly of the UGFC. The UGFC never became a multifunctional organization servicing the primary needs of the farmer. As in the case of the TUC, the Nkrumah regime intended the UGFC to be productionist- rather than consumptionist-oriented. Instead of pressuring the government to raise cocoa prices, the UGFC offered to increase production and to forego bonuses allegedly on behalf of the farmers. During this period a continuous decline in world market prices for cocoa and the preference of the Nkrumah regime to invest resources in large-scale industrial enterprises and state farms rather than to offer incentives to increase cocoa production led to a precipitous fall in the price of cocoa paid to the farmer. Favoritism toward party activists in the financing of loans, gross mismanagement of funds, cheating in the weighing and grading of crops, and the lowering of the prices for cocoa certainly did not endear the UGFC to the cocoa farmers of Ghana.

Few mourned its passing when the National Liberation Council officially disbanded the UGFC. Its role as the national marketing agent of the cocoa crop and almost all of its staff were transferred to a newly created Cocoa Marketing Board.[45] Many of the local cooperative societies sprang up again to deal with the new Cocoa Marketing Board. Most problems encountered in the system of marketing still remain, and present farmers' societies seem no better able to solve them than did their predecessors, let alone to become the vital multifunctional associations that could displace the ethnic networks of attachment of their members.

Other Associations

In the historical evolution of voluntary associations in Ghana, those without an occupational or economic base preceded the more functionally oriented organizations discussed above. Educated Gold Coasters sought to establish associations in imitation of their colonial administrators as a manifestation of their commitment to a modern, that is, European, way of life. One of the first kinds of associations to appear were alumni clubs or "old boys" organizations of graduates of particular secondary schools. Youth groups, many of which were affiliated with a church, constituted another type of early voluntary association. Still later, educated women founded associations to cater to others like them. Since members of all of these associations tended to be from the strata of Ghanaian society that had been most exposed to European culture, the values they espoused generally reflected middle-class Christian society. Hence, the importance of these associations is reduced by the fact that they reached only a small proportion of the population.

The Young Pioneers, officially launched in 1960, represented an effort to create a completely new type of youth organization in Ghana. Theoretically, the Young Pioneers was a mass organization with branches throughout the country for all school-age children. In actuality, the Young Pioneers never achieved this paramount position. At best, it nominally enrolled only 20 percent of the total primary and middle school-age population, and of this group less than 1 percent were uniformed activists.[46] Although the original intention had been to dissolve all other youth associations, the Boy Scouts and

Christian fellowships somehow eluded extinction. An envisioned Ghana Youth Authority, which was supposed to coordinate all youth movements in order to ensure their loyalty to the CPP, in much the same way as the UGFC and the TUC, never became operative.

Unlike its predecessors, the Young Pioneers actively sought to transform the value systems of its members in the direction of implanting greater loyalty to the Ghanaian nation and to the CPP. Nkrumah's inability to reform the educational system in the face of strong resistance by the professionals in the Ministry of Education led him to vest his hopes in the Young Pioneers as his major instrument of national political socialization. The experiment lasted for six years at best and in many areas even less, since along with the other party affiliates, the Young Pioneers organization was dissolved by the National Liberation Council in 1966. During the history of modern voluntary associations in Ghana, the Young Pioneers attempted more than any other organization to balance ethnic attachment with the greater commitment to the national community, but its efforts were dissipated by the opposition of the Ministry of Education to what they considered interference in their professional jurisdiction and by the fundamental problems the CPP encountered in attempting to establish and maintain its youth affiliates.[47] The perspective of many of the party functionaries who, for lack of alternative sources of leadership, often came to control regional and local branches, also biased the activities more toward instilling party loyalty than to concerning themselves with national identity. In some places the role of the Young Pioneers degenerated into a recitation of creeds pledging unswerving loyalty to Nkrumah and his ideology.

Class Membership

Class membership does not have the same potency in Ghana as a structuring principle in the social order as it does in more industrialized societies. Class differences exist in Ghana, probably to a greater extent than in many other African countries, but individuals still perceive their own identity and interests only to a very limited degree in terms of their class identity. Thus, as in the case of Lebanon, primordial bonds cut across class lines and both vitiate the effectiveness of class appeals and blur the implications of class distinctions. The tendency in Ghana to look to ethnically and regionally based political action as the channel through which to redistribute economic resources, along with the existence of many opportunities for socioeconomic mobility, have kept the less advantaged from becoming more class conscious. Class consciousness in the sense of perceiving common interests seems to be more articulated among members of the elite, but even there action on the basis of class only supplements and does not displace ethnic identity.

The most significant class differences in Ghana are modern rather than traditional in origin. The distinction in many of the traditional sociopolitical systems between the royal and commoner lineages has been supplanted by the gradations between the economic haves and have-nots. In the traditional society the material possessions of the chief constituted an important mark of his social status. This nexus between wealth and social position remains a vital element in the more modern status-class complex. Since cocoa farming and commerce, the earliest enterprises for accumulating wealth, were not limited to members of the royal lineages, the traditional and modern elites do not coincide, although there is some overlap in membership. One interesting factor affecting class interaction in Ghana is that the highest and lowest ends of the social scale tend to be peopled by foreigners. Large-scale expatriate enterprises still retain their paramount economic position in the Ghanaian economy. Until the Business Promotion Act took effect in 1971, foreigners, many of them Lebanese, virtually monopolized the middle-level retail trade as well. The distaste of many Ghanaians for manual labor has left many of the positions for agricultural laborers, household servants, and other employment involving strenuous physical work and low wages open to foreign Africans resident in Ghana.

Education has provided the principal channel of access to the elite. The early and sustained contact of the coastal areas with European civilization has produced some families with several generations of university-educated members. This old middle class spawned the first group of nationalist leaders and then later constituted the bulwark of the opposition to the CPP. Despite the advantaged position of certain families, it continues to be possible in Ghana for a child of an impoverished farmer to rise through the school system to the university. The class system is not rigid, largely because a person can nurture the hope of rising above his class of origin. The radical expansion of the educational system after independence combined with the greater state subsidization of school fees at all levels in Ghana than in most other African countries have permitted poor children with ability to receive the kind of education that enables them to eventually become part of the professional elite. As an indication of the background from which the university student body is drawn, most of the university students in both of our surveys of university students had parents with little or no education. Only 24 percent of the fathers in the first university survey and 10 percent in the second had completed the equivalent of secondary school. The equivalent figures for the mothers were 4 and 6 percent respectively. Only 7 percent of the university students described their fathers as professional men, whereas 41 percent said that they were farmers or fishermen.

One factor complicating the class structure in Ghana is the difficulty of dividing the population into a few neat layers. If the class distinctions were more obvious and clear-cut, they might have induced individuals to become more conscious of their class identity. In the rural areas farmers range from very wealthy cocoa producers to impoverished agricultural laborers with many gradations in between them. In Ghanaian society industrial laborers often seem to be an advantaged rather than the disadvantaged class that European class analysis usually assumes them to be. The expansion of the educational system now denies prestigious positions to many people whose level of education in the past would have automatically made them part of the elite. Even university graduates sometimes have problems gaining employment.

Tremendous differences exist in the income and life styles of the elite and the masses in Ghana. It is possible that the conspicuous consumption of many members of the elite combined with the decline in the per capita income and standard of living for the masses during the last ten years will engender more class consciousness in the future. At the present time, however, ethnic allegiance very much remains in the forefront.

Ghana has many elements of fragmentation resulting from its ethnic pluralism and the uneven development of the country. Ghanaians remain basically ethnically oriented, but at the same time they have some awareness of the national community and an emerging sense of Ghanaian citizenship. The expansion of the subjective boundaries of consciousness to the Ghanaian state reflects several factors: the small size of the country, which is linked together by one of the best road systems on the continent; the extent of internal migration; the centralized nature of the political system since independence; the higher proportion of the population in the market economy compared with the preponderance of subsistence farmers elsewhere in Africa; the national system of education; and the awareness of the political system through the various fundamental upheavals the national political system has undergone.

The attitudes of Ghanaians bear the fundamental imprint of their exposure to their particular ethnic environment but this childhood socialization does not impose unbridgeable discontinuities. The values that the traditional cultures seek to impart through proverbs, stories, myths, songs, and games, as well as explicit exhortation, are primarily those of virtue, honesty, proper comportment, respect of elders, and acceptance of social obligations. Ethnic groups differ somewhat in which of these elements they emphasize, but all of them relegate explicitly political indoctrination to a very minor role. Thus, national agents of political socialization in Ghana, like the schools, have relatively free scope. While Ghanaians continue to exhibit respect and attachment to their traditional institutions and customs, at the same time they subscribe to membership in a wider system beyond the village or traditional state. Ghanaians seem quite aware of the respective and distinctive roles of the traditional and national political systems and with the possible exception of some northern groups, traditional allegiances do not block participation in the modern system.

More problematically, some of the precolonial divergences, particularly between the northern and southern portions of Ghana, have been accentuated by uneven patterns of development. Thus, rates of school attendance, religious affiliation, knowledge of a lingua franca, and level of economic advancement reinforce the north/south division of the country. This may constitute a serious barrier to national accommodation if the northerners become more politically conscious and resentful of the situation.

Although the role of traditional agents of political socialization is on the decline and traditional political units are being superseded, ethnocentricity and intolerance may be on the ascendance in Ghana. The most significant contemporary ethnic identities are not traditional ones; they reflect ethnolinguistic boundaries that had little relevance until relatively recently. The crystallization of the Akan identity, especially if it continues to be accompanied by a sense of increasing social distance from other Ghanaian ethnic communities, may have increasing relevance for the progress of national accommodation.

NOTES

1. We have purposefully avoided the term "tribe" because of its negative connotations and because of its past use to refer confusingly to a variety of different types of ethnic groups.
2. See Meyer Fortes, *The Dynamics of Clanship among the Tallensi* (London: Oxford University Press, 1945); Madeline Manoukian, *Tribes of the Northern Territories of the Gold Coast* (London: International African Institute, 1951).

3. The full results of the 1970 census were not available at the time of writing due to the substantial time lag in processing and publishing the data. Because of the ban on references to ethnic groups introduced by the National Redemption Council, it is unlikely that the 1970 census data (when published) will have many breakdowns by ethnic categories. We therefore relied on B. Gil, A.F. Aryee, and D.K. Ghansah, *Population Census of Ghana, Special Report 'E', Tribes in Ghana* (Census Office: Accra, 1964), pp. xxxiii, xxxxiv.

4. Census Office, 1970 *Population Census of Ghana*, Vol. II, *Statistics of Localities and Enumeration Areas* (Accra: Ghana Publishing Corp., 1972), p. xxiv.

5. B.D.G. Folson, "The Traditional Political Systems," unpublished manuscript, is a good description of the varieties of traditional political systems.

6. The classic study on the dilemma of the traditional ruler, which was researched in the early 1940s, is K.A. Busia, *The Position of the Chief in the Modern Political System of Ashanti: A Study of the Influence of Contemporary Social Changes on Ashanti Political Institutions* (London: Oxford University Press, 1951).

7. For a more complete description, see Appendix on Survey Methodology. Briefly, our first survey was administered to 300 upper primary and middle school students in five rural communities, the second to a sample of 148 students at the University of Ghana, and the third to 175 university students at the University of Ghana and Cape Coast University. The Ministry of Education survey, in which we participated in the formulation of the questionnaire and sample and the analysis of the data, was given to a national sample.

8. See Fred M. Hayward, "Correlates of National Integration: The Case of Ghana," unpublished paper, 1972.

9. The Ministry of Education survey results were only partially analyzed at the time of this writing, so it was not possible to compare the magnitude of attitudinal differences occurring on the basis of ethnic distinctions with other configurations.

10. See, for example, Robert LeVine, "Political Socialization and Cultural Change," in Clifford Geertz, ed., *Old Societies and New States* (New York: The Free Press of Glencoe, 1963), pp. 281-289.

11. David W. Brokensha, *Social Change at Larteh, Ghana* (Oxford: The Clarendon Press, 1966), p. 269.

12. For a description of the festivals see A.A. Opoku, *Festivals of Ghana* (Accra: Ghana Publishing Corporation, 1970).

13. Gils, Aryee, Ghansah, op.cit., p. xliv.

14. John Caldwell, *African Rural-Urban Migration* (Canberra: Australian National University Press, 1969), pp. 141, 147, 153, 169; Margaret Peil, *The Ghanaian Factory Worker: Industrial Man in Africa* (London: Cambridge University Press, 1972), p. 213.

15. Ruth Simms Hamilton, "Urban Social Differentiation and Membership Recruitment among Selected Voluntary Associations in Accra, Ghana," unpublished PH.D. Diss., Northwestern University, 1966.

16. Peil, op.cit., pp. 172, 175–176.

17. Robert D. Hess and Judith V. Torney, *The Development of Political Attitudes in Children* (Garden City, N. Y.: Doubleday, 1968), pp. 100–119.

18. B. Gil, K.T. DeGraft-Johnson, and E.A. Colecraft, 1960 *Population Census of Ghana*, Vol. VI, *The Post Enumeration Survey* (Accra: Census Office, 1971), p. 238.

19. Gil, DeGraft-Johnson, and Colecraft, op.cit., pp. 238–243.

20. See Robert M. Price, "The Pattern of Ethnicity in Ghana: a Research Note,"*The Journal of Modern African Studies*, 11 (September 1973), p. 472; and Joseph M. Kaufert, "An Experimental Approach to Ethnic Unit Boundary Definition in Ghana," paper presented at the African Studies Association Conference, 1972.

21. *1970 Population Census of Ghana*, op.cit., p. xxiv.
22. Since there is a close correspondence between regional and ethnic group boundaries, we believe that the phrase "other regions" would serve as a surrogate for "other ethnic groups."
23. Roberta Koplin, "Education and National Integration in Ghana and Kenya," unpublished PH.D. Diss., University of Oregon, 1969, pp. 244, 252.
24. Kaufert, op.cit.
25. J.C. Caldwell, "Migration and Urbanization," in Walter Birmingham, I. Neustadt, and E.N. Omaboe, *A Study of Contemporary Ghana: Some Aspects of Social Structure*, Vol. 2 (Evanston, Ill.: Northwestern University Press, 1967), p. 112.
26. K.B. Dickson, "Development Planning and National Integration in Ghana," in David R. Smock and Kwamina Bentsi-Enchill, eds., *The Search for National Integration in Africa* (forthcoming).
27. Central Bureau of Statistics, *1963 Statistical Year Book* (Accra: Government of Ghana, 1966), p. 37.
28. *Educational Statistics 1968–1969* (Accra: Ministry of Education, 1972), pp. 2, 28, 46.
29. *1970 Population Census of Ghana*, op.cit., p. xxiv.
30. Gil, Aryee, Ghansah, op.cit., pp. lxxv-lxxvii.
31. For another and somewhat different analysis of the results, see Lynn Frederick Fischer, "Student Orientations toward Nation-Building in Ghana," in John N. Paden, ed., *National Integration in Africa: Research Reports* (forthcoming).
32. Hess and Torney, op.cit., pp. 33–35.
33. Gil, Aryee, and Ghansah, op.cit., p. lxxxv.
34. Ibid., p. lxxxi.
35. See Brokensha, op.cit., pp. 22–28; Maxwell Owusu, *Uses and Abuses of Political Power: A Case Study of Continuity and Change in the Politics of Ghana* (Chicago: University of Chicago Press, 1970), p. 110; D.K. Fiawoo, "Social Survey of Tefleh" (Legon, Ghana: Institute of Education, 1961), mimeographed.
36. *Educational Statistics 1968–1969*, op.cit., pp. 10–11.
37. Ibid., pp. 33, 34.
38. M.J. Marshall, "Christianity and Nationalism in Ghana," unpublished M.A. Thesis, University of Ghana, 1965, p. 3.
39. Noel Smith, *The Presbyterian Church of Ghana 1935–1960* (Accra: Ghana Universities Press, 1966), p. 259.
40. Emily Card, "The Politics of Underdevelopment: From Voluntary Associations to Party Auxiliaries in Ghana," unpublished PH.D. Diss., Columbia University, 1972, pp. 154–155.
41. Card, op.cit., p. 287.
42. Ibid., pp. 393–395.
43. Supplied by Trade Union Congress Secretariat.
44. M.S.M. Shea, "The Development and Role of Trade Unions in a Developing Economy: The Case of Ghana," unpublished PH.D. Diss., University of London, 1968, pp. 172–173.
45. Card, op.cit., pp. 192–200, 268–270, 300.
46. Ibid., 298, 299.
47. On the Young Pioneers see Charles A. Ballard, Jr., "A Contemporary Youth Movement: The Young Pioneers," unpublished M.A. Thesis, Institute of African Studies, University of Ghana.

7

Ethnicity and Politics in Ghana

In our consideration of the interaction between sectarianism and politics in Lebanon, we were able to confine our discussion to a single governmental system, since only one system has prevailed there since the time of independence. But a discussion of ethnicity and politics in Ghana necessitates attention to a series of governmental systems. Kwame Nkrumah moved from the competitive parliamentary system of the preindependence period to a one-party regime during his tenure in office, and following his overthrow in 1966, Ghana has had two different military governments and a parliamentary system. In view of the significant differences in political institutions, the nature of political competition, and programs pursued under the various regimes, our analysis of the role of ethnic factors in Ghana's political life as well as our appraisal of the adequacy with which ethnic conflict has been handled comes in the context of Ghana's successive types of governmental systems. Of Ghana's regimes, Nkrumah's Convention People's Party (CPP) administration lasted the longest and had the most articulated policy on the subject of ethnicity. For these reasons we will examine it in greater detail than its successors. As in the case of the division of chapters on Lebanon, this chapter concentrates on political dynamics within the framework of the overall political system, and Chapter 8 focuses on political change and

226

reform. In Chapter 8 we assess past policies and policy alternatives including those relating to law, economic planning, education, and language in terms of their actual and potential impact on national accommodation.

THE CPP GOVERNMENTAL SYSTEM

Ghana came to independence in 1957 under a classic Westminster parliamentary system. As a result of having won a majority of seats in the preindependence elections held in 1956, Kwame Nkrumah's CPP formed the government. Opposition to the CPP, much of which had an ethnic basis, seemed temporarily placated by the inclusion of regional assemblies having the power to bloc amendments to the constitution. Disturbances took place shortly after independence in the Volta Region among supporters of the Togoland Congress and in Accra after the formation of the Ga Adangme Shifmo Kpee (Ga Standfast Association), a Ga movement protesting against conditions in the capital city, but these were handled by the government without much difficulty. The CPP, however, never intended to maintain the kind of parliamentary system it inherited from the British or to countenance the existence of an organized opposition appealing to ethnic particularism. Gradually, Nkrumah moved toward the establishment of a one-party republican system in which he as president of the state and leader of the party wielded authoritarian powers. By 1961, when some opposition forces resorted to bombings and attempted assassination, the CPP government suppressed free political competition.

Many elements of Nkrumah's revision of the Ghanaian political system and centralization of power had their origin in his negative attitude toward ethnicity. As early as 1946 Nkrumah wrote that "all provincial and tribal differences should be broken down completely."[1] Nkrumah, perceiving the ethnic foundation of the parties in opposition and of much of the conflict within the CPP, thought it essential to confront and defeat these and all other manifestations of what he termed "tribalism."[2] But however serious a threat subnational loyalties posed for national integration, the CPP government did not consider ethnic divisiveness the only impediment it faced. For Nkrumah and CPP party militants, divisive ethnic forces constituted one link in a chain of obstacles that had to be overcome in pursuit of the party's long-term objectives. Their program envisaged nothing less than a complete transformation of the socioeconomic structure of Ghanaian society to make Ghana into an industrialized, socialist system. This transformation, which was expected to improve the economic well-being of all Ghanaians, necessitated the mobilization of the nation's entire population. This mobilization effort, which would entail the elimination of all major societal divisions, could best be achieved within the structure of a party-state, with the CPP constituting not merely the only party but also becoming identical with the state. In addition to national unification and mobilization providing the basis for an internal revolution, it would also propel Ghana into the vanguard of the movement for African unity, with the anticipated end result of the elimination of imperialist control in Africa and the creation of a United States of Africa.

The CPP's strategy for attaining national unification, for promoting mobilization, and for dealing with the forces of opposition encompassed the following: control of the chiefs and centralization of power in both geographic and institutional terms; repression of the opposition; creation of a one-party state; inculcation of a common ideology; control of the press and other mass media; and the absorption and reorganization of voluntary associations within the party as mobilizing party auxiliaries.[3] This statement of strategy, articulated with the advantage of historical hindsight, may give the somewhat misleading impression that a coherent CPP political program was fully developed at an early date. In fact, Nkrumah devised and redefined his strategy in reaction to specific events and predicaments. Moreover, depending upon which wing of the party was in ascendance at a particular moment, one or another component of the total program predominated. Nevertheless, the basic thrust of the CPP's goals evinced consistency throughout the period of postindependence CPP rule, that is, from 1957 to 1966.

The status and authority enjoyed by the chiefs during most of the colonial era posed a variety of challenges to the CPP's political strategy. As traditional authorities, they constituted obstacles to political modernization. Furthermore, they and their traditional states represented forces of division within the new state since they tended to arouse subnational ethnic sentiments and to exert pressure for a federal rather than a unitary state. Closely associated with this, they also controlled important powers that the CPP wished to bring under the party–state umbrella as part of its effort to centralize power. Admittedly, by the time of independence the chiefs were only shadows of their former selves, their decline in authority having commenced with the Local Government Ordinance of 1951. Their popular standing had also been steadily eroded by various forces of modernization, by their close ties to colonial authority, by their mismanagement of funds, and by some serious abuses of authority. They nevertheless remained a significant political force in 1957.

Following independence, the CPP launched a concerted attack on the authority remaining to the chiefs, and the regime was particularly severe with chiefs who backed the opposition.[4] The independence constitution did make provision for regional houses of chiefs, but they could concern themselves only with chieftaincy affairs, customary law, and other traditional institutions. The Constitution (Repeal of Restrictions) Act of 1958 further circumscribed their authority. In the following year the Stool Lands Control Act of 1959 granted to the government full control over revenues from stool lands traditionally managed by the chiefs, thus removing the financial basis of their authority. The Local Government (Amendment) Act of 1959 removed all chiefs from local and municipal councils, except for a single chief assigned to each council to serve as its ceremonial president. In a reorganization of the courts under the Courts Act of 1960, lay magistrates rather than chiefs and elders came to preside over local courts. In the Chiefs (Recognition Amendment) Act of 1959 the government reaffirmed its authority to recognize or withdraw recognition from chiefs, and even to send chiefs into exile from their traditional states. The CPP used these powers to punish opposition chiefs and to reward their supporters. Even the Asantehene, the king of the Ashantis, quickly learned the lesson that the CPP was attempting to teach, and he ended his opposition to the regime. The CPP did not intend to abolish entirely the institution of chieftaincy, and if a particular chief backed the CPP, he could continue to command ceremonial status in his area.[5] But the CPP managed to eliminate the remaining substantive authority of the chiefs and to assure that they desisted from leading any ethnically chauvinist and separatist movements.

Another measure adopted by the CPP for eliminating political divisions and conflicts within the country, and particularly ethnically based political opposition, was the suppression of all opposition and the creation of the one-party state. In fairness to the CPP, it needs to be conceded that the decline of the opposition after 1957 resulted partially from the band-wagon effect and the natural advantages enjoyed by a party in power. Many opposition MPs crossed the carpet to join the government side, and in two by-elections in 1959 in constituencies previously controlled by the opposition, the CPP won resounding victories.[6] Nevertheless, the CPP adopted repressive measures as well. The Avoidance of Discrimination Act of 1957, which rendered illegal political parties built primarily on a regional, ethnic, or religious base, constituted one of the first moves taken by the CPP against the opposition. The repugnance reflected in the act toward political activity motivated by primordial attachments was fully consistent with CPP ideology, but the act had a more immediate purpose. Under this act all the existing opposition parties became illegal bodies, and they were consequently forced to amalgamate, which they did in October 1957 by forming the United Party. But in part because the government forbade their holding public rallies, the United Party never beame an effective force.

A more direct and effective attack on the opposition came with the adoption of preventive detention in 1958. The government could imprison persons for up to five years to prevent their committing acts detrimental to state security. By the time the CPP was overthrown in 1966, 3000 persons, according to some estimates, had languished in prison under preventive detention. Many others who opposed the government went into exile, remained silent, or went underground to avoid being detained. By 1961 virtually all open opposition to the CPP had ended. The CPP's approach to elections provided an equally effective means of emasculating the opposition. The preindependence election of 1956 turned out to be the last free national election held under the CPP. In part, the CPP attitude toward the opposition seemed to derive from an exaggerated assessment of the opposition's potential strength and effectiveness. More fundamentally, however, the belief that political unity was essential to mobilization and to the desired social and economic unification of the pluralistic state underlay CPP policy. Less charitable observers have explained Nkrumah's attitude toward the opposition in terms of an insatiable hunger for power,[7] but this is not adequate.

We have already noted that the CPP considered a federal arrangement anathema because it would be inefficient and would tend to reinforce subnational ethnic-based loyalties. To achieve unity and mobilization, Nkrumah believed that authority must be centralized. For the sake of convincing the British to grant independence, Nkrumah accepted the inclusion of regional assemblies in the independence constitution, but as soon as the British were gone, the regional assemblies became merely advisory bodies, and thereafter the government permanently dissolved them. Centralization of authority had its institutional as well as its geographical aspects. Power was concentrated in Accra, and in Accra it was primarily lodged in the hands of Nkrumah. He held the key posts in both party and state, insofar as these could be differentiated. By June 1961 he had direct responsibility for thirty eight subjects and departments in the government.[8] During the early years Nkrumah shared authority with the party apparatus, but toward the end of the regime Nkrumah relied instead on key civil servants. No matter what structure he tried or what persons he relied upon, he never achieved a wholly efficient arrangement, in part because of the inherent contradictions in the dual structure of party and state authority. Nkrumah never seemed fully satisfied that he had succeeded in gathering the strings of power into his own hands nor into those of his subordinates. Control of major aspects of party and government activity remained elusive from central control, and Nkrumah considered this one reason why he was not able to impose the kind of unity on the country which he sought.

Consistent with the CPP's strategy for mobilization and national unification, a one-party state meant more than merely outlawing the opposition. The path to the new social order vested first the party branches and then the party auxiliaries with the task of providing a framework for participation and mobilization.[9] To render the party a more effective vehicle for social transformation, the party tried to expand its membership, even recruiting civil servants and members of the armed forces. CPP organizational activities at local levels and its contact with the masses increased after 1961 when the opposition had already been effectively silenced.[10] However, neither the party nor the auxiliaries actually fulfilled the roles planned for them. Despite its failure as a truly effective agent of mass mobilization, the party did promote Ghana's national unity. Some observers see its principal importance in this regard having been as a symbol or expression of unity in a pluralistic state,[11] but others have seen it as that of an active institutional agent of national unification.[12]

Nkrumah's lack of complete success in centralizing power became evident in the operation of the CPP itself.[13] Although the CPP's organizational framework theoretically incorporated and unified within its fold all rank-and-file party members, the achievement of real unity and cohesion exceeded the party's capabilities. Once the CPP's competitors were gone, internal party discipline and cohesion often lost out to internal competition and strife. As the party became more diffuse and inclusive, factionalism of both an ideological and an ethnic-geographic kind intensified. Local issues very often became obsessions at the expense of the party's national concerns. Local notables and chiefs were drawn into the party, and many of the localistic orientations and values that the CPP had hoped to suppress became evident in local party activities. While the party succeeded to some extent in molding Ghanaian society in its image, the fragmented character of Ghanaian society also left its clear imprint on the CPP.[14] The party constitution issued in 1962 stated that the CPP leadership "is faced with the danger of being swamped by tribal, regional, and other communal ideological influences which are penetrating the ranks of the more backward party membership."[15]

Local participation, another element of the CPP strategy vital to national unification and mobilization, also fell far short of the ideal. The party bureaucracy was active, but much of its energy was expended in sustaining itself rather than mobilizing the population. Dennis Austin goes so far as to assert that in the 1960s the party became little more than a massive propaganda machine.[16] Thus, the CPP lacked the capacity to involve the population in a sustained manner in a national party with a national developmental perspective. When it came, local participation often had a ritualistic quality with people mouthing CPP slogans that they rarely understood, let alone acted upon.

In part because of dissatisfaction regarding the factionalism and parochialism plaguing the regional, district, and local branches of the CPP, the party leadership decided in 1960 to restructure the party radically. Their blueprint involved a shift in the basis of affiliation and participation, from geographic-ethnic to functional. In the past, all persons of a particular locality were eligible for membership in the local branch, and branches were largely ethnically homogeneous, although at higher levels they were naturally affiliated to other ethnic groups. In the new plan of organization other statuses attained primacy. All industrial workers were expected to be members of the Trades' Union Congress (TUC), and their affiliation to the CPP was now to be within the framework of their union membership. In the party's eyes their economic and occupational status superseded their place of habitation and their ethnic group membership. Farmers, and particularly cocoa farmers, were to be active in the party on the basis of their membership in the United Ghana Farmers' Council (UGFC). For Ghana's market women the party organized the National Council of Ghana Women (NCGW), which became another party auxiliary. For young people the party created the Ghana Young Pioneers. Although the geographically defined branches of the party never actually disappeared, these four party auxiliaries had priority in the eyes of party leadership. Other organizations, like the Workers' Brigade, had strong ties to the party, but the above-mentioned four organizations constituted the officially designated party auxiliaries.

The party had several motives for restructuring itself along these lines, but one of the most important was the hope that the functional auxiliaries would provide vehicles for undermining ethnic identities and for forging crosscutting ties and interethnic affiliations. The creation of two new nationwide organizations, the Young Pioneers and the National Council of Ghana Women, and the reinforcement of the national character and perspective of the TUC and the UGFC thus had important implications for national integration. Through underscoring the importance of occupational and other functional ties at the expense of ethnic affiliations, party leaders intended these organizations to serve as a counterweight to the forces of localism and ethnic chauvinism. As David Apter described the hoped-for transformation: "Not local branches of Ashanti, or Fanti, or Ewe, or strangers, but farmers, workers, youth. Not local women's organizations fitting into the older forms of political and social life of a locality, but CPP women concerned with national problems."[17]

As with so many aspects of the CPP's strategy, the achievements of the party auxiliaries did not meet expectations. As already mentioned, they never completely supplanted the regional, district, and local branches, and this created conflicts between the two forms of organization.[18] Moreover, the auxiliaries inevitably became organized along ethnogeographic lines since this was the only sensible basis upon which to build their constituent units, and this diluted their functional character. Just as localistic orientations tended to characterize the local party branches, the local auxiliary branches had the same inclination. As David Brokensha has written of the Larteh branches of the Young Pioneers, the TUC, the UGFC, and the NCGW, "all the wings represent both the intrusion of external or national forces combined with the continuity of old groups and institutions, in a delicate balance. Despite the CPP's dislike of local, minority, or 'tribal' interests, it has had to accommodate itself to some extent."[19] Despite the avowed expectation that the auxiliaries would serve as channels for participation and instruments of mobilization, power in each one became highly centralized, and local participation was largely ritualistic. The absence of voluntarism also tended to dampen the enthusiasm of members. The party auxiliaries also suffered from a low-level institutionalization due to a shortage of qualified leaders, lack of organizational experience, inadequate financing, and the irresponsible management of the funds they received.[20]

The 1960 reorganization also accorded new importance to the inculcation of party ideology, in part to forge unifying and mobilizing ideological bonds among the population's disparate and competing groups. Through the medium of ideology, Nkrumah sought to replace self and communal interests as motivating forces with dedication to the nation and its development. The press, the party auxiliaries, and a newly established Kwame Nkrumah Ideological Institute all somewhat clumsily sought to instill the ideology of Nkrumahism, which was socialist-oriented. The Kwame Nkrumah Ideological Institute, opened in 1962, was expected to indoctrinate party leaders, chiefs, civil servants, and university students, but an ill-equipped staff, lack of clarity among lecturers regarding the precise nature of Nkrumahism, and other deficiencies made it less than fully adequate. Party auxiliaries also engaged in considerable ideological exhortation. Members of the Young Pioneers, for example, had to memorize party creeds. In addition the CPP posted ideological secretaries to the regions to help with doctrinal education of party members. The press served as another important instrument of ideological warfare. In its ranks were *The Spark*, a weekly publication of the CPP, whose explicit purpose was to project Nkrumahist ideology; daily newspapers, all of which had to accept party militants as editors to continue publishing; and the journals and newspapers of the party auxiliaries.

Nkrumah apparently failed to understand that despite the ideologically charged atmosphere of the mid-1960s, politics in Ghana was not primarily inspired by ideology. Even at its state of greatest ideological fervour, the CPP's popularity was deeply rooted in individual, local, and ethnic group self-interest. [21] As the tenets of Nkrumahism became more fully articulated and as the CPP turned Ghana into a repressive one-party state, only the fanatical vanguard of the party seemed to be aroused by its ideological exhortation. The party loyalty that remained primarily reflected whatever success the party had had in improving the lives of individual Ghanaians or groups of Ghanaians, either by stimulating economic development or by providing political patronage. Even within the one-party context, political interaction in Ghana largely represented competition, both ethnic-regional and functional-occupational, for economic benefit. Members of the party leadership themselves did not hesitate to qualify the party's socialist ideology when it suited their own economic interests; for example, one cabinet member, Krobo Edusei, asserted, "Socialism doesn't mean that if you've made a lot of money, you can't keep it." [22]

The CPP also sought to unify the population by inculcating loyalty to Nkrumah's person. At critical moments in a nation's history a charismatic leader can promote national cohesion. Although some analysts have exaggerated the level and signficance of Nkrumah's charisma,[23] there seems little question that Nkrumah had charismatic appeal. Through our own observation of the man and the testimony of those who knew him well and who understood the character of his leadership, it seems clear that during the late 1940s and the 1950s his charisma added legitimacy to the new state. Admittedly, the symbolism of unity provided by an individual leader is a tenuous, impermanent, and inadequate basis for the creation of sustained national cohesion, but at a critical point in Ghanaian history, Nkrumah's charisma made an important contribution to interethnic accommodation and the viability of the state.

As Nkrumah's charisma declined and finally disappeared in the 1960s, the CPP tried to substitute a personality cult of grotesque dimensions. The party press, party spokesmen, and all others making public reference to Nkrumah were expected to refer to the Osagyefo, the redeemer, the savior, and even the messiah. As Jon Kraus has explained, "The function of the cult was not only to create a national symbol with which Fanti, Ewe, Ashanti, Brongs, and Dagomba could identify but also to elevate his person and power beyond reproach or challenge."[24] This manufactured cult did not approach in effectiveness the charisma of the earlier years, and whether it played a useful role at all in encouraging national cohesion is doubtful.

The general pattern of geographic differentiation among Ghana's ethnic groups virtually dictated that with geographically defined, single-seat constituencies, Ghana's various ethnic groups would enjoy roughly proportional representation in the National Assembly. Efforts to delineate ethnically homogeneous constituencies further assured ethnic proportionality in the National Assembly. During the Nkrumah era Ghana had two parliamentary elections. Despite the fact that the same basic principles of representation held for both the 1956 and 1965 elections, the latter differed from the 1956 election in several important respects. First, by 1965 Ghana had become a one-party state, and so the CPP appointed the new members of the National Assembly rather than permitting contested elections. Second, the CPP leadership attempted to achieve not only proportional ethnic representation but also balanced representation of various functional groups.[25] This reflected the CPP's wish to restructure both the party and Ghanaian society as a whole along functional as opposed to ethnic lines. Although ethnic identity was too strong to neglect ethnic representation completely, it was clearly understood, as one commentator explained, "that the MPs drawn from different groups within the society are not to act as spokesmen for their own specific and parochial group interests, a concept of politics totally anathema to a party which views itself as a vehicle for national cohesion. . . ."[26] In terms of functional representation, the 1965 parliament included substantial delegations from the party hierarchy and the party auxiliaries, as well as from the party press and the Ideological Institute. In addition to the representation of cocoa farmers and industrial workers through their respective party auxiliaries, such other occupational groups as lawyers, teachers, and university lecturers also held seats. Playing a dual role, each of these functional representatives also at least nominally represented one of the country's 198 geographically defined, ethnically homogeneous constituencies.

Nkrumah also made concessions to persistent ethnic attachments when he appointed his early cabinets. As he conceded in retrospect, "While I believe we had largely eliminated tribalism as an active force, its by-products and those of the family system were still with us. I could not have chosen my government without some regard to tribal origins. . . ."[27] But, as indicated in Table 7-1, Nkrumah followed no fixed mathematical formula in allocating cabinet posts among Ghana's various ethnic communities. In fact, by 1965 the Akans were clearly overrepresented, and there was no Ewe representative. Moreover, the sixteen-member 1965 cabinet contained three Nzimas, Nkrumah's own ethnic community, a number quite out of proportion to the number of Nzimas in Ghana.

In comparison with other African states, Ghana's civil service during the time of Nkrumah was well trained and competent. Moreover, it carried heavy responsibilities for policy formulation and implementation. During the period of the party's reorganization in the early 1960s, the party did manage to encroach on the preserve of the civil service. For example, the UGFC took over the extension service and the cooperatives division from the Ministry of Agriculture, and the TUC held the right of veto over many activities of the

TABLE 7-1   *Ethnic Composition of Nkrumah's Postelection Cabinets*

	FANTI	NZIMA	ASHANTI	OTHER AKANS	EWE	GA	GUAN	NORTHERN
1952	1	1	1	0	1	2	1	1
1954	2	1	2	1	1	1	1	2
1956	2	2	2	2	1	1	1	2
1965	4	3	3	1	0	1	2	2

Department of Labour. As the decade progressed, however, Nkrumah turned more and more to trusted civil servants for assistance in policy-making, and the influence of the party leadership declined accordingly.

Because of the breadth of the bureaucracy's authority and the generally low status of the ordinary members of parliament, the particularistic demands of individual MPs and the ethnic groups they represented carried less weight than they do in many other states. Cabinet members and high party officials did often manage to benefit their particular constituencies, but political interference in the business of the bureaucracy and the impact of ethnic-regional interests on the bureaucracy did not reach the level found in Lebanon.

It should be evident from the discussion thus far that the CPP's attempts to mobilize and unify Ghanaian society fell far short of expectations. The CPP did succeed in undermining much of the remaining authority of the chiefs, thereby largely dismantling the traditional states. Moreover, by suppressing the opposition and declaring the CPP the sole party, the regime managed to stifle most dissent and most of the overt aspects of competitive politics, much of which had an ethnic base. But the party never created the kind of organic unity that Apter attributed to it when he asserted, "The party has generalized itself into the society. Party solidarity is translated into national solidarity."[28] In terms of promoting centralization of power, Nkrumah brought into being a unitary rather than a federal state; the constitutional authority originally ascribed to regional assemblies was quickly eliminated; and most government power and decision-making became concentrated in Accra. But Nkrumah never believed that he or anyone else achieved the control necessary to implement fully the revolutionary and homogenizing changes envisaged in the party ideology. Moreover, the inability of the party either to provide opportunities for meaningful participation to the rank-and-file members, or to arouse and sustain enthusiastic support for the government programs and the societal reforms that the party sought became painfully evident. Thus, the CPP failed both as a vehicle of effective mobilization and as a creator of societal solidarity. Although the party did exude a certain *élan* during the drive for independence, moral exhortations by party leaders rang hollow in later years, and attempts to inculcate Nkrumahism as an inspiring and unifying ideology attained only superficial results.

In drawing these basically negative conclusions about the CPP, one needs to see the Ghanaian situation in perspective. The shortcomings of the CPP's efforts at mobilization did not derive as much from the failures of individual leaders as from the limited capacities of most transitional political systems.[29] Moreover, the elimination of the chiefs and their traditional states as competitors for power with the central government removed a traditional source of division within Ghanaian society. Even though the party never evoked the universal support and commitment envisaged in its plans for mobilization, the CPP did have branches among all ethnic groups in the country and it did provide important institutional linkages among these groups. In coopting local notables into the party and in building on local institutions, as it frequently did, the CPP took on particularistic colorings in its branch organization, but it also added some national perspective to the otherwise localistic orientation of many village dwellers. Although the party was better at dispensing patronage than in making conversions to its ideology, it distributed this patronage relatively evenly among the country's ethnic groups and gave them a sizeable stake in the national system. The party auxiliaries, despite their limited success in suppressing ethnic identities, were multiethnic organizations with national institutional infrastructures.

A major difficulty facing the analyst in assessing the success that Nkrumah and the CPP had in managing communal conflict arises because the repressive character of the regime and the imposition of the one-party state eliminated open political competition. Thus, few opportunities existed for political action of an ethnic variety or of any other variety. Under these circumstances one has to pursue the elusive issue of the latent strength of ethnic conflict and tension. The conceptual and methodological tools do not exist for pushing such an inquiry very far, but it is significant that once Ghana reinstituted open competitive politics in 1969, political behavior of an ethnic character reasserted itself in very vigorous form.[30] It also may not be coincidental that the coup that overthrew the Nkrumah regime in 1966 was planned by three members of the same group, all Ewes, whom Nkrumah had excluded from representation in cabinets during the last five years of his regime.

To his credit, Nkrumah gained a reputation of being relatively ethnically blind. Toward the end of his regime when he became obsessed with his personal safety, he named fellow Nzimas to head both the special intelligence unit and the military intelligence operations, and the President's Own Guard Regiment is reputed to have contained a disproportionate number of Nzimas. We have already pointed to the disproportionate number of Nzimas and other Akans named to the 1965 cabinet. On the whole, however, Nkrumah tended to exhibit a national perspective in his handling of personnel matters and in his allocation of state resources. As will be discussed in the next chapter, the underrepresentation of northerners in the higher echelons of the civil service resulted from the insistence upon educational achievement as the basis of recruitment, not from ethnic bias. His appointment of some regional commissioners who were not members of any of the ethnic groups resident in that region, and his encouragement of some CPP candidates to stand for election in their place of residence rather than in their native area, offer testimony to his desire to have the CPP and his government think in national rather than in ethnic terms. His own constituency when he was a member of the National Assembly was Accra, which is Ga territory and many miles from Nzimaland, and he firmly believed that he should be a candidate in the nation's capital rather than in his own ethnic area.

While the period of 1958 to 1966 was not a period of persistent overt ethnic strife, this did not result from success in Nkrumah's effort to homogenize and unify the country by eradicating ethnic distinctions. Whatever ability he had in managing ethnic conflict depended heavily upon his own ethnic blindness and egalitarianism, personal qualities that could not be institutionalized, and on a repressive political system which most Ghanaians came to find repugnant and intolerable.

THE 1966 COUP AND THE NATIONAL LIBERATION COUNCIL REGIME

Testimony of army officers suggests that during the Nkrumah era Ghana's armed forces remained relatively free of ethnic-based conflict or tension. Although soldiers and officers were not subjected to any specific training expected to give them a national and ethnically tolerant perspective, they did submit to a discipline within which no particular ethnic groups enjoyed special advantage. Although officers did not attempt to organize ethnically balanced fighting units, the army command took care to assure that no unwarranted ethnic concentrations developed.[31] Some evidence of ethnic suspicion and hostility surfaced, but such instances did not create serious problems.[32]

The army's first active involvement in Ghana's political life came with the 1966 military and police coup that toppled Nkrumah from power.[33] Those who organized the coup shared the popular dissatisfaction with Ghana's economic deterioration and Nkrumah's repressive rule. It is likely that they, along with other members of the Ghanaian middle class, also had a distaste for the petit bourgeois orientation of the CPP. The armed forces themselves had special reasons for discontent, relating to Nkrumah's alleged plans for using the army to further his Pan-African ambitions. The regular forces also felt superseded in terms of status, equipment, and perquisites by the President's Own Guard Regiment.

Although ethnic factors were not explicitly cited as motivations by the coup's organizers, it may not be coincidental that the three key plotters were Ewes, a group that had not been represented in Nkrumah's cabinet since K. A. Gbedemah was removed in 1961. These three included the leader of the coup, Colonel Emmanuel Kotoka, Inspector General of Police John Harlley, and head of the Special Branch A. K. Deku.[34] However, it was not merely an Ewe affair, since Kotoka's chief aide, Major A. A. Afrifa,[35] is an Ashanti. Colonel A. K. Ocran, who is a Fanti, was drawn in at the last moment and became an important participant. Furthermore, the coup leaders asked a Ga, General J. A. Ankrah, to assume the position of head of state and Chairman of the National Liberation Council.

Ewe predominance among the coup leadership resulted in an ethnically imbalanced National Liberation Council. The Council as named on March 1, 1966, five days after the coup, consisted of three Ewes (Kotoka, Harlley, and Deku), two Gas (Ankrah and J. E. Nunoo), one Ashanti (Afrifa), one Fanti (Ocran), and one northerner (B. A. Yakuku). The ethnic imbalance in the NLC did not create much immediate concern, and except for the most loyal CPP supporters, the population gave broad backing to the NLC. But it came to be the source of considerable resentment later.

Ethnic conflict developed when many Ashantis and other Akans began to suspect the NLC of being an Ewe–Ga stronghold partial to Ga and Ewe interests. One accusation leveled by Akans was that Ewes and Gas were favored when officers were appointed to choice army posts. In turn, some Ewes suspected that the abortive countercoup in 1967, which led to the death of Kotoka and other Ewe officers, was an effort planned by Ashantis and Fantis to wrest control of the NLC from the Ewes and Gas.[36] In October 1967 Afrifa stated that Ghanaian "society is tending towards disintegration and the unity of our nation is facing its greatest challenge. The reason for this, as I see it, is that we are becoming too tribalistic in our outlook."[37] Ethnic tension within the NLC became exacerbated early in 1969 when thoughts turned to the anticipated return to civilian rule and the parliamentary elections that were to provide the basis for the transfer of power. Details of the interactions among members are not known, but Afrifa clearly favored the candidacy of his fellow Ashanti, Busia, while the Ewe members, Harlley and Deku, preferred his Ewe rival, K. A. Gbedemah. Gbedemah had been Nkrumah's Minister of Finance and the lone Ewe included in Nkrumah's cabinets until he was ousted and went into exile and opposition in 1961. Afrifa sought to have Gbedemah disqualified from the election, but Gbedemah's backers in the NLC and many Ewes in the armed forces strongly opposed his disqualification. The precise position of Ankrah is not clear, in terms of whether he backed Gbedemah or a third political group. Whatever his preference, he joined his Ewe colleagues in opposing Busia. Afrifa and others then discovered that Ankrah had received donations from business firms to use for his own political purposes, and they forced him to resign as chairman of the NLC. Afrifa then became chairman. Within a few days the other Ga on the Council, Nunoo, who may well have been implicated with Ankrah in a Ga-based political movement, was also forced out and was also replaced by an Akan. A later section of this chapter indicates the extent to which the election itself came to be waged largely along ethnic lines. Some of these maneuverings within the NLC prior to the election anticipated those subsequent developments.

The NLC never set forth or devised a clear policy for approaching Ghana's communal problems, but it opposed the strategy adopted by Nkrumah and the CPP. In fact, the NLC's only clearly articulated political ideology was one of anti-Nkrumahism. As an expression of this anti-Nkrumahism, the NLC banned and dismantled the CPP and the party auxiliaries (with the exception of the TUC), and sold some of Ghana's state enterprises to private companies. Although political activity was prohibited and the NLC did not permit much open opposition to its policies, NLC rule was not as repressive as Nkrumah's. In part this resulted from the fact that to the NLC, opposition did not constitute the same kind of threat that it did for Nkrumah, since unity was not considered so essential. The NLC concentrated on dismantling the CPP-created state superstructure and on conciliating the demands of competing interest groups. It displayed none of the CPP's interest in mobilizing the population.

Two NLC activities suggest that the NLC and its various civilian advisory groups adopted a more tolerant outlook toward the pluralistic character of Ghana than did Nkrumah. First, the NLC displayed a more conciliatory attitude toward chiefs than had Nkrumah. Although the range of chiefly authority was not extended, the NLC did give chiefs greater access to income from stool lands and permitted the reinstitution of traditional, nonpolitical procedures for the selection and dismissal of chiefs by their respective communities. Second, the Mills-Odoi Commission appointed by the NLC recommended a deconcentration of power from Accra.[38] Although the Commission's principal concern was the decentralization of administrative authority, it also proposed the creation of regional and district authorities to increase the control that local areas had over their own affairs. The NLC accepted the basic proposals of the Commission, but they were only partially implemented.[39]

Overall, the management of ethnic conflict did not command much attention from the NLC and its advisors. In the absence of political parties and competitive politics, ethnic groups did not have much opportunity for direct open competition. Even when rather severe ethnic tension developed in 1968 and 1969, largely because of ethnic imbalances within the NLC itself and concomitant fears regarding the NLC's ethnic partiality, the NLC did not pay explicit attention to the need for promoting ethnic accommodation.

THE 1969 ELECTIONS AND
THE PROGRESS PARTY REGIME

On October 1, 1969, after three and one-half years in office, the National Liberation Council handed over power to a civilian government headed by Dr. K. A. Busia, the former leader of the opposition to Nkrumah. For the first time in Africa a military regime abided by its promise to return the country to civilian rule under a new constitution and a popularly elected government. The dramatic and impressive inaugural ceremonies reflected the optimism in most parts of the country for the Second Republic and its new government. Despite the fears of some analysts that the multiplicity of political parties competing in the election would prevent any one party from emerging with majority support, Busia's Progress Party won 101 of 140 seats in the National Assembly. Moreover, the Progress Party attained this overwhelming victory in an honest election in which 70 percent of the eligible voters cast ballots.

Yet for all the hopeful signs, Ghana's political future contained portents of major problems. The most disturbing aspect of the political scene was the ethnic tension built up during the election. An absence of governmental concern and a lack of established mechanisms for managing such ethnic tension made the situation even more serious. We have already noted that during the period of NLC rule, resentment emerged among the Akan sub-

groups against Ewe (or Ewe-Ga) dominance. The Progress Party manipulated this growing Akan hostility toward the Ewes to its own advantage. The
core of Busia's supporters tended to be Akan, and they persuasively suggested that election of the Progress Party would assure safety from Ewe
control. The Progress Party apparently chose as a key element of its campaign
strategy the encouragement of a Pan-Akan identity, founded largely on fears
of purported Ewe chauvinism. The appeal of this campaign stemmed from
Akan reactions to the NLC, but it was directed against Busia's Ewe rival for
office, K. A. Gbedemah, who headed the National Alliance of Liberals
(NAL). It would have been foolhardy and out of character for Gbedemah to
focus his campaign strategy on the advocacy of Ewe interests, since the Ewes
constitute a relatively small portion of the total population and they could not
have provided an electoral base sufficiently large to win the elections. But the
success of the Progress Party strategy sapped most of the potential strength of
the NAL in non-Ewe areas, and in its reaction to the anti-Ewe attack of the
PP, the NAL fell into the PP's trap and gave the impression of being
primarily an Ewe party.

Despite the importance of these ethnic factors, it would be incorrect to
suggest that the appeal of Busia and his party derived solely from their
exploitation of ethnic factors. It was broadly popular during that period to be
anti-Nkrumah and anti-CPP, and probably no other politician could claim as
consistent an anti-Nkrumah record as Busia. Moreover, as chairman of the
NLC's National Advisory Committee and chairman of the Centre for Civic
Education, Busia had travelled widely and received extensive press coverage
during the preelection period when overt political activity was still prohibited.
His academic credentials and the variety of university posts he had held also
appealed to Ghana's education conscious public. Furthermore, he managed
to gather around him men with reputations for integrity and competence.

Nonetheless, an analysis of the electoral patterns attests to the influence
ethnic factors had on the election outcome. The Progress Party won 85
percent of the votes in Akan-dominant Brong Ahafo Region, 77 percent in
Akan-dominant Ashanti Region, and 71 percent in Akan-dominant Central
Region, while the NAL received 77 percent in the predominantly Ewe Volta
Region. The Progress Party swept all the seats in Ashanti, Brong Ahafo, and
Central Regions, and the NAL similarly made a strong showing in its
stronghold, taking fourteen out of the sixteen seats in Volta Region. The
NAL did not gain a single constituency in the Akan portions of the country.
Outside of the Volta Region the NAL had some success in Ga-dominated

Accra, in non-Akan portions of Eastern Region, and in the Upper and Northern Regions. In the parts of the country that are neither predominantly Akan or Ewe, the distribution of votes between the two parties tended to be less lopsided than in the Akan and Ewe areas. The only Akan area where the Progress Party lost came in Western Region, where two seats went to the People's Action Party in Nzima territory, Nkrumah's place of origin where old anti-Busia feeling remained high, and a third seat went to a member of the All People's Republican Party.[40]

The import of the 1969 elections surpassed the mere manipulation of ethnic factors. Developments under the NLC and during the election resulted in the forging of a Pan-Akan identity such as had never constituted an important social or political force in Ghana previously. Writing in 1967 prior to these developments, Dennis Austin asserted, "The Akan could, I suppose, be regarded as a tribe, but one cannot understand Ghanaian politics on that assumption. A distinguishing feature of local history—and of Ghanaian politics—has been the rivalry between the various divisions of the Akan . . ."[41] Antagonism between Akan-speaking Fantis and Ashantis extends back several centuries, and was apparent as recently as 1956 when Ashantis gave only 37 percent of their votes to the CPP, while 81 percent of the Fantis and others in the Colony voted for the CPP.[42] Although hostility between the Ashantis and the Brongs does not have as long or bitter a history, it has nevertheless reached crisis proportions at various times. For many years prior to independence, the Brongs insisted that they have a region of their own and be governed separately from the Ashantis, and Nkrumah successfully capitalized on this issue in soliciting Brong support for the CPP.

After the 1969 elections, many Ashantis, Brongs, Fantis, Akims, Akwapims, and others started referring to themselves as Akans, rather than by the names of their subgroups, in a manner and to a degree quite unknown previously. This new sense of Akan solidarity constitutes not merely a new interethnic alliance, a marriage of convenience for electoral purposes, but rather a new sense of ethnic identity. The cultural and linguistic similarities among Akan subgroups are obviously not new, but the relaxation of intra-Akan tension and the new sense of having a common "enemy" or antagonist—the Ewes—drew them together to an unprecedented degree. Survey data presented in Chapter 6 indicates the depth of Akan disdain for Ewes in 1972. Since the Akan subgroups together represent approximately 45 percent of Ghana's total population, the forging of a Pan-Akan identity and of an Akan political bloc potentially has widespread ramifications for Ghana's political future.

As could have been anticipated from their longstanding and bitter opposition to each other, Busia's political program and style of leadership contrasted sharply with that of Nkrumah. Although the Progress Party won the 1969 election by an overwhelming margin, Nkrumah's concept of a one-party state held no appeal for Busia. Despite some harrassment by the government, the opposition parties managed to survive and to voice their criticisms of the government. The government carefully circumscribed opposition by other interest groups without subjecting them to Nkrumah-style repression. Similarly, Busia's government never passed a Preventive Detention Act and had no political prisoners under detention at the time of its overthrow in 1972. On the side of party organization, the Progress Party leadership permitted its branches to continue their nominal existence following the election, but because of the magnitude of the Progress Party victory, party leaders did not believe it essential to intensify or even to sustain party activities at the local level, and no effective party organization persisted. Moreover, the Progress Party was not ideologically predisposed to the type of mobilization effort attempted by the CPP. An institutional attempt to organize grass-roots participation in community development, the National Service Corps, initially aroused considerable public interest but never managed to accomplish much beyond the construction of a few village meeting halls and health centers. In terms of leadership style, Busia commanded widespread respect for his intelligence, erudition, and moral rectitude. Unlike Nkrumah, however, Busia never had charismatic appeal, nor did the party attempt to fabricate a personality cult as the CPP had done with Nkrumah.

The lack of interest in mobilization and societal transformation on the part of the Progress Party did not derive from its having an alternative strategy for obliterating ethnic distinctions. In fact, problems of communalism did not command much attention from Busia or his colleagues. When they did, the response differed strikingly from that of Nkrumah. In sharp contrast to the tenets of Nkrumahism on this subject, Busia wrote in 1967 that "a sounder approach to the problem of tribalism in Africa is to accept the fact of pluralism, rather than fly in the face of the facts and attempt to achieve monolithic structures through coercion. It is no sign of backwardness to recognize the fact of the existence of different tribes and ethnic groups, nor is it reactionary to seek accommodation with tribal loyalties."[43]

Busia's philosophy regarding ethnic identities and subnational loyalties found expression in certain policies adopted by his government, and they reflect his recognition of the depth of ethnic attachments. For instance, his government fully sympathized with the steps taken by the NLC to restore some of the status to chiefs, which they had lost under Nkrumah. The framers of the constitution for the Second Republic contributed to this trend by creating both regional houses of chiefs and a national House of Chiefs. The Busia government then further augmented the authority of the chiefs by providing a new role for them in regional and district government. Although the 1972 coup intervened before the Local Administration Act (1971) could take full effect, under this legislation, one-third of the members of each district council and at least two members of each regional council were to be chiefs. In addition to the new status the Local Administration Act accorded to chiefs, it also promised geographical subunits of Ghana and the ethnic groups residing there somewhat greater control over their own affairs than had been the case under Nkrumah. The Act did not come close to creating a federal system or regional-ethnic autonomy, but it did accord somewhat greater recognition to the diversity of Ghana's population.

In practice, the Progress Party government demonstrated little clear concern with the management or amelioration of intergroup relations. One heard some exhortation against tribalism by PP politicians, and the Centre for Civic Education organized an educational program against tribalism. But on the whole, the government's attitude seemed to vacillate between indifference toward ethnic tensions and their exploitation for political ends. As analyzed in Table 7-2, the preponderance of Akans and the total exclusion of Ewes from the cabinet reconfirmed to many Ewes that the Progress Party government intended to exploit ethnic hostilities and undermine Ewe interests whenever possible. Admittedly, Busia's range of choice of Ewe MPs who were Progress Party members was severely limited, but if he had really sought to promote national reconciliation by reassuring the Ewes of his government's ethnic impartiality, he could have named an Ewe from another party.

The expulsion of Gbedemah, leader of the NAL and of the parliamentary opposition, from the National Assembly probably shocked the Ewes more than their exclusion from the cabinet. In November 1969 the Supreme Court ruled that Gbedemah could not take his parliamentary seat because he could not adequately account for approximately $30,000 he had been charged with misappropriating during the Nkrumah era. As a court decision, this was theoretically beyond the control of Busia, but, in fact, the legal action had been initiated by a Progress Party member who clearly had the party's sanction.[44]

The Ewe persecution complex gained reinforcement when they suspected the government of transferring Ewe army officers from key posts and of

TABLE 7-2   *Ethnic Composition of Busia's Cabinets*

		1969	1971
Ashanti		5	6
Brong		2	2
Akim		3	2
Fanti		1	1
Other Akan		3	2
	Akan	(14)	(13)
Ga		1	1
Northern		3	3
Guan		1	0
	Non-Akan	(5)	(4)
	TOTAL	19	17

giving Akans preference in army promotions and placements.[45] In February 1970 the government dismissed 568 civil servants and policemen without specifying clear-cut reasons for doing so. Although no list of those dismissed was ever made public, Ewe members of the National Assembly compiled their own roster and concluded that a disproportionate number of those affected were Ewes. In a parliamentary debate on these dismissals the Ewe leader of the opposition, Dr. Godfrey Agama, charged the Prime Minister with being a "tribalist." Speaking for the government, Victor Owusu, an Ashanti who was Minister of External Affairs, asserted that "Dr. Agama himself belongs to a tribe that has been notorious for its inward-looking tribalism. . . . It is a fact that when a particular member of his tribe was put in a responsible position as Manager of G.N.T.C. (Ghana National Trading Corporation), about 80 percent of the employees became Ewes overnight. It is also a fact that when a member of his tribe was made head of the C.I.D. (Criminal Investigation Division of the Police), 80 percent of the staff of the C.I.D. became Ewes. I can go on *ad nauseum* with these examples."[46] Not unexpectedly, when the dismissal of the 568 was challenged in court, a dismissed Ewe brought the suit against the government, giving it an ethnic flavor. The Supreme Court held that the plaintiff had been wrongfully dismissed, but Busia defiantly declared that his government would not reemploy the plaintiff or any of the other dismissed persons, regardless of the court's judgement.

The allocation of government revenues by the PP government for construction of new roads and the development of new water supplies, far from assuaging Ewe fears of persecution, only exacerbated them. While the government laid down seventy two miles of new roads in predominantly Ewe Volta Region in 1967 to 1969, and thirty miles during 1969–70, only one and a half miles were sponsored during 1970–71, the first full year of Progress Party government rule.[47] Although the rate of construction of government financed community water projects nearly doubled in the country as a whole during the first two years of Progress Party rule, the rate of construction in Volta Region declined by 30 percent.[48]

In one parliamentary debate an Ewe member of the opposition demanded that the government "eschew the policy of vindictiveness, the policy of victimization, and the policy of discrimination against non-Akan-speaking Ghanaians."[49] In a retrospective commentary on the Progress Party government, another Ewe contended that "open and veiled persecution of the minorities had become so pervasive that these classes of citizens moved about in fear and a deep sense of insecurity. . . . Tribalism . . . was being glaringly brandished through dismissals, transfers, postings, dispensation of development votes, contracts, licenses, and the like."[50] This sense of persecution is also reflected in the survey findings reported in Chapter 6.

In light of the more permissive attitude of the Progress Party government than the CPP government toward conflict among subnational ethnic groups, it is ironic that, in certain respects, the Progress Party government adopted a more nationalistic approach to Ghanaian affairs. Consistent with Nkrumah's Pan-Africanist orientation, the CPP government assumed a tolerant attitude toward the many non-Ghanaians, mostly from Nigeria, Togo, and Niger, who migrated to Ghana. However, the PP government could not countenance such a large noncitizen population: within six weeks of taking office, Busia's government issued the Aliens Compliance Order, which required that all noncitizens obtain residence permits within two weeks or be expelled from the country. This seemingly innocuous legislation resulted in the mass expulsion of foreign Africans, since the government would only consider applications from certain categories of workers, and even those were processed too slowly to comply with the two-week deadline. During the first three-month period after the Aliens Compliance Order went into effect, approximately 150,000 people left for lack of a permit.[51] A companion piece of nationalist legislation, the Ghanaian Business (Promotion) Act (1970), aimed at forcing foreigners out of many types of business activity, particularly by reserving small- and medium-size enterprises for Ghanaian nationals. Most of the petty traders affected were non-Ghanaian Africans, principally Nigerians, but many other businesses forced to close were owned by Lebanese and Indian businessmen. In its appeal to self-interest, the expulsion of aliens by the Progress Party and the reservation of many forms of business to Ghana nationals did evoke considerable popular support, and probably did arouse a stronger sense of Ghanaian nationality and national interest, at least during the several months that the anti-foreigner rhetoric featured in political speeches. These nationalist appeals did little over the long-term, however, to forge a sense of common interest among Akans and Ewes, whose relations continued to deteriorate.[52]

A group of army officers led by Colonel I. K. Acheampong staged a successful coup against the Busia government on January 13, 1972, and they installed the National Redemption Council (NRC), composed of military and police officers as the nation's governing body. Although he cited "economic chaos" as his principal provocation, Acheampong also indicated that among his foremost reasons for taking control of the state was the indifference of the Busia government to Ghana's growing ethnic tensions, stating that the NRC intended to bring an abrupt end to the "politics of tribalism" that developed under Busia. "I watched the seed of tribal conflict being slowly sown by the actions of the Busia regime, and with the blood of the millions of our Nigerian brothers to warn us, I acted to nip the threat in the bud. I cannot do this only to see the specter reappear in another guise and my colleagues and I are united in our determination to wage a direct offensive against it to uproot it from our society and give Ghanaians a chance to grow together in unity and strength."[53] It seems quite possible that a desire to combat the Akan chauvinism of Busia's government constituted the principal motive for the Ewes who joined Acheampong in staging the coup.

A review of some of the NRC's early efforts to grapple with Ghana's communal problems reveals some of the inherent complexities and some of the dilemmas that the NRC and any future Ghanaian government will face. The day after the coup Colonel Acheampong announced that the governing NRC would be composed of representatives of various functional and occupational groups. Presumably he planned to deemphasize ethnic factors in

Ghanaian political life by basing political representation on nongeographic and nonethnic factors, as the CPP did when it substituted party auxiliaries for local branches. Acheampong designated the following groups for representation on the NRC: the military, the Chamber of Commerce (for businessmen), the Bar Association (for lawyers), farmers, trade unions (for industrial workers), and chiefs. He inferred that chiefs would be included as an interest group in themselves, rather than as representatives of their particular ethnic constituents. The Christian Council and the Muslim community were also to be represented, thereby enhancing the political salience of religious identity.

Within a few days, however, Acheampong abandoned this notion of how the NRC should be constituted and he named a council composed of eleven military men and the Inspector General of Police. He never offered an explanation for why he did so, but it is clear that one principle guiding the appointments was the attempt to achieve ethnic balance on the council. The new NRC council contained an equal number of Akans and Ewes, four members of each community, two northerners and two Gas. (If the Chairman of the NRC had not been an Akan himself, the Akans could have felt themselves to be underrepresented since they constitute about 45 percent of the population and only 33 percent of the NRC.) Although he hoped to eventually restructure Ghanaian society on another basis, Colonel Acheampong apparently concluded that the most effective initial step toward defusing the tense ethnic situation he confronted upon taking office and toward bringing the "politics of tribalism" to an end, was to seek ethnic equilibrium within the ruling council. Paradoxically, but in recognition of the dilemma he faced in grappling with Ghana's communal problems, soon after naming an ethnically balanced ruling council, Colonel Acheampong issued a decree banning the use of the word "tribe" in all documents in Ghana, whether official or private.[54] Not long after issuing this decree Acheampong explained his attitude regarding ethnic distinctions by stating that "in the fatherhood of our God there is no Ga, no Fanti, no Ewe, no Dagomba, no Grunshie, no Nzima, no Ashanti, no Brong, but just all God's children destined in the greater scheme of things to live together on this portion of God's earth called Ghana."[55]

Despite the NRC's obvious concern over ethnic tension, after two years in office, Akan–Ewe hostility did not dissipate. Even though an Akan, Acheampong, continued as Chairman of the NRC, many Akans believed that the four Ewe members of the NRC were succeeding in getting a disproportionate number of Ewes named to key military and civilian posts. Provoking and aggravating this reaction, Akans still harbored hostility toward Ewes. On many issues the Akan and Ewe members of the NRC lined up as ethnic blocs opposed to each other, and it fell to the two northern members of the NRC to serve as mediators and arbiters. Thus, the greatest ethnic tension arose between southern groups, with north–south conflict still remaining latent. Adding to the heat, in 1973 an Ewe secessionist movement, reminiscent of the move before independence to reunite the Ewes of Ghana and Togo, reemerged.[56] When United Nations Secretary General Kurt Waldheim visited Togo in March 1974, a group of Ghanaian exiles living in Togo led by two former Ghanaian diplomats, all of them Ewes, presented Waldheim with a petition and led a demonstration demanding the reunification of former German Togoland. About the same time a group calling itself the National Liberation Movement of Western Togoland surfaced in Ghana and called for the merger of Volta Region with Togo. Although these movements lack broad mass support, they have provoked several government statements denouncing any efforts by portions of Ghana to secede, and their existence provides evidence of continuing Ewe malaise. The NRC made one concession (in late 1972) to popular sentiment for greater control by localities and regions over their own affairs by resurrecting a modified version of the Local Administration Act of 1971. The Local Administration (Amendment) Decree (1972) created the framework for the appointment by the NRC of regional, district, and local councils, approximately one-third of whose members are chiefs.[57]

THE BASIS OF POLITICAL ACTION

The political salience of ethnicity in Ghana is all too evident. Two fundamental features of the Ghanaian situation accentuate competition and conflict in the political arena among ethnic communities. The extensive involvement of the Ghana government in virtually all aspects of the nation's economic life means that competition for most economic benefits ultimately becomes political competition. The government not only provides roads, water, electricity, health facilities, and other amenities to selected localities, it also, for example, supplies farmers with fertilizers, with pesticides, credit, seeds and seedlings, as well as purchasing, processing, and marketing many agricultural commodities. In the Ghanaian economy of scarcity, limited resources generally preclude the distribution of these services and benefits to all localities and all individuals, so their acquisition becomes a source of intense competition. Along with civil servants, the government employs those who work for the schools, state farms, the railways, State Transport, Electricity Corporation, a vast array of industrial concerns, several mining operations, State Fishing Corporation, the armed forces, and other groups. In addition to controlling selection of employees for these concerns, the government naturally has ultimate responsibility for promotions and dismissals. We are not suggesting that personnel matters in these concerns are simply sources of political patronage, for each has a personnel department responsible for applying ethnically blind selection procedures, but these concerns are not completely immune from political and ethnic influences. Government control over the economy does not, in itself, create economic competition among ethnic groups, but it gives this competition a political character.

The second feature of the Ghanaian situation and of most other African states, which extends the scope of political competition among ethnic groups, is the extent to which the ethnic groups are geographically differentiated. In Lebanon competition for government assistance in the provision of water and electricity does not necessarily mean that some confessional groups will benefit to the exclusion of others, since most localities contain some confessional admixture. In Ghana, though, outside of the ethnically mixed urban areas, most localities approach ethnic homogeneity. Thus, political decisions regarding the citing of rural industries, feeder roads, secondary schools, health facilities, and other physical amenities result in some ethnic groups winning and others losing. To a considerable degree then, competition for any type of resource that will benefit persons living in a particular locality or region becomes not merely competition among localities or regions, but *ipso facto* competition among ethnic groups as well.

Despite the importance of the geographic distribution of amenities, ethnic competition is certainly not confined to competition among geoethnic groups for development projects and physical improvements—its scope is much greater. During the 1969 to 1972 period the focus of competition and conflict between Akans, Ewes, and other groups had only a limited geographical component. The competition involved the allocation of government construction contracts; the distribution of credit under the Ghana Business Promotion Act; and appointments to certain key military positions, key political posts, and high-level civil service and police jobs. Although in many cases the numbers of people involved in this kind of competition are relatively small, the ethnic overtones become strident because those competing constitute the elite of the respective ethnic groups. Those not directly benefiting often believe that if a member of their group obtains a key post or a key contract, he can use it to assist others in his group farther down the socioeconomic ladder through the provision of jobs, subcontracts, or other benefits. Consequently, large numbers watch closely and react to competition among the ethnic groups' elites. Because of this intense interest on the part of those not directly engaged in the competition, they tend to interpret all competition for elite posts as having an ethnic component, even in those cases where ethnic factors have been immaterial.

Unlike the situation in Lebanon where confessional groups tend to hold divergent ideological positions on key political issues, one rarely encounters clear ideological conflict among Ghana's ethnic groups. The northerners and the Ashanti, whose traditional political structures and chiefs enjoy somewhat greater contemporary influence, are probably more likely to favor a political system that accords a larger role to traditional institutions. This difference appeared most clearly just prior to independence when the northerners and the Ashanti led the fight for a federal constitution. The more impoverished ethnic groups, particularly the northerners, also understandably tend to favor special allocations to boost the development of the poorer portions of the country. Predominantly urban groups, like the Ga, have less inclination to support rural development schemes than do groups concentrated in rural areas. But such differences in political attitudes do not have major repercussions for the political system. Ideological divisions count for much less than the endemic competition among ethnic groups for scarce economic resources, for wealth, for power, and for prestige. In this competition, individuals are naturally most concerned about their individual and family success, but group competition and particularly ethnic group competition often serves as the most effective vehicle for attaining individual advantage.

Nkrumah and Acheampong indicated their recognition of the importance of ethnic factors in Ghanaian political behavior when they sought the representation of all major ethnic groups in their cabinets and ruling councils. The public discontent aroused by the absence of ethnic balance within the NLC and in Busia's cabinets underscores the political salience of ethnic identity. The question of whether parliamentary representation should be allocated proportionally among the nation's ethnic communities has never had to be faced in the way it has in Lebanon, since the geographic differentiation of ethnic groups means that geographically defined parliamentary constituencies give rise almost automatically to roughly proportional ethnic representation, at least in rural areas.

Ethnic factors are undoubtedly central to an understanding of political behavior in Ghana, but competition among monolithic and self-contained ethnic groups certainly does not fully describe the character of Ghana's political life. Not all Ashantis voted for the NLM in 1956 and not all Fantis supported the CPP. In the 1969 elections the Progress Party ran local candidates in all constituencies including the Ewe constituencies, and obtained some votes, while the NAL received votes in most Akan constituencies. Moreover, as described in Chapters 1 and 6, ethnic groups operating as cohesive units at one level of the system can divide into competing subunits at another level of the system. For instance, during the 1950s when the Brongs came into sharp conflict with the Ashantis over the subdivision of Ashanti Region into two parts, struggles among Brong subunits served as a counterpoint.[58] During the early 1970s when northerners demanded government allocations for development of water supplies in the north, intense conflict occurred within the north itself over which groups should benefit from the first water systems constructed.[59] Despite the emergence of a Pan-Akan identity in the late 1960s and early 1970s, the Ashanti and other Akan subgroups preserved some of their individual identities and each sought special advantages for themselves.

A type of politically relevant concern closely tied to ethnic politics might be termed traditional interests, or the interest among chiefs, other traditional office-holders, and their clients to sustain or reinstate traditional political institutions. The promotion of ethnic and traditional interests have at times represented closely joined issues, and the advancement of ethnic interests implied the preservation of the remnants of the traditional state structure. For instance, the NLM's demand in the mid-1950s for a federal system of government and retention of Ashanti autonomy was based on both appeals to Ashanti ethnic chauvinism and on a desire to safeguard the position of traditional authority.

But traditional interests later became more clearly differentiated from ethnic interests. As ethnicity became modernized in Ghana, the promotion of ethnic interests usually no longer entailed backing chiefs or traditional institutions. In the contemporary competition between ethnic groups for development projects, jobs, and political power, chiefs play a rather insignificant role, in terms of providing leadership and in terms of their status arousing much concern. In turn, chiefs from all parts of the country have tended to join together to form their own interest group, seeking benefits from the political system for themselves. The best illustration of this is the barrage of demands unleashed by chiefs following the 1966 coup for increased salaries, new authority, and added prestige.[60]

It should be apparent by this point in the discussion that religion has rarely served as an important factor in differentiating political interests in Ghana. We have observed that in the traditional setting, Ghanaians exhibited remarkable religious tolerance, based largely on their relativistic orientation to religious belief and practice. The spread of Islam and Christianity have tended to create somewhat sharper religious distinctions within Ghana, and since Christians predominate in the south and Muslims in the north, Christianity and Islam tend to reinforce existing cultural, linguistic, and socioeconomic divisions between north and south. If in the future, the north–south division becomes a major axis of political competition, the religious differences between these two regions could play a larger political role. The Northern People's Party did constitute an important force in the 1954 and 1956 elections, but religion did not seem to comprise a critical element in the party's sense of self-identity, as is clear from the fact that it had many Christian members.[61] Even the Moslem Association Party (MAP), which in the 1950s explicitly used religion as a basis for recruitment, sought to serve the special interests of non-Ghanaian and northern migrants living in southern towns rather than form a political movement for all Ghanaian Muslims. The limits of the MAP's political appeal is clear from its poor showing at the polls; it gained only 2.9 percent of the total vote in 1954 and 1.6 percent in 1956.

The incipient character of class formation in Ghana makes class identities weak and cautions against interpretations of political behavior in terms of class conflict. Granting this and granting that class competition often has an ethnic dimension, certain features of Ghana's recent political history can best be understood in quasi-class terms. In the late 1940s and the early 1950s the CPP successfully identified itself as an anti-chief and anti-intelligentsia organization based upon support from young primary school graduates and other members of the petite bourgeoisie, with leadership recruited primarily from the lower middle classes.[62] The opposing UGCC represented a coalition of traditional and modern elites, of chiefs and of an incipient professional class dominated by lawyers. Although the UGCC (like the CPP) sought independence for Ghana, it hoped that the transition to independence would not be traumatic and that the privileges enjoyed by the existing elites would not be threatened.

The CPP, on the other hand, promised new channels for mobility and a restructuring of society which appealed to its lower middle-class backers. It is erroneous, however, to see the CPP's socialism as a program for creating a workers' and peasants' state. As Bob Fitch and Mary Oppenheimer have pointed out, the CPP concept of socialism was largely confined to "a set of techniques and institutions which enabled rapid economic progress and economic independence in the face of a colonial heritage. . . ."[63] Insofar as a proletariat existed in Ghana, its representatives did not dominate the CPP or use it as a vehicle for satisfying the proletariat's class interests. Moreover, although the upper middle classes and professional groups remained largely alienated from the CPP, as the CPP leadership achieved economic and social mobility through their party positions, they lost much of their identification with the lower middle classes from which they originated. The transformation of Ghana into a party-state also undermined the concept of political parties representing particular class interests; all groups and classes were expected to join the CPP, and they all eventually became disenchanted with the CPP's economic program as the country's per capita income declined.[64]

Although some elements of class conflict are evident in Ghana's political past, it is more meaningful to identify particular occupational groups rather than whole socioeconomic classes as influencers of political and governmental behavior. The most successful of these groups are the unionized industrial workers, who constitute only a small portion of the population. The political character of industrial action derives primarily from the fact that the government is Ghana's principal employer. Apart from the transformation of the Trades' Union Congress into an auxiliary of the CPP, trade unions have not served as effective vehicles for political party opposition, but they have exerted substantial pressure against each regime, to improve the wages of particular sets of workers or to change government economic policy affecting industrial workers as a whole. They have done this despite tight government controls imposed on the unions by the CPP and all subsequent regimes. During the period 1966 to 1971 an average of fifty five strikes took place each year. In 1970, 20,000 workers were involved in strikes and in 1971, 32,000 workers were similarly engaged.[65]

In an attempt to build an unassailable electoral base following its accession to power in 1969, the Progress Party adopted what might be termed a rural strategy. By emphasizing development of rural areas and continually citing the neglect that Ghana's farming population had suffered in the past, Busia's government hoped to complement its ethnic appeal to the Akans by arousing united and sustained support in future elections from Ghana's farmers, who constitute a majority of the population. Although the government was undoubtedly correct in picking its economic priorities, it was a vulnerable political strategy. Farmers did not exhibit much corporate self-consciousness and the Progress Party failed to appreciate the disproportionate political strength of urban dwellers, particularly industrial workers, civil servants, and the military. In fact, new taxes imposed on salaried workers and urban wage earners and the loss of certain perquisites by civil servants and military officers helped to foment the 1972 coup.

In conclusion, we can rank in order of their overall importance the various bases of political action: (1) ethnic factors, (2) occupational interests, (3) class factors, and (4) traditional interests.

NOTES

1. Kwame Nkrumah, *Towards Colonial Freedom* (London: Heineman, 1962), p. xv.
2. See, for instance, Kwame Nkrumah, *Dark Days in Ghana* (New York: International Publishers, 1968), p. 66.
3. The parallelism between Nkrumah's strategy for promoting national integration and that advocated by the Soviet Union is striking. See Helen Desfosses Cohn, *Soviet Policy Toward Black Africa: The Focus on National Integration* (New York: Praeger, 1972).
4. For a comprehensive consideration of chieftaincy during the CPP regime, see John R. Schram, "Chieftaincy and Politics in Independent Ghana," unpublished M.A. Thesis, Institute of African Studies, University of Ghana, 1967.
5. See, for instance, the description of the interaction of the CPP and the chiefs of Larteh contained in David Brokensha, "Anthropological Enquiries and Political Science: A Case Study from Ghana," paper presented at the African Studies Association Meeting in October 1965, pp. 9–11.
6. For a discussion of these elections see David E. Apter, "Ghana," in James S. Coleman and Carl G. Rosberg, Jr., eds., *Political Parties and National Integration in Tropical Africa* (Berkeley: University of California Press, 1964), p. 292.
7. The most notable example is Henry Bretton, *The Rise and Fall of Kwame Nkrumah: A Study of Personal Rule in Africa* (New York: Frederick A. Praeger, 1966).
8. David J. Finlay, Ole R. Holsti, and Richard R. Fagen, *Enemies in Politics* (Chicago: Rand McNally, 1967), p. 157.
9. Nkrumah envisaged the state and the party becoming one. See Kwame Nkrumah, *I Speak of Freedom* (New York: Frederick A. Praeger, 1961), p. 209.
10. See Martin Kilson, "The Grassroots in Ghanaian Politics," in Philip Foster and Aristide R. Zolberg, eds., *Ghana and the Ivory Coast* (Chicago: University of Chicago Press, 1971), p. 114.
11. See Aristide R. Zolberg, *Creating Political Order: The Party-States of West Africa* (Chicago: Rand McNally, 1966), p. 62.
12. See, for instance, Maxwell Owusu, *Uses and Abuses of Political Power: A Case Study of Continuity and Change in the Politics of Ghana* (Chicago: University of Chicago Press, 1970), p. 328.
13. For a full discussion of this structure, see Kilson, op. cit., pp. 114–115.
14. For a full elaboration of this point, see Jon Kraus, "On the Politics of Nationalism and Social Change in Ghana," *Journal of Modern African Studies*, 7 (April 1969), pp. 122–123; and Brokensha, op. cit.

15. "The Constitution of the Convention People's Party," Revised version (Accra: Guinea Press, 1962), Part IV, p. 22.
16. Dennis Austin, *Politics in Ghana 1946–1960* (London: Oxford University Press, 1964), p. 418.
17. Apter, op. cit., p. 344.
18. This kind of conflict was admittedly not universal, as indicated in Harriet B. Schiffer, "Political Linkage in Ghana: Bekwai District, A Case Study," paper presented at African Studies Association, 1971, p. 14.
19. Brokensha, op. cit., p. 9.
20. For a careful elaboration of these points see Emily Card, "The Politics of Underdevelopment: From Voluntary Associations to Party Auxiliaries in Ghana," unpublished PH.D. Diss., Columbia University, 1972.
21. Maxwell Owusu provides convincing evidence of the importance of individual economic self-interest in motivating party loyalty in Swedru, but he unjustifiably asserts that this is virtually the only source of party loyalty. See Owusu, op. cit., Chapter 8.
22. Quoted by Conor Cruise O'Brien, *London Observer*, March 17, 1966.
23. David Apter, *Ghana in Transition* (New York: Atheneum, 1963), pp. 305–313; and David E. Apter, "Nkrumah, Charisma, and the Coup," *Daedalus*, 97 (Summer 1968), pp. 759–792. For another perspective, see I. M. Wallerstein, *The Road to Independence: Ghana and the Ivory Coast* (Paris: Mouton, 1964), pp. 156–163.
24. Jon Kraus, "Political Change, Conflict, and Development in Ghana," Foster and Zolberg, op. cit., p. 53.
25. For a full discussion of this see Jon Kraus, "Ghana's New 'Corporate Parliament'," *Africa Report*, 10 (August 1965), pp. 6–11.
26. Ibid., p. 8.
27. Kwame Nkrumah, *Dark Days in Ghana*, op. cit., p. 66.
28. Apter, *Ghana in Transition*, op. cit., p. 371.
29. See Audrey C. Smock, "Introduction," *Comparative Politics: A Reader in Institutionalization and Mobilization* (Boston: Allyn and Bacon, 1973), pp. 25–29.
30. For a discussion of the reemergence of ethnic conflict on the microlevel following Nkrumah's fall, see Enid Schildkrout, "Strangers and Local Government in Kumasi," *Journal of Modern African Studies*, 8 (July 1970), pp. 263–265.
31. For an example of such activity, see Peter Barker, *Operation Cold Chop* (Accra: Ghana Publishing Corp., 1969), p. 90.
32. For some examples, see L. H. Ofosu-Appiah, *The Life of Lt. General Kotoka* (Accra: Waterville Publishing House, 1972), pp. 76–78.
33. For a description of the coup and some of the factors motivating key participants, see Major-General A. K. Ocran, *A Myth Is Broken* (Accra: Longmans, Green, and Co., 1968); Colonel A. A. Afrifa, *The Ghana Coup* (London: Frank Cass and Co., 1967); Peter Barker, op. cit.; and Ofosu-Appiah, op. cit.
34. For an enumeration of the Ewes involved, see Ofosu-Appiah, op. cit., pp. 63–66.
35. Afrifa, in describing his involvement, stated that Ashantis and Ewes are traditional allies (Afrifa, op. cit., p. 40).
36. Ruth First, *The Barrel of a Gun* (London: The Penguin Press, 1970), p. 403.
37. Quoted in Jon Kraus, "Arms and Politics in Ghana," in Claude Welch, ed., *Soldier and State in Africa* (Evanston: Northwestern University Press, 1970), p. 204.
38. "Report of the Commission on the Structure and Remuneration of the Public Services in Ghana" (Accra: State Publishing Corp., 1967).
39. "White Paper on the Report of the Commission on the Structure and Remuneration of the Public Services in Ghana" (Accra: State Publishing Corp., 1968); see also Gene R. Harris,

"Some Aspects of Decentralization and the Formulation and Implementation of Agricultural Policy in Ghana," Institute of Statistical, Social, and Economic Research, University of Ghana, 1971, mimeographed.

40. Emily Card and Barbara Callaway, "Ghanaian Politics: The Elections and After," *Africa Report*, 15 (March 1970), p. 13.

41. Dennis Austin, "Opposition in Ghana, 1947–67," *Government and Opposition*, 2 (July–October 1967), p. 541.

42. Figures on the 1956 elections are taken from Austin, *Politics in Ghana, 1946–1960*, op. cit., pp. 353–354.

43. K. A. Busia, *Africa in Search of Democracy* (London: Routledge and Kegan Paul, 1967), p. 119.

44. The defiance of Gbedemah's constituents toward the government is clear from the results of the by-election to fill his vacated seat. The NAL candidate polled 6626 votes while the government supported PP candidate received only 314 votes. (*Daily Graphic*, December 22, 1969, p. 3).

45. Evidence on this point is contained in Victor LeVine, "Autopsy on a Regime: Ghana's Civilian Interregnum, 1969–1972," unpublished manuscript, 1972, p. 4.

46. *Parliamentary Debates*, Vol. 3, No. 23, June 17, 1970, pp. 878–880.

47. J. H. Mensah, "1971–72 Budget Statement" (Accra: Ministry of Finance, July 27, 1971), pp. 61–63.

48. Ibid, pp. 68–70.

49. *Parliamentary Debates*, Vol. 2, No. 23, p. 921.

50. G. Adali-Morty, "Facing the Music of Tribalism," *Daily Graphic*, March 25, 1972, p. 9.

51. For an explanation of this action see speech by Prime Minister Busia to the First National Congress of the Progress Party as quoted in *Daily Graphic*, August 29, 1970, p. 5. See also Margaret Piel, "The Expulsion of West African Aliens," *Journal of Modern African Studies*, 9 (July 1971), pp. 205–229.

52. We are not suggesting that the promotion of nationalistic fervor and national cohesion were central intentions of the Progress Party when they adopted these policies. Regardless of the "true" intentions of the party's leadership, which were no doubt complex and multiple, these policies did have important implications for national accommodation, and it is therefore legitimate for us to analyze them in these terms.

53. Acheampong quoted in *Daily Graphic*, February 25, 1972, p. 1.

54. Colonel I. K. Acheampong, *Speeches and Interviews*, Vol. 1 (Accra: Ghana Publishing Corporation, 1973); and National Redemption Council, "The Charter of Our Redemption" (Accra: n.p., 1973), p. 84.

55. Colonel I. K. Acheampong, *Speeches and Interviews*, op. cit., p. 158.

56. Interview data gathered by Fred Hayward in an Ewe village suggests that secessionist sentiment is stronger among Ewes in the older age group, since they had been exposed to or had been a part of the pan-Ewe movement in the 1950s. (Fred M. Hayward, "The Stability of Levels of National Integration: Projects from the Ghanaian Context," unpublished paper, June 1972, pp. 36–37.)

57. "N.R.C. Decree No. 138," December 22, 1972.

58. Dennis Austin, "Opposition in Ghana: 1947–67," op. cit., p. 542.

59. Interview with Regional Administrative Officer for Upper Region.

60. For a compendium of these demands, see Robert Pinkney, *Ghana Under Military Rule, 1966–1969* (London: Methuen, 1972), pp. 25–28.

61. Austin, *Politics in Ghana, 1946–60*, op. cit., pp. 229–230.

62. For various attempts to define the membership base of the CPP, see Owusu, op. cit., p. 331;

Jon Kraus, "On the Politics of Nationalism and Social Change in Ghana," op. cit., p. 118; and Apter, *Ghana in Transition*, op. cit., p. 311.

63.   Bob Fitch and Mary Oppenheimer, *Ghana: End of an Illusion* (New York: Monthly Review Press, 1966), p. 109.

64.   The Sekondi-Takoradi strike in 1961 revealed the opposition of many industrial workers to the government's economic program. See St. Clair Drake and Leslie Alexander Lacy, "Government Versus the Unions: The Sekondi-Takoradi Strike, 1961," in Gwendolen M. Carter, ed., *Politics in Africa* (New York: Harcourt, Brace & World, Inc., 1966), pp. 67–118.

65.   See Pinkney, op. cit., pp. 34–35; and *West Africa*, March 24, 1972, p. 370.

Political Change and Reform in Ghana

Consideration of the patterns of change in Ghana's communal problems over the past twenty or thirty years entails such questions as: (1) To what extent do Ghana's constituent traditional states still compete with the central government for legitimacy and authority? (2) What trends are apparent in terms of public awareness of and attachment to the modern state? (3) Is political and social conflict among the country's ethnic groups on the increase or decline? (4) Is progress toward national accommodation observable?

While in the case of Lebanon we differ from most other writers in seeing somewhat greater progress toward accommodation, our assessment of the Ghanaian situation accords communal problems more importance than do most other analysts. We disagree sharply with David Apter, for instance, when he asserts that "the nation has replaced the ethnic community,"[1] or with Maxwell Owusu, when he virtually denies that ethnic factors have an impact on political behavior in Ghana.[2] In differing with these authors we do not necessarily claim superior powers of analysis, but we do have the advantage of having observed firsthand the emergence of a resurgence of ethnic politics during the critical period of 1968 to 1973.

The strength and character of ethnic factors have not been constant throughout recent decades, and important developments over the past twenty

Portions of this chapter are printed with permission of The Free Press, from the forthcoming publication entitled *The Search for National Integration in Africa*, edited by David R. Smock and Kwamina Bentsi-Enchill. Copyright © 1975 by The Free Press, a Division of Macmillan Publishing Co., Inc.

or thirty years are clearly observable. Prior to 1950 the traditional states and their chiefs still functioned as important systems and institutions. During the period of indirect rule in the colonial era the role of the modern state was minimal and the distinction between traditional rule, emanating from the capital of each traditional state, and modern rule, emanating from Accra, was not so clear-cut as it later became. Nkrumah undermined indirect rule and helped dismantle the traditional states and the authority of the chiefs as a means of building the strength and power of a modern, centralized government. That battle is now essentially over, and the centralized, modern state has emerged the victor. This is not to imply that the central government is all-powerful, for its institutionalization and capabilities are still limited, but the limitations do not principally derive from threats posed to it by the traditional states. Accompanying the growing acceptance of the authority of the central government and the demise of the traditional states, the demands for a federal form of government that many Ashanti, northerners, and Ewes expressed in the mid-1950s have faded away, and the threats of secession uttered by some Ashanti are heard less frequently. These comprise no small achievements.

Improvements in road, rail, and water transportation, in telecommunications, and in the internal exchange of goods have helped tie all parts of Ghana into a national framework. Admittedly, Ghana's relatively small size has rendered this task less burdensome than in many other new states, but progress has nonetheless been considerable and commendable. Furthermore, as Maxwell Owusu has pointed out, a national civil service, police force, and army; a national school system; a national judiciary; centralized local government; and a national legislature have all helped bring the periphery near the center.[3] Other investigations already cited have indicated that sustained contact between government officials and rural communities has increased the sense of attachment the residents of those communities have to the state.[4] By comparing the obsession with issues of local importance on the part of voters in many constituencies in the 1954 elections[5] with the more nationally oriented struggle for power in 1969, the broadening of political perspective is manifestly clear.

Despite these developments, one cannot conclude that a trend exists toward improvement in relations among ethnic groups or in a lessening of interethnic political conflict. The situation has not remained static, but change has not been unidirectional. During the early years of the CPP's existence in the late 1940s and early 1950s, "class" factors appeared to take precedence over ethnic factors in political competition. Then the four years from 1954 to 1958 represented a period of intense ethnic conflict, with threats of secession and even the possibility of civil war. The years between 1958 and 1968 comprised a period devoid of strident, overt ethnic conflict, deriving largely from Nkrumah's repression of competitive politics and from his own ethnic blindness, as well as from his political strategy. Midway through the three years of NLC rule, ethnic conflict reemerged and then intensified at the time of the 1969 election and during the two and a half years of Progress Party rule. Concern over the rising crescendo of ethnic turmoil constituted one motive for the military takeover staged early in 1972, and since that coup the National Redemption Council has had to continue to contend with ethnic tension.

Our discussion has also pointed out changes in the character of Ghana's ethnic groups and the configuration of ethnic alliances. The 1950s witnessed a loose coalition among the Ashantis, the Ewes, and the northerners against the other groups. Between 1968 and 1972 a new Pan-Akan identity developed that bound the Ashantis to their Akan brethren, and the sharpest conflict came between the Akans and the Ewes. Some indication is now apparent of growing self-consciousness and increasing frustration among northerners arising from their disadvantaged socioeconomic position in the country, and from what K. A. B. Jones-Quartey has termed the "disgraceful habit of discriminatory treatment of the north as against the south."[6] As a result, sharper conflict could develop in the foreseeable future between ethnic groups from the north and those from the south.

The changes of governmental regime in Ghana have had something of a thesis-antithesis character in ethnic terms. The Nkrumah regime was essentially dominated by southern Akans, with the Ashantis never fully supportive. The military coup that overthrew Nkrumah in 1966 was led primarily by Ewes, and the National Liberation Council which the coup organizers established consisted preponderantly of Gas and Ewes. The Pan-Akan reaction against the NLC brought to power the Akan-dominated Progress Party government of Busia. Although the head of the National Redemption Council that toppled the Busia government is an Akan (Ashanti), Ewes have been thought by many observers (particularly Akans) to be the powers behind the throne, both in organizing the coup and in running the NRC government. This kind of a paradigm does not do justice to the complexities of Ghana's governmental changes, yet it does underscore the salience of ethnic factors in Ghana's political history. It also suggests the destablizing action-reaction character of ethnic conflict when it is not adequately managed by the prevailing political system.

Recent intense ethnic conflict in Ghana is based on a more modernized form of ethnicity than was ethnic conflict in the 1950s and earlier. During the 1968 to 1973 period various ethnic groups competed intensely, and sometimes hostilely, with each other for control of power and access to development resources, jobs, and prestige at the center. However, this conflict did not involve an effort to reinstate the chiefs or reconstitute the traditional states. Even though some of the competing ethnic groups, like the Akans and the Ewes, do not coincide with any preexisting traditional state, their sense of ethnic identity and self-interest are nonetheless clearly articulated.

Many educated Ghanaians have been unprepared to accept the persistence of ethnic identities in modern life because they consider ethnic identities to be traditional, primitive, and antimodern. They also have the conviction that the forces of modernization, if properly manipulated, will permit the total elimination of these anachronistic identities and the communal competition they generate. But contemporary ethnic conflict in Ghana is not a reversion to a tribal past; it is a modern phenomenon paralleling similar developments in many parts of the world. Although current ethnic identities and conflict do not constitute eternal features of Ghanaian social and political life, they will persist for a long time. Moreover, the difficulties being posed by this modernized form of ethnicity seem considerably more intractable than Ghana's more traditional ethnopolitical issue, namely, the dismantling of the traditional states. If government officials come to fully appreciate the character and strength of modern ethnicity in Ghana, they are more likely to be able to deal with Ghana's communal problems realistically and without embarrassment. They can also move beyond exhortations against tribalism to a more effective strategy for promoting national accommodation. The remainder of this chapter discusses some alternative strategies open to Ghana for grappling with communalism and for advancing national accommodation. The fields covered are political reform, government personnel policies, law, equitable economic development, language policy, and education. We analyze past policies pursued by various of the Ghanaian regimes in each of these spheres and consider policy alternatives currently open.

POLITICAL REFORM

Aside from the inherent complexity of the subject, consideration of political reform in Ghana is particularly difficult because of governmental instability. From 1966 to the present, Ghana has had a one-party state, a military regime, a parliamentary democracy, and another military regime. The analyst who tries to recommend adjustments to the governmental system therefore faces uncertainty regarding which system should be modified. Much of this discussion has relevance to all types of systems, but other portions relate only to a parliamentary democracy.

A popular response to a pluralist society in which the component ethnic groups are geographically differentiated is to advocate a federal system. Examples that come readily to mind include Belgium, India, Nigeria, and Canada. In some cases no real alternative exists to a federal system, but we believe that the federal approach generally can and should be avoided in a country the size of Ghana. Although the unitary system in Ghana has revealed some shortcomings, its strengths outweigh the weaknesses.

A federal approach tends to camouflage the most critical problem faced by communally fragmented states, which is the division of power at the center. In granting a measure of regional or ethnic autonomy, a federal system accords the constituent groups some sense of self-determination, but the problem of who is to control the center remains. Only when a system that gives the constituent groups a belief that they are equitably represented in the central decision-making organs can be devised, has the most fundamental issue been resolved. Moreover, federal systems frequently foster subnational political socialization. Rarely also do the federal units remain satisfied with the division of authority between themselves and the center. In a fragmented society the drawing of regional boundaries itself arouses controversy, particularly from ethnic minorities who may then agitate for regions of their own.[7]

Several types of policies designed to foster national unity can be better pursued in a unitary state. Although one needs to avoid being doctrinaire on this point, it is likely, for instance, that the rational allocation of resources leading to balanced and equitable regional economic development can most easily be achieved in a unitary state. In a federal system one expects a considerable proportion of the revenues for use in the region to be raised within the region itself, making it difficult to rationalize large-scale transfers of resources from wealthy portions of the country to less developed regions. Regional governments rarely accord high priority to programs fostering a national perspective, and the division of power in a federal state usually vests regional governments with responsibility for such subjects as education and language usage. Therefore, in a federal state the formulation and implementation of a national language policy that encourages national intercommunity communication and an educational policy that is national in scope and which promotes intergroup understanding and a national orientation, face serious impediments.

The advocacy by the opposition of a federal system for Ghana at the time of independence was based on several factors. Many northerners feared that their region would not enjoy equitable representation within the bureaucracy and in turn that the north would be controlled and manipulated by southern civil servants. They also believed that a unitary state under the CPP would shortchange the north and thus deny them the resources required to catch up with the rest of the country. Many Ashantis doubted that they would be adequately represented at the center in a CPP government, and that government expenditures in Ashanti Region would be commensurate with government revenues collected there. A unitary system that provided balanced ethnic representation in top political posts as well as in the higher echelons of the civil service would have largely satisfied the desires of both Ashantis and northerners for a just share of decision-making power. The economic interests of the northerners and of the Ashanti were, and continue to be, largely incompatible and cannot be fully reconciled by either a unitary or a federal system. But a unitary system that evidenced concern with equitable economic development, while also giving some recognition to the special claims of a region from which major portions of the state's revenues are extracted, would probably be more effective in meeting these conflicting demands than would a federal system. A recent study of various rural communities in Ghana revealed that those communities that exhibited the greatest desire for regional rather than central control were located in areas that have tended to be neglected by the central government.[8] The desire for regional control could be obviated by greater concern with equitable regional economic development, and the development of these neglected areas could be more rationally and effectively undertaken within a unitary context.

In arguing against a federal approach, we are not contending that there is no role for effective political representation and administrative competence at district and regional levels. Within the context of a unitary state, district and regional councils with carefully circumscribed powers can still be usefully established. As under the provisions of the Local Administration Act (1971), regional councils could serve as planning and coordinating bodies for their areas under the overall direction of the central ministries and subject to the priorities established by national bodies, and district councils could be responsible for certain types of public services.

The role of the chiefs raises a subsidiary question relating to the distribution of power within the state. It is conceivable that if the institution of chieftaincy had been managed differently during the colonial period, it might be possible to successfully incorporate chiefs into the modern state, but it would be a very difficult task. The status of the chiefs suffered badly during the colonial period from having been granted and having usurped excessive powers, as well as having been less than fully responsible in their management of stool funds. Many chiefs also became tainted from their close cooperation with the British and from their reluctance to support the independence movement. Moreover, since few chiefs attended school, they had problems fitting into a modern state. For these reasons and also because he saw their power as constituting a threat to an effective unitary state, Nkrumah systematically undermined what authority remained to the chiefs. Following this final blow to their prestige and status, they have survived largely as symbols of past glories and as representatives of the traditional cultures of their respective ethnic groups. It is probably useful to continue to accord chiefs a ceremonial status both locally and in a national House of Chiefs and to give them some role to play in local government, without permitting them to reestablish power bases from which they could compete with the center. Naturally, capable and educated chiefs could be accorded equal opportunity to seek national office with all other Ghanaian citizens.

This is not the occasion to indulge in an extensive discussion of the strengths and weaknesses of the three types of governmental system that Ghana has adopted since independence: an authoritarian one-party system, a military regime, and a parliamentary democracy. It is worth pointing out, however, that the character of intergroup relations has been influenced by the type of system in operation during a particular period. Ethnic conflict was probably most severe during the periods of parliamentary democracy, both in the early stages of the Nkrumah regime and during the Busia regime. To some extent, these antagonisms arose because the open democratic system permitted free political competition and much of this competition had an ethnic base. But the NLC period witnessed some ethnic tension as well. Moreover, when ethnic conflict is not evident under a military or one-party government, it may only be repressed and remain latent, waiting for a period of open political competition to find expression. If this is the case, then the fact that conflict is not readily apparent during a period of one-party or military rule does not mean that this type of regime is any more successful in promoting intergroup accommodation.

Regardless of the fundamental type of political system being employed, the successful promotion of intercommunity accommodation largely depends on the incorporation of the major communal groups in the central decision-making organs. At the top, one man usually has to have the greatest authority, and this person must necessarily be a member of a single ethnic group. Thus, it is difficult to achieve balance at this level. Supreme political power could be shared by requiring that the top post be rotated in some fashion among the various ethnic components of the population. Another possibility would be for free competition to prevail in the selection of the head of the government, but for a ceremonial head of state to be chosen on a rotational basis between the various regions or the major ethnic groups.[9] It might be advisable for a regime to have two positions of authority at the top, although one would naturally be clearly designated as the more important. These two posts could be president and prime minister, chairman and vice-chairman of a military council, or whatever. No restrictions would be imposed on who could succeed to the highest post, but the man holding the second post could not be selected from the same generic ethnic group.

In the Ghanaian context the most salient division is between Akan and non-Akan, which would mean that if the chairman is an Akan then the vice-chairman should be from a non-Akan group. The two leading candidates for the post of president of the Second Republic were Edward Akufo-Addo, the successful candidate, who is Akan, and N. A. Ollennu, a Ga. Many non-Akans suspected Prime Minister Busia, an Akan, to be partial to Akan interests and his support of Akufo-Addo for the post confirmed these apprehensions. If he had backed a non-Akan for the presidency so that one Akan and one non-Akan had held the two highest posts, fears of ethnic bias would have been at least partially allayed. Yet, if the constitution specified one of these posts for the Akans and the other for the non-Akans (in the manner of the Lebanese National Pact), this might have created considerable ethnic conflict, because the post of prime minister was more important than that of president: to reserve it for one of the two groups would have placed that group in an unacceptably privileged position. The somewhat unstable character of ethnic alignments in Ghana might necessitate the periodic reassessment of the allocation of the two highest posts. As discussed earlier, a sense of Pan-Akan identity has constituted an important psychological and political force since 1969, but it is conceivable that divisive competition among Akan subgroups could reassert itself in the future. In that eventuality the arrangement could be reformulated to take the new configuration of ethnic alignments into account.

At the level of the cabinet or the ruling military council, broader ethnic representation is possible. Ethnic balance can be achieved to some extent by having the head of a regime strive for ethnic diversity when he names his cabinet. It seems preferable, however, if formulae for distributing membership could be worked out for each successive regime to apply. This would minimize the chances of misunderstanding and suspicion. For instance, Prime Minister Busia may have thought that he provided for adequate ethnic diversity in his first cabinet by naming a Ga and three northerners as members. Although he may not have regarded the omission of an Ewe as giving rise to ethnic imbalance, the Ewes certainly perceived it in this manner. A broadly accepted formula for cabinet composition applicable to all regimes would have avoided this kind of ill-feeling.

The failure of Busia to name an Ewe to his cabinet in part resulted from the fact that his Progress Party fared so poorly in the Ewe areas that his choice of possible Ewe cabinet members was severely limited. If the opposing NAL had won the election, Gbedemah as prime minister would have had similar difficulty appointing Ashantis and other Akans to his cabinet, since NAL lacked major support among Akans. This tendency for parties to be ethnically based or at least to be stronger in some ethnic areas than in others commends a coalition approach to cabinet formation. If political parties were ethnically balanced, the electoral success of a particular party would not be perceived as a threat or danger to any ethnic group. But such genuinely multiethnic parties are not likely to emerge in the foreseeable future. Even the constitutional and legal provisions adopted prior to the 1969 election requiring that founding members of every political party come from all regions of the country did not assure that political parties were equally appealing to all ethnic groups. In fact, as already noted, the 1969 election turned largely into an ethnic contest. Obviously, the problem is more complex and deep-rooted than B. D. G. Folson, a Ghanaian political scientist, would have us believe when he states that "all that is required by way of formal enactments is the outlawing of parties that are based on ethnic or tribal entities."[10]

In Lebanon broadly based coalition cabinets result from two principal considerations. First, individual parties do not have sufficient popularity to win a majority of seats; to gain a vote of confidence in parliament a cabinet must include members of several political blocs and parties. Second, Lebanese political leaders regard cabinet formation as a means of fostering national cohesion. As a consequence, they strive to include balanced confessional representation as well as representatives of a wide spectrum of political viewpoints. During the two periods of parliamentary government in Ghana, single parties were able to form governments of their own. A "winner take all" philosophy prevailed, and the winning parties saw little virtue in using cabinet formation as an instrument of national reconciliation and intercommunity accommodation by asking members of the opposition to join the government. It may be that a coalition approach to parliamentary politics has sufficient merit that a constitutional provision should be adopted, as one analyst has recommended, requiring that all parties that win more than a certain minimum percentage of parliamentary seats be invited to join the government. [11] The coalition approach offers even greater assurance than a balanced cabinet that each ethnic group and other interest groups have a stake in the regime and in the political system as a whole. The Lebanese experience demonstrates the costs that the coalition approach extracts in terms of speed of government action and decisiveness, but it also reveals the benefits for the management of intercommunity relations.

In Ghana as in most of the ethnically divided states of Africa, the constituent ethnic groups tend to be divided geographically. Internal migration naturally results in more ethnic mixture today than in precolonial times, and this is particularly true in urban areas, which are quite heterogeneous. But in rural areas, even in communities that contain many strangers, local politics remains largely the business of the ethnic group indigenous to the area. The strangers usually vote and participate in political activities in their community of origin rather than in their place of residence. This means that parliamentary elections based on geographically defined, single-seat constituencies result in a distribution of seats among the ethnic groups which roughly corresponds to the portion of the total population each one comprises. To introduce multiseat constituencies in this situation would give rise to constituencies that are still largely ethnically homogeneous. The lists formed in such constituencies would be ethnically homogeneous as well, and the benefits for intercommunity accommodation that result from multiseat constituencies and list formation in Lebanon would generally not be realized. In fact, the system would tend to encourage the formation of ethnically homogeneous blocs. Such a system would in turn reinforce a more inclusive type of ethnic consciousness, and the resulting ethnolinguistic political forces would pose a greater problem for national accommodation than reconciling the demands of localities. The exception to this generalization, and it is an important exception, comes in urban areas where ethnic mixture is substantial. The shapers of new electoral laws in Ghana could usefully consider the advisability of delineating multiseat constituencies for Ghana's ethnically mixed urban areas and of reserving seats for members of particular ethnic groups proportional to their representation in the constituency. As in Lebanon, this approach in ethnically mixed areas would help assure minority group representation, minimize intercommunity political competition within the constituency, discourage the election of ethnic chauvinists, and foster the formation of interethnic political alliances.

GOVERNMENT PERSONNEL POLICIES

The Ghana government serves as the country's largest employer, incorporating within its various services persons from all the country's ethnic groups. Out of a total of 391,000 salaried and wage-earning workers in Ghana at the beginning of 1969, 284,000 were government employees. At the professional, technical, and clerical levels the proportion holding government posts is even higher.[12] Moreover, government service has generally been considered the most prestigious and desirable type of employment in Ghana. The mere fact of having brought within a common framework of employment such a large portion of the Ghanaian wage-earning population makes the government bureaucracy an important agent for accommodation. Common socioeconomic interests develop among government employees, and to some degree, a common perspective results from their having the same employer and being subjected to many of the same conditions of service. This transpires even more frequently within a particular service, like the educational service, or within a specific government corporation, like the railways.

Despite the potential of the bureaucracy for forging common bonds across ethnic boundaries, the process has not been as efficacious as it might have been because of ethnic imbalances within certain government sectors. This has three consequences. First, if a particular ethnic group is either absent or seriously underrepresented in a particular branch of government employment, members of that group will not have the same opportunity for forming bonds and shared understandings with others groups serving in that unit. Second, members of the excluded or underrepresented group may believe that they are being discriminated against and become resentful. Resentment directed against a private employer does not have the same negative implications for the system as does resentment directed against the government.

Moreover, in a state where government employment comprises such a large proportion of the total, the allocation of jobs naturally constitutes one of the most important resources the government has to distribute. If particular ethnic groups do not benefit from this resource to a degree commensurate with their size, they can become disaffected from a specific regime, or, if the situation persists, they can become alienated from the political system as a whole. Third, an ethnic group underrepresented in the civil service at the highest levels, where policy is set, may fear that the government will neglect their economic needs when policy is determined. Part of the reluctance among northerners to support early independence for Ghana arose from fear of discriminatory control of policy-making by southern civil servants and politicians.

Two aspects of this problem are distinguishable analytically. First, one can cite instances in which persons who are fully qualified in terms of education and experience for particular posts have been discriminated against in recruitment because of their ethnic identity. An example of this principle operating in reverse came in the disproportionate number of Ewes among the 568 government employees dismissed by the Busia regime early in 1970. Second, even when a criterion like educational achievement is impartially applied as the basis of recruitment, ethnic imbalances often arise because the levels of educational achievement vary considerably from one ethnic group to another. Ethnic imbalance in government employment in Ghana was more marked twenty years ago than it is now, but disparities in representation between ethnic groups from the north and the south are still pronounced, reflecting continuing disparities in educational achievement. Naturally, the greatest gap comes at the higher levels. For example, although a disproportionately large number of the rank and file of Ghana's army belong to northern ethnic groups, the officer corps contains relatively few northerners. Ga, Ewe, and Akan representation within the officer corps, on the other hand, surpasses their respective proportions of the total population.[13] At the higher levels of the civil service, similar north–south discrepancies exist. By the beginning of 1971 no northerner had yet been named to the post of principal secretary or principal assistant secretary. In May 1971 of the total administrative class, which constitutes the elite of the civil service, northerners held only 19 out of a total of 272 posts; a 7 percent northern inclusion in the administrative class as contrasted with 18.5 percent northern composition of the total population.

The introduction of some kind of an ethnic quota system in recruitment to government could serve both as a conflict-settling device and as an integrative mechanism. By enabling each ethnic group to have more equitable opportunity to benefit from government employment, such an ethnic quota system would remove a serious source of intergroup envy and hostility. Moreover, by bringing into regular relationship within the civil service large numbers of persons from diverse ethnic backgrounds, an important integrative end can be served.

Opposition to the introduction of ethnic quotas runs deep among southern civil servants. This results in part from the realization that such quotas would work to the disadvantage of southern ethnic groups. But this sentiment also reflects a genuine conviction that merit comprises the only legitimate basis for recruitment and promotion within the civil service. This principle, so fundamental to the British-style bureaucracy that was introduced during the colonial period, remains deeply imbedded. Shortly after independence the government undertook one experimental deviation from a strict merit standard by administering a special examination to northern candidates as a means of recruiting the first northerners to the administrative class. This examination was not as demanding as the regular selection exams, and four northerners passed and were admitted to the administrative class. None of the four proved to be well suited to their positions and gradually each one dropped out of the civil service. The experiment has been interpreted as a failure, and it is cited as sufficient grounds for belief that ethnic quotas or compensatory discrimination in civil service recruitment is counterproductive.[14]

As was clear in our discussion of the Lebanese experience, the introduction of ethnic quotas in civil service employment extracts its costs and should not be introduced without caution. Northerners seem to be making some headway in the race for employment because of recent educational advances in the north. But the educational gap between the north and south is still considerable and is not closing very quickly. One can expect northern resentment over educational and employment gaps to increase both in sophistication and stridency.[15] With special assistance in the field of education, the employment gap might conceivably be overcome without having to attack that problem directly, but such an outcome seems doubtful. At a minimum the problem should be given careful attention and alternative approaches seriously considered. After pointing out the disparities between representation in the civil service from the north and the south, Dr. Robert Gardiner, the Ghanaian Executive Secretary of the Economic Commission for Africa, warned that, "We cannot expect a nation half well-to-do, half miserably poor, half educated and half unskilled and unlettered, to enjoy stable social and political conditions."[16]

THE LEGAL SYSTEM

Reflecting a general belief that political activity should not be pursued primarily on the basis of ethnic interests, two legal measures have been adopted in the past to discourage the development and operation of ethnically based political organizations. In 1957 the National Assembly adopted the Avoidance of Discrimination Bill, the principal object of which was "to prevent organizations based on tribal, racial, religious, or local affiliations attempting to secure the return of members of parliament or to other bodies upon tribal, racial, or religious basis. . . ."[17] The act specifically provided that: "No organization established substantially for the direct or indirect benefit or advancement of the interests of any particular community or religious faith shall organize or operate for the purpose of engaging in any election."[18] Had it been utilized in disinterested fashion, this was potentially a very strong instrument. Whether it was realistic, given the depth of ethnic attachments in Ghana, is open to question. It did have the effect of forcing the various ethnically based opposition parties represented in the National Assembly at the time to join together to form the United Party. However, the potential effectiveness of the United Party as an opposition with a national perspective was never fully tested, because its members were soon subject to harrassment and detention or forced into exile. The members of the United Party saw this act as merely providing a legal rationale for the CPP's stifling of the opposition. Nkrumah himself admitted in retrospect that this law along with press censorship and the Preventive Detention Act was a means of insuring the security of the nation at a time when the opposition parties "began to undermine the state and to jeopardize its independence."[19]

The wish to encourage the formation of interethnic and interconfessional political parties motivated the framers of the constitution for the Second Republic to include Article 35, which sought to restrict the formation of organizations with sectional interests or bias. This article reads: ". . . no organization having as one of its aims or objects, the return of any member of the organization at public election, (a) shall be formed, the membership and leadership of which is restricted to members of any particular tribal group or religious faith; or (b) shall use any name, symbol, or color having any exclusive or particular significance or connotation to the members of any particular tribal group or religious faith; or (c) shall be formed for the sole purpose of securing whether directly or indirectly the welfare, advancement or interests of the members of any particular community or religious faith."[20] Two subsequent decrees by the NLC prior to the 1969 elections elaborated on this constitutional provision by making it mandatory for a political party to have among its founding members persons coming from each of Ghana's nine regions.[21] While all of the parties registered to contest the 1969 election met this provision and thereby had at least some members from each of several ethnic communities, the leaders and members of particular parties tended to be predominantly from the same ethnic group. The preceding chapter has described the extent to which the election ended up being waged largely in terms of appeals to ethnic sentiment.

Another provision in the constitution (Article 25) prohibited discrimination in the form of a law or an act by a public authority against any person on the basis of his ethnic, religious, or racial identity. An observer would be hard-pressed, however, to cite any instance in which this clause specifically influenced the behavior of any public official. The ineffectiveness of these measures makes it clear that a legal approach to the problems of intergroup relations is effective only if public officials and party leaders are furnished with the means for vigorously implementing provisions of the law and are motivated to do so.

The existence of multiple and ethnically differentiated legal systems also affects intercommunal relations. Just as Lebanon has separate laws covering personal status issues for each confessional community, Ghana's various culture areas have retained many of their traditional laws. So-called customary law covers, as in Lebanon, such personal status issues as marriage, divorce, and inheritance; but in Ghana it goes beyond issues of family law to govern such other spheres as land tenure. The area of greatest disparity among the various customary systems comes in terms of the principle by which family descent, clan membership, and inheritance is determined, since many of the culture groups in Ghana are predominantly matrilineal and others predominantly patrilineal. Although such disparities as these do at times provoke interethnic conflict and militate against interethnic marriages, a certain flexibility in the customary laws of Ghana reduces the frequency of intergroup legal confrontations. For instance, Brokensha describes the marriage laws of Larteh as providing a wide general framework of permissible actions rather than constituting a set of rigid rules.[22] This flexibility derives in part from the fact that, unlike Lebanon's personal status laws, customary law in Ghana is not generally written or codified and does not constitute a corpus of divinely revealed religious dogma. Nevertheless, a family from a matrilineal culture area would generally be reluctant to see their daughter marry someone from a group that follows a rule of patrilineal descent.

The problem of the conflict of laws has in certain respects been aggravated by developments during the colonial and postindependence eras. With greater geographical mobility and greater interethnic contact, the diverse customary legal systems more often interact. Moreover, a completely new and alien civil law was introduced by the British. Although the British may have seen its introduction as a means of achieving unification of law, this English law is more different from the customary systems than the customary systems are from each other. With increasing conversion to Christianity and rapidly expanding exposure to Western education, the English law has lost some of its alien character, at least among the more westernized portions of the population, but it still does not provide a commonly accepted basis for settling civil issues. Personal status issues in Ghana today are governed by diverse sets of customary laws, statutes based on English law, and the Marriage of Mohammedans Ordinance. An individual can choose whether to be married according to the customary law of his own ethnic group, under the Marriage Ordinance, or, if he is Muslim, under the Marriage of Mohammedans Ordinance. The form of marriage largely determines which set of laws shall regulate such other aspects of personal status as divorce and inheritance.

A unifying feature of the Ghanaian legal situation comes through a common system of courts that handles all cases, regardless of the type of law being applied in the particular instance. For each case the law being applied determines the form of evidence considered admissible. Moreover, as case law is built up, certain common principles are being applied in interpreting the various sets of laws. Some more direct attempts have been made to unify the various laws, for instance, in the enactment of the Maintenance of Children Act in 1963 and the Ghana Adoption Act (1962).[23]

The Ghanaian approach to conflict of laws has not been as aggressive as in some other African states. Tanzania, for example, has more energetically pushed the unification of customary law, and the Ivory Coast has adopted a comprehensive civil code patterned after the French code.[24] N. A. Ollennu has summed up the Ghanaian situation by stating that "there are a lot of customary laws peculiar to various tribes which are shown to be common, others are known to conflict, while even among those which apply universally or to more than one community, local variations exist which may amount to internal conflict. However, except to a very limited extent, there are no principles regulating internal conflicts in the laws in Ghana."[25]

Real advantages for national integration could be realized by having a single and universally accepted set of laws to cover personal status issues and land transactions. The adoption and acceptance of such a code could facilitate ethnic intermarriage and other types of interethnic contact. But there seems little likelihood that in the foreseeable future such a common law would be universally acceptable, and the adverse reaction to any effort to impose such law could have serious repercussions for national accommodation. Any attempt to adopt patrilineal succession and inheritance, for instance, would certainly provoke an outcry from the matrilineal culture groups. The elimination of polygamy might please doctrinaire Christians, but it would certainly anger Muslims and other non-Christians. Therefore, Ghana's laissez faire approach might be a realistic appraisal of what is feasible.

The processes of modernization, including urban migration, economic change, and social and educational development, are fundamentally altering the character of Ghanaian family life and family structure. For example, groups that have previously been matrilineal are now shifting perceptibly toward a more patrilineal system. When the long-term impact of these forces of change becomes more apparent it will undoubtedly be easier to prescribe a suitable approach for achieving greater unification of laws in Ghana. It may be that complete unification can never be accomplished, but it is likely that the range of variation will become reduced or else the variations will polarize around the magnets of Christian and Islamic concepts of personal status.

EQUITABLE ECONOMIC DEVELOPMENT

Disparities in levels of economic development between the different geographical regions of Ghana and between the different ethnic groups inhabiting those regions have constituted a source of alienation on the part of the poorer areas. At the same time, some richer regions (particularly Ashanti) have evidenced discontent because government taxation in the area has surpassed government expenditures. The conviction on the part of particular ethnic groups that they have been shortchanged or discriminated against by a particular regime, as was the perception of many Ewes during the Busia regime, has constituted an additional source of resentment. Over time, drastic inequalities among regions and among ethnic groups in levels of socioeconomic development probably stand as the most serious economic barrier to national accommodation. However, because the political leadership of underdeveloped regions is often inarticulate or lacking in political clout, the complaints from these areas usually command less attention than do complaints from other groups.

Because of discrepancies in natural resources and general economic potential, some regional disparities in development occur inevitably and must be countenanced. Sometimes, in an effort to overcome regional disparities, it is tempting to go overboard and to locate industries and other development projects primarily in these terms. When this is done the projects often turn out to be unviable and constitute more of a liability than an asset for the region. The construction of a $30,000,000 international airport in the relatively remote northern town of Tamale started during the last years of the Nkrumah regime provides one such example of this. Despite these dangers, the promotion of national accommodation necessitates that a degree of equity be attained in the levels of development enjoyed by the country's various ethnic groups. Consideration of the geographic aspect of economic growth can also contribute to the creation of further regional economic specialization and greater interregional economic interdependence, which also contributes to national accommodation.

An exchange that appeared in a leading Ghanaian newspaper during December 1970 and January 1971 illustrates the kind of controversy this issue can arouse. The initiator of the exchange, a northerner, asserted that special allocations should be set aside to assist northern development as a means of enabling northerners to attain greater equality. He wrote, "All the north wants is just something a bit special, unique to the area to catapult it into a situation in which they would not occupy a position of being a servant to the southerner." In the article he also warned that if northerners continued to be discriminated against by the south, "there is the great danger that the distrust and resentment the northerner has for the southerner could generate into an inevitable explosion of some sort."[26] Responses to this article by correspondents from the south contended that this method of combating ethnic hostility was "tribalistic," since it sought to have particular ethnic groups benefit at the expense of other ethnic groups.[27] One of the correspondents concluded, "Mr. Mahamah should find a means of helping to improve the lot of northerners rather than provoking tribalism in the country. By his tribalistic reasoning he widens the gap between the north and the south, rather than closing it, and consequently he has only succeeded in doing more harm than good."[28]

Patterns of government expenditure have had the effect of accentuating rather than mitigating some regional discrepancies. Divergences in the level of development existing among the regions, and particularly between the north and the south, are covered in Chapter 6. Table 8-1 indicates the wide differences in levels of government expenditure on various services provided to the different regions, using data on projected recurrent expenditures contained in the 1969–70 budget. This method of calculation obviously permits only a crude indication of the extent to which specific ethnic groups benefit from government expenditures. As already mentioned, regions are not completely ethnically homogeneous and urban areas are very mixed. Also, since capital (as opposed to recurrent) expenditures are not broken down in the budget according to region, that part of government spending does not figure in the calculations. Moreover, some items specified as being for a particular region may also aid persons coming from other regions; this would be true, for example, of major hospitals and some educational institutions. Despite these shortcomings, the table does offer some idea of the variations in expenditures, and the extent to which allocations of recurrent expenditures

TABLE 8-1 *Recurrent Government Expenditures Projected in 1969–70 Budget Calculated on Per Capita Basis for Each Region*

	AGRICULTURE	PUBLIC WORKS*	EDUCATION	HEALTH	TOTAL
1. Greater Accra	NȻ 1.0	NȻ 4.4	NȻ 8.1	NȻ 10.4	NȻ 23.9
2. Eastern	3.4	1.5	8.2	2.3	15.4
3. Volta	1.3	1.7	7.9	2.0	12.9
4. Western	1.3	2.3	6.5	2.5	13.6
5. Central	1.2	1.4	7.4	2.2	12.2
6. Ashanti	1.5	1.5	7.8	1.4	12.2
7. Brong-Ahafo	1.6	1.4	5.8	1.2	10.0
8. Northern	1.3	2.5	3.4	1.3	8.5
9. Upper	.8	1.1	3.0	1.2	6.1

SOURCE: *1969/70 Estimates; Regional Volumes* (Accra: Government Printer, 1969); using 1960 census population figures. Analysis done by Richard Taylor.

*Includes road maintenance figures listed under Development Expenditure.

have shortchanged the two least developed regions, Upper and Northern. Interestingly, the two regions supplying the greast amount of tax revenue per capita because of their cocoa and gold production, Ashanti and Brong-Ahafo, are disadvantaged in terms of government expenditures as well, ranking in sixth and seventh positions just ahead of Northern and Upper Regions. All four would seem to have legitimate grounds for complaint. [29]

Other bases can also be cited for the assertion that concern about equitable regional economic growth has not played a very large part in economic planning. Although regional inequalities did have some effect on decisions taken by the Nkrumah government regarding the location of individual industrial projects, [30] the Seven Year Development Plan published in 1964 devotes relatively little attention to regional or ethnic disparities in levels of development. Not a single table in the document gives a breakdown of economic statistics on the basis of regions or ethnic groups. [31] The Two Year Development Plan published in 1968 under the NLC states that the geographic aspect of planning has not yet received much attention and concedes that more consideration should be given to it. [32] Only one table in the plan, that relating to the number of telephone connections in the country, has an analysis by region. The One Year Development Plan published in 1970 under the Progress Party government expresses concern over regional inequalities, and emphasizes the need for greater utilization of regional, district, and local planning authorities. [33] But aside from mentioning a new program of the Ministry of Education for equalizing the regional distribution of qualified teachers and the continuation of special government aid for the construction of primary schools in Brong-Ahafo, Northern, and Upper Regions, the plan suggests few remedies for regional inequities. Of the sixty-five tables in the plan, only five present statistics on a regional basis.

Paralleling the formulation of the Seven Year Development Plan in 1963, the Town and Country Planning Division of the Ministry of Lands prepared a regional development plan. It presented a detailed comparison of the economic status and potential of the various geographical areas of Ghana and made proposals for balanced regional economic development. Unfortunately, this exercise was not an integral portion of the general planning effort and no reference is made to it in the Seven Year Plan. Its proposals were offered merely as suggestions to the executive ministries responsible for implementing the Seven Year Plan, [34] and never received official sanction.

The NLC and Busia regimes evidenced some interest in regional planning. The establishment of regional and district planning committees was seen as one component of the attempt to decentralize administration. Thirty regional planners with M.A. degrees were recruited by the Ministry of Finance and Economic Planning and stationed at regional headquarters. Unfortunately, they did little in determining the allocation of total resources and spent most of their time monitoring the implementation of projects in the development budget and assisting the executive ministries at the regional level prepare their development estimates.

A successful effort to promote balanced regional development requires much more than regional planners. The most fundamental requirement is technology, techniques, and development strategies appropriate to the various parts of the country. Recent dramatic advances in rice production in the Northern and Upper Regions indicate that in some spheres the technology and strategy are within reach. Moreover, a recent study of the most depressed area of Ghana, the so-called middle belt, which includes large portions of Northern and Upper Regions as well as portions of Brong-Ahafo, Volta and Eastern Regions, suggests a strategy for reversing the depopulation and economic decline of that area.[35] The success of Regional Development Corporations recently inaugurated by the NRC is yet to be fully tested.[36]

Northern displeasure with the inequitable geographic and ethnic distribution of national wealth is readily apparent, but the implications of uneven economic development should not be measured merely in terms of the public outcry it arouses. Portions of a population can be alienated from a state without even being fully cognizant of their alienation or without even complaining that they are being discriminated against. They merely sense that the system has little to offer them, and they are not drawn to identify with it. Moreover, a situation that does not immediately give rise to public protests may in time provoke outrage, once the population of a particular area and their leaders become more aware of and incensed over inequalities and become better able to articulate their displeasure. Such a development may well materialize in the less developed areas of Ghana, leading Ghanaian leaders to wish that they had confronted the problem more energetically many years before.

LANGUAGE POLICY

The promotion of some means of national intercommunity communication is of fundamental importance to the creation of a viable and cohesive state. We are not asserting that any existing language should be neglected or forgotten or that the state needs to promote a single mother tongue for all its citizens. For the foreseeable future, national communication in most African states will have to occur on the basis of bilingual or even multilingual competence of individual citizens. We are not prepared to prejudge whether the language of national communication in Ghana should be one of the Ghanaian vernaculars or English, which is the most widely spoken European language. But we are asserting the significance of national communication for the promotion of national accommodation and the improvement of intergroup relations, which must be recognized in the formulation of national language policy.

Despite the fact that approximately 45 percent of Ghana's population speaks one or another of the Akan dialects as their first language, linguistic diversity and fragmentation are considerable. Ghana's population incorporates ethnic groups with thirty-four distinct, mutually unintelligible languages, and fourteen additional languages are indigenous to large numbers of aliens.[37] As indicated in Table 8-2, thirteen of these languages have more than 100,000 native speakers.

This enumeration of the size of the country's various language communities only partially portrays the complete language situation. Unfortunately, few data are available regarding multilingualism in Ghana, which is an equally important aspect of the language picture. The follow-up survey of the 1970 census did include questions regarding multilingual competence, but at the time of this writing, these data have not been published. Madina, a suburb of Accra, offers an extreme case of linguistic diversity and of multilingualism. The 2000 residents of that small community speak 70 different mother tongues, but balancing this, 96 percent of Madina's residents are bilingual and 70 percent claim competence in three or more languages, and thereby share knowledge of one or more languages with many of the other residents.[38] Thus, despite the extremely fragmented character of Madina's linguistic situation, by means of multilingual competence, considerable intracommunity communication can occur, and this is the case for Ghana as a whole as well.

Even without precise survey data, one can assert with reasonable accuracy that of the Ghanaian languages Akan, or one or another of the Akan dialects (particularly Twi), serves as the most widespread lingua franca in Ghana. It is unfortunate that no accurate statistics exist regarding the use of Akan as a lingua franca and the rate at which its use is increasing. It is conceivable that with such statistics one might predict that within a specified number of years Akan will become a nearly universal lingua franca and thereby provide a

TABLE 8-2   *Numbers of Native-Speakers of Different Languages Living in Ghana in 1960*

1. Twi-Fanti (Akan)	2,657,020
2. Ewe	876,230
3. Guan	254,790
4. Adangbe	237,440
5. Ga	236,210
6. Dagbani	217,640
7. Dagarti	201,680
8. Gureni	193,500
9. Nzima	178,100
10. Kusal	121,610
11. Konkomba	110,150
12. Mole*	106,140
13. Yoruba*	100,560
14. Anyi-Bawle	88,740
15. Buli	62,620
16. Hausa*	61,730
17. Sisala	59,210
18. Mamprusi	58,710
19. Busa*	56,690
20. Kotokoli*	51,020
21. Tobote*	48,720
22. Wali	47,200
23. Lobi*	37,550
24. Kasem	37,030
25. Songhai*	35,930
26. Bambara*	34,180
27. Talene	32,780
28. Bimoda	32,270
29. Fula*	25,050
30. Pilapila*	24,790
31. Nabt	16,500
32. Buem	14,900
33. Ibo*	14,050
34. Chokosi	14,090
35. Nanume	13,700
36. Avatime-Nyangbo-Tafi	10,210
37. Mo	8,830
38. Akposo*	8,530
39. Likpe	7,140
40. Kru*	6,500
41. Akpafu	5,370
42. Bowiri	3,280
43. Santrokofi	3,230
44. Adele	2,900
45. Lolobi	2,860
46. Vagala	2,230
47. Logba	2,090
48. Akposo	1,780

*The majority of persons speaking these languages as their mother tongue are aliens or noncitizens.

SOURCE: B. Gil, A. F. Aryee, and D. K. Ghansah, *Special Report 'E': Tribes in Ghana, 1960 Population Census of Ghana* (Accra: Census Office, 1964), pp. 1–6 and Appendix A.

medium of national communication, even without official government en-couragement. Without accurate statistics, such an eventuality can be posited only with considerable uncertainty.

In light of the complexity of Ghana's linguistic situation, the government has laid down some guidelines concerning language use in particular situa-tions to enable effective communication to occur, and these guidelines constitute the government's language policies. English serves as the language for official government communication, and when Ghana has had civilian governments English has been the language prescribed for use in the National Assembly. The government conducts all official examinations in English. Occasionally a government department may issue a statement in one or more vernaculars, but this is usually a simplified version of the original official English version. The Bureau of Ghana Languages, which has the responsibil-ity for publishing books in the vernacular, produces a few books each year in eight different Ghanaian languages. The government-owned Ghana Broad-casting Corporation offers programs in English, and has some programs each week in the following five languages: Ewe, Akan, Nzima, Hausa, Dagbani, and Ga. The proportion of English programs to broadcasts in one or another of these five Ghanaian languages is in the ratio of approximately three to one.

The aspect of Ghana's language policy that is most critically important in shaping language usage and patterns of national communication is the manner in which language relates to education. The key questions in the educational sphere are: What language or languages are to be taught as compulsory and optional subjects for study? What proportion of the school curriculum is to be devoted to which languages? What language or languages are to be used as the media of instruction at various levels of the educational ladder?

Both primary and secondary schools offer courses in Ghanaian languages, and GCE examinations at the ordinary level offer four Ghanaian languages as optional subjects. Despite the fact that a substantial portion of teaching hours are devoted to Ghanaian languages, the Ministry of Education assumes that the student will be studying his mother tongue. Consequently, unless a child is resident in an area where his mother tongue is not the prevailing local language, he will generally not study a Ghanaian language other than his own. Thus, the teaching of Ghanaian languages has been seen not as a means of increasing communication across language boundaries but of increasing competence in one's own language. Multilingualism in Ghana has resulted from individual efforts to learn other Ghanaian languages rather than any official encouragement in the educational system or elsewhere. In November 1970 the Minister of Education revised the policy on languages, indicating that starting in 1971 pupils in Ghana's primary schools would be required to learn another Ghanaian language in addition to their mother tongue, with a choice of studying Ga, Nzima, Akan, Ewe, or Dagbani. This was the first major government attempt to promote multilingualism in Ghanaian languages in order to increase national communication. However, due to the lack of teachers and teaching materials, no serious effort has been made to see that the policy is implemented.

Probably the most lively subject for debate regarding language in most African countries is the issue of which language or languages should be used as media of instruction. The adoption of a particular language as the medium of instruction makes a considerable contribution to the students' competence in that language. Pressure is building in many countries to make greater use of the mother tongue as the medium of instruction in primary and even in the secondary schools. Although this policy is sound in terms of the educational benefits of giving instruction in a language with which the students are familiar, it has the disadvantage of delaying the moment when school children will become familiar with the language of broader usage, namely the national language.

From the earliest days of formal education in Ghana, controversy has surrounded the question of the medium of instruction, and divergent practices have been followed in various parts of the country and by different educational agencies. For instance, in the mid-nineteenth century the Basel Mission employed Ga and Twi as the media of instruction in their schools,[39] while the Wesleyans who worked in the coastal towns used English.[40] Throughout most of Ghana's educational history both English and the mother tongues have served as subjects for study and as media of instruction, but their respective roles have been subjected to a series of policy fluctuations. By 1960 government policy dictated that only the first year of primary school should be taught in the mother tongue and English was to take over as the medium of instruction in primary grade two. In 1963 and again in 1967 committees of educators recommended that the mother tongue be given a more prominent place as media of instruction,[41] but the government continued to energetically promote the utilization of English.[42]

The most recent policy statement by the Ministry of Education on this subject came in November 1970. It largely accepts the recommendation of the 1967 Education Review Committee that the language most widely spoken in the place where the school is located should be used as the medium of instruction for the first three years of primary school, and that the transition to English as the medium should commence in the fourth year. In advocating more extensive use of the mother tongues, educators have understandably been influenced by their professional concerns over the ease with which young children can absorb new information and the difficulties they have in doing this in a language foreign to them. These educators have also been anxious that children come to appreciate local traditions, which can probably be done best in the vernacular of the locality.

During the Nkrumah era, those with political responsibility demonstrated considerable concern over the possible divisive impact of a vernacular-medium policy. Despite the fact that English is a language alien to Ghana, policy-makers in the Nkrumah regime considered it to be the best vehicle for achieving national communication as well as social and political unification. They also promoted English because of its importance for international communication, not only with Europe and America but also with other African states, in the interests of African unity. The parents of Ghanaian school children have also tended to be a strong lobby for English, since command of English is seen as the avenue to social and economic mobility.

Professional linguists and secondary school language teachers have recently become a lobby against the ascendant position of English. They want to assure the preservation of all the Ghanaian languages and inculcate an appreciation for them among future generations of Ghanaians. They advocate that more classroom time be spent on studying the mother tongue and that increased use be made of the mother tongue as the medium of instruction. Hence, their principal interest is not in increasing multilingualism, but in improving facility in and the usage of one's mother tongue. Although this effort to preserve and promote the mother tongues is a worthy and commendable cause, its spokesmen seem to disregard the possible implications of the policies they advocate for multilingualism, national communication, and national integration. The danger exists that increased emphasis upon the local languages will inhibit the growth of lingua francas and increase the rigidity of existing boundaries between language communities.

Another position being advocated is that Ghana should have a single official language for national communication, but that it should be a Ghanaian language rather than English. The degree to which this point of view has gained strength over the past decade among Ghana's intelligentsia can be seen in two surveys of students at the University of Ghana conducted with a ten-year interval between them. Gilbert Ansre's survey in 1961 revealed that 93 percent of Ghana's university students favored the retention of English as the official language.[43] We conducted a survey among students at the University of Ghana in 1971 which indicated that only 30 percent favored the retention of English, and 56 percent advocated the adoption of a Ghanaian language as the national language.

Although neither of these movements against English represents a ground swell of public opinion, it does seem likely that Ghana's language policy will be the subject of continuing and increased debate. It is the particular concern of this discussion to explore what some of these policy alternatives might be, within the context of Ghana's need for improved intergroup relations and for national accommodation. Ghana's complex language situation has two clear implications: (1) national cohesion will require some means of achieving effective intergroup communication, and (2) the complexity of the situation resulting from the extent of linguistic fragmentation will make the task extremely difficult.

If the need for effective national communication is granted, four alternative approaches suggest themselves:

1. By encouraging or even requiring school children to learn a Ghanaian language other than their own, the educational system could contribute to greater interethnic understanding and communication. Consistent with this idea, the National Redemption Council has recently exhorted all Ghanaians to learn at least one Ghanaian language other than his own.[44] Through extensive multilingualism, certain members of each language group could communicate with one another. However, there would be no common, national language of intercommunication.[45] A more systematic approach toward the same end would be to require that every Ghanaian school child study another Ghanaian language and then specify that all non-Akan speaking children study Akan as this second language. The Akan-speaking children would have the option of learning one or another of Ghana's remaining major languages. If this policy was implemented, it would have the unstated effect of creating a certain level of competence in Akan among all those who have passed through Ghana's educational system. On the other hand, by requiring that all Akan-speakers learn some other Ghanaian language, they would not be placed in

a favored position vis-à-vis non-Akan speakers. Through this process Akan might become the country's lingua franca, but it would
not be designated as the official national language. Whether it is
realistic to expect a Ghanaian student to study his own language,
learn English, and learn another Ghanaian language, in addition
to his other academic requirements, would have to be explored; but
this approach offers an innovative and appealing, though partial,
solution to Ghana's linguistic fragmentation.

2.   Working within the current educational framework and adhering
to existing language and education policies, a vigorous effort could
be made to improve the teaching of English within the schools.
One important means toward this end, although not sufficient in
itself, would be the adoption of English as the medium of instruction as early as is educationally feasible and desirable. The precise
timing of the transition to English as the medium of instruction can
be decided only after carefully weighing a variety of important
factors. This would provide a basis for English to serve as the
principal vehicle for national communication. In an inconclusive
1971 parliamentary debate regarding the adoption of a national
language, one M.P. stated, "I just want to say that a lot of things
which were left us by the English people do not fit our status today;
but their language which they left us is binding all the tribes and all
the cultures which constitute Ghana as a nation into one. I think it
is important to cherish the English language, develop and add to it,
and make it our own, because it is the only thing which binds all of
us together as one people."[46]

3.   Alternatively, a single Ghanaian language could be chosen as the
vehicle for national communication. If a common national language is selected, it would need to be vigorously promoted by the
educational system; and if this language were to be given a prominent place in the curriculum, the current emphasis placed upon
both English and the mother tongue would correspondingly have
to be reduced. One effective means of encouraging use of this
language would be to make it the medium of instruction. Given its
numerical predominance in the country and its prestige, Akan
would probably be the most logical choice for this national
language.[47] Jack Berry has proposed a modification of this by
suggesting that Akan be chosen as the common language for

southern Ghana and Dagbani for northern Ghana,[48] but to encourage different languages for these two portions of the country
would only widen the gap which already exists between north and
south.

4.   A fourth approach would be to maintain current policies as an
interim arrangement, while keeping in mind the possibility that by
a natural process of selection one of Ghana's languages will become more widely used as a lingua franca and as a medium for
national communication, without official promotion. If one language gains ascendancy, it could be selected as the national language for use by schools and other institutions. Some linguists
contend that such a process is inevitable, with one stating that
"history has over and over again demonstrated that within sharply
defined political boundaries the most influential vernacular does in
time impose itself as a common or national tongue."[49] It seems
doubtful that such an outcome is so assured, but it could happen.
Some evidence exists to suggest that Akan is gaining ground as a
lingua franca, particularly in northern Ghana. Unfortunately,
insufficient data have been gathered to make any definitive statement regarding such a trend. Although the 1970 census did contain questions on second language competence, comparative data
suggesting trends over time will be available only following the
analysis of the 1980 census data.

If the government decided to select a single language as the national
language, there would be certain obvious advantages to having this language
be a Ghanaian language. The selection of a Ghanaian rather than a European
language would impart a sense of national uniqueness and pride, and a
Ghanaian language would serve as a more effective vehicle for transmitting
local and national culture from one generation to the next. Moreover, part of
the population would already be familiar with this language as a mother
tongue.

The problems that would be encountered as the result of such a step are
equally evident. The initial and most serious difficulty would be faced when
the government had to decide which of Ghana's many languages should be
the national language. Few issues would arouse as intense intergroup hostility
and conflict as the choice of a single Ghanaian language as the national
language. The twenty-year controversy over an Akan orthography that would

be mutually acceptable to both Twi and Fanti speakers suggests the intense emotion that language decisions arouse. In the 1971 parliamentary debate on the motion to consider the selection of a national language, one M.P. warned that, "This motion, if adopted, will divide this country. It will be a risk which any Government will undertake if it tries to press this matter too hard. It will be interesting to get from the Hon. Member for Berekum the particular language we should be using as Ghana's lingua franca. I must remind him right from the outset that if he inflicts Ga on the people of Ghana as lingua franca, his own people will beat him up; and if he presses that his own language be accepted as the lingua franca the rest of the language groups in Ghana will get together and oppose him. . . . Any government which deceives itself that the time is opportune to introduce a lingua franca in the country will be sitting upon a keg of gun powder. The motion can be described as a political dynamite. . . ."[50]

Only a few inconclusive studies have been undertaken in Ghana to assess people's attitudes toward the country's language policy. From his pilot survey of Ghanaian secondary and university students, Dr. D. K. Agyeman concluded that "the people who opt for a Ghanaian language as a national language are the very people who are tribally inclined and would opt for their own tribal languages as a national language."[51] In his sample only 20 percent of all non-Akans interviewed advocated Akan as a medium of instruction, whereas no Akans opted for any of the other languages. Our survey of students at the University of Ghana revealed the same tendency for respondents to prefer their own language as the national language, although this was much more frequently the case for Akan speakers than for non-Akan speakers.

Another problem created by the selection of a single Ghanaian language as the national language would be the educational burden it would place on the school system and on school children. Teachers would have to be trained and an enormous quantity of new educational material would have to be prepared for teaching the language and for its use as the medium of instruction. In those portions of the country where the national language is not spoken as the mother tongue, school children would contend with learning English as well as an additional Ghanaian language, both of which would be foreign to them.

We believe that because of the critical need for a national lingua franca and the difficulties involved in selecting a Ghanaian language for adoption as the national language, Ghana would be well advised to carefully preserve the present reliance upon English in the country's educational system, while finding means of improving the quality of language instruction for both

English and the mother tongue. Ghanaian languages should be accorded their proper place within the educational system and in national life generally, but the importance of English in Ghana as a lingua franca and as a vehicle for international communication should also be fully recognized. Careful attention can be given to the trends of language use in Ghana, and if Akan or another language is rapidly gaining ground as a second language, this is of considerable importance for policy formulation. Akan may unobtrusively become a medium for national communication without its having to be vigorously promulgated by the government. At the present time, however, the official declaration of a single Ghanaian language as the national language would give rise to a highly emotional reaction and possibly to interethnic violence.

THE EDUCATIONAL SYSTEM

In the absence of other potentially effective socialization agencies that reinforce the sense of national identity in longer established countries, the formal education system assumes a greater role in many new states as the exponent of the wider world beyond the village and beyond the ethnic group. As an expression of their faith in the ability of the educational system to contribute to the development of the country, many African states, including Ghana, invest a significant portion of their revenues in education. Ghana now spends about one-fourth of the national budget each year on education. However, the educational systems of virtually all African states are unable to effectively socialize students into a national identity and to promote intergroup tolerance. Their inability to do so results from the nature of the colonial educational system and the failure to undertake fundamental reforms after independence. Colonial education embodied the inadequacies of the metropolitan systems combined with the predispositions of colonial officials as to what constituted a proper education for Africans. Ministries of education have not often embarked upon a drastic reordering of the approach, objectives, and content of the curriculum inherited from the colonial period, sometimes because administrators do not perceive how serious the deficiencies of the present curriculum are, and also because of the great difficulties such a drastic reform entails. Moreover, throughout the continent the initial focus of ministries of education has tended to be on the expansion of the educational system.

As the first black African state to achieve its independence from colonial rule, Ghana provides an interesting example of the dilemmas of educational reform. For the first nine years of its independence, the Ghana government, under the leadership of Nkrumah, was explicitly committed to utilizing the educational system for the purpose of instilling a sense of loyalty to Ghana and its ideals. With the overthrow of Nkrumah and the installation of the National Liberation Council, Ghana established a Curriculum Research and Development Unit within its Ministry of Education, one of the first such governmental agencies in Africa. Yet, fifteen years after independence the educational program still reflected the colonial mold. Although Ghana's Ministry of Education moved quickly after independence to consolidate and expand the educational system and to introduce Ghanaian history, the curricula often exhibit the patterns and biases inherited from the colonial period.

For education to be an effective instrument of national accommodation, the public system should reach all parts of the country. In this respect Ghana has a distinct advantage over a country like Lebanon, since the Ghanaian educational system is clearly and carefully controlled by the Ministry of Education. This control extends even to schools being managed by religious missions. Yet, serious discrepancies exist in the level of educational development in different parts of the country. In 1950 the Northern Territories, which now are the Northern Region and Upper Region, had only 2.8 percent of the total number of primary and secondary school facilities.[52] By 1969 the same area had 10 percent of the public primary, middle, and secondary schools.[53] Although this proportion was still far below the 18.5 percent of the population that the 1970 census indicated were resident in these two regions, it represents a substantial improvement in educational opportunity, especially when it is remembered that the educational system as a whole expanded rapidly after 1960.

In comparing the expansion of educational facilities with the growth of enrollments (Table 8-3), it is clear that despite government efforts to favor somewhat the Northern and Upper Regions in siting schools, attendance has not kept pace with the increase in institutions. Although the Northern and Upper Regions have improved their relative standings in attendance, they still lag far behind the other regions in the number of children in school. The overall improvement in the position of the Northern Region from 1961 to 1970 was from 1.9 percent to 3.2 percent of the proportion of Ghanaian primary school students and from 1.8 to 2.9 percent of those in secondary

TABLE 8-3   *Growth of Enrollment in Schools by Region 1961–1970*

REGION	PRIMARY SCHOOL 1961	PRIMARY SCHOOL 1970	MIDDLE SCHOOL 1961	MIDDLE SCHOOL 1970	PERCENTAGE INCREASE 1960–1970
Accra		93,984		39,989	
	* 149,894		* 45,310		108.8
Eastern		194,586		79,007	
Central	63,145	109,848	20,689	47,125	87.2
Western	50,643	96,543	15,499	42,578	110.3
Volta	82,263	121,726	24,066	54,371	65.6
Ashanti	106,213	207,342	35,168	97,583	115.7
Brong-Ahafo	36,982	85,373	9,562	31,774	151.7
Northern	10,427	30,974	2,893	10,183	209.0
Upper	20,459	35,293	4,496	15,821	104.8
TOTAL	520,026	975,629	157,683	424,430	106.6

*In 1961 Accra was part of the Eastern Region. Therefore the 1961 data do not give separate statistics for Accra and Eastern Region.

SOURCE: *1963 Statistical Year Book* (Accra: Central Bureau of Statistics, 1966), p. 180; *Educational Statistics 1968-1969* (Accra: Ministry of Education, 1971), p. 1.

school. Primary school enrollment in the Upper Region actually did not advance as rapidly as the other regions, and it fell from 3.8 to 3.6 percent during the same period while middle school figures improved slightly from 2.9 to 3.7 percent. Hence, the lower rate of educational achievement in the northern portion of the country cannot be compensated for merely by opening more institutions.

Despite an apparent lack of general concern with balanced regional growth, the government has evinced disquietude over the disparity in the progress of education in the northern and southern parts of the country. As already mentioned, one manifestation of this has been in the siting of schools. During a period in which the number of primary schools almost doubled in number from 3574 to 7293 and the middle schools increased from 1234 to

3201, to accommodate the influx of students resulting from the introduction of ten years of universal free education, both the Northern and Upper Regions improved their relative positions. Unlike the policy in other portions of the country where the cost of school construction is a local responsibility, the government has borne all of the costs in the construction of new primary and middle schools in the north. Moreover, the government has favored this area in allocating qualified teachers. When fees for school texts were reintroduced after the 1966 coup, the primary and middle school students in the Upper and Northern Regions continued to receive theirs free. The government has given secondary school students from these two regions scholarships for tuition and full board, so that the students had to pay only for their uniforms and books. Northern university students have received special living and travel allowances.

Perhaps a more vigorous effort by the Ministry of Education or the Department of Social Welfare in going to northern towns and villages and promoting school enrollment would have made a difference, but factors other than the lack of opportunity now hold back the north. While traditional cultural values contribute to the reluctance to attend school, there are other reasons as well. The slower rate of social change and economic development has limited the utility of formal education. To families who assume that their progeny will follow in their footsteps, it seems more reasonable that they keep the children in the fields helping their parents farm, rather then have the children acquire a literary education that they may rarely use. The slower rate of change has meant that traditional life patterns and socialization agents have greater strength in the north. For parents there, the choice is perceived not simply as between school attendance or no education, but between a somewhat foreign, potentially alienating education and the traditional forms. In other regions, economic incentives, mainly the lure of a white-collar job in an urban center, have played a significant role in attracting children to schools. Even as these job openings decline in number, southern students continue to hope for them. These sometimes unrealistic aspirations and the habit within the community of school attendance keep the southern schools filled.

In bringing students into contact with members of other ethnic groups, heterogeneity in schools can foster toleration and lead to friendships across ethnic boundaries. The widespread expansion of the educational system at all levels since 1960 has unfortunately made the schools more homogeneous in ethnic composition. For primary age children, Ghana has achieved something close to the American concept of the neighborhood school. In ethnically heterogeneous neighborhoods in urban centers the composition of the primary school reflects that of the neighborhood, but most of the population still resides in the relatively homogeneous rural countryside. Middle schools draw their student bodies from a somewhat broader area; however, the pupils are usually still from the same ethnic group. The one exception is in the northern part of the country where some of the middle schools are boarding institutions, which bring together many different ethnic groups in order to have enough students to make the schools viable. In contrast with the older, elite secondary schools, which still recruit the best students from all ethnic groups, many of the more recently opened secondary schools with lower standards attract students only from the area in which they are located.

The three universities in Ghana, like the elite secondary schools from which they disproportionately recruit their students, remain heterogeneous. A survey we conducted of students at the University of Ghana in 1970 in which the sample was randomly selected from lists provided by the residence halls indicated that the composition of the student body roughly reflected that of the country's population. The major differences came in the overrepresentation of students from Volta Region and the underrepresentation from Northern and Upper Regions. Despite the long-term problem of educational development of the north, 7 percent of the sample (as compared with 18.5 percent of the total population) were members of northern ethnic groups. Thus, it is possible that a narrower gap exists between north and south at the more elite levels of education than amongst primary and middle school students.[54]

The Ministry of Education generally posts teachers without reference to their ethnic background or home community. This policy has derived primarily from the attempt to equalize the number of trained teachers throughout the country. With more than half of the present teachers now holding the minimum qualifications prescribed by the Ministry, and with teacher training facilities now established in every region, it is becoming increasingly feasible to regionalize assignments while maintaining some balance with regard to qualification. Along with the desire of teachers to work nearer their homes, another recent policy development, the greater emphasis on the vernacular language, will probably influence the Ministry of Education to attempt to take ethnic factors into greater account in posting teachers. The need for primary school teachers to be able to converse in the vernacular of their students conflicts with the earlier decision to achieve an element of integration in the posting of teachers, a policy that increased the exposure of students to members of other ethnic groups.

The content of the curriculum to a great extent determines the effectiveness of the educational system. A uniform social studies curriculum explicitly aimed at instilling a sense of national citizenship would assist the educational system to socialize students into a national political perspective. Since 1958 the Ministry of Education has prescribed the content of the curricula and prepared the list of recommended texts for all primary and middle schools in Ghana.[55] Although the Ministry had intended to offer a choice between several acceptable texts for each subject, in actuality, the yearly list has merely mentioned a single book. Thus, all primary and middle schools in Ghana, irrespective of their location or whether they are managed by a local authority or a church agency, follow the same program. The Ghanaian government does not directly control the secondary schools, but students prepare for uniform examinations set by the West African Examinations Council, an autonomous intergovernmental agency composed of educators from Ghana, Nigeria, Sierra Leone, and the Gambia.

Shortly after independence the Ministry of Education incorporated many Ghanaian-oriented teaching materials at all levels of the educational system.[56] At the time of independence the schools did have a few Ghanaian-oriented geography books, but they did not emphasize Ghanaian history. There was a series of texts entitled *Tropical Africa in World History* written by a colonial educational officer along with other books unrelated to Africa. By the 1961–1962 school year, the Ministry had introduced two Ghanaian history texts for primary school and one for middle school, and virtually all of the geography books were Ghanaian or West African-oriented. In civics, however, a more sensitive and, for the purpose of fostering a sense of national citizenship, a more significant subject, the Ministry of Education has missed many opportunities to promote national accommodation. The only civics text currently in use was written before independence by a colonial education officer for all of West Africa; it contains no material specifically oriented to the Ghanaian political system or experience. Under the auspices of the West African Examinations Council, secondary school examinations at both the ordinary and advanced levels in history and the social sciences assumed a more African orientation by 1967. At that time the West African Examinations Council replaced the exam on British Constitution with an exam on government, much of which dealt with West Africa, and economics and economic history also became more African-centered.[57] At the university level Ghana pioneered the concept of African studies centers, and students take a compulsory interdisciplinary course in African studies during their first year.

The Ministry of Education offers two forms of guidance to the schools for the teaching of social studies: a syllabus outlining the program and its objectives, and the list of approved texts. It also prescribes how many hours each week should be devoted to each subject. According to these materials, the study of history and geography begins in the fourth year of primary school and continues through the last year of middle school. The number of hours assigned to history and geography, though, indicates that the Ministry of Education considers it less important than religious instruction, arithmetic, physical education, or Ghanaian languages. Only 105 of the 1620 hours in each term are reserved for history and geography, while language studies (English and Ghanaian) receive 630, physical education 370, and arithmetic and religious instruction 150 each. Although the Curriculum Research and Development Unit has prepared a syllabus for civics at the primary level, the time sheet circulated by the Ministry does not allocate any periods to it. Moreover, the civics title that appears on the list of recommended texts for elementary schools has never actually been published, due to the poor quality of the draft version of the book that the State Publishing Corporation received. Hence, no book for primary civics exists. Interviews with teachers confirmed that civics is not taught now in primary schools and presumably never has been.

Out of a total of seven years of history, four and one-half of them focus exclusively on Ghana. An analysis of the contents of these texts, however, reveals that despite the fact that they were written by Ghanaians, a schoolchild is still exposed to an interpretation of Ghanaian history that strongly reflects European biases.[58] Ghana is described as an artificial creation of British colonial rule composed of disparate peoples whose precolonial contacts were in the form of military conflict. Historical chronologies focus on the establishment of European settlements, European relations with Africans, intertribal wars, and the British contribution to Ghana's development. Thus, the books portray Africans as passive subjects of European actors. These textbooks never seek to demonstrate that some basis for Ghana's nationhood preceded the imposition of colonial rule. Nor do they dwell on the cultural achievements of African people. The very superficial descriptions of the ethnic groups in Ghana, which are often little more than a catalogue of physical traits, together with the continuous mention of the intertribal wars, might lend themselves to aggravating rather than mitigating stereotypes and ethnic chauvinism. History books mention common elements of Ghanaian society only briefly, and then usually in the context of the mythological origin of the Ghanaian population in the Empire of Ghana or the coming together of the groups during the colonial period to constitute the contemporary state of Ghana.

Other deficiencies are the emphasis on the divisive years prior to the twentieth century and particularly the failure to deal with the independence movement in any detail. During the first four years of the study of history, the texts devote a total of eight pages to the period subsequent to the imposition of colonial rule. The eighth year of primary school does focus on modern history. In the last two years, half of one of the six books and sixteen pages in another describe the developments in the twentieth century. Therefore, it is quite conceivable that a Ghanaian schoolchild attempting to comprehend the deficiencies of the colonial period and the basis of the demand for independence would have some difficulty. Colonial figures, like George Maclean and Sir Gordon Guggisberg, receive more detailed and sympathetic attention than the architects of Ghana's independence, whether they were Nkrumahist or anti-Nkrumahist. The only twentieth-century Ghanaian who successfully competes with colonial governors for space is the educator, Kwegyir Aggrey, the first vice-principal of Achimota College. In editions published after Nkrumah's downfall, two books briefly mention his role as the leader of the independence movement as a background for discussing his faults and failures. Similarly, evaluations of colonialism attempt to be so balanced that the number of lines on the subject of the bad effects are then followed by a dissertation of equal length on the good results. Moreover, this extremely important topic was given only a single page in the fourth year history book for primary seven. At the middle school level the scramble for Africa and the resulting colonial system get nine pages. Particularly with regard to the grievances leading to the anticolonial movement and the extent of its support, the texts fail to clarify the motives of the leaders or even to provide much information about the manner in which the Ghanaians succeeded in achieving independence. This inadequate treatment of the independence movement deprives the student of knowledge of important events and of a source of pride in his national identity.

The Ghanaian approach to civics follows the English orientation, which centers on character training and includes little direct effort to inculcate a sense of national citizenship or pride in national symbols. Despite the obvious differences between Britain, a country that was able to achieve a large degree of national identity and loyalty in its population even before the inauguration of a mass educational system in the nineteenth century, and Ghana, where the very study of some historical period reactivates divisions in the society, the Ministry of Education continues to follow the British emphasis on history and character training. Only one book, the history text for the eighth year of primary school, ever discusses the contemporary Ghanaian political system. In that book fourteen pages are devoted to Ghana after independence and an additional eighteen to the organization of the political system and the duties of the citizen. An evaluation of Nkrumah's contribution and why he failed receives three further pages.

Results of the Ministry of Education survey, as discussed in Chapter 6, attest to the deficiencies of the curricula and teaching program. Although schooling was listed as the principal source of political information and appears to be the key agent of national political socialization, the education system dissipates much of its potential. The inability of students through secondary school to conceptualize key political institutions results, at least in part, from the failure to utilize the teaching of civics to impart knowledge about the Ghanaian political system. Lack of familiarity with national symbols, including the flag, similarly seems to reflect the refusal of the Ministry of Education to incorporate civic rituals in the schools or to emphasize national symbols more in the teaching programs. More students might have been attracted to historical and contemporary Ghanaians as the persons they most admired rather than to figures in their immediate environment if the school texts provided them with some national heroes. Similarly, increasing amounts of education might have produced greater intergroup tolerance if the history texts did not catalogue so many tribal wars and if the descriptions of ethnic groups did not dwell on superficial stereotypes.

In Ghana, as in most other African states, educators have not been fully aware of the potential critical impact of the content of the curriculum and the character of the teaching program in promoting national integration. With the massive efforts to expand the primary and middle school enrollments, the Ministry of Education has usually concerned itself with the number of children in schools, almost to the exclusion of what these students learn. The Curriculum Research and Development Unit never received adequate staff or resources to undertake a fundamental revision of the history, civics, and geography program. The Ghanaian experience demonstrates that the mere inclusion of national history in the curriculum far from resolves the intricate problems of directing education for the purpose of promoting national unity. The road to a relevant education must traverse the preparation of a new civics curriculum focused on the contemporary political system and the problems of political development and a reinterpretation of history toward a more African perspective. Furthermore, an anthropological and sociological orientation of social studies has more relevance than the current emphasis on history. The study of history in new countries generally, and as it is now taught in Ghana particularly, tends to reinforce divisions in society. Study of traditional cultural and institutional patterns would better enable a child to comprehend and appreciate the heritage of his country than a compendium of dates and historical incidents. A comparative analysis of the social and political organization, goals, values, and cultural symbols of the major ethnic components of the Ghanaian national community could profitably emphasize the similarities as well as the differences. Through such a study of the country's traditional heritage, students could develop respect for their past and tolerance for other groups. Many career bureaucrats in the Ministry of Education, however, cling to old practices and remain hostile to such fundamental innovations. It is all too apparent that the Ministry of Education in Ghana has missed many opportunities to build the educational system in a manner that would more effectively promote national accommodation.

NOTES

1. David Apter, *Ghana in Transition* (New York: Atheneum, 1963), p. 361.
2. Maxwell Owusu, *Uses and Abuses of Political Power: A Case Study of Continuity and Change in the Politics of Ghana* (Chicago: University of Chicago Press, 1970), p. 329.
3. Owusu, op. cit., p. 8.
4. Fred M. Hayward, "Government Performance and National Integration in Selected Ghanaian Communities," paper presented at the Annual Meeting of the African Studies Association, 1971.
5. For example, See Dennis Austin, *Politics in Ghana, 1946–60* (London: Oxford University Press, 1964), pp. 210, 211, 216, and 228.
6. K. A. B. Jones-Quartey, "Report From the Regions," *Legon Observer*, 6 (September 10, 1971), p. 62. Survey data collected by Fred Hayward among various ethnic groups in Ghana indicates the rather striking persecution complex many northerners have vis-à-vis the national government. See Fred M. Hayward, "Rural Attitudes and Expectations about National Government: Experience in Selected Ghanaian Communities," Madison, Wisconsin, August 1972, mimeographed, p. 19.
7. For an interesting discussion of this and other problems involved in a federal approach to the pluralistic states of West Africa, see B. D. G. Folson, "Single Parties, Tribes, Totalitarianism and Federalism in West Africa," *Economic Bulletin of Ghana*, 10 (2, 1966), pp. 31–34.
8. Fred M. Hayward, "Government Performance and National Integration in Selected Ghanaian Communities," op. cit., p. 20.

9. This idea is discussed in Kwamina Bentsi-Enchill, "Developments in Former British West Africa," in David Currie, ed., *Federalism and the New Nations of Africa* (Chicago: University of Chicago Press, 1964), p. 97; and in *Proceedings of the Constituent Assembly*, No. 12, February 5, 1969 (Accra: Ghana Publishing Corp., 1969), p. 521.

10. Folson, op. cit., p. 36.

11. W. Arthur Lewis has recommended that all parties winning 20 percent or more of the votes in a parliamentary election be included in the new government. See his *Politics in West Africa* (London: George Allen and Unwin Ltd., 1965), p. 83.

12. *Labour Statistics, 1968* (Accra: Central Bureau of Statistics, Series III, No. 13, December 1969), pp. 3 and 7. For illustrative data on ethnic mixtures in government departments, see Owusu, op. cit., p. 106.

13. Statistics regarding the size and ethnic composition of the Ghana armed forces are not obtainable. Our conclusions regarding the ethnic composition of the officer corps are drawn from an analysis of new commissions and promotions listed in the *Armed Forces Gazette* for the years 1968 and 1969. Only 6 percent of the officers listed were of northern origin, while northern ethnic groups constituted 18.5 percent of the total population according to the 1970 census. William Gutteridge indicates that in 1961, 60 percent of the rank and file members of the Ghana armed forces were northerners. See William Gutteridge, *Armed Forces in New States* (London: Oxford University Press, 1962), p. 35.

14. Interviews with officials of Public Service Commission and Establishments Secretariat.

15. See, for instance, J. A. Braimah, "Opening Speech," *Report of the Conference of Civic Club Representatives, March 27 to April 1, 1971* (Accra: Centre for Civic Education, 1971), p. 29; Bennett Mahamah, "Bridging the Gap Between the North and the South," *Daily Graphic*, December 30, 1970, p. 5; and *Parliamentary Debates*, Vol. 2, No. 23, March 23, 1970 (Accra: Ghana Publishing Corp., 1970), pp. 922–923.

16. Quoted in *Daily Graphic*, February 27, 1970, p. 9.

17. Avoidance of Discrimination Act, Dec. 1957, as quoted in *The Proposals of the Constitutional Commission for a Constitution for Ghana* (Accra: Ghana Publishing Corp., 1968), p. 68.

18. *The Proposals of the Constitutional Commission for a Constitution for Ghana*, op. cit., p. 69.

19. Kwame Nkrumah, *Dark Days in Ghana* (New York: International Publishers, 1968), pp. 63–64. See also William Burnett Harvey, *Law and Social Change in Ghana* (Princeton, N.J.: Princeton University Press, 1966), pp. 304–307.

20. *Constitution of the Republic of Ghana* (Accra: Ghana Publishing Corp., 1969), Article 35, p. 35.

21. Formation of Political Parties Decree NLCD 345 as amended by NLCD 347.

22. David Brokensha, *Social Change in Larteh, Ghana* (Oxford: The Clarendon Press, 1966), p. 221.

23. For a discussion of these, see W. C. Ekow Daniels, "Law Relating to Husband and Wife in Ghana," in (n.e.) *Integration of Customary and Modern Legal Systems in Africa* (Ife, Nigeria: University of Ife Press, 1971) p. 390.

24. For a discussion of the differing approaches adopted by Ghana and the Ivory Coast in this field, see Dorothy Dee Vellenga, "Attempts to Change the Marriage Laws in Ghana and the Ivory Coast," in Philip Foster and Aristide Zolberg, eds., *Ghana and the Ivory Coast: Perspectives on Modernization*, (Chicago: University of Chicago Press, 1971), pp. 125–150.

25. N. A. Ollennu, "The Law of Succession in Ghana," in *Integration of Customary and Modern Legal Systems in Africa*, op. cit., p. 301.

26. Mahamah, op. cit., p. 5.

27. See, for instance, *Daily Graphic*, January 4, 1971 and January 6, 1971.

28. *Daily Graphic*, January 6, 1971.
29. An interesting and detailed discussion of regional discrepancies in health expenditures is contained in Michael Sharpston, "The Regional Pattern of Health Expenditure," Accra, 1969, mimeographed.
30. "Seven Year Development Plan" (Accra: Office of the Planning Commission, 1964).
31. See for instance Town and Country Planning Division, Ministry of Lands, *National Physical Development Plan, 1963–1970* (Accra: State Publishing Corporation, 1965), Tables XXI and XXVI.
32. "Two Year Development Plan" (Accra: Ghana Publishing Corp., 1968), p. 20.
33. "One Year Development Plan, July 1970 to June 1971" (Accra: Ghana Publishing Corp., 1970), p. iii.
34. *National Physical Development Plan, 1963–1970*, op. cit., p. vii.
35. Dr. K. B. Dickson, "The Middle Belt of Ghana," *Bulletin de l'I.F.A.N.*, Vol. 31, Series B, No. 3 (1969), pp. 689–716.
36. "Outline of Government Economic Policy" (Accra: Ghana Publishing Corp., June 13, 1972), p. 18.
37. Work since 1960 by Prof. Gilbert Ansre and Dr. John Callow has led them to conclude that the 34 languages enumerated in the 1960 census should be further subdivided, giving a total of fifty-four Ghanaian languages. See Gilbert Ansre, "Language Policy and the Promotion of National Unity and Understanding in West Africa," Conference paper presented at the Institute of African Studies at the University of Ife, December 1970, mimeographed, p. 2.
38. Jack Berry, "The Madina Project: Ghana Language Attitudes in Madina," *Research Review*, Vol. 5 (Lent Term 1969), pp. 61–79.
39. Philip Foster, *Education and Social Change in Ghana* (London: Routledge and Kegan Paul, 1965), p. 88.
40. Ibid., p. 51.
41. See "Report of the Committee on Pre-University Education," May–June 1963, mimeographed, p. 19; and "Report of the Education Review Committee" (Accra: Ministry of Information, 1967), p. 55.
42. See "Report of the Committee on Pre-University Education," p. 19; and "White Paper on the Report of the Education Review Committee" (Accra: Ministry of Information, 1968), p. 6.
43. Gilbert Ansre, "A Study on the Official Language of Ghana," in *Colloque sur le Multilinguisme* (London: CCTA, 1962), p. 215.
44. National Redemption Council, "The Charter of Our Redemption" (Accra: Ghana Publishing Corp., 1973).
45. For a discussion of this approach see Ansre, "Language Policy for the Promotion of National Unity and Understanding in West Africa," op. cit.
46. *Parliamentary Debates*, Vol. 6, No. 37, May 5, 1971, p. 1583.
47. This has been proposed by E. A. Asamoa in "The Problem of Language in Education in the Gold Coast," *Africa*, XXV (January 1955), pp. 60–78.
48. Jack Berry, "Problems in the Use of African Languages and Dialects in Education," in UNESCO, *African Languages and English in Education*, Educational Studies and Documents, No. 11 (Paris: Education Clearing House, June 1953), p. 42.
49. Clifford H. Prator, *Language Teaching in the Philippines* (Manila: U.S. Education Foundation in the Philippines, 1950), p. 4.
50. *Parliamentary Debates*, Vol. 6, No. 37, May 5, 1971 (Accra: Ghana Publishing Corp., 1971), p. 1582.

51. D. K. Agyeman, "Ethnicity and Language Policy for our Schools," *Faculty of Education Bulletin*, University College of Cape Coast, I (July 1970), p. 17.

52. Foster, op. cit., p. 117.

53. *Educational Statistics 1968–1969* (Accra: Ministry of Education, 1971), p. 1.

54. Norman Uphoff points out that foreign aid donors have not done much to close the educational gap among Ghana's ethnic groups. Between 1957 and 1966 Gas and Akans received very disproportionate numbers of scholarships to foreign universities, while Ewes received somewhat fewer and northerners many fewer than their population size would warrant. See Norman Uphoff, "Ghana's Experience in Using External Aid for Development, 1957–1966" (Berkeley: Institute of International Studies, University of California, 1970), mimeographed, p. 400.

55. *Education Report for the Years 1958–1960* (Accra: Ministry of Information and Broadcasting on behalf of the Ministry of Education, 1962), p. 49.

56. Information about required books is from an analysis of the yearly lists published by the Ministry of Education from 1956 to 1971.

57. "The West African Examinations Council Annual Report for the Year Ended 31 March 1968" (Accra: West African Examinations Council Printer, 1969).

58. The textbooks used in this analysis are, for civics: J. R. Bunting, *Civics for Self-Government* (London: Evans Brothers Ltd., 1959); for primary school history: F. K. Buah, *An Elementary History for Schools, Book One* (London: Macmillan and Co. Ltd., 1st ed. 1963, 2nd ed. 1967); F. K. Buah, *History for Ghanaian Schools, Book Two* (London: Macmillan and Co. Ltd., 1964); F. K. Buah, *An Elementary History for Schools, Book Three, Africa and Europe* (London: Macmillan and Co. Ltd., 1966); F. K. Buah, *An Elementary History for Schools, Book Four, Ghana and Europe* (London: Macmillan and Co. Ltd., 1st ed. 1963, 2nd ed. 1967); F. K. Buah, *An Elementary History for Schools, Book Five, New Ghana* (London: Macmillan and Co. Ltd., 1968); for middle school history: Godfrey N. Brown and Philip M. Amonoo, *An Active History of Ghana, Book One—From Earliest Times to 1844* (London: George Allen and Unwin Ltd., 1961); Godfrey N. Brown, *An Active History of Ghana, Book Two—Since 1844* (London: George Allen and Unwin Ltd., 1964); M. I. Potts, *Makers of Civilization, Book One*, 3rd ed. (London: Longmans, 1961); M. I. Potts, *Makers of Civilization, Book Two*, 2nd ed. (London: Longmans, 1953); C. S. S. Higham, *Landmarks of World History* (London: Longmans, Green and Co. Ltd., 1947); C. M. O. Mate, *A Visual History of Ghana*, 2nd ed., (London: Evans Brothers Ltd., 1968). It should be noted that in this analysis we have followed the Ministry's required textbooks and divided the books into those for up to primary eight and then for form three and form four of middle school. Most schools, however, have six years of primary and four years of middle school classes. All of the authors of Ghanaian history texts except for Godfrey Brown are Ghanaians. None of the authors of European history books or the civics text are Ghanaian.

9

Conclusion

Any consideration of the past, present, or future of the political systems of Lebanon and Ghana would be incomplete without according a central role to communal loyalties. This study has documented that attachment to sect in Lebanon and to ethnic group in Ghana remains an omnipresent force in the political life of these states. Consequently, the stability and development of the two countries, as is true of other fragmented societies, depend on the management of communal relations to minimize conflict and tension. Since modernization frequently fuels rather than extinguishes the flames of communal sentiments, time is not on the side of those policy-makers who choose to ignore communalism in the hopes that it will expire of its own accord. To avoid the ravages of social and political strife, both modernizing and modernized plural states need to address themselves to the urgent task of promoting accommodation.

The successful promotion of national accommodation involves recognizing the legitimacy of communal groups by incorporating them in the structure and processes of the political system, while actively promoting a measure of common loyalty to the political system. It is necessary to recognize the intensity of attachments to parochial religious, ethnic, linguistic, regional, and racial subgroups, and attempt to harness these loyalties for the evolution

relations; whether social, spatial, and institutional separation facilitate or aggravate intercommunal relations; the circumstances under which individuals and groups alter their communal identities and the implications of these changes for the political system; the manner in which centrifugal and centripetal communal pressures vary in their impact; and how political structure, processes, and governmental policies affect the search for national accommodation. Here we will return to them and assess the Lebanese and Ghanaian experiences in an attempt to draw some tentative conclusions.

To summarize these conclusions, religious and ethnic communalism do not differ fundamentally, at least in the cases of Lebanon and Ghana. Although communal cleavages initially were deeper and more volatile in Lebanon, current communal conflict in Ghana has considerable disruptive potential. Social, spatial, and institutional separation do not necessarily impede the evolution of intercommunal understanding, but it is helpful to have some crosscutting links and common loyalties. Political structures and processes influence the formation of communal identities by determining which level of inclusiveness is most expedient; the more inclusive the communal blocs become the greater the tendency for conflict because of reduced flexibility. Centripetal communal pressures in Lebanon have involved communal groups in the substance as well as the form of political competition.

Communalism in Lebanon and Ghana, as elsewhere, rests on the foundations of the need for identity and belonging. It is not differences in religion *qua* religion or ethnic group *qua* ethnic group that give rise to the respective communal divisions, but instead the emotions and reactions that accompany membership in these groups. Thus, the nature and intensity of the social and political bonds that unite the individuals constituting the community, rather than the objective features differentiating them, determine the special character of communal entities. For this reason religious communalism and ethnic communalism play similar roles in the political systems of Lebanon and Ghana, and ethnicity and sectarianism in these two cases share much in common. Furthermore, the decline of religiosity in Lebanon and the increasing homogenization of the cultures of Ghana through the impact of modernization and mass education do not undermine the ability of the respective communal groups to provide a source of self-identification and a basis of political action. The import attributed to the attachment to the sect or to the ethnic group carries with it the belief that members of one's own community differ in fundamental ways from other members of the society. This conviction, often accompanied by an image of superiority, does not depend on objective reality. The basic human requirement for belonging to a social unit smaller and more intimate than a national community that can impart a sense of order, purpose, and security vests communal groups with a continuity and significance far beyond the actual divergences that may have once called them into being.

Theoretically, religious and ethnic communities differ in one fundamental respect. An individual can switch his religious affiliation by conversion, but it is impossible to change one's ethnic identity, except by deception or over a period of generations through assimilation. Yet the difference between them is not very great. Religious divisions in Lebanon, in much the same way as ethnic boundaries, rest primarily on birth and social grouping rather than on individual religious inspiration. Most conversion has historically been by clans or families as a unit: in some cases, a legal fiction of family descent was created to legitimate the transfer to the new religious community. Today, most conversions in Lebanon result from intermarriages in which the bride adopts the religion of the groom. Much the same kind of phenomenon occurs in Ghana; the children of an interethnic marriage generally adopt the ethnic identity of their father. Since the rate of interethnic marriages in Ghana is approximately twice the rate of intersect marriages in Lebanon,[1] ethnic "conversion" through marriage occurs more often than religious conversion through marriage in Lebanon.

Perhaps the question should be raised here as to why sectarianism in Lebanon and ethnicity in Ghana have come to dominate their respective social and political spheres. Specifically, why is religion not important in Ghana and ethnicity unimportant in Lebanon? In Lebanon only the Armenian community retains a sense of ethnic distinctiveness, a fact not unrelated to the fairly recent arrival of the Armenians in Lebanon and to their having a different language. The relative cultural homogeneity of Lebanon and the sharing of the Arabic language have obliterated the kinds of distinctions among groups from which ethnic considerations usually arise. One could argue, however, as has Ghassan Tueni, the editor of *al-Nahār*, Lebanon's paramount newspaper, that Lebanon's religious communities in some ways themselves constitute ethnic groups.[2] Insofar as Christians claim to be descendants of the Phoenicians and to be culturally akin to the other Christian Mediterranean countries, and as Muslims stress the Muslim religious roots of their Arabic heritage, sect does have some ethnic connotations, cultural similarities notwithstanding. The answer to why religion has counted for so little in Ghana as a source of social identity and as a focus of communal loyalty seems rooted in Ghana's traditional religious tolerance and sense of the relativity of religious beliefs. In those African countries like Sudan, in which religion does arouse more passions of a communal nature, religious groupings correspond more closely to ethnic divisions than they do in Ghana. In Ghana missionaries did not carve out territorial spheres of influence which would have resulted in relative denominational homogeneity within their ethnic zone, as they often did elsewhere. The members of Ghana's ethnic communities belong to a variety of sects. It is possible, however, that religion will come to be perceived with greater import as a factor distinguishing the predominantly Christian southern portion of the country from the north, where most of Ghana's Muslims originate. If this were to occur, religious differences might come to symbolize other cultural and economic characteristics setting apart the north and south, and in turn become more socially and politically significant.

In Lebanon and in Ghana, as in many other plural societies, the introduction of an open political system has tended to politicize communal groupings. Within both countries communal blocs have become a major ordering device for political and economic competition. On the eve of independence in Lebanon the National Pact, which is the unwritten agreement formulated by the first Maronite president and the first Sunni premier, allocated political offices to Lebanon's major religious communities. The electoral system in Lebanon, based on multimember constituencies with seats reserved for representatives of particular sects and a list system, has involved sects directly in the process of political recruitment of members of parliament. Similarly, the designation of all major political positions for persons from a specific religious community gives sects a voice in the selection of holders of these posts. The principle of the proportional distribution of political power has, over time, been extended to include other forms of political benefit, including scholarships, civil service posts, and grants to private schools; and sect representatives act as guardians of the interests of their group to ensure their fair share.

Ethnicity in Ghanaian politics has similarly revolved around issues of political recruitment and the distribution of amenities and patronage. However, in contrast with the Lebanese attempt to regularize and contain communal competition, none of the three types of governmental systems Ghana has had—parliamentary democracy, one-party rule, or military dictatorship—has openly recognized the legitimacy of ethnic interests or directly incorporated them into the political system. During the periods of parliamentary democracy, the apportionment of seats in parliament on a geographic basis has meant that most constituencies were ethnically homogeneous. Thus, ethnic factors weighed heavily in the recruitment and election of candidates. Members of parliament who were then appointed to cabinet posts contended among each other for political patronage for their ethnically defined constituencies. The installation of one-party rule or a military regime has forced ethnic rivalries underground, but the suppression of open political activity in the country at large has never eliminated ethnic antagonisms among members of the ruling councils. Ethnic considerations have entered into policy-making, investments in projects, and elite alignments, with each ethnic group trying to maximize its benefits.

Communal competition for economic benefits within the political system in Ghana has often been fiercer than in Lebanon with less predictable consequences, but this results from factors other than the difference between religious and ethnic parochialisms. Lebanon's continuing economic prosperity has taken some of the edge off sectarian economic rivalries by making more resources available for all communities. In contrast, Ghana's lower level of development and long periods of recession and balance of payments crises endow ethnic contention more with the character of a zero-sum game, because the location of a project in one area literally deprives all other groups from access to it or an opportunity to receive something comparable. Also, the Lebanese economy is less socialistic than Ghana's so that the government does not constitute such an exclusive source of jobs and other economic benefits. Moreover, the absence of clear geographical differentiation between Lebanon's sectarian groups means that, unlike Ghana, regional competition for development projects is not necessarily communal in character. It is even more significant that the recognition of a formula for distributing political offices and benefits among Lebanon's sects focuses much political competition inward among members of the same sect and also puts sectarian representatives in the position of safeguarding their legitimate share. Politics in Ghana, on the other hand, often involves an unprincipled scramble for all of the power and patronage the political system has to offer. In the absence of a defined formula, nothing prevents some groups from monopolizing political power to the exclusion of others, and when ethnic groups believe that they have been deprived of their due they become alienated from the incumbent regime. This in turn contributes to the bitterness and lack of trust that some ethnic groups exhibit toward others, and it leads to instability. The Lebanese system tends to elevate political and communal moderates to office: even though members of parliament and other office-holders have sectarian designations, members of parliament are elected by all of the citizens in their constituency and other office-holders are elected by all of the other representatives, and they therefore have to be acceptable to persons outside of their own community. Nothing comparable in Ghana has assured the acceptability of political leaders to a wide spectrum of communities: individual heads of government have ranged from being almost ethnically blind to being ethnically chauvinistic.

Although economic disparaties between communal groups exacerbate communal conflict in both Lebanon and Ghana, in neither country does the sharpest intergroup conflict arise between the most deprived group and the more advantaged. The deepest cleavage in Lebanon comes between the Maronites and the Sunnis, although the Shiites are the most disadvantaged group and seemingly would have the most legitimate grounds for complaint. Similarly in Ghana, the northern ethnic groups, although the most deprived, have not been effective or articulate demanders of their communal rights. In both cases, the more relatively advantaged groups are the most aggressive and abrasive competitors and are quicker to complain whenever they believe their rights to be infringed by other groups. It seems likely, however, that as the Shiites in Lebanon and the northerners in Ghana become more experienced political practitioners and have larger numbers of sophisticated spokesmen, they could each offer severe challenges to those in power, who have appeared to neglect their interests over the years.

At the time of independence, communal cleavages presented more of a problem in Lebanon than in Ghana. Yet, a comparison of these two systems seemingly points to the greater cultural homogeneity of Lebanon. In place of Ghana's thirty four distinct indigenous languages, Lebanon has one national tongue which plays a central cultural role. In contrast with the array of traditional cultural patterns in Ghana, Lebanese partake of an essentially shared culture, at least in its nonreligious characteristics. Rather than confronting the task of reconciling the traditional Ghanaian heritages with the superimposed Western civilization, Lebanon's culture reaches in two directions—back to a rich legacy and forward to modern elements deriving from centuries of close contact with Europe. The disappearance of the feudal order in the nineteenth century eliminated for Lebanon the task of dealing with the panoply of traditional political systems, which is still a part of the Ghanaian landscape. However, the depth of communal divisions depends on the subjective drawing of boundaries, and the intensity of the felt differences need not reflect actual cultural dissimilarities. Lebanon's physical location in a region of the world in which the preoccupation with religious affiliation has bordered on an obsession has made the things that divide the population seem more significant than what they have in common. Moreover, each confessional community believes that its particular traditions and belief system are divinely inspired and thus of eternal validity. Despite the deference Ghanaians publicly accord their traditional heritage, it constitutes something of a source of embarrassment because ethnic identity, traditional institutions, and customs are deemed antimodern vestiges of another age, which therefore should be eliminated. Doubtlessly, the colonial denigration of African cultures has colored the reaction Africans still have to their past. The relatively wholesale attempts of Ghana's elite to emulate European standards have rendered traditional divergences less of an obstacle to accommodation. The elite's immersion in European (essentially British) culture, which comes through their British-oriented education, provides a unifying element to a far greater extent than in Lebanon, where foreign cultural influences often have a divisive influence and where the educational system is less uniform.

Another element affecting the degree of fragmentation relates to the centripetal pressures Lebanon has had to cope with because its language and culture do not set it apart from the surrounding countries in its area. In Lebanon sectarianism sometimes becomes the substance as well as the form of political competition, but this does not derive from essential differences in the nature of religious and ethnic communalism. Lebanon's geographic position as part of a larger cultural area immediately raises questions about its relationship with other countries that speak the Arabic language. The framing of a foreign policy that would satisfy all elements within Lebanon has proved to be among the thorniest and most provocative problems which the Lebanese political system has confronted. Lebanon's language and culture, while drawing the country together on one plane, serve as sources of disunity and confessional fragmentation on another. Lebanese nationalists, mostly Christians, in their opposition to Pan-Arabism, argue as vociferously as do Ghanaian nationalists that linguistic homogeneity is not synonymous with nationality. Extreme Arab nationalists in Lebanon, mostly Muslims, contend that the Arabic language and culture that Lebanon shares with many other Arab states justify the erasure of existing national boundaries and the creation of a Pan-Arab state. Historically, Christians have defended the independence of Lebanon to avoid the fate of being submerged as a tiny minority in a predominantly Sunni Muslim state, while Muslims, particularly Sunnis, have seen some form of Arab federation as transforming their status from being one of Lebanon's many minorities, and not the most powerful one, into that of a majority community. Thus, the question of Lebanon's place in the Arab world has implications for personal freedom, religious ascendance, majority status, political power, and the prestige of the respective groups. A second dimension of the same issue comes from Lebanon's need to articulate a policy toward the 300,000 Palestinian refugees living within Lebanon's borders and the Palestinian commandos *(fedayeen)*. Greater Muslim sympathy for Arab causes has made them more willing to suffer the consequences of allowing the commandos to carry out operations on and from Lebanese soil, while Christians have favored greater control of the commandos with a concomitant reassertion of Lebanese sovereignty over the camps, to avoid or to minimize Israeli reprisals.

Ghana does not confront the same type of problem because an expansion of its territory would not fundamentally change the status of its constituent ethnic communities. Pan-African unity would just add more minorities and create a larger and more fragmented state. Therefore, it has never aroused the strong emotions and commitment of Pan-Arabism. Moreover, Pan-Arabism reflects concrete cultural similarities, including language, and for the vast majority of Arabs, a shared religion; whereas Pan-Africanism rests upon the less tangible notion that culturally and linguistically divided Africans should unite because of racial similarities, geographical contiguity, and the common experience of colonial oppression. Secession rather than federation constitutes the real boundary problem for African states. Relative to other African countries, Ghana has not suffered from serious efforts to sunder its territory. The only real clamor for a redefinition of borders has come from the Ewes, particularly in the period prior to independence, many of whom wished to redress the division of the Ewe community between Ghana and Togo after World War I. It is worth noting that the urge for secession in Ghana and other African states is motivated by much the same interests as the urge for federation in Lebanon; namely, the desire of particular constituent groups to change their status from that of minority to majority group within the redefined state.

Ironically, the full and open recognition of deep communal cleavages has often promoted more harmonious social patterns than their minimization. Lebanese sensitivity to the implications of strained communal relations, a struggle to achieve intergroup accommodation, and a will to live together as members of a common national society have produced an atmosphere conducive to greater political stability and increasing attitudinal convergence.

The opposite has occurred in Ghana. A failure of most Ghanaians to recognize the magnitude of societal divisions and to concede that their country suffers from serious ethnic tensions has encouraged irresponsible conduct and a drift into greater ethnic conflict and increasing ethnocentricity.

In the Introduction we asked whether social, spatial, and institutional separation facilitates or hinders accommodation. Most theorists concerned with plural societies have considered the evolution of crosscutting affiliations a prerequisite for stability, unity, and democracy. But Arend Lijphart has proposed the opposite, namely, that in a communally divided society encapsulation of communal groups may better serve improved relations.[3] In plural societies of all kinds persons tend to seek out members of their own groups and prefer their company. This is true in situations of both spatial isolation and mixture. In-group socializing in both countries reflects more the feeling of being at ease in one's own milieu than an active sense of prejudice, and the greater security derived from staying within a circle whose members have similar backgrounds, shared beliefs, and in the case of Ghana, a common language. It has little effect on national accommodation because such preferential social relations are considered natural and acceptable patterns of conduct in both Ghana and Lebanon: almost nowhere in the world do people choose friends without some attention to similar kinds of considerations.

From the experiences of Ghana and Lebanon, it seems that over the long term a mixed spatial distribution may be more conducive for national accommodation than regional homogeneity. Although neither country is a clear-cut example, Ghana is characterized by greater spatial separation of communal groups. The Lebanese historical experience of living side-by-side with members of other communities seems to facilitate the kinds of adjustments necessary for harmonious relations in a plural society. More important is the fact that the vast majority of Lebanon's districts and all its provinces include several sects: the competition for amenities and development resources has a geographic rather than an exclusively sectarian focus. Particularly in the case of South Lebanon, where divergence in attitudes toward the presence of commandos could potentially constitute a significant strain in sectarian relationships, the shared sense of regional identity and interests helps to offset other differences. In Ghana each ethnic community traditionally has had its own territory. Although internal migration has injected outsiders into once ethnically uniform villages and has given rise to multiethnic urban centers, it has not fundamentally altered the geographical concentrations of ethnically defined clusters of people.[4] Many migrants merely move within the area of their ethnolinguistic group; much of the movement is only temporary, since people return after short durations to their home villages; and the vast majority of people still remain in their original ethnic home-lands. Regionalism in Ghana therefore tends to be primarily an expression of ethnicity set in a geographical guise; in its most extreme form it could stimulate centrifugal secessionist tendencies.

In the short-term, communal conflict may be reduced by social and geographical isolation of the constituent communal groups, but within a heterogenous environment it becomes possible to form social relationships across communal boundaries. Even if intercommunal contacts remain primarily economic in nature and residents prefer socializing with members of their own group, the experience of living together with persons of diverse backgrounds can be beneficial. Intercommunal voluntary associations and intercommunal marriages occur more frequently in a communally mixed area, and both can gradually build bridges between different communities. A political system that expressly fashions institutional mechanisms in recogni-tion of heterogeneous residential patterns, as in the case of Lebanon, can also promote political moderation by making a candidate's election dependent on support from outside his own group. The reverse often takes place in homogeneous constituencies, such as in Ghana, where ethnic chauvinism and explicitly communal appeals have often been the key to electoral success, with each of the nominees seeking to outdo the others in the stridency of his ethnocentric call for votes. Fundamentally, national accommodation in-volves a process of social learning in which individuals and groups modify their conduct to be more acceptable to each other. The realization of the need for self-limitation comes more easily when citizens from a variety of groups live, work, participate in common organizations, and politick together.

Communally mixed environments bring with them problems as well as accommodative potential. Living accommodatively with people of diverse backgrounds becomes a daily exercise rather than an abstract issue, and more frequent contacts between members of different groups can give rise to an increased incidence of confrontation. Migration from a predominantly homogeneous to a heterogeneous atmosphere often precipitates a heightened sense of communal consciousness and a greater disposition for communal competition. Even so, intergroup experience ultimately constitutes more of an asset than a liability for national accommodation. Communal awareness and rivalry seem almost inevitable in this era of politicized pluralism, and they contribute a neutral input into the social and political system. What is critical is whether they are channeled into constructive, system-supporting, peaceful competition or mismanaged and allowed to degenerate into destabilizing conflict.

The existence of a network of communally exclusive institutions does not necessarily hinder national accommodation, but neither does it promote it. In Lebanon the sects sponsor a variety of voluntary associations and operate schools, hospitals, clinics, orphanages, presses, and in a few cases housing projects, giving people the option of virtually moving from the cradle to the grave within a sectarian environment. At present the remnants of the traditional political order comprise the primary institutional embodiment of ethnicity in Ghana and, as such, play a much smaller role. Politically relevant ethnic groups on the Ghanaian national scene do not coincide with the boundaries of the traditional Ghanaian states; ethnic blocs active in the national political system often encompass groups that formerly lacked a sense of identity. Nor do the communal actors primarily concern themselves with preserving prerogatives of the chiefs or the institutional integrity of these traditional entities. Significantly, intersectarian residential patterns considerably offset the impact of sectarian institutions in Lebanon, and the absence of extensive networks of ethnic associations and institutions in Ghana gives modern social, economic, and educational structures a thrust somewhat reducing the centrifugal pressures of geoethnicity.

The respective salience of sectarianism and ethnicity in Lebanon and Ghana as foci of loyalty, self-identity, and social categorization impedes the formation of effective voluntary associations that cut across communal cleavages. Moreover, in neither country has strong class-consciousness developed. The trade union movement in both remains confined to a small percentage of the working force, and the unions are beset with numerous organizational deficiencies. Professional syndicates in Lebanon and farmers' societies in Ghana perform a limited range of functions for their memberships, but for the large issues in the political arena, persons tend to revert to the communal mode of expression. Thus, the strength of communal bonds inhibits the development of economic and associational forms of social differentiation, and when class and occupational groupings intersect communal boundaries, communal considerations generally prevail. Although crosscutting loyalties and multiple affiliations cannot countervail communal considerations, their existence does contribute to national accommodation. National accommodation depends on a widening of horizons and the growth of a national perspective supplementing, but not supplanting, the communal frame of reference.

Even a weak sense of class-consciousness and relatively ineffective economic organizations and voluntary associations help to convey some awareness of belonging to a national system. Thus, the effectiveness of noncommunal forms of organization for promoting social learning cannot be measured solely in terms of their strength vis-à-vis communal ties.

Political structures and processes influence the formation of communal identities by determining which level of inclusiveness is most expedient. Contemporary ethnolinguistic communities in Ghana represent an adjustment to the exigencies of political competition within a national political system in much the same way as did the earlier development of a sense of common identity and interest amongst all members of the same sect in Lebanon. In both systems the propensity for communal conflict increases when competition takes the form of confrontation between two clearly defined blocs. Both Ghana and Lebanon can be thought of as congeries of minorities, and greater fluidity and flexibility accompanies a multipolar communal constellation in much the same way that the European state system of the nineteenth century allowed for easier balancing and adjustments than the post-World War II division between two superpowers. The Lebanese political system encourages the articulation of issues on both a multisect and intrasect basis, thereby moderating the Christian–Muslim division. The fact that the Lebanese system has been able to move back and forth between multipolar and more bipolar communal competition has enabled it to manage political crises that revolved around Christian–Muslim disagreement more easily than would otherwise have been the case. By structuring ethnic communities into two groups—those in power and those in opposition—the Ghanaian political system through its various forms of government has encouraged a thrust toward bipolar divisions. The contemporary Akan–non-Akan cleavage emerged more from political inspiration than from latent cultural similarities.

It seems unlikely that foreseeable economic, social, or political changes in either Lebanon or Ghana will substantially dispel the salience of communal considerations, but there may be some fluidity in the configurations of communal groupings and the intensity of conflict various issues arouse. The history of both countries attests to the fact that existing communal configurations do not represent fixed patterns on the social landscape. With regard to Lebanon, the most important development seems to be the growing sense of Arabness among Christians, based on a conception of Arab ethnic identity as separable from Muslim religious identity. It may be that for future generations, the shared sense of ethnic identity will provide a bond moderating some of the divisions deriving from religious differences. In turn, Christian acceptance of a secular version of Arab nationalism would facilitate the formulation of a consensus on the sensitive issues relating to Lebanon's role in the Arab world. In Ghana the relative recency of the emergence of the Akan–non-Akan cleavage in Ghanaian politics makes it difficult to predict its long term implications. A second factor of major importance is the possible political maturation of northerners. If northerners become more politically conscious and more articulate in their demands for a greater share of the national resources to overcome the disparities between the north and the south, it could alter the balance of power, particularly if northerners play off Akans against Ewes for their own advantage.

ACHIEVEMENT OF NATIONAL ACCOMMODATION IN LEBANON AND GHANA

As should be clear, Lebanon has come closer than Ghana to achieving national accommodation. Lebanese political structure distributes political offices and administrative positions approximately proportional to the percentage of the population the major communal groups constitute. In parliament and even more in the cabinet, sect representatives meet for discussion and bargaining. Lebanon's multiseat constituencies and its list system reduce incentives for communal appeals and increase pressures for cooperation, because candidates often depend on the votes of members of sects other than their own for election. In contrast, none of Ghana's political structures, neither the two parliamentary democracies, the two military regimes, nor the one-party system, has institutionalized mechanisms to assure the incorporation of the major ethnic groups into the political system in a meaningful manner. Some regimes have made more of an effort than others, but even under the more aware governments, cabinets have often been ethnically unbalanced and generally few efforts have been made to achieve ethnic equilibrium. Nor have ethnic considerations figured in civil service appointments, despite the central role that government employment occupies in the economy of the state. Furthermore, once ethnic groups accede to power, their delegates have utilized their position to favor themselves and sometimes punitively deprive their opponents. In Ghana every change of regime has given some groups a sense of being excluded from the seats of power.

An advantage of institutionalizing the equitable sharing of political power through the formation of broad-based governments is the moderating effect this has on opponents of a particular regime. A group, whether communal or political, that feels permanently excluded from political power has little incentive to play according to the rules of the game. In a kind of self-fulfilling prophecy, the Nkrumah regime declared that members of the opposition had subversive intentions; it then so entrenched itself and so emasculated the opposition that the latter was driven to attempting to overturn the CPP government by illegal means. Successor regimes in Ghana have tended to suffer from the same syndrome of considering any form of opposition illegitimate and using the institutions of power to consolidate its hold. Politicians out of power in Lebanon frequently make more explicitly communal appeals than members of the cabinet, but they are restrained by the knowledge that within a short period of time they may be once again invited to join the government in a coalition cabinet. Participation, or the hope of it, tends to vest politicians and the communities they represent with a stake in the system and with its concomitant responsibilities.

Lebanon's political processes have also facilitated national accommodation more than Ghana's by better providing for communal coalitions and by linking the masses with political leaders. Lebanese political dynamics bring together members of the major communal groups through elite coalitions more successfully than did past attempts in Ghana to unite the population in mass political parties. The management of sectarian conflict in Lebanon depends heavily on structured elite predominance by leaders who accept the need for reconciliation. Hence, the Lebanese political system rests on a sense of elite solidarity as well as some national consciousness among the elite, who hold together the rest of the system through their patron–client ties with the mass. Even though these vertical ties are usually uniconfessional, interconfessional elite alliances transmute the uniconfessional bond between the za'im and his constituents into relatively stable, multiconfessional blocs.

One encounters a lesser sense of solidarity among Ghana's economic and political elite because Ghana's elite is not as cohesive and does not have as deep historical roots. And there has been a tendency for politicians, especially during the Busia period, to exploit ethnic attachments for their own advantage. A more significant difference exists between the two political systems, however, in the effectiveness of patron–client relationships between the elite and the population. The absence of strong ties in Ghana in part reflects the weakness of democracy there, which has meant that the elite has often not felt it necessary to nurture such contacts among the masses. Although there is some sense of obligation on the part of elites from particular villages to assist their home towns, they do not as effectively draw these villages into the system. The weakness of client–patron networks results as well from the discontinuity in Ghana between traditional and modern leadership, unlike Lebanon, where the continuity has been much greater. Chiefs were traditional patrons, but with their fall no comparable patron–client relations have been established. Also, Ghana's civil service has been stronger, more disinterested, and less controlled by individual politicians than that of Lebanon, thus limiting the scope of political influence. Only at the ministerial level did politicians have much patronage to dispose of, and there were too few ministers to serve as effective broad-based patrons. The military rulers have not enjoyed these kinds of client relationships either.

In Ghana several political parties, particularly the CPP of Nkrumah, have attempted to incorporate the total population into an institutional vehicle transcending ethnic divisions. Although no political party has been rooted exclusively in a single ethnic community since the passage of the Avoidance of Discrimination Act of 1957, they have had differential degrees of support from different ethnic groups. The CPP approached being a truly national party far more than any of its opponents or successors, but even the CPP never won more than three-fifths of the popular vote in a fair election, and it was unable to inspire genuine broad endorsement among many ethnic groups. In taking the route of the mass party, the CPP had the intention of developing common institutions capable of offsetting communal allegiances and thereby effecting national integration. Few leaders of political parties and blocs in Lebanon have subscribed to such intentions. They have generally been content to erect interconfessional alliances solely for the purpose of electoral activity and parliamentary cooperation. Despite these more limited aspirations, though, the Lebanese political coalitions have been better able to sustain communal cooperation. In part, this reflects the difficulties the CPP and other Ghanaian parties have faced, both communal and institutional. In a country in which people have a basically ethnic rather than a national perspective, it is difficult to inspire support without making particularistic appeals, and no national program can manage to promote equally the interests of all communities. Moreover, the maintenance of a mass political party requires organizational skills and a level of institutionalization beyond the reach of most new states. Thus, CPP branches became colonized primarily by ethnics rather than by ideologues, and they gradually atrophied.

To the extent that national accommodation depends on skilled governance and self-consciousness, Lebanon has progressed far more than Ghana toward achieving this goal. Such considerations approach being an obsession in the Lebanese political system. Virtually every policy-maker keeps one eye on the proposal and one eye on its implications for intergroup relations. Along with being consummate political managers endowed with extraordinary ability for reconciling conflicting demands into a package that gives something to everyone and in the process evokes widespread support, Lebanese politicians frequently exhibit considerable sensitivity to the broad range of issues relating to intercommunal relations. However, Lebanese political processes so rest on the need to maintain consensus that they sometimes become immobilized because a regime often prefers not to act at all, even on a matter requiring immediate attention, rather than risk communal divisions. The Lebanese concern for avoiding dissension generally does not extend beyond this negative orientation to a more positive attempt to foster national unity. Moreover, one of the fundamental difficulties of the Lebanese accommodative and distributive system is that jobs, amenities, and political power can be apportioned, but foreign policy is not easily divisible or distributable and it often cannot be formulated in such a manner as to satisfy all the conflicting viewpoints. Consequently, foreign policy issues have often been the source of the greatest confessional conflict.

Although Ghana's various regimes have differed in their approach to ethnic problems, they have all underestimated the political implications of ethnicity. Nkrumah sought to eliminate ethnic distinctions as the first step toward realizing a new socialist order. Management of communal competition was certainly not at the top of his government's agenda. In the end Nkrumah created the facade of national unity through centralizing power in Accra at the expense of the traditional states and other regional interests and through eliminating the opposition. This interim measure was brought about at great cost to the political system which suppressed political manifestations of ethnicity. Nkrumah's successors have been even less concerned with ethnicity. Progress Party politicians perhaps evinced the greatest realization of the tenacity of ethnic bonds, but they used this primarily for the purpose of arousing support for the party among the Akan.

To promote full national accommodation, a political system needs to go beyond the creation of intergroup equilibrium to openly pursue measures that instill greater national unity. Lebanese policy-makers have been reluctant to go beyond the balancing of sectarian interests to attempting to foster a shared loyalty to the national community. Ghana under Nkrumah made some commitment to transform Ghanaians into national citizens, but these efforts did not succeed, and his successors have not been similarly motivated. Neither Lebanon nor Ghana has very actively sought to redress existing communal economic and educational inequalities. Greater communal economic disparities exist in Ghana than in Lebanon with the basic divide coming between the ethnic groups in the seven southern regions and the two northern ones. But there are considerable imbalances in Lebanon as well, particularly with regard to portions of predominantly Muslim South Lebanon, North Lebanon, and the Bekaa, as compared with Beirut and Mount Lebanon. The dynamics of Lebanon's politics assure more regional balancing in the expenditure of government revenues than has eventuated in Ghana, while patterns of expenditure in Ghana tend to reinforce rather than to correct regional inequalities. Ghana has undertaken a significant compensatory program intended to assist the north in only one field, education, which has managed to narrow the gap somewhat. During the administration of President Chehab, Lebanon instituted a number of programs to reduce disparities between regions and between the less and more affluent sects, but successor regimes have not pursued this equalization policy as vigorously.

Language policy does not have the same consequences in Lebanon as in Ghana due to the existence of a single national tongue in the former as against the considerable linguistic fragmentation in Ghana. In Lebanon differences exist among sectarian groups in their foreign language competence; these disparities do not, however, significantly detract from the unity that the Arabic language provides. In Ghana the question of a national language, especially when it relates to the medium of instruction adopted in the schools, has aroused considerable debate. Nkrumah's preference for English entrenched it in the political and education system of the country until recently. In succumbing to pressures from linguists and educators to increase the use of the mother tongue in the education system, policy-makers have frequently neglected the larger consideration of national accommodation. Obviously, a country with thirty four indigenous languages must promote a lingua franca in order to facilitate communication between its citizens. Whether this lingua franca is English or a Ghanaian language, like Akan, is not as important as the awareness of the implications of decisions regarding language for the future of the national community.

A national system of education provides the most feasible means by which a government can instill a sense of national citizenship. In this regard, the greater national control of education in Ghana makes its educational system a more effective vehicle of national political socialization than the more decentralized and predominantly private educational system in Lebanon. Neither country has given the curriculum sufficient attention to assure that the teaching of social studies inculcates national awareness and pride, tolerance toward other groups, and appropriate political values. At least in Ghana, all students are exposed to the same textbooks and teaching materials which the Ministry of Education has endorsed and adopted. Although the curriculum has many inadequacies, none of the courses present an interpretation from a particular ethnic perspective, and all of the students gain some similarity of perspective on the basis of what they have learned. Freedom for religious groups in Lebanon to operate their own schools, the weaker role of the Ministry of National Education, and the relative confessional homogeneity of the student bodies of each type of educational institution have weakened the ability of the system of education in Lebanon to serve a national role. Education in Lebanon, particularly in private religious schools, often reinforces particularistic orientations more than it fosters a national frame of reference.

In the Introduction we mentioned that as a political system moves toward national accommodation, it will be characterized by decreasing strife and decreasing political instability arising from communal confrontation; increasing attachment to the political system; more accommodative behavior on a personal level; greater acceptance of a national frame of reference; and convergence in basic political values pertaining to the major goals of the political system. Although it is not possible to measure precisely the degree to which either the Lebanese or the Ghanaian political system has moved in these directions, it is useful to consider the subject. Generally, the Lebanese system exhibits decreasing strife and instability whereas the incidence is rising in Ghana. Nevertheless, the distance between Lebanon and Ghana on the continuum of national accommodation should not be exaggerated. Lebanon still has some way to go and Ghana, although making less progress, began its independent political life with not as severe problems.

Since achieving independence some thirty years ago, Lebanon has maintained the same basic constitutional order and a democratic political process, something few other newly independent states have managed to do. Although Lebanon has been caught between the pressures of the commandos and the counterpressures of the Israelis in recent years, in the period after the 1958 civil war, Lebanon has been increasingly able to cope with problems having communal overtones. A comparison of the circumstances leading up to and the resolution of the two major crises the system has faced in recent years, the

1969 and 1973 commando confrontations, demonstrates how far Lebanon has progressed.

Ghana's adoption of five different types of governmental systems in the first fifteen years of independence attests to its lack of political stability. Although changes of regimes in Ghana have not had the overtly ethnic causes of the Nigerian civil war or the human toll of ethnic warfare in Burundi, communal conflict has been a contributing factor. Under every Ghanaian government the population has observed that some ethnic groups have benefited at the expense of others. Nkrumah, particularly toward the end of his tenure, favored the Akans. Political control was balanced toward the Ewes and Gas during most of the NLC period and toward the Akans in the Busia period; the struggle between the two blocs is not yet clearly resolved under the NRC. This continuing battle for political dominance, with its pendulum swinging between the Akans and the non-Akans, creates considerable tension and impedes the search for legitimacy. Exclusion from power on ethnic grounds breeds alienation and accompanying rationalizations for resorting to extraconstitutional means to topple the incumbent administration. On two occasions, the 1968 coup which displaced Nkrumah and the 1972 coup which brought the National Redemption Council into power, deteriorating economic conditions following the drop in the world price of cocoa and unwise economic policies played important roles as well. Nevertheless, Ghana's political history indicates that the failure to come to terms with pluralism has extracted a price.

A will to live together pervades the Lebanese system. One of the most important shared understandings is the urge for reconciliation and the desire on all sides of responsible opinion to pull back if it looks as if events are leading to conflict that might get out of control. A basic underlying force that sustains these sentiments is fear, borne out of a realization that disasters occurred both in 1860 and in 1958, and they could happen again. There is also growing appreciation among all communities of the value of a viable and cohesive state and the kind of intergroup accommodation upon which this depends. In contrast, the belated recognition of the incipient dangers in unrestrained communal competition has not similarly inspired Ghanaians to moderation in the framing of political demands. The Lebanese readiness to compromise and to accord to each group its legitimate share does not yet characterize the Ghanaian political culture with its winner-take-all ethos. For this reason "tribalism," or discordant ethnic ethnocentricism, appears to be on the ascendance in Ghana.

The Lebanese also exhibit a greater acceptance of a national frame of reference. This results in part from the greater political consciousness and sense of participation the Lebanese political system provides, but it also reflects an attachment to the national political community. With the exception of some sporadic efforts by the Ewe to reunite with their ethnic brethren in Togo, Ghana has never faced the kind of controversy over its national boundaries that Lebanon has. In Lebanon it has not been possible to be nationally oriented in merely a passive fashion. The resolution of the tension between Arab nationalism and Lebanese statism in favor of pride in Lebanese citizenship within a looser definition of Arab unity has considerably enhanced the prospects for national accommodation in Lebanon. Our survey results attest to how far the Lebanese have travelled from an exclusively parochial to a national cum sectarian focus. Increasing penetration by education, mass media, and government economic policy seems to be stimulating greater awareness of belonging to a national community in Ghana as well. Unlike the situation in Lebanon though, greater national consciousness has not motivated a disposition for concerns or actions more commensurate with a national rather than an ethnic frame of reference. Thus, in Ghana people may be in the process of simultaneously becoming more nationally cognizant and more ethnically inclined.

Lebanon, more than Ghana, has evolved a consensus regarding the internal structure of political authority and the legitimate limits of political action, but Ghanaians agree to a greater extent on the goals the political system should pursue. These developments reflect the continuing sectarian differences regarding Lebanon's foreign policy and the disagreements over whether the state should assume a more activist role in achieving social justice. Although Lebanese widely subscribe to the sharing of political power among the sects, reservations exist, particularly among the Muslims, about the distribution of political offices. Our adult survey results, for example, evinced considerable dissatisfaction with the reservation of the presidency for a Maronite and the premiership for a Sunni. It is difficult to evaluate the significance of calls for reform though, because it has always been fashionable to criticize the system and most Lebanese who do so have no clear idea of what should be substituted. Much of the criticism also reflects the success of the current confessional system, since many Lebanese believe that a sufficient level of accommodation has been achieved for Lebanon to move on to a more flexible arrangement. Few of the students we questioned exhibited much concern with changes in the structure of the confessional system, but nearly two-thirds of them advocated that the government promote greater regional equality and social equity. In Ghana ethnic groups generally do not have divergent ideological positions on foreign policy or domestic issues. As already noted, political competition in Ghana relates to the substance of politics, but the intensity of this competition does have destructive implications for the form of the political system. Lebanon is one of the few states that received its independence after World War II which maintains a democratic political system. Ghana, in contrast, underwent four major changes in the form of its political system in its first fifteen years.

Data from our adult survey of Lebanon show a clear trend towards convergence of political opinion between Christians and Muslims on a wide variety of issues which have divided these two groups in the past. Discrepancies still remain, but a comparison of the responses of the younger with those of the older and the more educated with the less educated indicates that within the foreseeable future many of the Christian–Muslim differences may decrease in magnitude or even disappear. Lebanon has by no means resolved all of its disagreements and established a consensual political culture. Substantial and significant differences still exist. A comparison of the statements of Christian and Muslim politicians during the 1973 commando crisis, for instance, demonstrates the growing similarity in Christian–Muslim perspectives as well as the gap still separating them. Both groups framed the issue in terms of how to reconcile the legitimate needs of the Palestinian people with the integrity of the Lebanese state, but Christian politicians were more concerned with the prerogatives of Lebanese sovereignty, while the Muslim politicians emphasized the rights of the Palestinians.

In the foreseeable future, neither Lebanon nor Ghana may be able to go beyond accommodation to integration and the subordination of communal attachments to national loyalty. Whether full integration occurs seems of secondary importance to the establishment of a political system that satisfies the legitimate aspirations and needs of their respective communal components while strengthening national bonds among these groups, so that the needs of the national community are not lost sight of at decisive moments in the shuffle of particularistic considerations. From the viewpoint of the world community, it may be preferable that Lebanon and other fragmented states do not become completely integrated, since their rising nationalism is a much tempered form of the emotional fervor that has inspired so many historical excesses in the name of the national interest. It seems more than a coincidence that Lebanon is one of the least militaristic states in the world. The level of reconciliation between the sects is sufficiently high to not propel the government into foreign adventures to divert the population. Moreover, under present conditions foreign intervention might have a divisive impact.

COSTS AND BENEFITS OF THE LEBANESE AND GHANAIAN APPROACHES TO PLURALISM

Probably the most notable aspect of the Lebanese approach is the explicit recognition given to the depth of communal identities and divisions. The relative stability of the political system in Lebanon, the growth in support for the system, the increase in attachment to the national community, and its economic prosperity all attest to the benefits that the maintenance of confessional balance and reconciliation has helped accrue in Lebanon. Lebanon has not eliminated all of its communal problems, but it has institutionalized procedures for conflict resolution. Lebanon confronts each new situation with a wealth of experience in sectarian tensions. As Ali Mazrui has written, "The experience of jointly looking for a way out of a crisis, of seeing mutual hostility subside to a level of mutual toleration, of being intensely conscious of each other's position and yet sensing the need to bridge the gulf—these are experiences which, over a period of time, should help two groups of people move into a relationship of greater integration."[5] Although, unlike Mazrui, we do not consider integration a likely or necessarily even a desirable goal for a plural society, we concur that the legacy of facing and resolving crises immeasurably strengthens the fabric of national accommodation. National accommodation does not presume the increasing homogenization of society with a concomitant reduction in the role of communal political actors. In a fragmented society competition between communal groups is inevitable, and with that competition may come some friction. What matters is that members of the political system have the will to live together, and that the political system itself has a means to grapple with the conflict when it occurs. Lebanon has achieved this to a considerable extent.

Lebanon's achievements have not been free of cost. Timidity and a fear of upsetting the balance between communities has prevented the system from going beyond reconciliation to actively promoting unity in diversity. Increased loyalty to the country and convergence in attitudes has occurred in part because of a fortuitous confluence of economic prosperity and a change in the nature of Pan-Arabism, but Lebanon may not be as lucky in the future. An obsession with maintaining balance and not offending any group has sometimes left the system immobilized and indecisive. Lebanon's political system has not been well suited for grappling with some of the country's outstanding social and economic problems. This deficiency would be more acute if Lebanon did not have the good fortune of continued economic prosperity even without economic planning or energetic government management of resources. Some of Lebanon's problems derive from particularly Lebanese patterns of political life: an obsession with rigidly adhering to a sectarian balance; a concern to always postpone acting until a consensus is formed; and the inclusion of diverse ranges of political ideology as well as sectarian and regional interests in the cabinet. Nevertheless, some reduction in efficiency and decisiveness may be the cost that any political system that adopts the model of national accommodation will have to pay. The laissez-faire attitude of the government has brought with it an unequal distribution of the benefits of Lebanon's development, with some confessional groups not profiting to the same extent as others. Such a situation has obvious implications for confessional balance and the future of Lebanon. Shiites, Lebanon's poorest and least educated sect, particularly feel themselves left behind economically. They also complain that they do not receive their fair share of benefits from development projects and government appointments. In our survey results Shiites diverged significantly from other Lebanese communities in attributing less importance to their citizenship and believing less frequently that loyalty to Lebanon was increasing. Shiites, alone of all groups, ranked their extended family ahead of their country in their hierarchy of loyalties.

In the last interview he granted before his death in 1973, President Fuad Chehab stated that, "Le problème fondamental du Liban, aujourd'hui et demain, est social. Il faut établir au Liban un équilibre social qui n'existe pas. . . . Ainsi, l'établissement de la justice sociale peut seul assurer au Liban un véritable équilibre. Certes, le compris entre les communautés constitue un autre élément de cet équilibre: mais cet élément est devenu moins important que la justice sociale."[6] Not only is social justice involved, but a greater equalization would facilitate the maintenance of sectarian harmony. Shiites' relatively low level of political consciousness and lack of political articulateness has bought time for the system in the past. If Lebanon cannot move beyond political balance to compensatory aid for the Shiites, the system will probably face greater strains deriving from Shiite dissatisfaction in the future, and the likelihood that the Shiites now constitute the most numerous sect further accentuates the significance of dealing with the issue.

Lebanon's political system has also not responded adequately to modifications in demographic composition. The distribution of political offices, seats in parliament, and cabinet posts reflects the relative size of the sects in the 1932 census. Lebanon has refrained from undertaking a new census during the past forty years because of the major repercussions for the political system that differential rates of population growth among the sects would entail. The only adjustment came during the Chehab regime when a decision was made to maintain parity at each level in posts for Christians and Muslims in civil service recruitment. However, leading members of all groups privately admit that the sectarian balance has changed. It is confirmed by the 1971 survey done by the Family Planning Association of Lebanon, that the Shiites, who comprised the third largest community in 1932, have had a much higher fertility rate than other groups, and are probably now the most numerous. Moreover, the slight preponderance of Christians in the 1932 census has very likely given way to a Muslim majority because of differential rates of fertility and emigration. For a variety of reasons, little active pressure exists presently to reform the Lebanese political formula. Maronite and Sunni politicians realize that both might lose under a new formula, and they act in concert to some extent to preserve the present order. Shiite reticence reflects their low level of political consciousness and the awareness of some Shiite leaders that demands for a new census and a reallocation of political offices based on the census results could engender political instability. Despite the imbalance in favor of the Christians, the political system has achieved some legitimacy from all sections of the population. Nevertheless, rigidity in the face of uneven sectarian population growth may bring problems in the future.

An issue central to the evaluation of the Lebanese approach is whether the explicit recognition of confessional groups and their incorporation into the political system has strengthened sectarian identity at the expense of national unity. Lebanese critics of their own political system often claim that this is one of its major deficiencies. Kwame Nkrumah also believed that any compromise with ethnicity in the form of according it a place in the Ghanaian political system would hinder the growth of national consciousness. Evidence does not now exist to refute this assumption conclusively or to affirm it. Unless Lebanon adopted a closed political system which attempted to repress political competition in any form, sectarianism would assert itself even if it were not explicitly incorporated as a building block of the system. By according legitimacy to communal interests, the present political system brings sectarian competition into the open while containing it within manageable limits. A political system that forced confessionally oriented political actors to camouflage their real concerns and to operate behind the scenes would probably suffer from greater conflict and instability. The Lebanese political order may freeze the confessional frame of reference for posterity, but it is a restrained and tolerant form of communalism. Moreover, as Charles Rizk has advised, "Pour surmonter un obstacle, il faut le reconnaitre. Pour transcender le confessionalisme, la seule attitude virile et constructive consiste à l'accepter. C'est déjà le demystifier."[7]

Although the Lebanese political system may reinforce confessional groups, this does not mean that it inhibits the development of national loyalty or national consciousness. As we have said before, communalism and national identity should not be considered as two conflicting and irreconcilable allegiances. National accommodation does not necessitate the weakening of communal attachments. By according sectarian groups security, the Lebanese political system has facilitated the growth of a sense of national citizenship and attachment to the system. The refusal or inability of Lebanese policy-makers to engage more actively in promoting national cohesion partially accounts for some critics' belief that the confessional political arrangements retard the development of national consciousness. Our theme has been that Lebanon's confessional system does not preclude greater efforts to instill a sense of national identity and shared values, and that the National Pact is compatible with measures that go beyond balance to unity in diversity.

In assessing the costs and benefits of Ghana's approach to ethnic pluralism, it is necessary to distinguish between Nkrumah's efforts to eliminate ethnic distinctions in favor of integration and the benign neglect or active exploitation of ethnicity by his successors. All of these have had a common tendency to underestimate the strength of ethnic ties and their impact on the political system. Of Ghana's regimes, the CPP government under Nkrumah, more than any other government, kept ethnic conflict and resultant tensions to a minimum. There were, however, two different facets to the policies Nkrumah employed to bring about relative peace among Ghana's constituent ethnic groups. To some extent he defused the ethnic tensions that had riddled the preindependence political system by attempting to infuse a national perspective into all political actors and by endorsing some programs designed to instill a greater national perspective. The other side of his war against ethnicity, though, inflicted great costs on the political system. By creating a one-party state and putting many of his opponents in preventive detention, Nkrumah eliminated open ethnic competition, but at the expense of many political freedoms. Nkrumah did not succeed in instilling national consciousness as much as he refused to countenance expressions of ethnic identity. Nkrumahism did not change people's beliefs and their hierarchy of loyalties to the extent that Nkrumah believed that he had. Once open political competition was restored, communalism reemerged just as strong as ever.

One of the major instruments of Nkrumah's approach, the one-party state, has been adopted by many other African states for most of the same reasons that it appealed to Nkrumah. Other African leaders have also hoped that the elimination of opposition and the discipline of a political party with a national orientation and developmental objectives would increase the prospects for national unity in their country. They have assumed that open political competition would exacerbate ethnic tension and would subvert the prospects for rapid economic development. These fears do have considerable validity. Certainly, Ghana's experiences under parliamentary democracy do not inspire confidence. The point is, however, that it is wrong to perceive the monolithic one-party state or untrammelled ethnic competition as the only two alternatives available. Moreover, any political system in a plural society that does not allow for the expression of communal interests will have to resort to the use of repression. Preventative detention, the absence of freedom of expression, a controlled press, and the lack of real political participation are not conducive to the growth of national loyalty any more than unrestrained ethnic competition. Hence, the one-party states in Africa that have retained support tend to be regimes like the Ivory Coast, which engage in careful ethnic arithmetic in the composition of governing councils and the allocation of amenities, and regimes such as Tanzania, which allow a measure of genuine participation.

In theory, national accommodation can be achieved in a one-party system or in a military regime just as well as in a parliamentary democracy. What matters more than the form of the political system is the incorporation of meaningful communal representation, an awareness of the implications of policies for communal relations, and an active effort to instill loyalty to the national community over existing networks of particularistic loyalties. In Ghana, as elsewhere in similar circumstances, though, when governors do not have to account for their actions to the populace via elections, they have often forgotten the requirements of the disparate communal groups in their society, failing to distribute political offices and amenities equitably. Moreover, politicians faced with active constituencies more frequently develop the skills necessary to moderate and conciliate conflicting demands.

To keep communal competition within manageable limits, a parliamentary democracy needs more institutional safeguards than the Ghanaian systems have adopted. The winner-take-all ethos that characterizes the Westminster model does not suit many plural societies because it almost assuredly means that some communal groups will be in power at the expense of others. In Ghana, as in other new states, politicians have manifestly lacked the self-restraint that is so much a part of the British system of government, and government and opposition soon turn into an entrenched in-group and a permanent out-group. In a system in which ideology, class, occupation, or other associational interests bind voters to political parties, each regime will have a national perspective. Such cannot be assured in a communally fragmented system, and the temptation will always be there, as it was for the Progress Party, to treat communal groups that supported the opposition vindictively. Moreover, even if the administration makes an effort to share resources equitably, it will have a difficult time gaining the confidence of communal groups represented by opposition members of parliament. For these reasons a coalition government based on an established formula for distributing key positions proportionately among the constituent communities seems far preferable.

IMPLICATIONS FOR OTHER PLURAL SOCIETIES

The experiences of Lebanon and Ghana attest to the strength and tenacity of communal affiliations in plural political systems. Communal concerns will almost assuredly continue to significantly influence the social and political processes of communally fragmented countries for years to come. Since communalism rests on man's fundamental needs for identity and security, it will resist efforts to be eradicated. Moreover, many contemporary social, economic, and political conditions tend to enhance the relevance of communal attachments in both new and more established systems. Attempting to hide or to deny the existence of communal identities merely postpones the day when the problems posed by communalism can come to be managed more successfully. Communal political competition reflects real interests based on meaningful societal divisions that have just as much legitimacy as the class, ideological, and associational bonds that social scientists and policy-makers often consider more modern and therefore proper to espouse.

Assimilation of communal groups into a common nationality through the elimination of communal loyalties does not seem to be feasible or completely desirable. Some individuals may transcend their communal attachments, but such communal blindness cannot be expected of the mass of people. Even a political system as developed as the Soviet Union's, which has had the resources and the willingness to engage in repression and radical social engineering, has not succeeded in erasing the communal frame of reference. The lower capabilities of transitional political systems foreclose the systematic application of the same techniques the Soviet Union has employed without complete success. Furthermore, many aspects of this strategy (e.g., suppression of the opposition and restrictions on personal and civil liberties) are repugnant, whether they are practiced by a new country like Ghana or a more established one like the Soviet Union.

Political systems do not stand helpless before the specter of destructive communal confrontation. As the Lebanese experience shows, it is possible to manage communal competition and to reduce tensions even in a society with deep communal divisions. A political system that recognizes the legitimacy of communal interests and incorporates communal groups in a meaningful manner has a far better opportunity to effect moderation and conciliation than one that refuses to come to terms with communal political actors. This acceptance of the legitimacy of communal attachments constitutes the first step toward the achievement of national accommodation.

National accommodation depends equally on the willingness to undertake programs and to pursue policies that strengthen the bonds of the national community. By fostering a sense of national citizenship and loyalty to the political system, plural states ensure that unity will not be lost in diversity. The conciliation of communal entities by according them a role in the political system and with it the security that enables them to recognize the needs of others, and the inculcation of a common perspective beyond the more particularistic frame of reference, both comprise essential dimensions of a successful strategy of national accommodation. Conciliation of communal entities and inculcation of common bonds complement each other.

We have mentioned several ways that the political system may facilitate the search for national accommodation. A democracy that allows for communal competition at the same time that it moderates it has the best chance of bringing skilled political managers to the fore and of evolving procedures for conciliating conflicting communal interests and demands. Along with abstaining from action that may upset the communal balance, the government has several mechanisms available to it to foster attachment to the national community. Equality of opportunity, balanced regional growth, and compensatory programs to reduce existing disparities—all help to provide the economic foundations for national accommodation. A language policy that promotes knowledge and use of a lingua franca helps compensate for the linguistic fragmentation from which many plural societies suffer. The reform of the educational system to establish greater uniformity; to substitute a social studies curriculum more able to instill tolerance, an appreciation for the diversity of cultures within the state, and a national perspective; and to introduce communal mixing at least at some levels of schooling would make a considerable contribution. Carefully devised cultural programs and use of the mass media may also provide instruments for stimulating greater unity.

Beyond these institutional and policy approaches to national accommodation, the will to live together and to make the system work constitute essential ingredients. No formulae for sharing power and no structural arrangements can compensate for the absence of the subjective requirement that the constituent groups want to be part of the same political system. The confessional distribution of offices is only one aspect of the success of the Lebanese experience. The system rests primarily on shared understandings and on unwritten agreements that cannot function without the existence of a solid psychological basis of support—the kind of sentiment that permits democracy to function in Great Britain. As the Lebanese have themselves perceived, dialogue, moderation, reason, and tolerance must pervade the system.

In many plural societies, the population neither has the same spirit of reconciliation and compromise as does Lebanon nor does it have strong feelings against the integrity of the political system. In these countries the adoption of the institutional arrangements and policy directives outlined above can prevent the drift toward irreconcilability. Once the constituent communal groups develop the kind of antipathy that characterized Bengalis and West Pakistanis, no political structure or formulae can bridge the immense gap between them. The disintegration of Pakistan stands as testimony to the fact that the search for national accommodation must be viewed as an urgent task if the chances of success are not to be lost forever.

NOTES

1. Although no figures exist for Lebanon comparable to the 1960 Ghanaian census tables on rates of communal intermarriage, as mentioned in Chapter 3 the Catholic Church reported that approximately 9 percent of all marriages it performed in 1971 were intersectarian. This

rate probably represents recent increases. During the thirteen years since the 1960 Ghanaian census data was compiled, the rate of ethnic intermarriages in Ghana has probably increased also.

2. Ghassan Tueni, *L'Orient-Le Jour*, Supplement, March 13–19, 1971, p. xiv.

3. Arend Lijphart, *The Politics of Accommodation: Pluralism and Democracy in the Nether-lands* (Berkeley: University of California Press, 1968).

4. It should be remembered that the Ghanaians employ the figure of 5000 as the urban/rural baseline and the Lebanese use 10,000. Even so, the figure for Lebanon is twice that for Ghana.

5. Ali A. Mazrui, *Cultural Engineering and Nation-Building in East Africa* (Evanston, Ill.: Northwestern University Press, 1972), p. 285.

6. Maurice Duverger, "Chehab, l'homme et le système," *L'Orient-Le Jour*, April 29, 1973, pp. 1, 3. "Lebanon's fundamental problem, both now and in the future, is social. It is necessary to establish in Lebanon a social equilibrium which does not currently exist. . . . Only the establishment of social justice can assure Lebanon of a true equilibrium. The pact among the communities constitutes another element of this equilibrium: but this element has become less important than social justice."

7. Charles Rizk, *L'Orient*, October 2, 1966, p. 6. "To surmount an obstacle, one must recognize it. To transcend confessionalism, the only manly and constructive attitude is to accept it. That already demystifies it."

Appendix on
Survey Methodology

We are acutely aware of the shortcomings of survey research: respondents may give answers intended to please the interviewer; except under the most ideal circumstances, it is impossible to attain a completely randomized sample; and responses can be influenced by the sociopolitical circumstances prevailing at the moment the interview is conducted. In Africa and the Middle East the researcher faces the added problems of translation and comparability of terminology and concepts in different languages.

Nevertheless, systematically posing the same questions to a wide range and large numbers of respondents imposes a healthy discipline upon the researcher. Although the difficulties of undertaking survey research in foreign cultures are considerable, their significance for the American researcher is very likely greater. Working in a relatively unfamiliar setting and using other methodological approaches, it is easy to end up gathering information from too narrow a spectrum of the population. Moreover, we have been uniformly impressed by the preparedness of respondents in Lebanon and Ghana to agree to be interviewed and to cooperate with interviewers.

During the period of our research in these two countries we conducted five different surveys and we cooperated with the Ghana Ministry of Education in conducting an additional survey. The various approaches employed for the survey were dictated by circumstances and the kinds of data we needed to amass. Each questionnaire used was pretested and revised following pretesting. The other aspects of the methodology employed for each survey are detailed below.

LEBANESE ADULT SURVEY

This survey entailed individual interviews with a carefully stratified sample of one thousand adult Lebanese during July and August 1972. We tried to assure a roughly representative distribution of the sample in terms of age, religious identity, region of residence, size of community, and socioeconomic status. As a reflection of the relative importance of men and women in Lebanese political life, we constituted the sample to consist of 76 percent males and 24 percent females. All sample members were over the age of twenty, and half were between twenty and forty years old and the remaining half were forty one years or more. Of the sample members, 30 percent lived in cities with populations above 100,000, 45 percent lived in towns with populations between 10,000 and 100,000, and the remaining 25 percent lived in rural communities of less than 10,000. Because of the delicate political situation prevailing at the time in the South, all the sample members were selected from among those residing in Lebanon's remaining four *mohafazats*. Twenty five percent lived in the North, 25 percent in Mount Lebanon, 30 percent in Beirut and its suburbs, and the remaining 20 percent in Bekaa. In terms of socioeconomic status, the interviewers ranked 19 percent of the sample members as being upper class, 61 percent as being middle class, and 19 percent as being lower class. However, using such other indices as education and occupation, our sample tended to be somewhat skewed toward the upper ranges. For instance, estimates for the total adult population of Lebanon indicate that 70 percent have attended school, but 88 percent of our sample had attended school. The actual discrepancy is probably not as great because our sample was confined to Lebanese citizens, while estimates of educational level for the total population of Lebanon include many immigrants who tend to have less education. In terms of religious identity, our sample contained 60 percent Christians and 40 percent Muslim, while the Lebanese figures are closer to half and half. This discrepancy arose from our inability to interview in the South, which is predominantly Muslim.

The interviewing was conducted orally and in Arabic, and each interview took an average of forty five minutes. Our ten interviewers were university students from the social science faculties of two universities: eight from the Lebanese University and two from the American University of Beirut. Five of the interviewers were Muslim and five were Christian. Each interviewer interviewed fifty persons in each of two different localities assigned to him. The localities were selected on the basis of the following criteria: (1) geographic location, (2) population size, (3) religious identities of inhabitants, and (4) ecological setting. The interviewer was instructed to interview in each locality six women between the ages of twenty and forty and six women forty one or over; nineteen men between the ages of twenty and forty and nineteen men forty one years or over. Moreover, his selection of sample members in the designated locality had to roughly reflect the confessional composition of the community and the distribution of that community's population among the major socioeconomic strata. Only about 5 percent of those selected to be sample members refused to be interviewed. Of those interviewed, the interviewers rated 93 percent as being either "cooperative" or "very cooperative." The seventy five questions included in each interview included both open-ended questions and fixed alternative questions.

LEBANESE STUDENT SURVEY

This survey involved administering written questionnaires to intermediate and secondary students. The questionnaire consisted of fifty one items, all of them fixed alternative questions. The questionnaire was translated into Arabic and French; the version selected for use in a particular school depended upon the relative levels of competence of the students in written Arabic and French. The testing was done in March and April 1973 in six selected private schools, five of which were in Beirut and one in Mount Lebanon. The questionnaires were administered in selected classrooms in first and second year intermediate levels, and first year, second year, and third year of secondary. Of the questionnaires completed in each of these grades, one hundred were selected from each grade by random methods for inclusion in the sample (five of these questionnaires were incomplete and had to be discarded). The final sample therefore consisted of 495 students distributed equally among the five grades. Of this group, 288 were Christians and 207 Muslims; 331 were boys and 164 were girls.

FIRST GHANA SURVEY
(PRIMARY AND SECONDARY STUDENTS)

During 1970–1971 the authors, with the aid of a graduate research assistant, did field work in five rural communities in Ghana: Komenda, a Fanti town in the Western Region; Akropong, an Ashanti community in the Ashanti Region; Agotime Kpetoe, an Ewe town in the Volta Region; Oyibi, a Ga village in the hinterland of the Greater Accra area; and Tongo, a Tallensi village in the Upper Region. The five villages thus represented the five major generic ethnic groupings in Ghana. According to the results of the 1960 census, about half of the population of Ghana lived in small villages or dispersed homesteads of less than one thousand people. Two of the communities, Tongo (population 231) and Oyibi (population 518) fit this category with a third, Akropong (population 1098), being slightly larger. Another fourth of the population in 1960 resided in large villages of between 1000 and 5000. Agotime Kpetoe (population 3021) and Komenda (population 4261) fit into this grouping.

A questionnaire of forty seven (mostly open-ended) items was administered after a period of key informant interviewing to a sample of sixty children in each of the five communities, making a total of three hundred participants. Ten students were randomly selected from each of the following classes: primary five, primary six, middle form one (equivalent to junior high school), middle form two, middle form three, and middle form four. The interviewing was done orally in the child's mother tongue. A single version of the questionnaire was employed in each of the six classes, but the final question, which dealt with traditional history, was specially prepared for each local situation and consequently differed for each of the five communities.

SECOND GHANA SURVEY
(UNIVERSITY STUDENTS)

This survey, conducted in 1970, involved a sample of 148 university students chosen randomly from residence hall lists at the University of Ghana. The questionnaire, which was administered in written form, contained eighty six items and was written in English. Most of the questions were open-ended. The questions covered much of the same ground as the first Ghana survey. The students completed the questionnaires individually in their place of residence.

THIRD GHANA SURVEY
(UNIVERSITY STUDENTS)

This survey entailed the administration of a written questionnaire to selected classes at the University of Ghana and Cape Coast University. A total of 175 students completed the questionnaires, under the supervision of their classroom professors. The fifty one open-end questions, which were presented in English, sought to elicit intellectual biographies for each respondent with a view toward learning more about the agents of socialization and their relative impact.

GHANA MINISTRY OF EDUCATION SURVEY

The authors and Professor Lynn Fischer of Cape Coast University and Northwestern University worked with officials of the Ministry of Education (primarily Walter Blege) to prepare and conduct this survey, and to analyze the results. Thirty eight education officers of the Ministry of Education administered a questionnaire orally at preselected schools during the last two weeks of January 1972. These interviewers had previously been trained at a briefing session and a workshop on survey interviewing. Each primary and middle school student was interviewed individually in his mother tongue, which meant that the questionnaire was translated into seven different Ghanaian languages, a task undertaken by the Ghana Institute of Languages. Secondary school students were presented with an English version of the questionnaire in written form and they responded to the questions in writing. Most of the eighty items on the questionnaire were open-ended.

The schools where interviewing was done were selected in the following fashion: a primary. middle, and secondary school were randomly selected in the largest urban center of each of Ghana's nine regions. A rural district was randomly selected within each region as well, and then a primary, middle, and secondary school were randomly selected within that district. Thus, nine urban centers and nine rural districts were covered. In order to have a roughly equal distribution of the sexes, whenever a selected school restricted its admissions to one sex, a companion school for the opposite sex within that geographical unit was also picked. Thus students were interviewed in a total of sixty schools. Interviewers followed a quota plan to insure that approximately equal numbers of students would be sampled from each grade within each school. In addition, they employed random methods to select respondents within each grade. The total sample consisted of 1757 respondents, of which 1040 were distributed almost equally among six grades of primary school, 359 distributed among four grades of intermediate school, and 358 among five grades of secondary school.

Bibliography

BOOKS

Abou, Sélim. *Le Bilinguisme Arabe-Francais au Liban: Essai d'Anthropologie Culturelle*. Paris: Presses Universitaires de France, 1962.
Acheampong, I. K. *Speeches and Interviews*. I. Accra: Ghana Publishing Corp., 1973.
Afrifa, A. A. *The Ghana Coup*. London: Frank Cass and Co., 1967.
Agwani, M. S. *The Lebanese Crisis, 1958*. London: Asia Publishing House, 1965.
Almond, Gabriel A., and Bingham G. Powell, Jr. *Comparative Politics: A Developmental Approach*. Boston: Little, Brown and Co., 1966.
———, and Sidney Verba. *The Civic Culture: Political Attitudes and Democracy in Five Nations*. Princeton, N. J.: Princeton University Press, 1963.
Antonius, George. *The Arab Awakening*. London: Hamish Hamilton, 1938.
Apter, David E. *Ghana in Transition*. New York: Atheneum, 1963.
——— *The Politics of Modernization*. Chicago: University of Chicago Press, 1965.
Attwater, Donald. *The Christian Churches of the East, Vol. I, Churches in Communion with Rome*. London: G. Chapman, 1961.
Austin, Dennis. *Politics in Ghana, 1946–1960*. London: Oxford University Press, 1964.
Barker, Peter. *Operation Cold Chop*. Accra: Ghana Publishing Corp., 1969.

Bell, Daniel. *The End of Ideology: On the Exhaustion of Political Ideas in the Fifties.* Glencoe, Ill.: Free Press, 1960.

Binder, Leonard. (ed.). *Politics in Lebanon.* New York: John Wiley & Sons, Inc., 1966.

Bourret, F. M. *Ghana: The Road to Independence, 1919–1957.* London: Oxford University Press, 1960.

Braimah, J. A. *The Two Isanwurfos.* London: Longmans, 1967.

Bretton, Henry. *The Rise and Fall of Kwame Nkrumah: A Study of Personal Rule in Africa.* New York: Frederick A. Praeger, 1966.

Brokensha, David. *Social Change at Larteh, Ghana.* Oxford: The Clarendon Press, 1966.

Brown, Godfrey N. *An Active History of Ghana, Book Two—Since 1844.* London: George Allen and Unwin Ltd., 1964.

———, and Philip M. Amonoo. *An Active History of Ghana, Book One—From Earliest Time to 1844.* London: George Allen and Unwin Ltd., 1961.

Buah, F. K. *An Elementary History for Schools, Book One.* London: Macmillan and Co., Ltd., 1st ed. 1963, 2nd ed. 1967.

———. *History for Ghanaian Schools, Book Two.* London: Macmillan and Co. Ltd., 1964.

———. *An Elementary History for Schools, Book Three, Africa and Europe.* London: Macmillan and Co. Ltd., 1966.

———. *An Elementary History for Schools, Book Four, Ghana and Europe.* London: Macmillan and Co. Ltd., 1st Ed. 1963, 2nd Ed. 1967.

———. *An Elementary History for Schools, Book Five, New Ghana.* London: Macmillan and Co. Ltd., 1968.

Bunting, J. R. *Civics For Self-Government.* London: Evans Brothers Ltd., 1959.

Busia, K. A. *Africa in Search of Democracy.* London: Routledge and Kegan Paul, 1967.

———. *The Position of the Chief in the Modern Political System of Ashanti: A Study of the Influence of Contemporary Social Changes on Ashanti Political Institutions.* London: Oxford University Press, 1951.

Bustani, Emile. *March Arabesque.* London: Robert Hale, 1961.

Caldwell, John. *African Rural–Urban Migration.* Canberra: Australian National University Press, 1969.

Cardinall, A. W. *The Natives of the Northern Territories of the Gold Coast.* London: George Routledge and Sons, 1920.

Catala, Pierre, and André Gervais. eds. *Le Droit Libanais.* Paris: Librairie Générale de Droit et de Jurisprudence, 1963.

Charmes, Gabriel. *Voyage en Syrie: Impressions et Souvenirs.* Paris: Levy, 1891.

Chamoun, Camille. *Crise au Moyen-Orient.* Paris: Gallimard, 1963.

Chevalier, Dominique. *La Société du Mont Liban a l'Epoque de la Révolution Industrielle en Europe.* Paris: Librairie Orientaliste P. Geuther, 1971.

Chiha, Michel. *Politique Intérieure.* Beirut: Trident, 1964.

Christensen, James Boyd. *Double-Descent Among the Fanti.* New Haven: Human Relations Area Files, 1954.

Churchill, Charles. *The Druzes and the Maronites Under Turkish Rule from 1840–1860.* London: Bernard Quarith, 1862.

Cohen, Abner. *Custom and Politics in Urban Africa: A Study of The Hausa Migrants in Yoruba Towns.* Berkeley and Los Angeles: University of California Press, 1969.

Cohn, Helen Desfosses. *Soviet Policy Toward Black Africa: The Focus on National Integration.* New York: Praeger, 1972.

Corm, Georges G. *Contribution à L'Etude des Sociétés Multi-Confessionnelles.* Paris: Librairie Générale de Droit et de Jurisprudence, 1971.

Daaku, Kwame Yeboa. *Trade and Politics on the Gold Coast, 1600–1720.* London: Oxford University Press, 1970.

Dahl, Robert A. *Polyarchy: Participation and Opposition.* New Haven: Yale University Press, 1971.

Davidson, Basil. *Black Star: A View of the Life and Times of Kwame Nkrumah.* London: Allen Lane, 1973.

Dawson, Richard E., and Kenneth Prewitt. *Political Socialization.* Boston: Little, Brown and Co., 1969.

Deutsch, Karl W., et. al. *Political Community in the North Atlantic Area: International Organization in the Light of Recent Experience.* Princeton, New Jersey: Princeton University Press, 1957.

Development Studies Association. *Lubnān wa'l- 'Amal al-Fidā'ī al-Filasṭīnī (Lebanon and the Palestinian Guerillas).* Beirut: Nadwat al-Dirāsāt al-Inmā'iyya, 1969.

Devolve, Pierre. *L'Administration Libanaise.* Paris: Institut International d'Administration Publique, 1971.

Dibs, Joseph. *Perpétuelle Orthodoxie des Maronites.* trans. by Vazuex. Beirut: Imprimerie Moderne d'Arras, 1896.

Dib, Pierre. *History of the Maronite Church.* trans. by Seely Begianni. Beirut: Imprimerie Catholique, 1971.

Dickson, Kwamina B. *A Historical Geography of Ghana.* Cambridge: Cambridge University Press, 1969.

Dunn, John and A. F. Robertson. *Dependence and Opportunity: Political Change in Ahafo.* Cambridge: Cambridge University Press, 1973.

Easton, David, and Jack Dennis. *Children in the Political System: Origins of Political Legitimacy.* New York: McGraw-Hill Book Co., 1969.

Emerson, Rupert. *From Empire to Nation.* Cambridge: Harvard University Press, 1960.

Encyclopedia of Religion and Ethics. VI. New York: Charles Scribners, 1955.

Enloe, Cynthia. *Ethnic Conflict and Political Development.* Boston: Little, Brown and Co., 1973.

Esman, Milton. *Administration and Development in Malaysia: Institution Building and Reform in a Plural Society.* Ithaca, N. Y.: Cornell University Press, 1972.

Fage, J. D. *Ghana: A Historical Interpretation.* Madison: University of Wisconsin Press, 1959.

Fallers, Lloyd. *The Social Anthropology of the Nation-State.* Chicago: Aldine, 1974.

Field, M. J. *Akim-Kotoku: An Oman of the Gold Coast.* London: The Crown Agents for the Colonies, 1948.

———— *Religion and Medicine of the Ga People.* London: Oxford University Press, 1961.

Finlay, David J., Ole R. Holsti, and Richard R. Fagen. *Enemies in Politics.* Chicago: Rand McNally & Co., 1967.

First, Ruth. *The Barrel of a Gun.* London: The Penguin Press, 1970.

Fitch, Bob, and Mary Oppenheimer. *Ghana: End of an Illusion.* New York: Monthly Review Press, 1966.

Forde, Enid R. *The Population of Ghana.* Evanston: Northwestern Studies in Geography, No. 15, 1968.

Fortes, Meyer. *The Dynamics of Clanship Among the Tallensi.* London: Oxford University Press, 1945.

———— *The Web of Kinship Among the Tallensi.* London: Oxford University Press, 1949.

Fortescue, Adrian. *The Uniate Eastern Churches.* 2nd Ed. New York: Ungar, 1957.

Foster, Philip. *Education and Social Change in Ghana.* London: Routledge and Kegan Paul, 1965.

Fuller, Anne H. *Buarij: Portrait of a Lebanese Muslim Village.* Cambridge, Mass.: Harvard University Press, 1961.

Furnivall, J. S. *Colonial Policy and Practice.* London: Cambridge University Press, 1948.

Fynn, J. K. *Asante and Its Neighbours 1700–1807.* Evanston: Northwestern University Press, 1971.

Gemayel, Pierre. *Connaissance des Kataeb.* Beyrouth: n.p., 1948.

Glazer, Nathan and Daniel P. Moynihan. *Beyond the Melting Pot: The Negroes, Puerto-Ricans, Jews, Italians, and Irish of New York City.* Cambridge: Massachusetts Institute of Technology Press, 1963.

Goody, J. R. *The Social Organization of the LoWilli.* London: HMSO, Colonial Research Studies, No. 19, 1956.

Grassmuck, George and Kamal Salibi. *Reformed Administration in Lebanon.* Beirut: American University of Beirut, 1964.

Greenstein, Fred I. *Children and Politics.* New Haven, Conn.: Yale University Press, 1965.

Gulick, John. *Social Structure and Cultural Change in a Lebanese Village.* New York: Wenner-Gren Foundation, 1955.

———— *Tripoli, A Modern Arab City.* Cambridge, Mass.: Harvard University Press, 1967.

Gutteridge, William. *Armed Forces in New States.* London: Oxford University Press, 1962.

Haddad, George. *Fifty Years of Modern Syria and Lebanon.* Beirut: Dar al-Hayat, 1950.

Haddad, Robert M. *Syrian Christians in Muslim Society.* Princeton, N.J.: Princeton University Press, 1970.

Ḥaqqī, Ismāʿil. *Lubnān Mabāḥith ʿIlmiyyah wa-ʾIjtimāʿiyyah. (Lebanon's Scientific and Social Research).* Beirut: Al-Maṭbaʿat al-ʿArabiyyah, 1969.

Harfouche, Jamal K. *Social Structure of Low-Income Families in Lebanon.* Beirut: Khayats, 1965.

Harik, Iliya. *Man Yahkum Lubnān. (Who Rules Lebanon).* Beirut: Al-Nahār, 1972.

———. *Politics and Change in a Traditional Society: Lebanon, 1711—1845.* Princeton, N.J.: Princeton University Press, 1968.

Al-Ḥasan, Ḥasan, *Al-Qanūn al-Dustūrī fī Lubnān (Constitutional Law and the Constitution in Lebanon).* Beirut: Dār Maktabat al-Ḥayāt, 1963.

Ḥaydar, Aḥmad Muṣṭafā. *Al-Dawlat al-Lubnāniyyah 1920–1953 (The Lebanese State, 1920–1953).* Beirut: Al-Najma Press, 1954.

Harvey, William Burnett. *Law and Social Change in Ghana.* Princeton, N.J.: Princeton University Press, 1966.

Hess, Robert D., and Judith V. Torney. *The Development of Political Attitudes in Children.* Garden City, N.Y.: Doubleday and Co. Inc., 1968.

Higham, C. S. S. *Landmarks of World History.* London: Longmans, Green and Co. Ltd., 1947.

Hill, Polly. *The Occupations of Migrants in Ghana.* Ann Arbor, Mich.: University of Michigan, Museum of Anthropology, Anthropological Papers, 1970.

Hitti, Philip K. *Lebanon in History.* New York: St. Martin's Press, 1967.

Holland, T. E. *The European Concert in the Eastern Question.* London: Oxford University Press, 1885.

Hourani, Albert. *Arabic Thought in the Liberal Age, 1798–1939.* London: Oxford University Press, 1962.

———. *Syria and Lebanon.* London: Oxford University Press, 1946.

———. *A Vision of History: Near Eastern And Other Essays.* Beirut: Khayats, 1961.

Hudson, Michael C. *The Precarious Republic: Political Modernization in Lebanon.* New York: Random House, 1968.

Iskandar, Adnan G. *Bureaucracy in Lebanon.* Beirut: American University of Beirut, 1964.

Jouplain, M. *La Question du Liban.* Paris: Arthur Rousseau, 1908.

Jumblatt, Kamal. *Fī-Majrā al-Siyāsat al-Lubnāniyyah Awḍā'a wa-Takhṭīṭ (In the Course of Lebanese Politics, Situations and Plans).* Beirut: Dar-al-Tali'a, 1960.

———. *Haqīqat al-Thawrat al-Lubnāniyyah (The Truth About the Lebanese Revolution).* Beirut: Dar al-Nashir al-'Arabiyya, 1959.

Kerr, Malcolm. *Lebanon in the Last Years of Feudalism, 1840–1868: A Contemporary Account by Anṭūn Ḍāhir al-'Aqīqī.* Beirut: American University of Beirut, 1959.

Khalaf, Samir, and Per Kongstadt. *Hamra of Beirut: A Case of Rapid Urbanization.* Leiden: E. J. Brill, 1973.

Khatir, Lahad. *Ahd al-Muta ṣarrifīn fī Lubnān 1861–1918 (The Mandate Era in Lebanon, 1861–1918).* Beirut: Al-Jāmi'at al-Lubnāniyyah, Qism al-Dirāsāt al-Tarīkhiyyah, 1967.

Al-Khouri, Bishara. *Ḥaqā'iq Lubnāniyyah. (Lebanese Truths).* Vol. 3. Harissa: Basil Brothers Press, 1961.

Kimble, David. *A Political History of Ghana.* Oxford: Clarendon Press, 1963.

Kothari, Rajni. *Politics in India.* Boston: Little, Brown and Co., 1970.

Koury, Enver M. *The Operational Capability of the Lebanese Political System.* Beirut: Catholic Press, 1972.

Langton, Kenneth P. *Political Socialization.* New York: Oxford University Press, 1969.

Lewis, W. Arthur. *Politics in West Africa.* London: George Allen and Unwin Ltd., 1965.

Lijphart, Arend. *The Politics of Accommodation: Pluralism and Democracy in the Netherlands.* Berkeley: University of California Press, 1968.

Longrigg, Stephen Hemsley. *Syria and Lebanon Under French Mandate.* Beirut: Librairie du Liban, 1958.

Mahmassani, Maher, and Ibtissam Messarra. *Statut Personnel: Textes en Vigueur au Liban.* Beyrouth: Faculté de Droit et de Sciences Economiques, 1970.

Manoukian, Madeline. *The Ewe-Speaking People of Togoland and the Gold Coast.* London: International African Institute, 1952.

———— *Tribes of the Northern Territories of the Gold Coast.* London: International African Institute, 1951.

Maté, C. M. O. *A Visual History of Ghana.* 2nd Ed. London: Evans Brothers, Ltd., 1968.

Mazrui, Ali A. *Cultural Engineering and Nation-Building in East Africa.* Evanston, Ill.: Northwestern University Press, 1972.

Meo, Leila M. T. *Lebanon: Improbable Nation.* Bloomington: University of Indiana Press, 1965.

Meyerowitz, Eva L. R. *The Akan of Ghana.* London: Faber and Faber, 1958.

Mughaizil, Joseph. *Lubnān wa'l-Qaḍiyyat al-'Arabiyyah. (Lebanon and the Arab Problem).* Beirut: Manshūrāt, 'Awaydat, 1959.

Murphy, Robert. *Diplomat Among Warriors.* London: Collins, 1964.

Morrison, Donald G., Robert C. Mitchell, John H. Paden, and Hugh M. Stevenson. *Black Africa: A Comparative Handbook.* New York: Free Press, 1972.

Nantet, Jacques. *Histoire du Liban.* Paris: Les Editions de Minuit, 1963.

Nkrumah, Kwame. *Dark Days in Ghana.* New York: International Publishers, 1968.

———— *Ghana, The Autobiography of Kwame Nkrumah.* Edinburgh: Thomas Nelson & Sons, 1959.

———— *I Speak of Freedom.* New York: Frederick A. Praeger, 1961.

———— *Towards Colonial Freedom.* London: William Heinemann, Ltd., 1962.

Nordlinger, Eric A. *Conflict Resolution in Divided Societies.* Cambridge, Mass.: Harvard University, Center for International Affairs, Occasional Papers in International Affairs, No. 29, January 1972.

Nukunya, G. K. *Kinship and Marriage Among the Anlo Ewe.* London: The Athlone Press, 1969.

Ocran, A. K. *A Myth is Broken.* Accra: Longmans, Green & Co., 1968.

Ofosu-Appiah, L. H. *The Life of Lt. General Kotoka.* Accra: Waterville Publishing House, 1972.

Opoku, A. A. *Festivals of Ghana.* Accra: Ghana Publishing Corp., 1970.

Owusu, Maxwell. *Uses and Abuses of Political Power: A Case Study of Continuity and*

Change in the Politics of Ghana. Chicago: University of Chicago Press, 1970.

Patai, Raphael. *The Republic of Lebanon*. New Haven, Conn.: Human Relations Area Files, 1956.

Peil, Margaret. *The Ghanaian Factory Worker: Industrial Man in Africa*. London: Cambridge University Press, 1972.

Pinkney, Robert. *Ghana Under Military Rule, 1966–1969*. London: Methuen & Co. Ltd., 1972.

Polk, William R. *The Opening of South Lebanon, 1788 – 1840*. Cambridge, Mass.: Harvard University Press, 1963.

Potts, M. I. *Makers of Civilization, Book One*. 3rd Ed. London: Longmans, Green & Co. Ltd., 1961; *Makers of Civilization, Book Two*. 2nd Ed. London: Longmans, Green & Co. Ltd., 1953.

Prator, Clifford H. *Language Teaching in the Philippines*. Manila: U.S. Education Foundation in the Philippines, 1950.

Prothro, Edwin Terry. *Child Rearing in the Lebanon*. Cambridge, Mass.: Harvard University Press, 1967.

Prothro, Edwin Terry and Nutfy Najib Diab. *Changing Family Patterns in the Arab East*. Beirut: American University of Beirut, 1974.

Qubain, Fahim I. *Crisis in Lebanon*. Washington, D.C.: Middle East Institute, 1961.

Rabbath, Edmond. *La Formation Historique du Liban Politique et Constitutionnel*. Beyrouth: Librairie Orientale, 1973.

Rabushka, Alvin, and Kenneth A. Shepsle. *Politics in Plural Societies: A Theory of Democratic Instability*. Columbus, Ohio: Charles E. Merrill Publishing Co., 1973.

Rattray, R. S. *The Tribes of the Ashanti Hinterland*. Vol. 2. Oxford: The Clarendon Press, 1932.

El-Rayyes, Riad N. and Dunnia Nahas. *Politics in Uniform: A Study of the Military in the Arab World and Israel*. Beirut: Al-Nahār Press Services, 1972.

Rizk, Charles. *Le Régime Politique Libanais*. Paris: Librairie Générale de Droit et de Jurisprudence, 1966.

Rondot, Pierre. *Les Chrétiens d'Orient*. Paris: J. Peyronnet et Cie., n.d.

———— *Les Institutions Politiques du Liban*. Paris: Institut d'Etudes D'Orient Contemporain, 1947.

Sa'ad, Ma'rūf, and Muḥammad Majdhūb. *'Indamā Qawamnā*. *(When We Resisted)*. Beirut: Dār al-'Ilm lil-Malāyīn, 1959.

Salem, Elie A. *Modernization Without Revolution: Lebanon's Experience*. Bloomington: Indiana University Press, 1973.

Salem, Jean. *Le Peuple Libanais: Essai d'Anthropologie*. Beyrouth: Librairie Samu, 1968.

Salibi, K. S. *The Modern History of Lebanon*. London: Weidenfeld and Nicholson, 1965.

Sayigh, Yusif A. *Entrepreneurs of Lebanon*. Cambridge, Mass.: Harvard University Press, 1967.

Smith, Donald E. *Religion and Political Development*. Boston: Little, Brown and Co., 1970.

Smith, M. G. *The Plural Society in the British West Indies*. Berkeley and Los Angeles: University of California Press, 1965.

Smith, Noel. *The Presbyterian Church of Ghana, 1935–1960*. Accra: Ghana Universities Press, 1966.

Smock, Audrey C. *Ibo Politics: The Role of Ethnic Unions in Eastern Nigeria*. Cambridge, Mass.: Harvard University Press, 1971.

Stewart, Desmond. *Turmoil in Beirut*. London: Allen Wingate, 1958.

Suleiman, Michael W. *Political Parties in Lebanon*. Ithaca, N.Y.: Cornell University Press, 1967.

Szereszewski, Robert. *Structural Changes in the Economy of Ghana, 1891—1911*. London: Weidenfeld and Nicholson, 1965.

Al-Ṭāʾifiyyah. *(Sectarianism)*. Beirut: al-Nahār, December 1972–January 1973.

Tordoff, William. *Ashanti Under the Prempehs, 1888–1935*. London: Oxford University Press, 1965.

Touma, Toufic. *Un Village de Montagne au Liban*. Paris: Mouton and Co., 1958.

Valin, Emile Jean-Pierre. *Le Pluralisme Socio-Scolaire au Liban*. Beyrouth: Imprimerie Catholique, 1969.

Wallerstein, I. M. *The Road to Independence: Ghana and the Ivory Coast*. Paris: Mouton, 1964.

Welch, Claude E. Jr. *Dream of Unity*. Ithaca, N.Y.: Cornell University Press, 1966.

Wilks, Ivor. *The Northern Factor in Ashanti History*. Legon: Institute of African Studies, University College of Ghana, 1961.

Williams, Judith R. *The Youth of Haouch el Harim: A Lebanese Village*. Cambridge, Mass.: Harvard University Press, 1968.

Yamak, Labib Zuwiyya. *The Syrian Social Nationalist Party: An Ideological Analysis*. Cambridge, Mass.: Harvard Middle Eastern Monographs, No. 14, 1966.

Yaukey, David. *Fertility Differences in a Modernizing Country*. Princeton, N.J.: Princeton University Press, 1971.

Al-Zaylaʿ, Naʿīm. *Shamʿūn Yatakallam*. *(Chamoun Speaks)*. Beirut: n.p., 1960.

Zeine, Zeine N. *Arab-Turkish Relations and the Emergence of Arab Nationalism*. Beirut: Khayat's, 1958.

Zolberg, Aristide. *Creating Political Order: The Party-States of West Africa*. Chicago: Rand McNally, 1966.

Zuwiyya, Jalal. *The Parliamentary Election of Lebanon, 1968*. Leiden: E. J. Brill, 1972.

ARTICLES

Abu-Laban, Baha. "Social Change and Local Politics in Sidon, Lebanon," *Journal of Developing Areas*, 5, (October 1970), 27–42.

Agbodeka, Francis. "The Fanti Confederacy, 1965–69," *Transactions of the Historical Society of Ghana*, VII (1964), 82–123.

Agyeman, D. K. "Ethnicity and Language Policy for our Schools," *Faculty of Education Bulletin*, University College of Cape Coast, I (July 1970), 11–18.

Alem, Jean-Pierre. "Troubles Insurrectionels au Liban," *Orient*, 2, No. 6 (1958), 37–47.

Ansre, Gilbert. "A Study on the Official Language of Ghana," in (n.e.) *Colloque sur le Multilinguisme* (London: CCTA, 1962).

Apter, David E. "Ghana," in James S. Coleman and Carl G. Rosberg, Jr., eds., *Political Parties and National Integration in Tropical Africa*. (Berkeley: University of California Press, 1964, 259–317.

————. "Nkrumah, Charisma, and The Coup," *Daedalus*, 97 (Summer 1968), 759–792.

Arhin, Kwame. "Diffuse Authority Among the Coastal Fanti," *Ghana Notes and Queries*, 9 (November 1966), 66–70.

Asamoa, E. A. "The Problem of Language in Education in the Gold Coast," *Africa*, XXV (January 1955), 60–78.

Austin, Dennis. "Opposition in Ghana, 1947–67," *Government and Opposition*, 2 (July-October 1967), 539–556.

Ayoub, Victor F. "Resolution of Conflict in a Lebanese Village," in Leonard Binder, ed., *Politics in Lebanon*. New York: John Wiley & Sons, Inc., 1966, 107–126.

Azrael, Jeremy R. "Patterns of Polity Directed Educational Development: The Soviet Case," in James S. Coleman, ed., *Education and Political Development*. Princeton, N.J.: Princeton University Press, 1965, 233–271.

Barakat, Halim. "Social and Political Integration in Lebanon: A Case of Social Mosaic," *Middle East Journal*, 27 (Summer 1973), 301–318.

Barth, Frederik, "Introduction," in Frederik Barth, ed., *Ethnic Groups and Boundaries: The Social Origins of Cultural Differences*. Boston: Little, Brown and Co., 1969, 9–38.

Bates, Robert H. "Ethnicity and Modernization in Contemporary Africa," Social Science Working Paper, No. 16. Pasadena, California: California Institute of Technology, 1972.

Bawarshi, Tawfiq. "The Lebanese Labour Scene," *Middle East Forum*, XXXIX (June 1963), 21–26.

Bentsi-Enchill, Kwamina. "Developments in Former British West Africa," in David T. Currie, ed., *Federalism and the New Nations of Africa*. Chicago: University of Chicago Press, 1964, 75–100.

Beresday, George L. F., and Bonnie B. Stretch, "Political Education in the U.S.A. and U.S.S.R.," *Comparative Education Review*, 7 (June 1963), 9–16.

Berry, Jack, "The Madina Project: Ghana Language Attitudes in Madina," *Research Review*, 5 (Lent Term 1969), 61–79.

————. "Problems in the Use of African Languages and Dialects in Education," in UNESCO, *African Languages and English in Education*, Educational Studies and Documents, No. 11 (Paris: Education Clearing House, June 1953).

Boahen, A. Adu. "Asante and Fante A. D. 1000–1800," in Ade Ajayi and Ian Espie, eds., *A Thousand Years of West African History* (Ibadan: Ibadan University Press, 1965).

Boulos, Jawad. "L'Influence des donées géographiques et historiques sur la personalité du Liban," *Action Proche-Orient*, XXI (Juin 1963), 17–26.

Braimah, J. A. "Opening Speech," *Report of the Conference of Civic Club Representatives March 27 to April 1, 1971*. Accra: Centre for Civic Education, 1971, 27–35.

Caldwell, J. C. "Migration and Urbanization," in Walter Birmingham, I. Neustadt, and E. N. Omaboe, A Study of Contemporary Ghana: Some Aspects of Social Structure, Vol, 2. Evanston, Ill.: Northwestern University Press, 1967, 111–146.

Card, Emily, and Barbara Callaway. "Ghanaian Politics: The Elections and After," Africa Report, 15 (March 1970), 10–15.

Chamoun, Mounir. "La Famille au Liban," Travaux et Jours, 25 (Octobre–Décembre 1967), 13–40.

Coleman, James S. "Introduction: Education and Political Development," in James S. Coleman, ed., Education and Political Development. Princeton: Princeton University Press, 1965, 3–34.

Connor, Walker. "Nation-Building or Nation-Destroying," World Politics, XXIV (April 1972), 319–335.

———— "The Politics of Ethnonationalism," Journal of International Affairs, 27 (1, 1973), 1–21.

Crow, Ralph E. "Parliament in the Lebanese Political System," in Allan Kornberg and Lloyd D. Musolf, eds., Legislatures in Developmental Perspective. Durham: Duke University Press, 1970, 273–302.

———— "Religious Sectarianism in the Lebanese Political System," Journal of Politics, 24 (August 1963), 489–520.

Daniels, W. C. Ekow. "Law Relating to Husband and Wife in Ghana," in (n.e.) Integration of Customary and Modern Legal Systems in Africa. Ife, Nigeria: University of Ife Press, 1971, 352–393.

Dekmejian, R. H. "The Arab World After Nasser," Middle East Forum, 47 (Autumn and Winter 1971), 37–46.

Deutsch, Karl W. "Social Mobilization and Political Development," American Political Science Review, LV (September 1961), 493–514.

Dib, George, "Selections from Riad Solh's Speech in the Lebanese Assembly, October 1943," Middle East Forum, 34 (January 1959), 6.

Dickson, K. B. "Development Planning and National Integration in Ghana," in David R. Smock and Kwamina Bentsi-Enchill, eds., The Search for National Integration in Africa (Forthcoming).

————. "The Middle Belt of Ghana," Bulletin de l'I.F.A.N., 31, Series B, No. 3 (1969), 689–716.

Drake, St. Clair, and Leslie Alexander Lacy. "Government Versus the Unions: The Sekondi-Takoradi Strike, 1961," in Gwendolen M. Carter, ed., Politics in Africa. New York: Harcourt, Brace & World, Inc., 1966, 67–118.

Esman, Milton. "The Management of Communal Conflict, Public Policy, 21 (Winter 1973), 49–78.

Faris, Nabih A. "The Summer of 1958," Middle East Forum, 38 (January 1961), 32.

Farsoun, Sameh K. "Family Structure and Society in Modern Lebanon," in Louise Sweet, ed., Peoples and Cultures of the Middle East, I. Garden City, N.Y.: The National History Press, 1970, 257–307.

Fischer, Lynn Frederick, "Student Orientations toward Nation-Building in Ghana," in John N. Paden, ed., *National Integration in Africa: Research Reports* (Forthcoming).

Folson, B. D. G. "Single Parties, Tribes, Totalitarianism and Federalism in West Africa," *Economic Bulletin of Ghana*, 10, No. 2 (1966), 22–38.

Fortes, Meyer, "Some Aspects of Migration and Mobility in Ghana," *Journal of Asian and African Studies*. VI (January 1971), 1–20.

"Forum Interviews Pierre Gemayel," *Middle East Forum*, 34 (March 1959), 30.

Geertz, Clifford. "The Integrative Revolution: Primordial Sentiments and Civil Politics in the New States," in Clifford Geertz, ed., *Old Societies and New States*. New York: The Free Press of Glencoe, 1963, 105–153.

Glazer, Nathan and Daniel P. Moynihan. "Why Ethnicity." *Commentary*, 58 (October 1974), 33–39.

Golins, Frank R. "Patterns of Libyan National Integration," *Middle East Journal*, 24 (Summer 1970), 338–352.

Goody, Jack. "Introduction," to J. A. Braimah, *The Two Isanwurfos*. London: Longmans, 1967.

Gubser, Peter. "The *Zuama* of Zahlah: The Current Situation in a Lebanese Town," *Middle East Journal*, 27 (Spring 1973), 173–189.

Gulick, John. "Conservatism and Change in a Lebanese Village," in Abdulla M. Lutfiyya and Charles W. Churchill, eds., *Readings in Arab Middle Eastern Societies and Cultures*. The Hague: Mouton & Co., 1970, 314–327.

Harik, Iliya. "The Ethnic Revolution and Political Integration in the Middle East," *International Journal of Middle East Studies*, 3 (July 1972), 303–323.

Hess, Clyde G. Jr., and Herbert L. Bodman Jr. "Confessionalism and Feudality in Lebanese Politics," *The Middle East Journal*, 8 (Winter 1954), 10–26.

Hottinger, Arnold. "Zu'amā' and Parties in the Lebanese Crisis of 1958," *Middle East Journal*, 15 (Spring 1961), 127–140.

———. "Zu'amā' in Historical Perspective," in Binder, *Politics in Lebanon*, 85–105.

Hourani, Albert H. "Lebanon from Feudalism to Modern State," *Middle Eastern Studies*, 2 (April 1966), 256–263.

Hourani, Albert H. "Race, Religion and the Nation-State in the Near East," in Abdullah M. Lutfiyya and Charles Churchill, eds., *Readings in Arab Middle Eastern Societies and Cultures*, 1–19.

Hudson, Michael. "The Electoral Process and Political Development in Lebanon," *The Middle East Journal*, 20 (Spring 1966), 173–186.

Huntington, Samuel. "Foreword," in Eric A. Nordlinger, *Conflict Resolution in Divided Societies*, Cambridge, Mass.: Harvard University, Center for International Affairs, Occasional Papers in International Affairs, No. 29 (January 1972), n.p.

——— "Political Modernization: America vs. Europe," *World Politics*, 18 (April 1966), 378–414.

Jones-Quartey, K. A. B. "Report From the Regions," *Legon Observer*, 6 (September 10, 1971), 6–8.

Kerr, Malcolm H. "Lebanese Views on the 1958 Crisis," *Middle East Journal*, 15

(Spring 1961), 211–217.

———. "Political Decision Making in a Confessional Democracy," in Leonard Binder, *Politics in Lebanon,* 137–212.

Khalaf, Samir, "Family Associations in Lebanon," *Journal of Comparative Family Studies,* II (Autumn 1971), 236–250.

———. "Industrial Conflict in Lebanon," *Human Organization,* 24 (Spring 1965), 25–33.

———. "Lebanese Labor Unions: Some Comparative Structural Features," *Middle East Economic Papers.* Beirut: American University of Beirut, 1968, 111–138.

———. "Primordial Ties and Politics in Lebanon," *Middle Eastern Studies,* 4 (April 1968), 243–269.

Khalil, Khalil Ahmad. "Al-Zaʿāmat al-Istizlamiyyah fī Lubnān," (The Leadership of Clientele in Lebanon), *Dirāsāt ʿArabiyyah* (September 1972), 27–38.

Khan, Rais A. "Lebanon at the Crossroads," *World Today,* 25 (December 1969), 530–536.

Khuri, Fuad I. "Al Ṭabaqāt al-Ijtimaʿiyyah fī Lubnāna wa-Dawruhā al-Siyāsī," (Social Classes in Lebanon and Their Political Role), *Revue Libanaise des Sciences Politiques,* No. 2 (1970), 25–32.

———. "The Changing Class Structure in Lebanon," *Middle East Journal,* 23 (Winter 1969), 29–44.

Kilson, Martin. "The Grassroots in Ghanaian Politics," in Philip Foster and Aristide R. Zolberg, eds., *Ghana and the Ivory Coast.* Chicago: University of Chicago Press, 1971, 103–123.

Kraus, Jon. "Arms and Politics in Ghana," in Claude Welch, ed., *Soldier and State in Africa.* Evanston: Northwestern University Press, 1970, 154–221.

———. "Ghana's New 'Corporate Parliament'," *Africa Report,* 10 (August 1965), 6–11.

———. "On the Politics of Nationalism and Social Change in Ghana," *Journal of Modern African Studies,* 7 (April 1969), 107–130.

———. "Political Change, Conflict, and Development," in Philip Foster and Aristide Zolberg, eds., *Ghana and the Ivory Coast,* 33–72.

Kuper, Leo. "Plural Societies: Perspectives and Problems," in Leo Kuper and M. G. Smith, eds., *Pluralism in Africa.* Berkeley: University of California Press, 1969, 7–26.

Laude, Carl H. "Patterns of Polity Directed Educational Development: The Philippines," in James S. Coleman, ed., *Education and Political Development,* 313–349.

LeVine, Robert. "Political Socialization and Cultural Change," in Clifford Geertz, ed., *Old Societies and New States,* 280–303.

Lijphart, Arend. "Consociational Democracy," *World Politics,* 21 (January 1969), 207–225.

———. "Typologies of Democratic Systems," *Comparative Political Studies,* I (April 1968), 17–35.

Mazrui, Ali A. "Pluralism and National Integration," in Leo Kuper and M. G. Smith, eds., *Pluralism in Africa,* 333–349.

Melikian, Levon. "By Their Names," *Middle East Forum*, XXXIX (April 1963), 34–39.

———. "The Family in Lebanon," in *Cultural Resources of Lebanon*. Beirut: Librarie du Liban, 1969, 160–172.

Melson, Robert, and Howard Wolpe. "Modernization and the Politics of Communalism: A Theoretical Perspective," in Melson and Wolpe, eds., *Nigeria: Modernization and the Politics of Communalism*. East Lansing: Michigan State University Press, 1971, 1–42.

Mercier, Paul. "On the Meaning of Tribalism in Black Africa," in Pierre L. van den Berghe, ed., *Africa: Social Problems of Change and Conflict*. San Francisco: Chandler Publishing Company, 1965, 483–501.

Messarra, Antoine. "La Répartition Confessionnelle Permanente ou Provisoire?" *Action Proche-Orient*, 23 (December 1964), 35–40.

Morrison, Donald G. and Hugh Michael Stevenson. "Integration and Instability: Patterns of African Political Development," *American Political Science Review*, LXVI (September 1972), 902–927.

Nour, Francis. "Particularisme Libanais et Nationalisme Arabe," *Orient*, 2, No. 7 (1958), 29–42.

Ollennu, N. A. "The Law of Succession in Ghana," in *Integration of Customary and Modern Legal Systems in Africa*, 294–310.

Oppong, Christine. "Local Migrations in Northern Ghana," *Ghana Journal of Sociology*, 3 (February 1967), 1–16.

Paden, John N. "Urban Pluralism, Integration, and Adaptation of Communal Identity in Kano, Nigeria," in Ronald Cohen and John Middleton, eds., *From Tribe to Nation in Africa: Studies in Incorporation Processes*. Scranton, Pa.: Chandler Publishing Co., 1970, 242–270.

Peters, Emrys L. "Aspects of Rank and Status Among Muslims in a Lebanese Village," in Louise Sweet, ed., *Peoples and Cultures of the Middle East*, 76–123.

Piel, Margaret. "The Expulsion of West African Aliens," *Journal of Modern African Studies*, 9 (July 1971), 205–229.

Price, Robert. "The Pattern of Ethnicity in Ghana: A Research Note." *The Journal of Modern African Studies*, II (September 1973), 470–475.

Rondot, Pierre. "La Crise du Liban," *L'Afrique et L'Asie*, No. 43 (1958), 45–53.

———. "Quelques Réflexions sur les Structures du Liban," *Orient*, 2, No. 6 (1958), 23–36.

Rubinstein, Aryeh. "Israel's Integration Problem," in Benjamin Rivlin and Joseph S. Szyliowicz, *The Contemporary Middle East: Tradition and Innovation*. New York: Random House, 1965, 388–396.

Saab, Hassan. "The Rationalist School in Lebanese Politics," in Binder, *Politics in Lebanon*, 271–282.

Salem, Elie, "Cabinet Politics in Lebanon," *The Middle East Journal*, 21 (Autumn 1967), 488–501.

———. "Local Elections in Lebanon: A Case Study," *Midwest Journal of Political Science*, IX (November 1965), 376–387.

Salibi, Kamal. "The Lebanese Crisis in Perspective," *The World Today*, 14 (September 1958), 369–380.

————. "The Lebanese Emirate," *Al-Abḥāth*, 20 (September 1967), 1–16.

————. "The Lebanese Identity," *Journal of Contemporary History*, 6, No. 1 (1971), 76–84.

————. "Lebanon Since The Crisis of 1958," *The World Today*, 17 (January 1961), 32–42.

Salzman, Philip C. "National Integration of the Tribes in Iran," *Middle East Journal*, 25 (Summer 1971), 325–336.

Schildkrout, Enid. "Strangers and Local Government in Kumasi," *Journal of Modern African Studies*, 8 (July 1970), 251–269.

Shils, Edward. "The Prospect for Lebanese Civility," in Binder, *Politics in Lebanon*, 1–12.

Smith, M. G. "Institutional and Political Conditions of Pluralism," in Kuper and Smith, eds., *Pluralism in Africa*, 27–65.

Smock, Audrey C. "Introduction," in Audrey C. Smock, ed., *Comparative Politics: A Reader in Institutionalization and Mobilization*. Boston: Allyn & Bacon, 1973, 1–33.

Spagnolo, J. P. "Constitutional Change in Mount Lebanon, 1861–1864," *Middle Eastern Studies*, 7 (January 1971), 25–48.

Suleiman, Michael W. "Elections in a Confessional Democracy," *The Journal of Politics*, 29 (February 1967), 109–128.

Tannous, A. I. "Group Behavior in the Village Community of Lebanon," in Lutfiyya and Churchill, eds., *Readings in Arab Middle Eastern Societies and Cultures*, 99–108.

Vellenga, Dorothy Dee. "Attempts to Change the Marriage Laws in Ghana and the Ivory Coast," in Philip Foster and Aristide Zolberg, eds., *Ghana and The Ivory Coast*, 125–150.

Van Dusen, Michael H. "Political Integration and Regionalism in Syria," *Middle East Journal*, 26 (Spring 1972), 123–136.

Wilks, Ivor. "The Growth of the Akwapim State," in Jan Vansina, R. Mauny, and L. V. Thomas, eds., *The Historian in Tropical Africa*. London: Oxford University Press, 1964, 390–411.

————. "A Medieval Trade-Route from the Niger to the Gulf of Guinea," *Journal of African History*, III, No. 2 (1962), 337–341.

Ziadeh, Nicola A. "The Lebanese Elections, 1960," *The Middle East Journal*, 14 (Autumn 1960), 367–381.

Zolberg, Aristide A. "Patterns of National Integration," *Journal of Modern African Studies*, V (December 1967), 449–468.

————. "Tribalism Through Corrective Lenses," *Foreign Affairs*, 51 (July 1973), 728–739.

UNPUBLISHED MATERIALS AND PAMPHLETS

Al-Amīn, 'Alī Ḥasan. "Al-Shī'a fī Lubnān" (The Shiites in Lebanon), 1972, mimeo.

Ansre, Gilbert. "Language Policy and the Promotion of National Unity and Understanding in West Africa," conference paper presented at the Institute of African
Studies at the University of Ife, December 1970, mimeo.

Ballard, Charles A. Jr. "A Contemporary Youth Movement: The Young Pioneers,"
M.A. Thesis, Institute of African Studies, Univesity of Ghana, 1967.

Bell, Daniel. "Ethnicity and Social Change," paper presented at Conference of
Ethnic Problems, Boston, October 1972.

Bitar, Edward. "Personnel Administration in a Developing Country: A Study of the
Lebanese Bureaucracy," PH.D. Diss., Louisiana State University, 1970.

Brokensha, David. "Anthropological Enquiries and Political Science: A Case Study
from Ghana," paper presented at the African Studies Association Meeting in
October 1965.

Card, Emily. "The Politics of Underdevelopment: From Voluntary Associations to
Party Auxiliaries in Ghana," PH.D. Diss., Columbia University, 1972.

Chehab, Camille. "Les Elections Législatives de 1964," Beirut, 1964, mimeo.

_____ "Les Elections Législatives de 1968," mimeo.

Deeb, Mary-Jane Anhoury. "The Khazin Family: A Case Study of the Effect of Social
Change on Traditional Roles," M.A. Thesis, American University of Cairo, 1972.

Dekmedjian, R. H. "The Entrepreneur in Lebanese Politics: A Case of Overlapping
Elites," paper presented at Middle East Studies Association Annual Meeting,
Milwaukee, November 9, 1973.

Donato, Joseph. "Le Plan du Développement Social au Liban," Beyrouth: Juin 1960.

Early, Evelyn A. "The 'Amiliyya Society of Beirut: A Case Study of an Emerging
Urban Za'im," M.A. Thesis, American University of Beirut, 1971.

Effah-Apenteng, Victor. "Gold Coast Politics: The Federalist Agitation, 1954–1957,"
M.A. Thesis, Institute of African Studies, University of Ghana, 1970.

Entelis, J. P. "The Lebanese Kataeb: Party Transformation and System Maintenance
in a Multiconfessional Society," PH.D. Diss., New York University, 1970.

Fayyad, Halim Faris. "The Effects of Sectarianism on Lebanese Administration," M.A.
Thesis, American University of Beirut, 1956.

Ferkiss, Victor C. and Barbara Ferkiss. "Race and Politics in Trinidad and Guyana,"
paper, n.d.

Fiawoo, D. K. "Social Survey of Tefleh," Legon, Ghana: Institute of Education,
1961, mimeo.

Frankel, Ephraim Jr. "The Maronite Patriarchate and its Role in Lebanese Politics: A
Case Study of the 1958 Lebanese Crisis," M.A. Thesis, American University of
Beirut, 1971.

Folson, B. D. G. "The Traditional Political System," n.d. mimeo.

Ghana Youth Council, "Report for 1959–1960," mimeo.

_____ "Report for 1970," mimeo.

Goody, Jack. "The Ethnography of the Northern Territories of the Gold Coast, West
of the White Volta," Cambridge, 1952, mimeo.

Gubser, Peter. "The Politics of Economic Interest Groups in a Lebanese Town,"
Washington, D.C., 1972, mimeo.

Hamilton, Ruth Simms. "Urban Social Differentiation and Membership Recruitment Among Selected Voluntary Associations in Accra, Ghana," PH.D. Diss., Northwestern University, 1966.

Harris, Gene R. "Some Aspects of Decentralization and the Formulation and Implementation of Agricultural Policy in Ghana," Institute of Statistical, Social and Economic Research, University of Ghana, 1971, mimeo.

Hayward, Fred. "Correlates of National Political Integration: The Case of Ghana," paper, 1972.

———— "Government Performance and National Integration in Selected Communities," paper presented at the Annual African Studies Association Meeting, 1971.

———— "Rural Attitudes and Expectations about National Government: Experience in Selected Ghanaian Communities," Madison, Wisconsin, August 1972. mimeo.

———— "The Stability of Levels of National Integration: Projects from the Ghanaian Context," June 1972, mimeo.

Horner, Norman. "A Statistical Survey of Christian Communities," Beirut, 1972, mimeo.

Jeranian, Panos S. "Catholic Armenia and Maronite Religions in Mount Lebanon 1720–1840," M.A. Thesis, American University of Beirut, 1971.

Kaufert, Joseph M. "An Experimental Approach to Ethnic Unit Boundary Definition in Ghana," paper presented at African Studies Association, 1972.

———— . "Impact of Multiple Ethnic Loyalties and Linkages Upon Integration Potential Among Student Elites in Ghana." PH.D. Diss., Northwestern University, 1973.

Khalaf, Samir. "Lebanon," draft version of article prepared for *Encyclopedia Britannica*, 1971.

————, and Linda Schatkowski, "The Convergence of Tradition and Modernity: The Case of the Islamic Maqased of Beirut," 1969, mimeo.

Khuri, Fuad I. "A Profile of Family Associations in Two Suburbs," paper for the Middle East Social Anthropology and Sociology Conference, Nicosia, 1970.

———— "Sectarian Loyalty in Two Lebanese Suburbs: A Stage Between Family and National Allegiance," n.d., mimeo.

———— "Two Suburbs of Beirut," manuscript, 1972.

Kilbourne, Mary A. "The Greek Orthodox Community of Syria and Lebanon in the Twentieth Century," M.A. Thesis, American University of Beirut, 1952.

Kisirwani, Marun Y. "Attitudes and Behavior of Lebanese Bureaucrats: A Study in Administrative Corruption," PH.D. Diss., University of Indiana, 1971.

Koplin, Roberta. "Education and National Integration in Ghana and Kenya." PH.D. Diss., University of Oregon, 1969.

LeVine, Victor. "Autopsy on a Regime: Ghana's Civilian Interregnum 1969–1972," manuscript, 1972.

Al-Majlis al-Islāmī al-Shī'ī al-A'lā fī Lubnān, (The Higher Shiite Islamic Council of Lebanon), untitled, undated pamphlet.

Marshall, M. J. "Christianity and Nationalism in Ghana," M.A. Thesis, University of Ghana, 1965.

Messerlian, Zaven Meguerditch. "Armenian Representation in the Lebanese Parliament," M.A. Thesis, American University of Beirut, 1963.

Middle East Economic Consultants. "The Green Plan: A General Evaluation of Performance," Beirut, 1972, mimeo.

Nikoi, Amon. "Indirect Rule and Government in the Gold Coast Colony 1844–1954," PH.D. Diss., Harvard University, 1956.

Paden, John N. "Situational Ethnicity in Urban Africa with Special Reference to the Hausa," paper presented at the African Studies Association Meeting, New York, 1967.

Peterson, William. "Ethnic Structures in Western Europe," paper presented at the Conference on Ethnic Problems," Boston, October 1972.

Pipes, Richard. "Reflections on the Ethnic Problems in the Soviet Union," paper presented at the Conference on Ethnic Problems, American Academy of Arts and Sciences, Boston, 1972.

Sa'adah, Mounir R. "The Fifth Lebanese Legislative Assembly, 1943–44," M.A. Thesis, American University of Beirut, 1945.

Sharpston, Michael. "The Regional Pattern of Health Expenditure," Accra, 1969, mimeo.

Schatkowski, Linda. "The Islamic Maqassed of Beirut: A Case Study of Modernization in Lebanon," M.A. Thesis, American University of Beirut, 1969.

Schiffer, Harriet B. "Political Linkage in Ghana: Bekwai District, A Case Study," paper presented at African Studies Association Meeting, 1971.

Schram, John R. "Chieftaincy and Politics in Independent Ghana," M.A. Thesis, Institute of African Studies, University of Ghana, 1967.

Shea, M. S. M. "The Development and Role of Trade Unions in a Developing Economy: The Case of Ghana," PH.D. Diss., University of London, 1968.

Simonian, Teny Anoushavian. "Assimilation Patterns of Rural and Urban Armenian Communities in Lebanon," M.A. Thesis, American University of Beirut, 1971.

Spencer, Noel. "The Role of the Maronite Patriarchate in Lebanese Politics from 1840 to the Present," M.A. Thesis, American University of Beirut, 1963.

Uphoff, Norman. "Ghana's Experience in Using External Aid for Development, 1957–1966." Berkeley: Institute of International Studies, University of California, 1970, mimeo.

World Food Programme, "Plan of Operations: Integrated Development of the Lebanese Mountain Areas," Beirut, May 1971, mimeo.

OFFICIAL PUBLICATIONS

Armed Forces Gazette. Accra: Government of Ghana, 1968 and 1969.

Census Office, *1970 Population Census of Ghana,* Vol. II, *Statistics of Localities and Enumeration Areas.* Accra: Ghana Publishing Corp., 1972.

Central Bureau of Statistics, *1963 Statistical Year Book.* Accra: Government of Ghana, 1966.

"The Constitution of the Convention People's Party," Revised version, Accra: Guinea Press, 1962.

"Constitution of the Republic of Ghana," Accra: Ghana Publishing Corp., 1969.

"Al-Dustūr al-Lubnānī" (The Lebanese Constitution), Beirut: Bureau of Lebanese and Arab Documentation, 1969.

"Education Report for the Years 1958–1960," Accra: Ministry of Information and Broadcasting on behalf of the Ministry of Education, 1962.

"Educational Statistics 1968–1969," Accra: Ministry of Education, 1971.

"L'Enquête par Sondage sur la Population Active au Liban, Novembre 1970," Beyrouth: Ministère du Plan, 1972.

Gil, B., A. F. Aryee and D. K. Ghansah, *Special Report 'E', Tribes in Ghana, 1960, Population Census of Ghana*. Accra: Census Office, 1964.

Gil, B., K. T. DeGraft-Johnson, and E. A. Colecraft, *1960 Population Census of Ghana, Vol. VI, The Post Enumeration Survey*. Accra: Census Office, 1971.

The Gold Coast Handbook. Accra, 1937.

Institut International de Recherche et de Formation en vue du Développement Intégral et Harmonisé, *Besoin et Possibilité de Développement*, Tome I. Beyrouth: Ministère du Plan, 1961.

"Jadāwil Manhāj al-Ta'līm" (Program of Instruction). Ministry of Education, Beirut, 1969.

"Jam'īyāt al-Khidmat al-Ijtimā'iyyah fī Lubnān" (Social Welfare Organizations in Lebanon), Beirut: Ministry of Planning, 1965.

Al-Jarīda al Rasmiyyah (Official Gazette), Beirut, various volumes and dates.

Labour Statistics, 1968. Accra: Central Bureau of Statistics, Series III, December 1969.

Al-Majlis al-Islāmīal-Shī'ī al-A'lā (The Higher Shiite Islamic Council. "Qānūn Inshā' al Majlis al Islāmī al Shī'ī al A'la (Law on the Establishment of the Higher Shiite Islamic Council), Beirut: Sadir Press, 1969.

"Manhāj al-Ta'līm" (The Program of Instruction), Beirut: Ministry of Education, 1946.

Maşlaḥat al-In'ash al-Ijtimā'ī, "Al-Taqrīr al Sanawī li'ām 1969 wa 1970" (Annual Report of the Department of Social Development), Beirut, 1969 and 1970, mimeographed.

Mensah, Hon. J. H., "1971–72 Budget Statement," Accra: Ministry of Finance, July 27, 1971.

Ministère du Plan, "Plan Sexennal de Développement, 1972–1977," Beyrouth: La Direction Centrale de la Statistique, 1972.

National Redemption Council, "The Charter of Our Redemption," Accra: Ghana Publishing Corp., 1973.

"One Year Development Plan, July 1970 to June 1971," Accra: Ghana Publishing Corp., 1970.

"Outline of Government Economic Policy," Accra: Ghana Publishing Corp., June 1972.

Parliamentary Debates. Accra: Government Printer, several volumes and dates.

Population Bulletin of the United Nations Economic and Social Office in Beirut. Beirut, July 1972.

Proceedings of the Constituent Assembly. Accra: Ghana Publishing Corp. 1969.

The Proposals of the Constitutional Commission for the Constitution for Ghana. Accra: Ghana Publishing Corp., 1968.

"Report of the Committee on Pre-University Education," Accra, May–June 1963, mimeo.

"Report of the Commission on the Structure and Remuneration of the Public Services in Ghana," Accra: Ministry of Information, 1967.

"Report of the Education Review Committee," Accra: Ministry of Information, 1967.

"Report from the Select Committee on Federal System of Government and Second Chamber for the Gold Coast," Accra: The Government Printer, 1955.

"Seven Year Development Plan," Accra: Office of the Planning Commission, 1964.

"Statement by the Government on the Report of the Commission Appointed to Enquire into the Matters Disclosed at the Trial of Captain Benjamin Awhaitey before a Court Martial, and the Surrounding Circumstances," Government White Paper, 1959, Accra: Government Printer, 1959.

"Statistical Data on Education and Manpower in the Arab Countries," Paris: OECD Directorate for Scientific Affairs and Development Centre, 1966.

Statistiques Scolaires Années 1969–1970, 1970–1971. Beyrouth: Le Bureau de la Statistique, 1972.

"Taqrīr Ra'īs Majlis al Khidma al-Madaniyyah 'an A'māl al-Majlis Khilāl al-Sanawāt al-Thalātha 1966–1967–1968" (Report of the Chairman of the Civil Service Board on the Activities of the Board During the Three Years 1966–1967–1968) Official Gazette, Annex, No. 26, March 31, 1969.

Al-Tarbiya al-Madaniyyah (Civics). 2nd ed., Beirut: Mudīriyyat al-Ta'līm al Mihanī, 1970.

Town and Country Planning Division, Ministry of Lands, *National Physical Development Plan, 1963–1970.* Accra: State Publishing Corporation, 1965.

"Two Year Development Plan," Accra: Ghana Publishing Corp., 1968.

"The West African Examinations Council Annual Report for the Year Ended 31 March 1968," Accra: West African Examination Council Printer, 1969.

"White Paper on the Report of the Commission on the Structure and Remuneration of the Public Services in Ghana," Accra: Ministry of Information, 1968.

"White Paper on the Report of the Education Review Committee," Accra: Ministry of Information, 1968.

NEWSPAPERS AND PERIODICALS CITED

Al-'Amal
Al-Anwār
Arab World
Arab World Weekly
Al-Bayraq
Daily Graphic
Daily Star
Ghanaian Times
Al-Hayāt
Al-Jarīda
London Observer
Le Monde
Al-Muḥarrir
Al-Nahār
L'Orient-Le Jour
Al-Ṣayyād
West Africa

Index

DATE DUE	
SEP 3 0 1997	

GAYLORD   PRINTED IN U.S.A.